Ment

Students

Practical Life Strategies for Stress, Anxiety, Depression, and More: Backed by Research

Ryan Patel DO, FAPA

Copyright and Disclaimer

© 2023 RKLB1 Corp.

professional the appropriate discipline with a license to practice in their jurisdiction, any strategy, idea, recommendation, or anything from this book, and only do things under the care, approval, and guidance of said health professional.

For rights and permissions, please contact:

RKLB1 Corp.

Ohio, United States.

info@mentalhealthforcollegestudents.com

ISBN: 979-8-86606292-8

Dedication

This book is dedicated to anyone who wants to become a better version of themselves by taking charge of their mental health using positive life strategies.

Acknowledgment

I want to acknowledge Karen and Lizzy for their love and support. My parents, for always encouraging me to do my best. To Thomas Carrigan and John Delaney −I appreciate our friendship. To coach Tom Gabel for teaching us that football is more than just a game—it is a lesson to succeed in life. To coach Jerald Cheeks for teaching us underdogs how to face pressure, adversity, and win—in football and in life. There are many other people that have influenced and shaped me—thank you.

About the Author

Ryan Patel, D.O. FAPA, is a college psychiatrist at The Ohio State University Office of Student Life Counseling and Consultation Service and a Professor of Psychiatry in the Department of Psychiatry and Behavioral Health at The Ohio State University Wexner Medical Center. He is a sought-after speaker and consultant regarding young and emerging adult mental health in the public and private sectors.

He is a board member (2023-2025 term) of the American College Health Association. He has served various leadership roles over the years, including chair of their Mental Health Section and chair of the 2023 conference planning committee.

Dr. Patel has over ten years of experience working with college students and young professionals, using a personalized approach combining lifestyle strategies, medication, and counseling.

He has participated in numerous clinical research projects, committees, programs, media, and legislative efforts in the field of college mental health.

His self-help blog quickly reached over 120,000 page views. His nutrition, sleep, and exercise strategies for mental health workshop program is one of the most popular programs of its type at OSU. Dr. Patel is on a mission to help improve the mental health of others using individual-level and large-scale strategies.

Originally from Oklahoma, Dr. Patel graduated from The University of Oklahoma with a Bachelor of Science in Zoology/Behavioral Neuroscience. He attended medical school at Oklahoma State University Center for Health Sciences. He received world-class training by completing his psychiatry residency training at The Cleveland Clinic Foundation, where he also served as a chief resident in psychiatry and received the department's Intern of the Year award. He was recognized for his service to the Cleveland Clinic Housestaff Association with a certificate of recognition. Dr. Patel is board-certified by the American Board of Psychiatry and Neurology and is a fellow of the American Psychiatric Association.

Prior to joining OSU, Dr. Patel served as a psychiatry section chief for Advocate Bromenn Medical Center and has experience in both office-based and hospital-based psychiatry, working with professionals, executives, and young adults.

Contents

Chapter 1: Introduction

"Within the labyrinth of the mind lies the power to heal and thrive." -Anonymous

Yes, you can! You can take steps to improve your mental health.

Thoughts, emotions, feelings, and behaviors are all interconnected. Changing one can change the others. This is a commonly understood concept in the mental health world.

This book is about behaviors backed by research that can help improve your mental health. As you read this book, I hope you'll start seeing connections you may not have realized before. You'll also explore how your behaviors impact your mental health and how you can change them for the better.

As a psychiatrist, I have spent over ten years studying, teaching my patients, and writing about research-backed behaviors that can improve mental health. I also shine a light on life behaviors that can interfere with good mental health.

During medical school at Oklahoma State University, I realized that a holistic and personalized approach was the most effective way to help people improve their health. However, the training and knowledge of life behaviors and mental health were still emerging.

I continued to incorporate this approach into my practice during my psychiatry training at the Cleveland Clinic Foundation. Over the last decade, I have refined and improved this technique while working as a college psychiatrist at The Ohio State University.

In addition to my clinical work, my knowledge and experience have been further deepened by numerous research projects, programs, and committees that I have participated in at OSU and through my work in numerous leadership roles with the American College Health Association. Through my professional speaking and consulting work, I have helped numerous entities improve their systems to better the mental health of young people, including their employees, customers, and students.

Every day, I think about, study, and look for life behaviors that can improve mental health. What started as a blog to educate my patients between appointments about healthy life behaviors for mental health has transformed into educating the wider student body.

Over time, I realized that writing this book was a way to reach more people. Many people want to improve their mental health, but they may be engaging in behaviors that interfere with mental health without even realizing it.

This book is organized by topic area. In each chapter, I will briefly discuss research studies and draw strategies from them to improve mental health. In the expanded knowledge section, I will also provide my experience in helping people apply these strategies and various considerations in applying them effectively. Readers will find that some of my posts and studies repeat. This is done intentionally for two reasons. First, the post and research cover more than one topic area, making it more appealing for readers who just look at specific topic areas to see the information. The second reason for the repetition is to emphasize certain strategies' importance and potential benefits. Even if you are interested in just some of the topics, you will find useful strategies in other chapters due to the overlapping benefits of various strategies on mental health. Some mental health concerns facing young adults are not covered in this book as they are better addressed by other modalities or books specific to those topics.

The healthy life behaviors discussed in this book do not replace professional treatment. They are a complement to medical, psychiatric, and counseling treatments. You should always check with your health professional to ensure anything discussed in this book is right for you.

As research on various life behaviors and mental health continues to accumulate, so does my own observation that many people do not realize how their lifestyle impacts their mental health.

If you don't realize it, how can you change it?

The average effect size of any single life strategy to improve mental health will vary: some with a small effect size and others with a large effect size. But "average" implies an average of high and low. When you apply a personalized strategy stack based on your situation using the strategies discussed in this book, you may find that the total effect on you is significant. In my work with patients, I have seen this happen to numerous people over the years.

In my experience, when people optimize their life behaviors using the strategies I discuss in this book, they often need less medication. In some cases, I have helped people come off psychiatric medications altogether. In other cases, we have been able to be more targeted with medications when life behaviors and counseling are addressed. In my experience, this targeted approach reduces the risk of over-medication and potential side effects.

Doing things in your daily life to improve your mental health will require skill, will, knowledge, practice, and adjustment over time as your situation changes or more information emerges. Healthy living for good mental health is a process, and I hope this book begins that journey for you.

As you will see in this book, many strategies exist to improve mental health. The combination that specifically works best for you will likely vary from person to person.

This book is about empowering you with knowledge of strategies to improve your mental health. It's up to you to apply and practice those skills under the supervision of your health professional.

Are you ready? Let's go.

P.S. Visit my website at mentalhealthforcollegestudents.com and register for my blog and newsletter to continue the journey of life strategies for mental health.

Chapter 2: Transitioning to College

This chapter delves into the multifaceted world of college life, encompassing its exciting opportunities, inevitable challenges, and vital coping strategies.

The chapter is divided into two segments, Part A and Part B.

Part A primarily focuses on the critical transition phase of stepping into college. This section comprises a collection of studies that provide valuable insights on adjusting to the new environment, making social connections, coping with homesickness, and planning for a successful semester's conclusion. It further extends to offering guidance for parents and families to understand and support their wards' mental health needs during these transformative years, including a discussion about health insurance for mental health.

The journey continues as Part B explores the student's journey into more specialized topics. It looks at the influence of interruptions on mental health, study skills to improve memory and the importance of self-care for graduate students. The section doesn't shy away from addressing grave issues like the long-term impact of bullying and the mental health implications of returning to campus amidst a pandemic. Furthermore, it enlightens readers about maximizing spring breaks for mental health rejuvenation and readjusting to college life.

Altogether, this chapter aims at a variety of strategies and considerations to help young adults successfully start their college journey.

Part A: To College!

Part A of this chapter provides a series of strategies drawn from studies of topics important during the college transition.

These topics range from making new social connections and strategies for concluding a semester successfully to coping mechanisms for homesickness. Understanding these elements can greatly influence the experiences and outcomes of this transformative period, ensuring that students navigate these changes with confidence and resilience.

Recognizing the essential role of a support system in this phase, this part of the chapter also offers a comprehensive guide for parents and families. This section is designed to equip them with the understanding and tools to support their college-going wards effectively. By doing so, it seeks to foster a supportive and understanding environment that can contribute positively to students' mental well-being.

Coping with Loneliness and Isolation

Many young adults struggle with loneliness. For example, a national survey found that almost 70% of

Gen-Zers and 71% of millennials are lonely vs. 50% of baby boomers.[12]

In 2023, the United States Surgeon General issued an advisory on the epidemic of loneliness and isolation.[3]

For some, this was further increased by COVID-19-related social distancing, quarantine, isolation, and increasing use of technology.

Feelings of loneliness can increase symptoms of depression[4] and, over time, worsen cognitive function.[5]

The American Psychological Association offers the following strategies to cope with loneliness/isolation[6]:

When possible, plan ahead by considering how you might spend your time, who you can contact for psychosocial support, and how you can address any physical or mental health needs.

Create and follow a daily routine. This can help with a sense of order and purpose. As needed, include regular daily activities, such as work, exercise or learning, and other healthy activities. Maintain virtual contact through other

---

[1] https://www.scientificamerican.com/article/how-to-prevent-loneliness-in-a-time-of-social-distancing/

[2] https://www.cigna.com/static/www-cigna-com/docs/about-us/newsroom/studies-and-reports/combatting-loneliness/cigna-2020-loneliness-factsheet.pdf

[3] https://www.hhs.gov/sites/default/files/surgeon-general-social-connection-advisory.

[4] Cacioppo JT, Hawkley LC, Thisted RA. Perceived social isolation makes me sad: 5-year cross-lagged analyses of loneliness and depressive symptomatology in the Chicago Health, Aging, and Social Relations Study. *Psychol Aging*. 2010;25(2):453–463. doi:10.1037/a0017216

[5] Cacioppo JT, Cacioppo S. Older adults reporting social isolation or loneliness show poorer cognitive function 4 years later. *Evidence-Based Nursing* 2014;17:59-60.

[6] https://www.apa.org/practice/programs/dmhi/research-information/social-distancing

mediums such as phone calls, text messages, video chat, and social media to access social support networks.

Maintain a healthy lifestyle. Get enough sleep, eat well, and exercise in your home when you can do so. Try to avoid using alcohol or drugs as a way to cope with the stresses of isolation and quarantine.

Limit excessive news consumption to reliable sources because too much exposure to media coverage can increase feelings of fear and anxiety.

Balance this time with other activities unrelated to quarantine or isolation, such as reading, listening to music, or learning a new language.

Psychological Strategies To Manage Stress And Stay Positive During Times Of Loneliness/Isolation[7]:

Take a look at your worries and aim to be realistic in your assessment of the actual concern and your ability to cope. Keeping a diary may help.

Focus on what you can do and accept what you can't change.

Keep a daily gratitude journal. This will help you appreciate the positives, which can help reduce stress. This will be further discussed in a future chapter.

Practice mindfulness and relaxation exercises. Specific strategies will be discussed in later chapters.

---

[7]https://www.apa.org/practice/programs/dmhi/research-information/social-distancing

Focusing on what you can gain from this challenging time can also be useful. Some examples include giving you more time to reflect on your life, work on a life or career goal, identify people from the present or past that you want to take steps to become closer to and identify and reduce or remove negative influences from your life.

Other Strategies:

For some, periodic isolation can be a time of solitude—an opportunity to step back from your daily life and re-focus on your priorities and longer-term goals. This can help you better deal with shorter-term challenges. This can also help you identify things you could add or subtract when returning to your usual life.

What tasks or goals have you been putting off that you can now address because of this time?

Can you research future goals?

Change the scene. Take a walk outside when possible. Find another place to work. Fresh air and seeing others, even at a distance, may help reduce feelings of loneliness.

Consider online discussion groups based on hobbies such as books, movies, shows, crafts, gaming, video games, professional interests, sports, community areas, etc.

Consider a discussion group with your classmates.

Many places now offer online group fitness, yoga, and virtual races.

Schedule a time for virtual visits with friends or family.

Participate in sports leagues in your community or volunteer as a helper or a referee.

Expanded Knowledge

Loneliness is particularly prevalent among young adults and millennials, and the onset of COVID-19 only exacerbated it. As we move forward, it's essential to remember that loneliness is a state, not a trait; it's temporary, and with the right tools and mindset, we can effectively navigate through it.

Study: Concussion and Head Injury's Impact on Grades and Emotions[8]

Anyone is susceptible to head injuries (from a fall, sports injury, trauma, etc.) leading to a concussion.

Concussions can cause various physical and emotional symptoms that can last for several weeks.[9] This can impact classwork, job performance, relationships, etc.

---

[8]https://u.osu.edu/emotionalfitness/2016/07/20/study-concussion-and-head-injurys-impact-on-grades-and-emotions/

[9] McCrory P, et. al. Consensus statement on concussion in sport: the 4th International Conference on Concussion in Sport held in Zurich, November 2012. Br J Sports Med. 2013 Apr;47(5):250-8.

What Is A Concussion?[10]

In short, a concussion is a brain injury with the following features[11]:

- It may be caused by a direct blow to the head, face, neck, or elsewhere on the body with an 'impulsive' force transmitted to the head, with or without loss of consciousness.

- Neurologic symptoms can start quickly and resolve spontaneously.

- In some cases, symptoms and signs may evolve over minutes to hours.

- Symptoms may impact brain or nerve functioning in many cases, but brain scans and other tests may be normal.

What Are Some Physical And Emotional Symptoms Of A Concussion?

Within minutes to hours of an injury:

- Headache, dizziness, lack of awareness of surroundings, and nausea and vomiting.[12]

Over hours and days of an injury, victims might have:

---

[10] McCrory P, et. al. Consensus statement on concussion in sport: the 4th International Conference on Concussion in Sport held in Zurich, November 2012. Br J Sports Med. 2013 Apr;47(5):250-8.

[11] McCrory P, et. al. Consensus statement on concussion in sport: the 4th International Conference on Concussion in Sport held in Zurich, November 2012. Br J Sports Med. 2013 Apr;47(5):250-8.

[12] Kelly JP, Rosenberg JH. Diagnosis and management of concussion in sports. Neurology. 1997;48(3):575.

- Changes in mood, thinking, or sleep.[13]

- Become more sensitive to light, noise, and sleep disturbances.[14]

What Are Some Observable Signs That Someone May Have Had A Concussion Following An Injury?[15]

Signs observed in someone who might be experiencing a concussion after an injury might be[16]:

- Confusion (acting, appearing, making confusing remarks, being slow to respond or follow instructions.

- In-attention or easily distracted or difficulty with follow-through.

- Emotional difficulties (appearing distraught, crying for no apparent reason).

- Having difficulties with memory.

- Loss of consciousness.

- Becoming less coordinated (stumbling, inability to walk tandem/straight line).

---

[13] Cantu RC. Posttraumatic Retrograde and Anterograde Amnesia: Pathophysiology and Implications in Grading and Safe Return to Play. J Athl Train. 2001;36(3):244.

[14] Cantu RC. Posttraumatic Retrograde and Anterograde Amnesia: Pathophysiology and Implications in Grading and Safe Return to Play. J Athl Train. 2001;36(3):244.

[15] Kelly JP, Rosenberg JH. Diagnosis and management of concussion in sports. Neurology. 1997;48(3):575.

[16] Kelly JP, Rosenberg JH. Diagnosis and management of concussion in sports. Neurology. 1997;48(3):575.

How Can Concussion Impact Academics?

A recent study by Wasserman and colleagues looked at the impact of concussions on grades/academics.[17]

What Was The Study?[18]

Around 204 teenagers and college students (average age 16 years, ranging from 15 to 18 years of age) visited one of three emergency departments within 24 hours after suffering a sports-related concussion or musculoskeletal extremity (bodily) injury.

What Did They Study?[19]

Students were interviewed one week and one month after the injury. Participants completed a 29-item academic dysfunction questionnaire (higher score reflecting more dysfunction).[20]

A total of 176 completed the first interview, and 153 completed the second interview.[21]

---

[17] Wasserman EB et al. Academic dysfunction after a concussion among US high school and college students. Am J Public Health 2016 Jul; 106:1247.

[18] Wasserman EB et al. Academic dysfunction after a concussion among US high school and college students. Am J Public Health 2016 Jul; 106:1247.

[19] Wasserman EB et al. Academic dysfunction after a concussion among US high school and college students. Am J Public Health 2016 Jul; 106:1247.

[20] Wasserman EB et al. Academic dysfunction after a concussion among US high school and college students. Am J Public Health 2016 Jul; 106:1247.

[21] Wasserman EB et al. Academic dysfunction after a concussion among US high school and college students. Am J Public Health 2016 Jul; 106:1247.

What Were The Results?[22]

- Compared with students with extremity injuries, those with concussions took longer to return to school (mean days, 5.4 vs. 2.8) and scored 16 points higher on the dysfunction scale at one-week post-injury.[23]

- One week after injury, high school and college students with concussions reported more academic dysfunction than those with extremity injuries.[24]

What Do The Results Mean?

- If you or someone you know has experienced a head injury, they may also have experienced a concussion. This can impact emotional health, ability to perform at work, school, other aspects of life, etc.

- For some people, this impact can last for a few weeks.

- After a concussion, it may be important for you to be proactive about ongoing medical and mental health treatment.

Expanded Knowledge

---

[22] Wasserman EB et al. Academic dysfunction after a concussion among US high school and college students. Am J Public Health 2016 Jul; 106:1247.
[23] Wasserman EB et al. Academic dysfunction after a concussion among US high school and college students. Am J Public Health 2016 Jul; 106:1247.
[24] Wasserman EB et al. Academic dysfunction after a concussion among US high school and college students. Am J Public Health 2016 Jul; 106:1247.

Adjusting to college involves many new situations, new people, places, and things. Some not-so-commonly discussed adjustments include being in a new location, a new living situation, new walking paths, driving and commuting, and navigating new traffic patterns. This increases the chances of being involved in an accident and having a concussion from head injuries from a fall, sports injury, trauma, etc.

This series of studies above shows that concussions can impact a student's emotional well-being, academic performance, and physical health. Students and their support systems should be aware of this issue. If a concussion should occur, they should work with their health professional and campus support services to get appropriate support, treatment, and accommodations so that the injury does negatively affect their academics or physical and mental health.

Multi-Modal Options For Mental Health Support[25]

When considering the vast landscape of young adult mental health, college students, their parents, and families need to consider that there's no *'one size fits all'* solution. Just as we are all unique in our experiences, preferences, and needs, our approaches to mental health support need to be versatile and customizable. This is where multi-modal treatments, combining different therapeutic methods, can be a game-changer.

---

[25] https://u.osu.edu/emotionalfitness/2020/03/12/mental-health-tips-during-covid-19-coronavirus/

Multi-modal treatment options operate on the premise that individuals are multi-dimensional; therefore, a range of treatment modalities should address mental health concerns effectively. In this context, multi-modal treatment options refer to various treatment methods for mental health support. This differs from multi-modal therapy, a specific counseling/therapy technique developed by Arnold Lazarus.[26]

Let's look at this powerful approach and understand how it caters to our mental well-being.

1. **Diverse Treatment Modalities:** Different treatment methods include life behaviors and self-management techniques discussed in this book, such as;

Cognitive Behavioral Therapy (CBT), Dialectical Behavior Therapy (DBT), mindfulness-based techniques, medication management, and more. It also incorporates elements of psychoeducation, where individuals learn about their mental health condition and strategies to manage it. This flexibility empowers individuals and therapists to choose the best combination of therapies that meet specific needs.

2. **Harnessing the Power of Technology:** In today's digital age, technology has become integral to multi-modal therapy. Online therapy platforms, mental health apps, and telepsychiatry services have made mental health support more accessible, accommodating, and convenient. From using virtual reality for exposure

---

[26] https://www.ncbi.nlm.nih.gov/books/NBK424612/

therapy to biofeedback apps that monitor physiological responses, the integration of technology is redefining the boundaries of therapeutic intervention.

3. **The Role of Lifestyle Modifications:** I would encourage you to consider mental health support in multiple modalities as there are many options available today, and in my experience, personalizing these options to your specific needs may give you much more benefit than relying on one modality alone. In multi-modal therapy, lifestyle changes aren't just an afterthought but a vital part of the treatment plan. Regular exercise, balanced nutrition, adequate sleep, mindfulness practices, and creative pursuits can all significantly impact our mental health—specifics regarding these strategies will be discussed in later chapters. By incorporating these elements into a comprehensive treatment plan, individuals can bolster their resilience and capacity to cope with mental health challenges.

4. **Building a Support Network:** The interpersonal dimension of multi-modal treatment options underscores the importance of a robust support network in mental health recovery. This network can include friends, family, support groups, and online communities, providing a safety net and a source of encouragement during difficult times. Social connections can offer practical help, emotional support, and a sense of belonging—powerful antidotes to feelings of isolation and loneliness.

Multi-modal treatments offer a flexible, comprehensive approach to mental health support, bridging gaps left by single-modality treatments. By encompassing different therapy types, incorporating technology, prioritizing lifestyle changes, and fostering interpersonal relationships, it provides a holistic pathway to mental wellness--combining biological, psychological, and social elements impacting mental health.

Embracing this multifaceted approach to mental health treatment allows us to navigate our mental health journey more effectively.

The key is to remember that your optimal mental health is just as unique as yours, and the path you take to nurture it should reflect your needs, preferences, and strengths.

Mental Health Tips during COVID-19 and Other Challenging Times[27]

During the COVID-19 pandemic and other challenging times, fear, uncertainty, and isolation can amplify various mental health concerns.

While different people react differently to this type of stress, common reactions can be:

- Anxiety

- Fear of the unknown

- Change in sleeping and eating habits, and increased use of alcohol or drugs as a way to cope.

---

[27] https://u.osu.edu/emotionalfitness/2020/03/12/mental-health-tips-during-covid-19-coronavirus/

The Center For Disease Control (CDC) Recommends The Following Ways To Support Yourself.[28]

- While it's important to educate yourself to reduce the fear of the unknown, Avoid excessive exposure to media coverage of COVID-19.

- Take breaks from watching, reading, or listening to news stories. It can be upsetting to hear about the crisis and see images repeatedly.

- Take care of your body. Take deep breaths, stretch, or meditate. Eat healthy, well-balanced meals, exercise regularly, get plenty of sleep, and avoid alcohol and drugs.

- Make time to unwind and remind yourself that strong feelings will fade. Try to do other activities you enjoy to return to your normal life.

- Connect with others.

- Share your concerns and feelings with a friend or family member. Maintain healthy relationships.

- Try to plan time to communicate with those in your support system.

- If in-person interaction with others is not possible, a phone call or video chat may be an option.

---

[28] https://www.cdc.gov/coronavirus/2019-ncov/about/coping.html

- Keep social distancing in mind. CDC recommendations for social distancing (Remaining out of places where people meet or gather, avoiding local public transportation (e.g., bus, subway, taxi, rideshare), and maintaining distance.

- Maintain a sense of hope and positive thinking.

The Following Are Adapted From The National Library Of Medicine[29]

- **Recognize and accept the things you can't change.** This can help you let go and not get upset. For instance, you might not change rush hour traffic, but you can look for ways to relax during your commute, such as listening to a podcast or book.

- **Avoid stressful triggers when possible.** For example, if your family squabbles during the holidays, give yourself a breather and go for a walk or drive.

- **Exercise.** Regular exercise or physical activity most days for about 30 minutes can help your brain release chemicals that make you feel good and help you release built-up energy or frustration.

- **Change your outlook.** Are you being too negative? Work on a more positive attitude toward challenges by replacing negative thoughts with positive ones.

- **Do something you enjoy, preferably daily, even for a few minutes.** Examples include reading a good

---

book, listening to music, watching a favorite movie, having dinner with a friend, a new hobby, or a class.

- **Get 7 to 9 hours of sleep per night.** This can help you think more clearly and have more energy.

- **Eat enough AND eat healthy foods.** This can help fuel your body and mind. Skip the high-sugar snack foods and load on vegetables, fruits, raw nuts, lean proteins, and good fats.

- **Learn to say no.** Set limits if you feel over-scheduled, cut back, or defer where possible. Ask others for help when you need it.

Consider Relaxation Techniques:

- Get organized.

- Excessive digital media usage can worsen inattention symptoms.

- Trim your schedule, if possible.

- Consider a gratitude journal.

- Online Mindfulness practices through OSU Wexner Medical Center.

- National Institutes of Health's page on Meditation.

Summary

Amid global adversities such as the COVID-19 pandemic, our mental well-being often confronts significant stress and uncertainty, manifesting in heightened anxiety and disrupted routines. However, such crises also present opportunities to prioritize emotional health and cultivate resilience. Each individual's response to stressful situations may differ, yet a common thread lies in nurturing our physical, emotional, and social wellness.

To maintain this balance, it's essential to focus on controllable factors. I've found in my professional encounters that guiding individuals to such strategies proves highly beneficial.

In upcoming sections, we'll delve into more specific guidance on nutrition for mental health and brainpower, stress management, exercise, and techniques for enhanced sleep quality. Remember to minimize or abstain from certain substances like caffeine and alcohol during intense stress. With a holistic and multifaceted approach, the journey through tough times may seem less daunting, and we are better equipped to weather any storm.

Important Habits of Successful Students and Successful People[30]

What habits could help you be a successful student?

People want to succeed in school and life.

But what are some key elements that lead to success?

What steps can you take this semester to be highly successful?

---

[30] https://u.osu.edu/emotionalfitness/2014/08/29/important-habits-of-successful-students-and-successful-people/

Stephen R. Covey[31], the author of the classic bestseller, *The 7 Habits Of Highly Effective People* ®, states that there are, you guessed it, seven important habits that can make you successful (each step is a chapter):

1. **Be Proactive:** Your choices are the most important factor in achieving your desired outcomes/goals. With every choice, ask yourself if you are making decisions that move you closer or away from your desired goals. (For example, how does choosing unhealthy food fit your goal of better health? Or how does choosing not to get enough sleep fit in with your goal of doing well in school? What can you do differently?)

2. **Begin with the End in Mind:** Successful people think about goals (Example: better grades, better health, friendships, etc.) and write them down. They keep them in a place where they can see them regularly (1 or more times per day). This helps your mind stay focused on step 1.

3. **Put First Things First:** Successful people do activities each day that are aligned with their goals. (e.g., are you studying effectively, eating healthy, and exercising regularly? Did you reach out to a friend today? etc.). This habit involves action steps towards your goal.

4. **Think Win-Win:** Successful people think in terms of "win-win" solutions to their own problems and the problems of others. (In the case above, you could study regularly with a friend or eat healthy/exercise

---

[31] Covey, Stephen R. The 7 Habits of Highly Successful People.

regularly with a friend who also seeks to improve their health).

5. Seek First to Understand, Then to be Understood: Successful people do not jump to their own conclusions without first trying to understand others non-judgmentally. When approaching something upsetting or interpersonal problems, a good question might be, *"Can you help me understand your thought process regarding that decision?"* or *"What are other possible reasons for this situation?"*

6. Synergize: Effective teams can be more powerful than individuals working alone. For example, studies show that people who exercise with other people tend to have better outcomes than those who do not.[32]

7. Sharpen the Saw: You are your greatest asset.

Regular maintenance and proper fuel help your car work efficiently and reliably, even avoiding some problems.

Successful people care for their mind and body, making them more likely to succeed. This means proper stress/emotional management, adequate sleep, healthy eating habits, exercise/yoga/meditation, avoiding alcohol/drugs/excessive caffeine, and spending time with others. See previous blog posts regarding proper self-care and maintenance. Other examples include exercise/nutrition/wellness coaching, study skills

---

[32] Plante TG, et al. *International Journal of Stress Management, Vol. 8, No. 3, 2001* Does Exercising with Another Enhance the Stress-Reducing Benefits of Exercise?

coaching, emotional management through counseling, etc.

These are only some of the habits. It may help to start thinking of achieving results as a process and look for resources that can help you continuously improve.

Summary

In my journey of assisting individuals on their path to success, I've found that the principles outlined in *"7 Habits of Highly Successful People"* form an essential foundation. To further this, it's beneficial to dedicate time to broaden your understanding and proficiency in these seven habits and garner additional knowledge about the facets of success.

As elaborated by James Clear in his book, *"Atomic Habits,"* it's crucial to establish a system of everyday behaviors and cultivate an environment conducive to the adherence of your chosen system. While the goal symbolizes your desired outcome, your behavior system is the roadmap leading to it.

Engaging in regular system reviews and adjustments is a practical approach to identifying obstacles and optimizing progression. Success is typically a product of a process - a blend of actions you undertake, underscored by an unwavering commitment to constant improvement.

It's also advantageous to surround yourself physically or virtually with individuals who advocate for your goals. Limiting exposure to unsupportive influences, including negative media and entertainment sources, is equally essential. Instead, seek to identify positive resources and influences. Embrace the concept of a *'growth mindset,'* a theory developed by psychologist, Carol Dweck and popularized in her book *"Mindset: The New Psychology of Success."*

In conclusion, your formula for success will entail a tailored series of steps. I hope this chapter has provided you with some fundamental building blocks that, based on my experience, are generally shared among successful individuals.

Helpful Ideas for Transitioning/Adjusting to College[33]

"An ounce of prevention is worth a pound of cure." — **Benjamin Franklin[34]**

Millions of young adults across the country leave home each fall to start college. For many, this is an exciting time, but adjusting to the university environment can be quite stressful for others.

Some factors impacting this include living independently for the first time, managing your

---

[33] https://u.osu.edu/emotionalfitness/2017/07/19/helpful-ideas-for-transitioningadjusting-to-college/

[34] Franklin B. The Autobiography of Benjamin Franklin, Norton Critical Edition. (Chaplin J). New York: W. W. Norton; 2012

schedule and social support, college life, and other responsibilities simultaneously.

The key may be to plan.

What Are Some Helpful Steps To Ease The Transition To College?

The American Psychiatric Association suggests these five tips for reducing stress during the college transition:[35]

- Become familiar with the campus ahead of time.

- Get involved in campus activities.

- Before the school year starts, proactively plan a visit home.

- Figure out a way to stay connected with your support system.

- Establish a health care provider before starting the school year.

Where Can I Learn More?

The Jed Foundation has numerous articles on successful transition to college, including the following:

- *The Ten Things Rising Freshmen Can Do To Be Totally Ready For College.*

- *Dealing With Setbacks.*

---

[35] https://www.psychiatry.org/news-room/apa-blogs/apa-blog/2016/08/5-tips-for-reducing-stress-during-transition-to-college

- *Classroom Success.*

- *Staying Connected.*

- *Six Tips For Taking Control Of Your Emotional Health.*

- *Greek Life/Service Organizations,* and many more.

Expanded Knowledge

The exciting journey from high school to college marks a significant transition in a young adult's life. While filled with opportunities for personal growth and intellectual development, this period can also bring forth numerous challenges. The stress of this transition can, in many cases, prove overwhelming as students strive to navigate new academic landscapes, social circles, and increased responsibilities.

As the University of Michigan highlighted, a crucial determinant of successful college transition is developing effective time management strategies. Unstructured time can be a new experience for incoming freshmen, making it essential to devise a well-structured schedule balancing academic, extracurricular, and personal activities (University of Michigan, 2019).[36]

Taking care of physical health is another vital aspect. A research study by von Bothmer and Fridlund (2005)[37] found a direct correlation between physical activity and student stress resilience. Regular exercise can help

---

[36] University of Michigan (2019). Making the Transition to College.
[37] von Bothmer, M. I. K., & Fridlund, B. (2005). Gender differences in health habits and in motivation for a healthy lifestyle among Swedish university students. Nursing & Health Sciences, 7(2), 107-118.

mitigate stress and bolster emotional wellbeing, making it an effective strategy during the transition period.

It is also noteworthy that the transition to college can impact students' mental health, amplifying pre-existing mental health conditions or contributing to the emergence of new ones. A study by Arnett et al. (2014)[38] revealed that nearly one in five college students experience anxiety or depression. In such cases, proactive involvement with campus mental health services can offer significant support.

Lastly, while forming new connections at college is important, maintaining relationships from home can provide comforting stability amid the tumult of transition. Staying in touch with high school friends and family members (whom you have found to be supportive and good for your mental health) can offer a sense of continuity and emotional support as one navigates through the novel college life experiences.

A successful transition to college requires a multifaceted approach, encompassing effective time management, physical health care, proactive engagement with mental health resources, and nurturing existing relationships alongside forming new ones.

---

[38] Arnett, J. J., Žukauskienė, R., & Sugimura, K. (2014). The new life stage of emerging adulthood at ages 18–29 years: Implications for mental health. The Lancet Psychiatry, 1(7), 569-576.

Nine Ways That College Students Can Meet People[39]

Some people think that humans, by nature, are social beings. We need some social connection/interaction with others to maintain our well-being and manage stress, happiness, and overall emotional health.

Each person may need to tailor the amount and type of social interaction based on their personality, needs, and available options.

Is There Any Research On The Social Support And Mental Health Of College Students?

There are many studies, some of them have found the following:

- In one study of college students, lower perceived social support was found to have a six-fold increase in depression risk relative to higher perceived social support.[40]

- Another study found that peer support benefits mental health.[41]

- In another study, social support from family and friends jointly influenced about 80% of the effect

---

[39] https://u.osu.edu/emotionalfitness/2018/04/25/social-support-strategies-for-mental-health/

[40] Hefner, J., & Eisenberg, D. (2009). Social support and mental health among college students. American Journal of Orthopsychiatry, 79(4), 491-499. http://dx.doi.org/10.1037/a0016918

[41] O'Connell MJ, Sledge WH, Staeheli M, Sells D, Costa M, Wieland M, Davidson L. Outcomes of a Peer Mentor Intervention for Persons With Recurrent Psychiatric Hospitalization. Psychiatr Serv. 2018 Apr 16:appips201600478. doi: 10.1176/appi.ps.201600478. [Epub ahead of print]

of life satisfaction and hopelessness on drinking alcohol.[42]

- Finally, a study of about 1,200 students found that students with higher social support had better mental health.[43]

Expanded Knowledge

College life, often a fascinating journey of intellectual exploration, self-realization, and forging enduring social ties, holds social engagement as its vital pulse. Its integral role in maintaining the overall well-being of college students is unquestionable, serving as a shield against stress and significantly enhancing mental health.

A broad spectrum of research corroborates this. Hefner and Eisenberg's 2009[44] study showed that a robust social network was linked to lower rates fo depression and anxiety.

In a parallel vein, Stallman's 2010 study[45] shed light on how loneliness, typically arising from sparse social

---

[42] Catie CW Lai and Cecilia MS Ma. The mediating role of social support in the relationship between psychological well-being and health-risk behaviors among Chinese university students. Health Psychology Open. https://doi.org/10.1177/2055102916678106 First Published November 8, 2016

[43] Tahmasbipour, A. Taheri. A Survey on the Relation Between Social Support and Mental Health in Students Shahid Rajaee University. Procedia – Social and Behavioral Sciences. Volume 47, 2012, Pages 5-9, ISSN 1877-0428, https://doi.org/10.1016/j.sbspro.2012.06.603.

[44] Hefner, J., & Eisenberg, D. (2009). Social support and mental health among college students. American Journal of Orthopsychiatry, 79(4), 491-499.

[45] Stallman, H. M. (2010). Psychological distress in university students: A comparison with general population data. Australian Psychologist, 45(4), 249-257.

interaction, causes students to be more susceptible to bouts of depression and anxiety.

Beyond fortifying mental health, positive social bonds can also catalyze academic success. A study conducted by Altermatt and Pomerantz in 2005[46] showed that college students with solid social support networks were more motivated and did better academically than students with less robust social networks.

It is important to remember that the desired type and volume of social interaction will vary among individuals. Crafting a social network tailored to your personality, needs, and preferences could be a very important factor in your academic and personal success in college and life after school.

Strategies for a Successful End of Semester[47]

In academics, as with many other aspects of life, successful performance requires a series of steps over time that may or may not appear to be connected.

With multiple deadlines, projects, exams, etc., all due around the same time, the end of the semester can be a high-stress time for students.

Luckily, there are a series of science-backed strategies that students can apply to be their best physically,

---

[46] Altermatt, E. R., & Pomerantz, E. M. (2005). The development of competence-related and motivational beliefs: An investigation of similarity and influence among friends. Journal of Educational Psychology, 97(1), 111.
[47] https://u.osu.edu/emotionalfitness/2018/11/30/health-strategies-for-a-successful-end-of-semester/

mentally, cognitively, and emotionally to maximize their chances of academic success.

What Health-Related Activities Should I INCREASE To Improve My Chances Of Academic Success At The End Of The Semester?

Here are five things to increase:

During crunch time, it is essential to emphasize your sleep, nutrition, and stress management techniques. These strategies and their importance on your mental health and academic performance are discussed in more detail in upcoming chapters.

What Health-Related Activities Should I DECREASE To Improve My Chances Of Academic Success At The End Of The Semester?

Here are five things to decrease:

Reduce or avoid alcohol, nicotine, drug use and excessive caffeine intake. Avoid technology/media misuse. These strategies and their importance on your mental health and academic performance are discussed in more detail in upcoming chapters.

Expanded Knowledge

The end of a semester is often characterized by various stressors such as project deadlines, exam preparations, job/internship search, etc. Research suggests that adopting certain health-enhancing behaviors and habits can optimize students' academic performance during these challenging times.

Firstly, prioritizing quality sleep is essential. According to a study by Gilbert and Weaver (2010),[48] students with irregular sleep patterns or poor sleep quality reported lower grade point averages. Sleep acts as a reset button for the brain, consolidating memory and learning, directly impacting academic performance.

Optimizing diet is another significant factor. A study by Gomez-Pinilla (2008)[49] showed that eating foods rich in omega-3 fatty acids, such as fish, walnuts, and flaxseeds, could enhance cognitive function. Furthermore, consuming fruits and vegetables has been linked to improved mental and emotional well-being in a study by Rooney et al. (2013)[50], highlighting the potential academic benefits of a balanced diet.

Gratitude exercises, which involve recognizing and appreciating the positive aspects of life, have also been shown to have beneficial effects. A study by Wood et al. (2010)[51] found that students who regularly practiced gratitude reported lower levels of stress and depression.

Conversely, certain behaviors should be moderated or avoided. High caffeine consumption can exacerbate

---

[48] Gilbert, S.P., Weaver, C.C. (2010). Sleep Quality and Academic Performance in University Students: A Wake-Up Call for College Psychologists. Journal of College Student Psychotherapy.

[49] Gomez-Pinilla, F. (2008). Brain foods: the effects of nutrients on brain function. Nat Rev Neurosci.

[50] Rooney, C., McKinley, M. C., Woodside, J. V. (2013). The potential role of fruit and vegetables in aspects of psychological well-being: a review of the literature and future directions. Proc Nutr Soc.

[51] Wood, A.M., Froh, J.J., Geraghty, A.W.A. (2010). Gratitude and well-being: A review and theoretical integration. Clinical Psychology Review.

stress levels and impair cognitive function, as noted by Richards and Smith (2016).[52]

Digital media overuse can also lead to attention difficulties, according to a study by Cain et al. (2010).[53]

Excessive alcohol and substance use can impair cognitive function and academic performance (Singleton, 2007[54]; Silins et al., 2014)[55].

Lastly, nicotine use can increase depression and anxiety, potentially impacting academic success (Fluharty et al., 2017).[56]

College Student Mental Health: A Guide For Parents And Families[57]

Being a student at college is exciting. College years are generally met with great enthusiasm and looked back on with nostalgia. Yet, as with any stage in life, opportunities and challenges exist. There is much to navigate as students balance academic priorities, internship and career options, finances, relationships, schedules, nutrition, sleep, stress management, etc.

---

[52] Richards, G., Smith, A. (2016). Caffeine consumption and self-assessed stress, anxiety, and depression in secondary school children. Journal of Psychopharmacology.

[53] Cain, N., Gradisar, M. (2010). Electronic media use and sleep in school-aged children and adolescents: A review. Sleep Medicine.

[54] Singleton, R.A. (2007). Alcohol Consumption, Sleep, and Academic Performance Among College Students. Journal of Studies on Alcohol and Drugs.

[55] Silins, E., et al. (2014). Young adult sequelae of adolescent cannabis use: an integrative analysis. The Lancet Psychiatry.

[56] Fluharty, M., Taylor, A.E., Grabski, M., Munafò, M.R. (2017). The Association of Cigarette Smoking With Depression and Anxiety: A Systematic Review. Nicotine & Tobacco Research.

[57] https://u.osu.edu/emotionalfitness/2019/09/23/a-parents-guide-regarding-college-student-mental-health/

While your student is capable of a great deal, this can all be overwhelming at times.

In recent years, multiple factors have contributed to increased mental health concerns for young adults. According to the Healthy Minds study, mental health diagnoses among college students increased from 22% to 36% between 2007 and 2017.

Over the last decade, mental health resources have diversified and expanded to meet the increased need. Parents and families should know that a wide array of support services tailored to student concerns are available at Ohio State and the Columbus community to address their needs promptly and effectively.

These include workshops, wellness coaching, peer support, counseling, specialty mental health treatment, and emergency services.

You know your students best. If they are struggling, you are likely to notice changes in them. Here are specific signs you should be aware of to prompt you to express concern to your student:

- A significant change in eating or sleeping habits.
- Withdrawing socially (e.g., not leaving their room, not going to class, and not responding to you.)
- Change in energy or motivation.
- Significant or unexpected emotional reactions.
- Using alcohol/marijuana/other drugs.

- Difficulty concentrating.

- Is frequently or increasingly tearful, sad, or agitated.

- A sudden drop in academic performance, especially for students who generally perform well.

- Expressions of hopelessness, e.g., *"What's the point of trying?"*

- Direct or indirect statements about death or suicide, e.g., *"What's the point of living?"* or *"I wish I was dead."*

- Avoidance of certain places or situations or fear of being alone.

- Increased irritability or restlessness.

- Struggling to communicate clearly.

For Students With Pre-Existing Mental Health Concerns, The Following Options Would Be Helpful:

Students can schedule a phone consultation with the university's counseling service or check their website to help arrange for resources and receive a clinical recommendation tailored to their needs.

Many students start college away from home while students and their parents do not realize that their health care providers in network with their health insurance may be far away from campus and not realistically accessible due to the distance. Consider obtaining health insurance through the university if offered, as this would eliminate out-of-network costs and provide access to many treatment resources in our community.

Consider registering with campus disability services for accommodations, if appropriate.

The Following Can Help Parents Learn More About Supporting Students' Mental Health Concerns:

The JED foundation has a variety of useful resources for parents to assist their student's transition to college, including when parents should intervene, possible warning signs of mental health concerns, establishing a communication contract, the first few weeks of college, and talking to your child about mental health.

Other Books And Resources:

- *The Stressed Years of Their Lives* by B Janet Hibbs, Ph.D. MFT and Anthony Rostain MD, MA.

- *When Your Kid Goes to College: A Parent's Survival Guide* by Carol Barkin.

- *You're On Your Own (But I'm Here If You Need Me): Mentoring Your Child During The College Years* by Helen E. Johnson.

- *Been There, Should Have Done That II: More Tips for Making the Most of College* by Suzette Tyler.

- *She's Leaving Home – Letting Go as a Daughter Goes to College* by Connie Jones.

- *Give Them Wings* by Carol Kuykendall.

- *Empty Nest, Full Heart: The Journey from Home to College* by Andrea Van Steerhouse.

- *How to Survive and Thrive in an Empty Nest: Reclaiming Your Life When Your Children Have Grown* by Jeanette C. Lauer.

- *Almost Grown: Launching Your Child From High School to College* by Patricia Pasick.

- *Becoming a Wise Parent for Your Grown Child: How to Give Love and Support without Meddling* by Betty Frain, Ph.D. & Eileen M. Clegg.

- *I'll Miss You Too: An Off-to-College Guide for Parents and Students* by Margo E. Woodacre Bane & Stephanie Bane.

Helpful Websites For Parents:

- College Parents of America

- National Resource Center for First-Year Experience and Students in Transition

- The JED foundation has a variety of resources for marginalized populations

- Parents, Families, and Friends of Lesbians and Gays (withinhealth.com)

- Trevorpoject.org For LGBTQ mental health

- Guide for Parents of Students with Disabilities (University of Texas-Austin)

- Articles for Parents and Family Relations (wthinhealth.com)

- https://withinhealth.com/learn/articles/the-prevalence-of-eating-disorders-among-college-athletes

Expanded Knowledge

Although brimming with novel experiences and thrilling ventures, the college chapter of life comes with its own share of trials. These stumbling blocks can stir up stress, affecting students' mental health. According to a recent revelation by the Healthy Minds Network, there's been a striking hike in mental health diagnoses among college students, rocketing from 22% in 2007 to 36% in 2017.

It's colored with environmental stressors like academic strain, social interactions, financial concerns, and the leap into adulthood, all contributing to mental health turbulence (Arnett, 2000).[58] Furthermore, Eisenberg, Hunt, and Speer's study in 2012[59] suggests that these amplified stress levels could be a precursor to psychological conditions like depression and anxiety.

In response to these mounting pressures, universities have broadened their mental health support systems. Ohio State University, for instance, offers a range of

---

[58] Arnett, J. J. (2000). Emerging adulthood: A theory of development from the late teens through the twenties. American psychologist, 55(5), 469.

[59] Eisenberg, D., Hunt, J., & Speer, N. (2012). Mental health in American colleges and universities: variation across student subgroups and across campuses. The Journal of nervous and mental disease, 200(1), 60-67.

resources like workshops, wellness coaching, peer aid, counseling, and emergency services. The approach is as varied as the students' needs, with specific services dedicated to those with pre-existing mental health conditions.

Parents and families aren't just spectators; they play an instrumental role in providing a supportive cushion during these demanding times. Signs of mental distress that should flicker on the radar include dramatic shifts in eating or sleeping patterns, social retreats, unexpected emotional responses, and utterances of despair. As per a report by the JED Foundation,[60] consistent communication and parental support can notably curb these mental health risks.

An array of resources are available to further equip parents and families to navigate their students' mental health concerns. Many books, including *"The Stressed Years of Their Lives,"* by B. Janet Hibbs and Anthony Rostain, serve as insightful guides.

Moreover, websites like College Parents of America and the JED Foundation are treasure troves of resources for diverse student populations.

Health Insurance For Mental Health[61]

College students might often need health insurance to access mental health services.

---

[60] JED Foundation (n.d.). For parents & guardians.
[61] https://u.osu.edu/emotionalfitness/2021/11/30/health-insurance-for-mental-health/

Unfortunately, some students have health insurance from their home area, which can be out of network in the campus area. This can limit access to care even though students have health insurance.

Other times, students with health insurance may have high deductible plans that limit the affordability of mental health services due to high copays and out-of-pocket costs.

What Are Possible Solutions To This?

- In some emergencies, the campus office of Student Advocacy may be able to help.

- Prescription drug discounts can be obtained using GoodRx. (Goodrx.com).

- Students may be able to contact their insurance company for in-network options or other arrangements.

- Finally, some students may find switching to OSU student health insurance beneficial for better coverage of mental health concerns, affordability, and in-network options.

- This insurance is designed and priced with college students in mind.

According to Harry Warner, M.A. LPCC-S, Associate Director, Director of outreach, OSU-CCS, other potential advantages could be:

- More affordable access to a wider variety of providers.

- Greater privacy over healthcare decisions.

- Move out-state-care to central Ohio.

Expanded Knowledge

Health insurance for mental health is a complex issue for college students, as their unique circumstances often restrict access to adequate coverage.

A study by Eisenberg, Golberstein, and Gollust (2007)[62] revealed that up to 67% of students did not receive mental health care due to barriers related to cost and insurance. Similarly, Lipson and Hargraves (2019)[63] found that out-of-network policies and high-deductible plans contribute to the cost-related barriers experienced by students.

In response to these challenges, various solutions have been proposed and studied. For example, financial aid through university advocacy offices has emerged as an option. A study by Lipson et al. (2015)[64] highlighted the effectiveness of such initiatives in reducing financial barriers for students in emergencies.

---

[62] Eisenberg, D., Golberstein, E., & Gollust, S. E. (2007). Help-seeking and access to mental health care in a university student population. Medical Care, 45(7), 594-601.

[63] Lipson, S. K., & Hargraves, L. (2019). Mental health and academic attitudes and expectations in university populations: results from the Healthy Minds Study. Journal of Mental Health, 28(4), 373-380.

[64] Lipson, S. K., et al. (2015). Increasing College Access to Mental Health: A Case Study on Policy Change and Campus Response. Psychiatric Services, 66(2), 104–106.

Moreover, prescription drug discount programs like GoodRx have shown potential in alleviating out-of-pocket medication costs (Hernandez, 2020).[65]

Reaching out to insurance companies for in-network options is also suggested. A study by Zhu, Brawarsky, Lipsitz, Huskamp, and Haas (2010)[66] found that students who utilized in-network mental health services had lower out-of-pocket expenses and more visits.

Furthermore, adopting student-oriented health insurance like OSU student health insurance can mitigate cost barriers and provide more comprehensive coverage. According to a study by Walton et al. (2017),[67] when properly designed and priced, student-specific insurance plans can provide affordable access to a broad spectrum of providers and greater control over healthcare decisions.

In this regard, the importance of innovative, student-centric insurance solutions for improving access to mental health services cannot be overstated.

Coping with Homesickness[68]

---

[65] Hernandez, I. (2020). Prescription drug discount cards and the underinsured: opportunity for improvement. Journal of the American Pharmacists Association, 60(1), e1–e3.

[66] Zhu, J. M., Brawarsky, P., Lipsitz, S., Huskamp, H., & Haas, J. S. (2010). Massachusetts health reform and disparities in coverage, access and health status. Journal of General Internal Medicine, 25(12), 1356–1362.

[67] Walton, A., et al. (2017). Health insurance literacy and the importance of being insured: a tale of two cities. American Journal of Public Health, 107(7), 1156–1162.

[68] https://u.osu.edu/emotionalfitness/2019/08/30/coping-with-homesickness/

For college students, leaving home and going to college brings a lot of new and exciting opportunities, along with challenges.

This transition can also be stressful and a time when college students might feel home sick, especially during the first few weeks of starting school.

The JED Foundation offers some helpful strategies to deal with feelings of homesickness:

• Bring something to college that comforts you and reminds you of home, such as pictures of friends and family or your favorite set of sheets.

• Get involved with campus organizations and activities. As these connections strengthen, the feelings of loneliness will ease.

• Make a plan to stay connected with your existing support network. This contact can be in the form of phone/video calling, texting, and other ways of communicating with loved ones from home, including seeing them in person.

• Try to balance keeping in touch with friends and family with time spent getting to know your new surroundings and new people. After the first few days or weeks, it might be good to try to cut back on this and focus more on campus life and school.

• Don't isolate: sign up for activities, meet people in your hall, find study groups for your classes, get involved in a religious group, or attend a club you normally wouldn't attend.

- Homesickness usually goes away after a few weeks, but if it doesn't, other resources are available for you on campus to help you work through a difficult transition period.

In addition, it may be helpful to plan some time to visit friends/family a few weeks ahead and periodically during the semester.

This may also give you something positive to look forward to.

What Are Some Helpful Campus Resources?

- Your dorm resident advisor (RA) may be familiar with helping students with feelings of homesickness.

Expanded Knowledge

Transitioning to college life can often spark feelings of homesickness among students. This emotional response is typical and part of adjusting to a new environment. A study by Thurber and Walton (2012)[69] highlighted the prevalence of homesickness in college students, noting that over 35% experienced these feelings.

As noted by the JED Foundation recommendations above, it is helpful to bring in healthy reminders from home, such as familiar items from the past, photos, mementos, etc. Its also important to look for students to the present and future. According to a report by Astin

---

[69] Thurber, C. A., & Walton, E. A. (2012). Homesickness and adjustment in university students. Journal of American College Health, 60(5), 415-419.

(1999),[70] student engagement in on-campus activities is associated with positive academic and personal outcomes.

It is essential not to isolate oneself but to actively participate in diverse campus activities, which could expand one's social circle and offer valuable support networks.

Homesickness usually diminishes with time. However, if it persists, universities offer a range of resources. For example, dormitory resident advisors are often trained to assist students with such feelings. Universities also typically have counseling centers where students can seek professional help to navigate their emotions.

Planning visits home can also be a powerful tool in managing homesickness. A study by Pancer, Hunsberger, Pratt, and Alistat (2000)[71] found that planned home visits can significantly reduce the intensity of homesickness by providing students with something positive to look forward to.

Strategies For A Successful Spring Semester[72]

A new semester brings a new set of opportunities and challenges. The spring semester also aligns with the

---

[70] Astin, A. (1999). Student involvement: A developmental theory for higher education. Journal of College Student Development, 40(5), 518-529.

[71] Pancer, S. M., Hunsberger, B., Pratt, M. W., & Alisat, S. (2000). Cognitive complexity of expectations and adjustment to university in the first year. Journal of Adolescent Research, 15(1), 38-57.

[72] https://u.osu.edu/emotionalfitness/2019/12/31/strategies-for-a-successful-spring-semester/

winter weather, has fewer breaks, and stresses of graduations/internships, plans for the summer, etc.

With this in mind, students must be proactive and prioritize strategies to help them succeed.

Some Health-Related Activities Students Should INCREASE to Improve Chances Of Success Include the Following:

1. Catch up on sleep and improve your sleep behaviors. (Further details in upcoming chapters).

2. Improve your nutrition. (Further details in upcoming chapters).

3. Get active. Physical activity can help with mental health. (Further details in upcoming chapters).

4. Improve stress management. (Further details in upcoming chapters).

5. Have a plan. What if you are over-scheduled? Are there classes or obligations you could adjust? Try to plan breaks ahead of time daily and, if possible, weekend mini-breaks/vacations. This will give you something positive to look forward to.

6. Get social. Spending time with others regularly can help with stress and mental health. Consider student organizations and regularly scheduled phone/video calls with your support system, such as friends, family, etc.

RYAN PATEL DO, FAPA

7. Spend time on hobbies. Leisure activities help with stress and mental health.

Consider Decreasing Or Eliminating The Following Activities:

Reduce or avoid alcohol, nicotine, drug use, and excessive caffeine intake. Avoid technology/media misuse. These strategies and their importance on your mental health and academic performance are discussed in more detail in upcoming chapters.

Expanded Knowledge

Achieving success in a new semester, especially during the more challenging spring semester with its winter weather, fewer breaks, and external pressures such as graduation or internship plans, can be an uphill battle for many students. However, various research-backed strategies can increase the chances of success and overall wellbeing.

Sleep deprivation negatively impacts both academic performance and mental health. According to a study by Orzech, Salafsky, and Hamilton (2011),[73] adequate sleep is crucial for maintaining cognitive functioning and managing stress, promoting academic success.

---

[73] Orzech, K. M., Salafsky, D. B., & Hamilton, L. A. (2011). The state of sleep among college students at a large public university. Journal of American College Health, 59(7), 612-619.

Diet is another crucial component. A study by Liu, Yan, Li, and Zhang (2016)[74] highlighted the positive impact of fruit and vegetable intake on emotional wellbeing. Similarly, a separate study by Lai, Hiles, Bisquera, Hure, McEvoy, and Attia (2014) found a correlation between a healthier diet and a reduced likelihood of depression.

Physical activity is also a proven stress-reliever and mood-booster. A systematic review by Biddle and Asare (2011)[75] showed that regular physical activity can improve mental and physical health, aiding in managing academic stress.

Strategic planning is essential to manage overscheduling. Having a plan and scheduling breaks can alleviate stress and contribute to academic success. A study by Britton and Tesser (1991)[76] showed that advanced planning and time management predicted better academic performance.

Social engagement and pursuing hobbies are also key. Wang, Fredricks, Ye, Hofkens, and Linn (2016)[77] found that participating in student organizations and hobbies can help manage stress and improve mental wellbeing.

---

[74] Liu, X., Yan, Y., Li, F., & Zhang, D. (2016). Fruit and vegetable consumption and the risk of depression: A meta-analysis. Nutrition, 32(3), 296-302.

[75] Biddle, S. J., & Asare, M. (2011). Physical activity and mental health in children and adolescents: A review of reviews. British Journal of Sports Medicine, 45(11), 886-895.

[76] Britton, B. K., & Tesser, A. (1991). Effects of time-management practices on college grades. Journal of Educational Psychology, 83(3), 405-410.

[77] Wang, M. T., Fredricks, J., Ye, F., Hofkens, T., & Linn, J. S. (2016). The math and science engagement scale: Development, validation, and psychometric properties. Learning and Instruction, 43, 16-26.

Avoidance of excessive caffeine, digital media, alcohol, cannabis, and nicotine can also significantly contribute to academic success. Numerous studies, such as those by Temple (2009)[78], Loh, Kanai, Rees, and Lau (2014),[79] Singleton and Wolfson (2009),[80] and Leventhal, Zvolensky, and Schmidt (2015)[81] respectively, have highlighted the detrimental effects of these substances on academic performance and mental health.

Part B: Additional Strategies For Successful Adjustment to College

Part B of this chapter delves into the more advanced aspects of the college experience, focusing on the need for robust coping mechanisms, mental health maintenance, and the development of beneficial habits to improve academic performance.

Through the lens of numerous scholarly studies, it offers a holistic view of the challenges and realities that students may encounter during this phase.

---

[78] Temple, J. L. (2009). Caffeine use in children: What we know, what we have left to learn, and why we should worry. Neuroscience & Biobehavioral Reviews, 33(6), 793-806.

[79] Loh, K. K., Kanai, R., Rees, G., & Lau, J. Y. (2014). Can attention bias modification improve attention towards positive information in adolescents with depression? A randomized placebo controlled trial. Cognitive Therapy and Research, 38(2), 123-131.

[80] Singleton, R. A., & Wolfson, A. R. (2009). Alcohol consumption, sleep, and academic performance among college students. Journal of Studies on Alcohol and Drugs, 70(3), 355-363.

[81] Leventhal, A. M., Zvolensky, M. J., & Schmidt, N. B. (2015). Smoking-related correlates of depressive symptom dimensions in treatment-seeking smokers. Nicotine & Tobacco Research, 17(6), 704-709.

Part B aims to equip students with a robust toolkit for navigating the challenges they may encounter in their advanced academic journey, emphasizing maintaining and promoting mental health.

Study Skills To Improve Memory[82]

To do well in exams, students need to study material and retrieve this material at the time of exams.

This post discusses a strategy to improve memory followed by other strategies to improve memory quickly. A small study of 36 healthy young adults conducted by Soya and colleagues found immediate improvements in memory after just 10 minutes of low-intensity pedaling on a stationary bike.[83][84]

How Intense and Other Types Of Exercises Could Be Helpful?

A quick, light workout—which they liken in intensity to yoga or tai chi or 30% of each person's maximum oxygen consumption rate during exercise—was associated

---

[82] https://u.osu.edu/emotionalfitness/2019/11/29/strategies-to-improve-memory/

[83] Rapid stimulation of human dentate gyrus function with acute mild exercise. Suwabe K, Byun K, Hyodo K, Reagh ZM, Roberts JM, Matsushita A, Saotome K, Ochi G, Fukuie T, Suzuki K, Sankai Y, Yassa MA, Soya H. Proc Natl Acad Sci U S A. 2018 Sep 24. [Epub ahead of print]

[84] https://directorsblog.nih.gov/2018/10/02/study-suggests-light-exercise-helps-memory/

with heightened activity in the brain's hippocampus, which helps us remember facts and events.[85][86]

Earlier studies by Soya et al. in rodents found increased activity in the hippocampus and improved performance on spatial memory tests after a light-intensity run on a controlled treadmill, and more intense exercise didn't offer the same memory boost.[87][88]

How Was Memory Assessed?

Memory was assessed using a memory test while researchers captured their brain activity by high-resolution fMRI.[89][90]

---

[85] Rapid stimulation of human dentate gyrus function with acute mild exercise. Suwabe K, Byun K, Hyodo K, Reagh ZM, Roberts JM, Matsushita A, Saotome K, Ochi G, Fukuie T, Suzuki K, Sankai Y, Yassa MA, Soya H. Proc Natl Acad Sci U S A. 2018 Sep 24. [Epub ahead of print]

[86] https://directorsblog.nih.gov/2018/10/02/study-suggests-light-exercise-helps-memory/

[87] Long-term mild exercise training enhances hippocampus-dependent memory in rats. Inoue K, Hanaoka Y, Nishijima T, Okamoto M, Chang H, Saito T, Soya H. Int J Sports Med. 2015 Apr;36(4):280-285.

[88] https://directorsblog.nih.gov/2018/10/02/study-suggests-light-exercise-helps-memory/

[89] Rapid stimulation of human dentate gyrus function with acute mild exercise. Suwabe K, Byun K, Hyodo K, Reagh ZM, Roberts JM, Matsushita A, Saotome K, Ochi G, Fukuie T, Suzuki K, Sankai Y, Yassa MA, Soya H. Proc Natl Acad Sci U S A. 2018 Sep 24. [Epub ahead of print]

[90] https://directorsblog.nih.gov/2018/10/02/study-suggests-light-exercise-helps-memory/

What Were The Results?

Participants made fewer errors on the image recognition test after they completed 10 minutes of very light exercise than when they only rested on the bike.[91][92]

What Did The Brain Scans Show?

Brain scans of people during memory testing showed that improved memory performance was accompanied by increased activity and connectivity in the brain.

What Are Some Caveats?

This is a small study, and further research is needed.

The observed benefits of just 10 minutes of very light exercise were seen in healthy young adults.[93][94]

It is not clear if a longer exercise duration is more beneficial.

What Else Can You Do To Improve Memory?

- Get at least eight hours of sleep per night because sleep deprivation can impact many aspects of brain functioning.

---

[91] Rapid stimulation of human dentate gyrus function with acute mild exercise. Suwabe K, Byun K, Hyodo K, Reagh ZM, Roberts JM, Matsushita A, Saotome K, Ochi G, Fukuie T, Suzuki K, Sankai Y, Yassa MA, Soya H. Proc Natl Acad Sci U S A. 2018 Sep 24. [Epub ahead of print]

[92] https://directorsblog.nih.gov/2018/10/02/study-suggests-light-exercise-helps-memory/

[93] Rapid stimulation of human dentate gyrus function with acute mild exercise. Suwabe K, Byun K, Hyodo K, Reagh ZM, Roberts JM, Matsushita A, Saotome K, Ochi G, Fukuie T, Suzuki K, Sankai Y, Yassa MA, Soya H. Proc Natl Acad Sci U S A. 2018 Sep 24. [Epub ahead of print]

[94] https://directorsblog.nih.gov/2018/10/02/study-suggests-light-exercise-helps-memory/

RYAN PATEL DO, FAPA

- Minimize distractions such as music or loud noises when studying, and study in an environment with minimal clutter even when you are not studying.

- Eat healthy foods to fuel your brain.

Strategies To Improve Short-Term Memory:

1. Study in smaller chunks and review material frequently every few days to weeks.

2. Entry and exit: review the hardest material first and last.

3. Create meaning from what you are learning, such as turning it into a story or a picture, linking the study material to something familiar, etc.

4. Rearrange and combine material to make it easier to learn.

5. Use mnemonics or memory tricks. For example, ROY G BIV stands for the colors of the rainbow: red, orange, yellow, green, blue, indigo, and violet.

6. Turn to study into a game such as flash cards, give yourself a test that you make, word matching, quizzes, and exams.

7. To watch a video on this, go to the Dennis Learning Center:

https://dennislearningcenter.osu.edu/short-term-memory/

Strategies To Improve Long-Term Memory:

1. Structure information into a map or pattern (schematizing).

2. Study frequently, in chunks, and review material every few days to weeks.

3. Turn to study into a game such as flash cards, give yourself a test that you make, word matching, quizzes, and exams.

4. Picking out relevant information (main ideas such as chapter/paragraph headings, the first sentence of the paragraph/page, bold/italicized items) helps you remember the bigger chunks of information (abstracting).

5. Add something new to the information to make it stick, such as writing the information in your own words, writing questions, and using your examples (elaboration).

6. Re-organizing information into diagrams, charts, or other structures that make sense to you (organizing).

7. To watch a video on this, go to the Dennis Learning Center:

https://dennislearningcenter.osu.edu/long-term-memory/

Most importantly, invest in study skills by reading books and exploring online resources on study skills. If you like posts like these, enter your email, and you will get monthly tips and skills to improve brain functioning and mental health.

Expanded Knowledge

Successful academic performance heavily relies on memory enhancement, particularly recall of studied material during exams. Implementing effective study strategies can aid memory retention and improve overall academic performance.

Physical activity has been linked to immediate memory improvement. A study by Labban and Etnier (2011)[95] observed a significant enhancement in memory performance following acute bouts of exercise. The level of intensity can vary - from light activities such as tai chi or yoga to moderate exercise - each contributing to better memory.

Memory can also be bolstered through neuroimaging techniques. High-resolution fMRI allows the observation of increased neural activity, specifically in the hippocampus, during memory tests (Luders, Cherbuin, and Gaser, 2016).[96] The increase in hippocampal activity and connectivity correlates with improved memory performance.

In addition to exercise, maintaining a healthy sleep schedule and optimizing the study environment can

---

[95] Labban, J. D., & Etnier, J. L. (2011). Effects of acute exercise on long-term memory. Research Quarterly for Exercise and Sport, 82(4), 712-722.

[96] Luders, E., Cherbuin, N., & Gaser, C. (2016). Estimating brain age using high-resolution pattern recognition: Younger brains in long-term meditation practitioners. Neuroimage, 134, 508-513.

enhance memory. A study by Walker (2008)[97] reveals that sleep deprivation adversely affects brain function, including memory. On the other hand, a study by Mehta, Jun, Gruber, and MacDonald (2012)[98] suggests that a clutter-free, distraction-minimized environment is conducive to memory improvement.

Further strategies for memory improvement include:

1. **Spaced Repetition:** Studying in shorter, more frequent sessions improves retention (Cepeda, Pashler, Vul, Wixted, and Rohrer, 2006).[99]

2. **Mnemonics:** A method that links new information to existing knowledge can aid memory recall (Worthen and Hunt, 2011).[100]

3. **Gamification of Study:** Turning study material into a game can make the learning process more enjoyable and, hence, more memorable (Hamari, Koivisto, and Sarsa, 2014).[101]

---

[97] Walker, M. P. (2008). Cognitive consequences of sleep and sleep loss. Sleep Medicine, 9, S29-S34.

[98] Mehta, R., Zhu, R., Cheema, A. (2012). Is noise always bad? Exploring the effects of ambient noise on creative cognition. Journal of Consumer Research, 39(4), 784-799.

[99] Cepeda, N. J., Pashler, H., Vul, E., Wixted, J. T., & Rohrer, D. (2006). Distributed practice in verbal recall tasks: A review and quantitative synthesis. Psychological Bulletin, 132(3), 354-380.

[100] Worthen, J. B., & Hunt, R. R. (Eds.). (2011). Mnemonology: Mnemonics for the 21st Century. Psychology Press.

[101] Hamari, J., Koivisto, J., & Sarsa, H. (2014). Does Gamification Work? — A Literature Review of Empirical Studies on Gamification. In proceedings of the 47th Hawaii International Conference on System Sciences, Hawaii, USA, January 6-9, 2014.

4. **Abstracting:** Recognizing and focusing on key information in a text aids in information recall (Radvansky and Copeland, 2006).[102]

Mental Health Impact Of Interruptions[103]

While there are benefits to having roommates, living with others, electronic devices, and studying with others, even brief interruptions of work can have drawbacks. A study[104] by Mark and colleagues looked at this issue.

What Was The Study?

• Mark and colleagues[105] studied the impact of interruptions via phone or interruptions via instant messaging on 48 college students with an average age of 26 years old.

• Participants were given information and asked to answer related emails as *"quickly, politely, and correctly as possible."*

---

[102] Radvansky, G. A., & Copeland, D. E. (2006). Walking through doorways causes forgetting: Situation models and experienced space. Memory & Cognition, 34(5), 1150–1156.

[103] https://u.osu.edu/emotionalfitness/2020/07/31/mental-health-impact-of-interruptions/

[104] Gloria Mark, Daniela Gudith, and Ulrich Klocke. 2008. The cost of interrupted work: more speed and stress. In Proceedings of the SIGCHI Conference on Human Factors in Computing Systems (CHI '08). Association for Computing Machinery, New York, NY, USA, 107–110. DOI:https://doi.org/10.1145/1357054.1357072

[105] Gloria Mark, Daniela Gudith, and Ulrich Klocke. 2008. The cost of interrupted work: more speed and stress. In Proceedings of the SIGCHI Conference on Human Factors in Computing Systems (CHI '08). Association for Computing Machinery, New York, NY, USA, 107–110. DOI:https://doi.org/10.1145/1357054.1357072

- During the task, participants were subjected to phone or instant messaging interruptions related or unrelated to the task or no interruptions.

What Were The Results?

- Mark and colleagues[106] found that people in the interrupted conditions experienced a higher workload, more stress, higher frustration, more time pressure, and effort.

- Depending on the type of interruption, they also found that it could take up to 23 minutes to return to the original task.[107]

What Are Some Potential Strategies To Minimize Interruptions?

- When studying, minimize/turn off unnecessary notifications on your electronic devices.

- Students may want to time some of their studying around the schedules of others in their living situation (house with family members, roommates, etc.) and parts of the day when there are fewer interruptions by others. It may be helpful to proactively communicate

---

[106] Gloria Mark, Daniela Gudith, and Ulrich Klocke. 2008. The cost of interrupted work: more speed and stress. In Proceedings of the SIGCHI Conference on Human Factors in Computing Systems (CHI '08). Association for Computing Machinery, New York, NY, USA, 107–110. DOI:https://doi.org/10.1145/1357054.1357072

[107] Gloria Mark, Daniela Gudith, and Ulrich Klocke. 2008. The cost of interrupted work: more speed and stress. In Proceedings of the SIGCHI Conference on Human Factors in Computing Systems (CHI '08). Association for Computing Machinery, New York, NY, USA, 107–110. DOI:https://doi.org/10.1145/1357054.1357072

with others about your wish not to be interrupted at certain times of the day.

• Identify study areas on campus that have few interruptions.

• Some students may benefit from white noise or instrumental music to help maintain focus. Others may prefer a quiet space.

• Studying or doing a key task or two first thing in the morning may be useful before using electronic devices or doing other tasks.

• Try keeping a notepad handy to make a note of any ideas or thoughts that may occur while you are working on a task.

• Experiment with doing one task at a time in various chunks to determine how long an ideal piece of time is for you to stay focused on a single task. This may help you schedule things more effectively in the future.

• Consider meditation practice to improve your focus. This and stress management strategies are discussed in later chapters.

• Consider your campus study/learning center to improve your study skills.

Other Thoughts:

• This is a small study, and further research is needed.

• Some people may work better in high-interruption environments.

- It is also possible that interruptions have a different impact depending on the type of work you are doing and they type of interruption.

- Further research in this area is needed.

Expanded Knowledge

Interruptions, especially in study or work environments, are a pervasive concern impacting cognitive workload, stress levels, and overall mental health. This phenomenon has been observed in various studies, expanding the argument of Mark and colleagues.

Trafton and Monk (2007)[108] investigated the effects of task interruptions on individuals, providing substantial evidence of the negative impacts. They found that individuals who experienced task interruptions took notably longer to complete tasks and made double the errors compared to those without interruptions. This supports Mark's findings about heightened stress, frustration, and time pressure following disruptions.

Furthermore, a study by Stothart et al. (2015)[109] looked specifically at cell phone notifications as interruptions. Their research demonstrated that even a simple notification could cause significant distraction, reducing performance in tasks requiring constant focus.

---

[108] Trafton, J.G., & Monk, C.A. (2007). Task Interruptions. Reviews of Human Factors and Ergonomics, 3(1), 111–126.
[109] Stothart, C., Mitchum, A., & Yehnert, C. (2015). The Attentional Cost of Receiving a Cell Phone Notification. Journal of Experimental Psychology: Human Perception and Performance, 41(4), 893-897.

To minimize these interruptions, several strategies could be applied. Bailey and Konstan (2006)[110] recommended a technique of batching tasks together based on their complexity to maintain focus. This method could optimize productivity and reduce the negative impacts of interruptions.

For a more tech-focused approach, Kushlev and Dunn (2015)[111] suggested setting specific times to check electronic devices and making conscious efforts to disconnect periodically.

This minimizes interruptions and reduces the negative effects of constant digital engagement.

Furthermore, meditation has been proven effective in improving focus and reducing susceptibility to interruptions (Tang et al., 2015).[112] Regular practice can help maintain mental well-being in high-interruption environments.

Self-Care Strategies for Graduate Students[113]

Graduate students face a variety of stressors, such as increased time spent on schoolwork, financial stress,

[110] Bailey, B.P., & Konstan, J.A. (2006). On the Need for Attention-aware Systems: Measuring Effects of Interruption on Task Performance, Error Rate, and Affective State. Computers in Human Behavior, 22(4), 685-708.

[111] Kushlev, K., & Dunn, E.W. (2015). Checking Email Less Frequently Reduces Stress. Computers in Human Behavior, 43, 220-228.

[112] Tang, Y.Y., Hölzel, B.K., & Posner, M.I. (2015). The Neuroscience of Mindfulness Meditation. Nature Reviews Neuroscience, 16, 213–225.

[113] https://u.osu.edu/emotionalfitness/2020/11/18/self-care-strategies-for-graduate-students/

graduate/teaching assistantships, career planning, and family issues.[114][115][116]

Other stressors include increased time spent on research and often starting at a new school, which can increase isolation; graduate school often requires shifting work style from semester to semester to projects that can take months to years, with limited breaks in between.

Graduate students must also manage work style, personality, and other relationship dynamics with their lab mates and advisors, whom they may not have known when entering their program. These and other factors can impact graduate student mental health.

What Are Some Mental Health Concerns Among Graduate Students?

According to the American College Health Association, graduate students experienced the following mental health concerns in the previous 12 months:[117]

---

[114] Mazzola JJ, Walker EJ, Shockley KM, Spector PE. (2011). Examining stress in graduate assistants: Combining qualitative and quantitative survey methods. Journal of Mixed Methods Research, 5(3), 198-211.

[115] Oswalt SB, Riddock CC. (2007). What to do about being overwhelmed: graduate students, stress, and university services. College Student Affairs Journal, 2007, 27 (1), 24-44.

[116] Fox JA. (2008). The troubled student and campus violence: new approaches. Chronicles of Higher Education, 55(12), A42-A43.

[117] ACHA grad student survey data: (from January 22, 2020 Michael J. Stebleton Lisa Kaler. Promoting Graduate Student Mental Health: The Role of Student Affairs Professionals and Faculty. JCC Connexions, Vol. 6, No. 1. Feb. 2020 https://www.naspa.org/blog/promoting-graduate-student-mental-health-the-role-of-student-affairs-professionals-and-faculty

- Around 63% of students reported feeling overwhelming anxiety.

- Roughly 58% of students reported feeling very lonely.

- A total of 46% of students reported that academics had been traumatic or very difficult to handle.

- Nearly 41% of students felt so depressed it was difficult to function.

- However, 24% of students reported that stress had negatively influenced their academics.

What Factors Can Improve Graduate Student Well-Being?

One study found that the top ten predictors of graduate student wellbeing include overall health, living conditions, social support, sleep, academic preparation, career prospects, feeling valued and included, advisor relationships, academic engagement, and financial confidence.[118]

What Is A Potential Self-Care Plan For Graduate Students?

Daly and colleagues suggest a self-care strategy unique to graduate students.[119] Graduate students could

---

[118] University of California Berkeley. Graduate Student Happiness & Well-Being Report 2014. http://ga.berkeley.edu/wp-content/uploads/2015/04/wellbeingreport_2014.pdf Page 128. Accessed November 2020.

[119] Self care strategies in grad school. Daly BD, Gardner RA. A Case Study Exploration into the Benefits of Teaching Self-Care to School Psychology Graduate Students [published online ahead of print, 2020 Oct 23]. Contemp Sch Psychol. 2020;1-12. doi:10.1007/s40688-020-00328-3

consider customizing a self-care plan based on these domains and example strategies.[120]

Physical/Body[121]

- I would encourage students to consider these healthy nutrition strategies for mental health (Discussed in a subsequent chapter).

- Exercise regularly (4–5 times a week) (Discussed in subsequent chapter).

- Take a walk.

- Posture adjustment.

- Get at least six hours or more of sleep per night (Discussed in subsequent chapter).

Mind/Mental[122]

- Allow for internet and video game breaks.

- Engage in 'brain breaks' such as reading novels and doodling.

---

[120] Self care strategies in grad school. Daly BD, Gardner RA. A Case Study Exploration into the Benefits of Teaching Self-Care to School Psychology Graduate Students [published online ahead of print, 2020 Oct 23]. Contemp Sch Psychol. 2020;1-12. doi:10.1007/s40688-020-00328-3

[121] Self care strategies in grad school. Daly BD, Gardner RA. A Case Study Exploration into the Benefits of Teaching Self-Care to School Psychology Graduate Students [published online ahead of print, 2020 Oct 23]. Contemp Sch Psychol. 2020;1-12. doi:10.1007/s40688-020-00328-3

[122] Self care strategies in grad school. Daly BD, Gardner RA. A Case Study Exploration into the Benefits of Teaching Self-Care to School Psychology Graduate Students [published online ahead of print, 2020 Oct 23]. Contemp Sch Psychol. 2020;1-12. doi:10.1007/s40688-020-00328-3

- Maintain realistic goals and expectations regarding school and grades.

- Break down large tasks into small tasks.

Social/Relationships[123]

- Spend time doing something active with <significant other> on weekends.

- Spend one day a week with a cohort or friends (no school work, actual fun).

- Schedule Facetime with a partner.

Emotional[124]

- Make a note of gratitude daily.

- Cry and deep breath.

- Listen to music to calm down/ release whatever you are feeling.

- Write for fun.

[123] Self care strategies in grad school. Daly BD, Gardner RA. A Case Study Exploration into the Benefits of Teaching Self-Care to School Psychology Graduate Students [published online ahead of print, 2020 Oct 23]. Contemp Sch Psychol. 2020;1-12. doi:10.1007/s40688-020-00328-3
[124] Self care strategies in grad school. Daly BD, Gardner RA. A Case Study Exploration into the Benefits of Teaching Self-Care to School Psychology Graduate Students [published online ahead of print, 2020 Oct 23]. Contemp Sch Psychol. 2020;1-12. doi:10.1007/s40688-020-00328-3

Spiritual125

- Spend weekends in nature.

- Practice mindful positivity: look for the best in a situation.

- Sing during class breaks.

- Go to church (Sundays) or read several Bible verses.

Work/Professional[126]

- Schedule breaks to avoid burnout (90-min on, 10-min off, etc.)

- Ask cohort members for advice.

- Make lists and stick to them with due dates.

- Celebrate task accomplishment.

- Adjust plan, time management, and seeking out counseling support.

Other Strategies To Consider:

- Daily routines and short-term hobbies and goals outside of work (fitness/nutrition goals, cooking/recipes, arts and crafts, sports, etc.) can help create a sense of control, which can help

---

[125] Self care strategies in grad school. Daly BD, Gardner RA. A Case Study Exploration into the Benefits of Teaching Self-Care to School Psychology Graduate Students [published online ahead of print, 2020 Oct 23]. Contemp Sch Psychol. 2020;1-12. doi:10.1007/s40688-020-00328-3

[126] Self care strategies in grad school. Daly BD, Gardner RA. A Case Study Exploration into the Benefits of Teaching Self-Care to School Psychology Graduate Students [published online ahead of print, 2020 Oct 23]. Contemp Sch Psychol. 2020;1-12. doi:10.1007/s40688-020-00328-3

balance some of the stress from uncertainties associated with graduate school.

- Work on creating smaller tasks out of bigger projects.

- Regularly meet with other graduate students or students in your field via support groups.

- A regularly scheduled meeting with your advisor can help establish structure and accountability and increase focus.

- Identify people you find supportive or enjoy being around and set up regularly scheduled times to meet in person or electronically (friends, family, colleagues, etc.).

- Avoid drugs, excessive alcohol, and excessive caffeine.

Expanded Knowledge

Embarking on the graduate school journey can feel like a roller coaster ride. It's a time of intellectual blossoming but also an encounter with stress-inducing hurdles, such as the emotional toll of isolation, financial burdens, and the quest for work-life equilibrium. Unsurprisingly, these factors can impact the mental health of graduate students.

Imagine self-care as a well-rounded toolkit filled with physical, mental, social, emotional, and professional implements. On the physical front, regular exercise has been associated with decreased symptoms of anxiety and depression, as per Rosenbaum et al. (2014).[127] Similarly, nutrition, the fuel for our bodies, plays a pivotal role. The correct intake of micronutrients has been tied to mood upliftment (Sarris et al., 2015).[128]

As for mental upkeep, cognitive hacks like setting achievable goals, portioning grand tasks into bite-sized pieces, and practicing mindfulness can bolster mental fortitude (Kabat-Zinn, 2013).[129]

Social connection and drawing wisdom from peers can significantly decrease stress (Cohen & Wills, 1985).[130] Emotional maintenance tools, such as expressing gratitude or engaging in leisure activities, can infuse positivity and deflate anxiety (Watkins, 2014).[131]

Treading the path of spiritual practices can offer refuge and a fresh perspective (Cotton et al., 2006).[132] And lastly, professional strategies like setting boundaries and celebrating accomplishments can boost productivity and hold burnout at bay (Schaufeli et al., 2009).[133]

---

[127] Rosenbaum, S., et al. (2014). Physical activity interventions for people with mental illness: a systematic review and meta-analysis. The Journal of Clinical Psychiatry, 75(9), 964-974.

[128] Sarris, J., et al. (2015). Nutrient-based therapies for mental disorders: a systematic review. The Lancet Psychiatry, 2(5), 472-482.

[129] Kabat-Zinn, J. (2013). Full catastrophe living, revised edition: how to cope with stress, pain and illness using mindfulness meditation. Hachette UK.

[130] Cohen, S., & Wills, T. A. (1985). Stress, social support, and the buffering hypothesis. Psychological Bulletin, 98(2), 310.

[131] Watkins, P. (2014). Gratitude and the Good Life. Springer.

[132] Cotton, S., et al. (2006). Spirituality and religion in patients with HIV/AIDS. Journal of General Internal Medicine, 21(S5), S5-S13.

[133] Schaufeli, W. B., et al. (2009). How changes in job demands and resources predict burnout, work engagement, and sickness absenteeism. Journal of Organizational Behavior, 30(7), 893-917.

Returning To Campus And Mental Health During COVID[134] (Or Other Large-Scale Stressful Events)

According to a public opinion poll conducted March 26 – April 5, 2021, among a sample of 1,000 adults 18 years of age and older, released by the American Psychiatric Association (APA), young adults from the ages of 18 to 29 (49%) are more likely to say they are more anxious now compared to last year, despite available vaccinations for COVID-19.[135]

The American Psychological Association recommends the following strategies to cope with Covid related stress as a student:[136]

Practice Self-Care[137]

- Get enough sleep.

- Exercise regularly.

- Eat well.

- Find activities that engage different parts of yourself.

- Occupy your mind with puzzles.

- Engage your senses with hot baths or fragrant candles.

---

[134] https://u.osu.edu/emotionalfitness/2021/08/20/returning-to-campus-and-mental-health-during-covid/
[135] https://www.psychiatry.org/newsroom/news-releases/new-apa-poll-shows-sustained-anxiety-among-americans-more-than-half-of-parents-are-concerned-about-the-mental-well-being-of-their-children
[136] https://www.apa.org/topics/covid-19/student-stress.pdf
[137] https://www.apa.org/topics/covid-19/student-stress.pdf

- Look for tasks you can postpone or simply eliminate from your to-do list.

Find Ways To Focus[138]

- You might feel unmotivated now. Recognize that the current circumstances are hard for everyone. Don't judge yourself; just do the best you can.

- Establish a routine. Get up, go to bed, and do your work simultaneously every day.

- Frequent breaks can help you re-engage in your work.

- Try to create a separate work space, although you should reserve your sleeping area for sleeping. If family members are distracting you, use *"I statement"* to explain the problem— *"I'm worried about my exam next week"*—and work together to develop solutions.

Seek Out Social Support[139]

- To combat isolation, plan ahead to schedule time to connect with friends and family.

Help Others Cope[140]

- Your classmates and family members may be anxious, too.

---

[138] https://www.apa.org/topics/covid-19/student-stress.pdf
[139] https://www.apa.org/topics/covid-19/student-stress.pdf
[140] https://www.apa.org/topics/covid-19/student-stress.pdf

- You don't have to fix their problems. It's enough to let them know they're not alone.

Find Ways To Manage Disappointment[141]

- Grieve losses, then reframe how you think about these life events. Think about how you can honor what you've achieved.

- Find new ways to celebrate. Consider recreating important events once it's safe.

Limit Your Media Consumption[142]

- While staying informed is important, too much news—especially social media—can increase anxiety. Set limits on your media consumption and smartphone use to avoid being overwhelmed.

- Technology and mental health are discussed in more detail in an upcoming chapter.

Focus On Things You Can Control[143]

- Your classmates, friends, or family members may disobey the rules about physical distancing or doing other things that add to your stress.

- While modeling good behavior and staying safe yourself, recognize that you can't control what other people do.

---

[141] https://www.apa.org/topics/covid-19/student-stress.pdf
[142] https://www.apa.org/topics/covid-19/student-stress.pdf
[143] https://www.apa.org/topics/covid-19/student-stress.pdf

- Instead of worrying about our ambiguous future, focus on solving immediate problems.

Other Thoughts:

- While returning to campus during COVID can be anxiety-provoking for some, practicing self-care and being realistic with your self can help.

- With this in mind, having a backup plan or willingness to adjust may be useful if things are not going as well as expected despite your best efforts.

Expanded Knowledge

The global tsunami of COVID-19 or other large-scale stressful events can stir up a storm in the minds of students, especially those setting foot on campus amid a sea of unknowns. Echoing this sentiment, a study by Son et al. (2020)[144] reveals a worrying surge in stress, anxiety, and depression among students during these testing times. This underscores the pressing need for tailored coping strategies and resources to navigate mental health.

Imagine three pillars of self-care: sleep, physical activity, and nutrition, each with solid ties to mental well-being. Bei et al. (2016)[145] unfurled an intriguing link between poor sleep quality and heightened anxiety and

---

[144] Son, C., et al. (2020). Effects of COVID-19 on College Students' Mental Health in the United States: Interview Survey Study. Journal of Medical Internet Research, 22(9), e21279.
[145] Bei, B., et al. (2016). Sleep and Mood in Adolescents: A Perfect Storm. Journal of Adolescence, 52, 105–112.

depression levels in students. Diving deeper, Meyer et al. (2011)[146] corroborated how regular physical activity is a buoy to drift away from stress and lift the mood. And lest we forget, a balanced diet functions as a lighthouse, guiding the way to mental well-being (Jacka et al., 2010).[147]

Regularity and focus serve as faithful companions on this journey. Research by Schönfeld et al. (2016)[148] showed the importance of daily routine in helping reduce stress. During large-scale social stress, avoiding getting caught in the whirlpool of excessive media is especially important. Overexposure can worsen stress and anxiety (Garfin et al., 2020).[149] Lastly, concentrating on things you can control can boost resilience and coping skills (Folkman et al., 1986).[150]

Maximizing Spring Break For Mental Health[151]

- Many college students look forward to March and spring break as a way to take time off from school

[146] Meyer, J. D., et al. (2011). Physical Exercise and Psychological Health. Sports Medicine, 19(3), 180–190.

[147] Jacka, F. N., et al. (2010). Association of Western and Traditional Diets with Depression and Anxiety in Women. American Journal of Psychiatry, 167(3), 305–311.

[148] Schönfeld, P., et al. (2016). Coping with stress in medical students: results of a randomized controlled trial using a mindfulness-based stress prevention training (MediMind) in Germany. BMC Medical Education, 16(1), 316.

[149] Garfin, D. R., et al. (2020). Unprecedented pandemic, unprecedented stress, and unprecedented resilience. Psychological Trauma: Theory, Research, Practice, and Policy, 12(S1), S1–S5.

[150] Folkman, S., et al. (1986). Dynamics of a stressful encounter: cognitive appraisal, coping, and encounter outcomes. Journal of Personality and Social Psychology, 50(5), 992–1003.

[151] https://u.osu.edu/emotionalfitness/2019/02/28/maximizing-spring-break-for-mental-health/

and relax, recharge for the second half of the spring semester, etc.

- There are healthy and unhealthy options to consider when considering a rejuvenating spring break.

- This is important because unhealthy choices during spring break could create more problems for the rest of the semester.

What Are Unhealthy Spring Break Patterns To Avoid?

- Excessive alcohol, including short-term binge drinking, has been shown to impact brain functioning[152] and grades,[153] depression,[154] and increased risk of sexual assault.[155]

- This can also increase your anxiety for the weeks and months to follow.

- Low-risk drinking recommendations can be found here.[156]

---

[152] Zeigler DW, Wang CC, Yoast RA, Dickinson BD, McCaffree MA, Robinowitz CB, et al. The neurocognitive effects of alcohol on adolescents and college students. Prev Med. 2005;40:23–32.

[153] https://u.osu.edu/emotionalfitness/2014/09/12/does-alcohol-use-impact-your-grades/

[154] Boden JM1, Fergusson DM. Alcohol and depression. Addiction. 2011 May;106(5):906-14. doi:10.1111/j.1360-0443.2010.03351.x. Epub 2011 Mar 7.

[155] https://u.osu.edu/emotionalfitness/2015/10/21/study-alcohol-impacts-sexual-assault/

[156] https://u.osu.edu/emotionalfitness/2018/02/26/alcohol-and-grades/

- Cannabis use can worsen depression and suicidal ideation,[157] brain functioning,[158][159] sleep[160] , and anxiety.[161]

- Sleep deprivation can impact academic performance.[162]

- Consider minimizing caffeine intake since excessive caffeine intake can impact stress[163] and sleep.[164][165]

What Are Healthy Spring Break Options To Consider?

- Catch up on sleep.

---

[157] Gobbi G, Atkin T, Zytynski T, et al. Association of Cannabis Use in Adolescence and Risk of Depression, Anxiety, and Suicidality in Young Adulthood: A Systematic Review and Meta-analysis. JAMA Psychiatry. Published online February 13, 2019. doi:10.1001/jamapsychiatry.2018.4500

[158] Doss MK et al. Δ9-Tetrahydrocannibinol at retrieval drives false recollection of neutral and emotional memories. Biol Psychiatry 2018 May 9; [e-pub]. https://doi.org/10.1016/j.biopsych.2018.04.020.

[159] Schuster RM, Gilman J, Schoenfeld D, et al. One month of cannabis abstinence in adolescents and young adults is associated with improved memory. J Clin Psychiatry. 2018;79(6):17m11977 .

[160] Hser YI, Mooney LJ, Huang D, et al. Reductions in cannabis use are associated with improvements in anxiety, depression, and sleep quality, but not quality of life. J Subst Abuse Treat. 2017;81:53-58.

[161] Hser YI, Mooney LJ, Huang D, et al. Reductions in cannabis use are associated with improvements in anxiety, depression, and sleep quality, but not quality of life. J Subst Abuse Treat. 2017;81:53-58.

[162] https://u.osu.edu/emotionalfitness/2017/12/31/poor-sleep-and-poor-grades-might-go-together/

[163] https://u.osu.edu/emotionalfitness/2017/04/19/study-caffeine-stress-and-brain-function/

[164] T. Roehrs, T. Roth. Caffeine: sleep and daytime sleepiness. Sleep Med Rev, 12 (2) (2008), pp. 153–162.

[165] 13. H.P. Landolt, E. Werth, A.A. Borbely, D.J. Dijk. Caffeine intake (200 mg) in the morning affects human sleep and EEG power spectra at night. Brain Research, 675 (1–2) (1995), pp. 67–74.

- Rest your brain. If you've been studying intensely, reading, writing, analyzing, etc., it may be useful to rest those areas of the brain by doing different types of activities.

- Minimize screen time, if possible. If you've spent a lot of time doing schoolwork on your computer, it may be useful to rest that part of your brain by doing different types of activities that don't involve screens.

- Eat well to fuel yourself properly and for optimal mental health. Examples include plenty of fresh fruit, vegetables, nuts, lean meats, etc..[166] This might also enhance recovery.

- If you've spent a lot of time indoors, spending time outside, safely and to a point, may be helpful for mental health.[167][168]

- Reduce isolation by spending time with others, if possible.

- Other options include hiking/camping/other activities in nature, playing recreational sports, traveling to museums, art exhibits, beaches, shows, etc.

---

[166] https://u.osu.edu/emotionalfitness/2018/06/28/food-choices-to-improve-depression/

[167] Avery DH, Kouri ME, Monaghan K, Bolte MA, Hellekson C, Eder D. Is dawn simulation effective in ameliorating the difficulty awakening in seasonal affective disorder associated with hypersomnia? J Affect Disord. 2002 May;69(1-3):231-6.

[168] https://www.cdc.gov/cancer/skin/basic_info/sun-safety.htm

- You might improve your mental health by doing something good in the community where you travel through programs like BUCK-I-SERV and other service trips.[169]

Tips On How To Stay Safe During Spring Break:

- Since the number one cause of death in young adults is accidents, it may be wise to minimize/avoid high-risk-hazardous activities.[170]

- This is a very useful link for travel safety tips for spring break.[171]

Expanded Knowledge

Spring break, a much-awaited event for many college students, serves as a pivotal period for rest and rejuvenation amidst academic stress. However, decisions made during this time can significantly affect students' mental health and academic performance.

Drinking patterns during spring break, particularly binge drinking, can negatively impact cognitive function and academic performance, as found in a study by Balsa, Giuliano, and French (2011).[172] They noted increased depressive symptoms, heightened risk of sexual assault,

[169]https://u.osu.edu/emotionalfitness/2017/11/22/mental-health-benefits-of-volunteering/
[170] https://www.cdc.gov/family/springbreak/index.htm
[171] https://www.limcollege.edu/safety/are-you-prepared/spring-break
[172] Balsa, A. I., Giuliano, L. M., & French, M. T. (2011). The effects of alcohol use on academic achievement in high school. Economics of Education Review, 30(1), 1–15.

and subsequent anxiety associated with heavy alcohol consumption.

Cannabis use can exacerbate depressive feelings, suicidal ideation, and anxiety, as per Fergusson, Horwood, & Swain-Campbell's (2002)[173] research. Its effects on cognitive function and sleep can be detrimental. Sleep deprivation, on its own, affects academic performance, as reported by Gaultney (2010).[174]

Excessive caffeine intake, closely linked to sleep disturbances and heightened stress, as revealed by a study by Richards and Smith (2015),[175] might be worth minimizing.

Healthy spring break choices include catching up on sleep, resting the brain, minimizing screen time, and maintaining a balanced diet. There's evidence suggesting spending time outdoors can improve mental health (Beyer et al., 2014),[176] and reducing isolation can enhance well-being (Seppala et al., 2013).[177]

---

[173] Fergusson, D. M., Horwood, L. J., & Swain-Campbell, N. (2002). Cannabis use and psychosocial adjustment in adolescence and young adulthood. Addiction, 97(9), 1123-1135.

[174] Gaultney, J. F. (2010). The prevalence of sleep disorders in college students: impact on academic performance. Journal of American College Health, 59(2), 91-97.

[175] Richards, G., & Smith, A. P. (2015). Caffeine consumption and self-assessed stress, anxiety, and depression in secondary school children. Journal of Psychopharmacology, 29(12), 1236-1247.

[176] Beyer, K. M., Kaltenbach, A., Szabo, A., Bogar, S., Nieto, F. J., & Malecki, K. M. (2014). Exposure to neighborhood green space and mental health: evidence from the survey of the health of Wisconsin. International journal of environmental research and public health, 11(3), 3453-3472.

[177] Seppala, E., Rossomando, T., & Doty, J. R. (2013). Social connection and compassion: Important predictors of health and well-being. Social Research: An International Quarterly, 80(2), 411-430.

Other activities like hiking, museum visits, and community service can also enrich mental health.

Safety during spring break is also essential, as accidents are the leading cause of death among young adults (Rockett et al., 2012).[178] Following travel safety guidelines can minimize risk during this period.

The Lasting Negative Impact Of Bullying[179]

Many students might be aware of the emotional harm that can occur as a result of bullying.

People may not know that being bullied as a child or a young person might lead to emotional problems that occur when you are an adult.

This was highlighted in a recent study.

What Was Studied?

Exposure to bullying and childhood maltreatment was assessed among 5466 children aged 8 to 16 years old.

Then, at 18 years of age, symptoms of anxiety, depression, self-harm, and suicidality were measured.

What Did The Study Show?

This study showed that adults who were bullied during their childhood had an increased risk of anxiety,

---

[178] Rockett, I. R., Regier, M. D., Kapusta, N. D., Coben, J. H., Miller, T. R., Hanzlick, R. L., ... & Smith, G. S. (2012). Leading causes of unintentional and intentional injury mortality: United States, 2000–2009. American journal of public health, 102(11), e84–e92.
[179]https://u.osu.edu/emotionalfitness/2015/07/31/the-lasting-negative-impact-of-bullying/

depression, and self-reported harm in the past year compared to the other groups.

What Do The Results Mean?

While we know from studies that victims of maltreatment during childhood are at an increased risk of various mental health problems during adulthood, this study suggests that bullying during childhood also has serious mental health consequences as the victims become adults.[180]

It is hoped that future research will shed further light on this topic.

Have you experienced bullying in the past?

Are you experiencing emotional problems now?

Have you considered professional help?

Expanded Knowledge

Bullying, often dismissed as a rite of passage, packs a punch much stronger than the immediate emotional distress it causes. Its grasp extends far into adulthood, morphing into significant psychological distress. This issue comes to light in a series of compelling longitudinal studies.

---

[180] Adult mental health consequences of peer bullying and maltreatment in childhood: two cohorts in two countries. Suzet Tanya Lereya, William E Copeland, E Jane Costello, Dieter Wolke. www.thelancet.com/psychiatry Published online April 28, 2015 http://dx.doi.org/10.1016/S2215-0366(15)00165-0

Copeland, Wolke, Angold, and Costello (2013)[181] found that children who were bullied from the ages of 9 to 16 were more likely to experience anxiety disorders, depression, tendencies of self-harm, and suicidality as adults.

Adding weight to these findings, a riveting study by Lereya, Copeland, Costello, and Wolke (2015)[182] divulged that the adverse effects of childhood bullying continue to cast a long shadow, with victims still grappling with poor mental health and diminished life satisfaction even at age 50.

Bowes et al. (2015)[183] took a step further to study children experiencing both bullying and maltreatment. They found these children bore the brunt, as they displayed the most severe levels of mental health problems in adulthood.

A case can be made for bullying as a public health challenge. It underscores the urgency of not just prevention and early intervention measures but also robust mental health support for victims so they can heal from the wounds that bullying inflicts, even long after the incidents have passed.

---

[181] Copeland, W. E., Wolke, D., Angold, A., & Costello, E. J. (2013). Adult psychiatric outcomes of bullying and being bullied by peers in childhood and adolescence. JAMA Psychiatry, 70(4), 419-426.

[182] Lereya, S. T., Copeland, W. E., Costello, E. J., & Wolke, D. (2015). Adult mental health consequences of peer bullying and maltreatment in childhood: two cohorts in two countries. The Lancet Psychiatry, 2(6), 524-531.

[183] Bowes, L., Joinson, C., Wolke, D., & Lewis, G. (2015). Peer victimisation during adolescence and its impact on depression in early adulthood: prospective cohort study in the United Kingdom. BMJ, 350, h2469.

In my experience, this can be a particularly important issue for college students as they navigate life outside of their homes and cope with bullying, trauma, and pain of the past.

Students need to recognize this and seek out counseling from campus or the surrounding community while enhancing healthy life behaviors to improve their mental health.

Chapter 3: Strategies to Improve Anxiety

Anxiety is one of the top mental health concerns among young people. In a national survey of over 33 thousand college students, about 31% reported being diagnosed or treated with anxiety in the past 12 months.

Anxiety was the second most common mental health concern, followed by stress (38.9%), and 51% of students reporting anxiety said that anxiety impacted their academic performance.[184] Anxiety and stress are related, and stress management can help improve anxiety. Chapter 5 covers stress in more detail.

There are a variety of anxiety disorders, and when thinking of lifestyle strategies to address anxiety, we want to consider reducing or eliminating factors that worsen anxiety while increasing factors that improve anxiety. This chapter will discuss those factors. The end of this chapter will add my insights and clinical experiences related to those factors and put the life strategies together.

As always, this book is intended for informational purposes. Check with your healthcare professional to see if any strategies discussed here are right for you. If you choose to apply them, do it under the care and guidance of your health professional.

---

[184] American College Health Association. American College Health Association-National College Health Assessment III: Reference Group Executive Summary Fall 2022. Silver Spring, MD: American College Health Association; 2023.

Study: Omega-3 May Help With Anxiety[185]

A previous blog post discussed probiotics and anxiety[186]. A recent review article examined whether omega-3 fatty acid treatment is associated with an improvement in anxiety.[187]

What Are Omega-3 Fatty Acids?

Omega-3 are polyunsaturated dietary fatty acids (PUFAs) that include alpha-linoleic acid (ALA), which are then converted to eicosapentaenoic acid (EPA) and docosahexaenoic acid (DHA).[188]

They are nutrients that the human body cannot make, so we must get them through foods or supplements.[189]

What Was The Study?

The study authors[190] reviewed 19 clinical trials, including 2240 participants from 11 countries.

[185] https://u.osu.edu/emotionalfitness/2019/05/29/study-omega-3s-may-help-with-anxiety/
[186] https://u.osu.edu/emotionalfitness/2019/05/29/study-omega-3s-may-help-with-anxiety/
[187] Su KP, Tseng PT, Lin PY, et al. Association of Use of Omega-3 Polyunsaturated Fatty Acids With Changes in Severity of Anxiety Symptoms: A Systematic Review and Meta-analysis. JAMA 0Netw Open. 2018;1(5):e182327. Published 2018 Sep 14. doi:10.1001/jamanetworkopen.2018.2327
[188] https://ods.od.nih.gov/factsheets/Omega3FattyAcids-Consumer/
[189] https://ods.od.nih.gov/factsheets/Omega3FattyAcids-Consumer
[190] Su KP, Tseng PT, Lin PY, et al. Association of Use of Omega-3 Polyunsaturated Fatty Acids With Changes in Severity of Anxiety Symptoms: A Systematic Review and Meta-analysis. JAMA 0Netw Open. 2018;1(5):e182327. Published 2018 Sep 14. doi:10.1001/jamanetworkopen.2018.2327

What Were The Results?

- The authors[191] found an association of improved anxiety symptoms with omega-3 treatment compared to control groups in placebo-controlled and non-placebo-controlled trials.

- They also found a stronger anti-anxiety effect of omega-3 when anxiety symptoms were more severe (clinical) than less severe (subclinical) populations.[192]

How Much Omega-3 Was Used In The Studies?

In the review of 19 clinical trials,[193] anti-anxiety benefits occurred when using at least 2 grams per day of omega-3, DHA, and EPA combined.

The results did not differ whether the amount of EPA was more than or less than 60% of total omega-3.

---

[191] Su KP, Tseng PT, Lin PY, et al. Association of Use of Omega-3 Polyunsaturated Fatty Acids With Changes in Severity of Anxiety Symptoms: A Systematic Review and Meta-analysis. JAMA 0Netw Open. 2018;1(5):e182327. Published 2018 Sep 14. doi:10.1001/jamanetworkopen.2018.2327

[192] Su KP, Tseng PT, Lin PY, et al. Association of Use of Omega-3 Polyunsaturated Fatty Acids With Changes in Severity of Anxiety Symptoms: A Systematic Review and Meta-analysis. JAMA 0Netw Open. 2018;1(5):e182327. Published 2018 Sep 14. doi:10.1001/jamanetworkopen.2018.2327

[193] Su KP, Tseng PT, Lin PY, et al. Association of Use of Omega-3 Polyunsaturated Fatty Acids With Changes in Severity of Anxiety Symptoms: A Systematic Review and Meta-analysis. JAMA 0Netw Open. 2018;1(5):e182327. Published 2018 Sep 14. doi:10.1001/jamanetworkopen.2018.2327

What Are Some Caveats?

- The populations studied were broad, which makes it difficult to generalize to specific populations like college students.

- Some of the studies had a small sample size.

- There was a broad range of benefits in different studies.

- Omega-3s can interact with medications and supplements.

- Talk to your health provider before considering omega-3.

Based on the research findings, not everyone will have the same benefits from omega-3.

What Are Some Sources Of Omega-3?

According to the National Institute of Health,[194] sources of omega-3 include:

- Fish and other seafood (especially cold-water fatty fish, such as salmon, mackerel, tuna, herring, and sardines).

- Nuts and seeds (such as flaxseed, chia seeds, and walnuts).

- Plant oils (such as flaxseed oil).

- Fortified foods (such as certain brands of eggs, yogurt, juices, milk, soy beverages, and infant formulas).

---

[194] https://ods.od.nih.gov/factsheets/Omega3FattyAcids-Consumer

- Omega-3 dietary supplements include fish oil, krill oil, cod liver oil, and algal oil (sourced from algae). They come in a wide range of doses and forms.

How Much Omega-3s Do I Need Per Day?

The U.S. Food and Drug Administration recommends consuming no more than 3 grams/day of EPA and DHA combined, including up to 2 grams/day from dietary supplements.[195]

Expanded Knowledge

Omega 3 have been heavily studied for mental health. They have been implicated in memory, learning, and a range of cognitive functions, essential ingredients for the vitality of our mental lives (Innis, 2007).[196] Not stopping at that, these fatty acids also help sculpt the very nerve cells that form the physical basis of our thoughts and feelings.

Through the lens of empirical evidence, a meta-analysis of 13 studies encompassing 1,233 participants revealed the power of omega-3 as a force against anxiety (Su et al., 2018).[197] The data show us a meaningful picture

---

[195] https://ods.od.nih.gov/factsheets/Omega3FattyAcids-Consumer
[196] Innis, S. M. (2007). Dietary omega 3 fatty acids and the developing brain. Brain Research, 1187, 35–50.
[197] Su, K. P., Tseng, P. T., Lin, P. Y., Okubo, R., Chen, T. Y., Chen, Y. W., & Matsuoka, Y. J. (2018). Association of Use of Omega-3 Polyunsaturated Fatty Acids With Changes in Severity of Anxiety Symptoms: A Systematic Review and Meta-analysis. JAMA Network Open, 1(5), e182327.

- Omega-3 supplementation has statistically significant effects in alleviating the clinical symptoms of anxiety. This suggests a potential weapon in our armamentarium against severe anxiety disorders and their subtler, often overlooked, subclinical counterparts.

Yet, this story of omega-3 does not unfold the same way in every individual. Just as we carry a unique genetic blueprint, our metabolic processes and genetic backgrounds imprint personal signatures on how we respond to omega-3 treatments. Indeed, certain genetic variations can impact how these fatty acids are metabolized and utilized in the body, ultimately influencing the effects of supplementation (Caspi et al., 2007).[198]

It is important to understand that many plant-based omega-3s do not efficiently convert to the active form, DHA and EPA.

Another important factor to remember is that the ratio of omega-3 to non-omega-3 may also be important. In my experience, increasing omega-3 while decreasing non-omega-3 may provide the most benefit.

It is important to note that the journey with omega-3 fatty acids must be undertaken with prudence. The promise they hold for anxiety treatment, while exciting, necessitates caution. Prior consultation with a healthcare provider is indispensable, given the potential

---

[198] Caspi, A., Williams, B., Kim-Cohen, J., Craig, I. W., Milne, B. J., Poulton, R., ... & Moffitt, T. E. (2007). Moderation of breastfeeding effects on the IQ by genetic variation in fatty acid metabolism. Proceedings of the National Academy of Sciences, 104(47), 18860-18865.

for interactions with other medications and the natural variation in individual responses.

Omega-3 has been heavily studied for mental health. They have been implicated in memory, learning, and a range of cognitive functions, essential ingredients for the vitality of our mental lives (Innis, 2007).[199] Not stopping at that, these fatty acids also help sculpt the very nerve cells that form the physical basis of our thoughts and feelings.

Through the lens of empirical evidence, a meta-analysis of 13 studies encompassing 1,233 participants revealed the power of Omega-3s as a force against anxiety (Su et al., 2018).[200] The data show us a meaningful picture - Omega-3 supplementation has statistically significant effects in alleviating the clinical symptoms of anxiety. This suggests a potential weapon in our armamentarium against severe anxiety disorders and their subtler, often overlooked, subclinical counterparts.

Yet, this story of omega-3 does not unfold the same way in every individual. Just as each carries a unique genetic blueprint, our metabolic processes and genetic backgrounds imprint personal signatures on how we respond to omega-3 treatments. Indeed, certain genetic variations can impact how these fatty acids are metabolized and utilized in the body, ultimately

---

[199] Innis, S. M. (2007). Dietary omega 3 fatty acids and the developing brain. Brain Research, 1187, 35−50.

[200] Su, K. P., Tseng, P. T., Lin, P. Y., Okubo, R., Chen, T. Y., Chen, Y. W., & Matsuoka, Y. J. (2018). Association of Use of Omega-3 Polyunsaturated Fatty Acids With Changes in Severity of Anxiety Symptoms: A Systematic Review and Meta-analysis. JAMA Network Open, 1(5), e182327.

influencing the effects of supplementation (Caspi et al., 2007).[201]

It is important to understand that many plant based omega 3s do not efficiently convert to the active form, DHA and EPA.

Another important factor to remember is that the ratio of omega-3 to non-omega-3 may also be important. In my experience, increasing omega-3 while decreasing non-omega-3 may provide the most benefit.

It is important to note that the journey with omega-3 fatty acids must be undertaken with prudence. The promise they hold for anxiety treatment, while exciting, necessitates caution. Prior consultation with a healthcare provider is indispensable, given the potential for interactions with other medications and the natural variation in individual responses.

Sedentary Behavior Activity/Exercise and Anxiety[202]

---

[201] Caspi, A., Williams, B., Kim-Cohen, J., Craig, I. W., Milne, B. J., Poulton, R., ... & Moffitt, T. E. (2007). Moderation of breastfeeding effects on the IQ by genetic variation in fatty acid metabolism. Proceedings of the National Academy of Sciences, 104(47), 18860-18865.

[202] https://u.osu.edu/emotionalfitness/2023/04/29/sedentary-behavior-activity-exercise-and-anxiety/

According to a review of 31 studies, anxiety is associated with sedentary behavior.[203]

They defined sedentary behavior as low levels of energy expenditure (1.0 to 1.5 of the metabolic equivalent of task [MET]), usually occurring while sitting, during work or leisure activities, including screen behaviors (e.g., TV watching), hobbies (e.g., reading books), lying down, in transit, or during driving a car.[204][205][206]

What Was The Study?[207]

In a meta-analysis, the authors[208] did a systematic review and found k = 31 original studies (total N = 99,192) and k = 17 (total N = 27,443.

[203] Stanczykiewicz, B., Banik, A., Knoll, N. et al. Sedentary behaviors and anxiety among children, adolescents and adults: a systematic review and meta-analysis. BMC Public Health 19, 459 (2019). https://doi.org/10.1186/s12889-019-6715-3

[204] Stanczykiewicz, B., Banik, A., Knoll, N. et al. Sedentary behaviors and anxiety among children, adolescents and adults: a systematic review and meta-analysis. BMC Public Health 19, 459 (2019). https://doi.org/10.1186/s12889-019-6715-3

[205] Tremblay MS, Colley RC, Saunders TJ, Healy GN, Owen N. Physiological and health implications of a sedentary lifestyle. Appl Physiol Nutr Metab. 2010;35(6):725–40. https://doi.org/10.1139/h10-079.

[206] Owen N, Healy GN, Matthews CE, Dunstan DW. Too much sitting: the population health science of sedentary behavior. Exerc Sport Sci Rev. 2010;38(3):105–13. https://doi.org/10.1097/jes.0b013e3181e373a2.

[207] Stanczykiewicz, B., Banik, A., Knoll, N. et al. Sedentary behaviors and anxiety among children, adolescents and adults: a systematic review and meta-analysis. BMC Public Health 19, 459 (2019). https://doi.org/10.1186/s12889-019-6715-3

[208] Stanczykiewicz, B., Banik, A., Knoll, N. et al. Sedentary behaviors and anxiety among children, adolescents and adults: a systematic review and meta-analysis. BMC Public Health 19, 459 (2019). https://doi.org/10.1186/s12889-019-6715-3

What Were The Results?[209]

The authors[210] concluded that higher levels of SB are associated with higher anxiety symptoms.

A separate systematic review found exercise as helpful for anxiety[211]

What Is A Reasonable Amount Of Activity, Or How Much Should I Exercise?

The recommended exercise or activity duration according to The Department of Health and Human Services *"Physical Activity Guidelines for Americans"*[212][213]:

- For moderate-intensity activity, 20 to 42 minutes a day (150 to 300 minutes per week).

- For vigorous intensity activity, 10 to 21 minutes a day (75 to 150 minutes a week).

---

[209] Stanczykiewicz, B., Banik, A., Knoll, N. et al. Sedentary behaviors and anxiety among children, adolescents and adults: a systematic review and meta-analysis. BMC Public Health 19, 459 (2019). https://doi.org/10.1186/s12889-019-6715-3

[210] Stanczykiewicz, B., Banik, A., Knoll, N. et al. Sedentary behaviors and anxiety among children, adolescents and adults: a systematic review and meta-analysis. BMC Public Health 19, 459 (2019). https://doi.org/10.1186/s12889-019-6715-3

[211] Stonerock, Gregory L. et al. "Exercise as Treatment for Anxiety: Systematic Review and Analysis." Annals of behavioral medicine : a publication of the Society of Behavioral Medicine 49.4 (2015): 542–556. PMC. Web. 9 May 2018.

[212] https://www.cdc.gov/physicalactivity/basics/adults/index.htm

[213] https://health.gov/sites/default/files/2019-09/Physical_Activity_Guidelines_2nd_edition.pdf

What Are Some Examples Of Moderate And Vigorous Intensity Activities (Exercise)?[214]

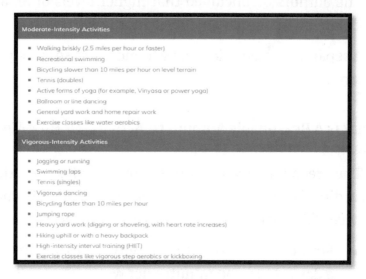

What Are Some Precautions?

- It may be best to check with your healthcare provider to make sure it's safe for you to start an exercise program.

- Individuals with a history of disordered eating or disordered exercise should check with their health professional before exercising.

- It may be wise to stop exercising and seek professional help if you notice:

- Increased depression, disordered eating, and other mental health concerns due to exercise.

- Injury, pain, or decreased motivation

---

[214] https://health.gov/sites/default/files/2019-09/Physical_Activity_Guidelines_2nd_edition.pdf

- Obsessive behaviors

- Other symptoms.

- Exercise may not help without proper nutrition, so it may be wise to learn about proper nutrition, proper exercise technique, and exercise/nutrition plans before starting to exercise.

- It may be helpful to gradually start exercising to give yourself time to adjust to an active lifestyle.

- It might take weeks, months, or longer for some people to get used to and enjoy the minimum activity guidelines.

- Occasional weeks without exercise or light activity may be important to prevent injury.

- Figuring out what works best for you may give you lasting benefits.

Expanded Knowledge

Anxiety increasingly intrudes on our collective lives as we navigate the modern world. The way we live our lives and the things we do each day can worsen or improve anxiety. One such factor is the scope of our physical activity, or perhaps more critically, our lack thereof: our sedentary behavior.

However, starting a new exercise regime is a journey best taken with careful consideration. Consultation with a healthcare provider is strongly advised before stepping onto the fitness path. Individuals with a history of disordered eating or exercise should heed this counsel with particular care.

Adjusting your nutrition to account for activity level is also important; otherwise, one may not receive as much anxiety benefit from exercise.

In this endeavor, remember that patience is an essential ally. Acclimating to an exercise routine can take weeks, even months. Sometimes, a pause of lighter activity or rest could be the much-needed antidote to prevent injuries.

The quest for an active lifestyle is deeply personal. In finding what resonates best with you, the reward could be a trove of enduring benefits. Working with a fitness trainer and or a nutritionist may be especially helpful as you master your own physical activity plan.

Mindfulness Meditation vs. Escitalopram for Anxiety[215]

Mindfulness meditation has been shown to have various mental health benefits. For example, a review of 13 studies showed improved ADHD symptoms with mindfulness meditation.[216]

---

[215] https://u.osu.edu/emotionalfitness/2022/12/21/mindfulness-meditation-vs-escitalopram-for-anxiety/

[216] Poissant, H., Mendrek, A., Talbot, N., Khoury, B., & Nolan, J. (2019). Behavioral and Cognitive Impacts of Mindfulness-Based Interventions on Adults with Attention-Deficit Hyperactivity Disorder: A Systematic Review. Behavioural neurology, 2019, 5682050. doi:10.1155/2019/5682050

Also, 41 trials show mindfulness meditation helped improve stress-related outcomes such as anxiety, depression, stress, positive mood, etc.[217]

A review of 14 clinical trials shows meditation is more effective than relaxation techniques for anxiety.[218]

A recent study examined whether mindfulness-based stress reduction (MBSR) was as effective as the anti-anxiety medication Lexapro (escitalopram).[219]

Who Was In The Study?[220]

- Around 102 participants in MBSR and 106 in the escitalopram group, with a median age of 33 years.[221]

- Participants were mostly female.[222]

---

[217] Goyal M, Singh S, Sibinga EMS, et al. Meditation Programs for Psychological Stress and Well-Being [Internet]. Rockville (MD): Agency for Healthcare Research and Quality (US); 2014 Jan. (Comparative Effectiveness Reviews, No. 124.)Available from: https://www.ncbi.nlm.nih.gov/books/NBK180102/

[218] Montero-Marin, J., Garcia-Campayo, J., Pérez-Yus, M., Zabaleta-del-Olmo, E., & Cuijpers, P. (n.d.). Meditation techniques v. relaxation therapies when treating anxiety: A meta-analytic review. Psychological Medicine,1-16. doi:10.1017/S0033291719001600

[219] Hoge, Elizabeth A et al. "Mindfulness-Based Stress Reduction vs Escitalopram for the Treatment of Adults With Anxiety Disorders: A Randomized Clinical Trial." JAMA psychiatry, e223679. 9 Nov. 2022, doi:10.1001/jamapsychiatry.2022.3679

[220] Hoge, Elizabeth A et al. "Mindfulness-Based Stress Reduction vs Escitalopram for the Treatment of Adults With Anxiety Disorders: A Randomized Clinical Trial." JAMA psychiatry, e223679. 9 Nov. 2022, doi:10.1001/jamapsychiatry.2022.3679

[221] Hoge, Elizabeth A et al. "Mindfulness-Based Stress Reduction vs Escitalopram for the Treatment of Adults With Anxiety Disorders: A Randomized Clinical Trial." JAMA psychiatry, e223679. 9 Nov. 2022, doi:10.1001/jamapsychiatry.2022.3679

[222] Hoge, Elizabeth A et al. "Mindfulness-Based Stress Reduction vs Escitalopram for the Treatment of Adults With Anxiety Disorders: A

How Was Anxiety Measured[223]?

- Clinical Global Impression of Severity scale (CGI-S) was performed by blinded clinical interviewer at baseline, week eight endpoint, and follow-up visits at 12 and 24 weeks.[224]

- The primary patient-reported measure was the Overall Anxiety Severity and Impairment Scale (OASIS).[225]

What Was The Intervention?[226]

- Participants were randomized 1:1 to 8 weeks of the weekly MBSR course or the antidepressant escitalopram, flexibly dosed from 10 to 20 mg.[227]

Randomized Clinical Trial." JAMA psychiatry, e223679. 9 Nov. 2022, doi:10.1001/jamapsychiatry.2022.3679

[223] Hoge, Elizabeth A et al. "Mindfulness-Based Stress Reduction vs Escitalopram for the Treatment of Adults With Anxiety Disorders: A Randomized Clinical Trial." JAMA psychiatry, e223679. 9 Nov. 2022, doi:10.1001/jamapsychiatry.2022.3679

[224] Hoge, Elizabeth A et al. "Mindfulness-Based Stress Reduction vs Escitalopram for the Treatment of Adults With Anxiety Disorders: A Randomized Clinical Trial." JAMA psychiatry, e223679. 9 Nov. 2022, doi:10.1001/jamapsychiatry.2022.3679

[225] Hoge, Elizabeth A et al. "Mindfulness-Based Stress Reduction vs Escitalopram for the Treatment of Adults With Anxiety Disorders: A Randomized Clinical Trial." JAMA psychiatry, e223679. 9 Nov. 2022, doi:10.1001/jamapsychiatry.2022.3679

[226] Hoge, Elizabeth A et al. "Mindfulness-Based Stress Reduction vs Escitalopram for the Treatment of Adults With Anxiety Disorders: A Randomized Clinical Trial." JAMA psychiatry, e223679. 9 Nov. 2022, doi:10.1001/jamapsychiatry.2022.3679

[227] Hoge, Elizabeth A et al. "Mindfulness-Based Stress Reduction vs Escitalopram for the Treatment of Adults With Anxiety Disorders: A Randomized Clinical Trial." JAMA psychiatry, e223679. 9 Nov. 2022, doi:10.1001/jamapsychiatry.2022.3679

- The MBSR group was taught MBSR as a manualized 8-week protocol with 45-minute daily home practice exercises, weekly 2.5-hour long classes, and a day-long retreat weekend class during the fifth or sixth week.[228]

- Participants were taught several forms of mindfulness meditation, such as breath awareness (focusing attention on the breath and other physical sensations), a body scan (directing attention to one body part at a time and observing how that body part feels), and mindful movement (stretching and movements designed to bring awareness to the body and increase interoceptive awareness).[229][230]

---

[228] Santorelli SF, Kabat-Zinn J, Blacker M, Meleo-Meyer F, Koerbel L. Mindfulness-Based Stress Reduction (MBSR) Authorized Curriculum Guide. Center for Mindfulness in Medicine, Health Care, and Society at the University of Massachusetts Medical School. Revised 2017. Accessed December 14, 2017.
https://www.bangor.ac.uk/mindfulness/documents/mbsr-curriculum-guide-2017.pdf
[229] Hoge, Elizabeth A et al. "Mindfulness-Based Stress Reduction vs Escitalopram for the Treatment of Adults With Anxiety Disorders: A Randomized Clinical Trial." JAMA psychiatry, e223679. 9 Nov. 2022, doi:10.1001/jamapsychiatry.2022.3679
[230] Santorelli SF, Kabat-Zinn J, Blacker M, Meleo-Meyer F, Koerbel L. Mindfulness-Based Stress Reduction (MBSR) Authorized Curriculum Guide. Center for Mindfulness in Medicine, Health Care, and Society at the University of Massachusetts Medical School. Revised 2017. Accessed December 14, 2017.
https://www.bangor.ac.uk/mindfulness/documents/mbsr-curriculum-guide-2017.pdf

What Were The Results?[231]

Participants who completed the trial at week 8 showed noninferiority for CGI-S score improvement with MBSR compared with escitalopram[232]—meaning MBSR was as effective as escitalopram.

What are some caveats?

- This is the first study to compare MBSR to medication.[233]

- The study did not use commonly used instruments to measure anxiety in clinical settings, such as GAD-7, Hamilton rating scale for anxiety, or the Beck anxiety inventory.

- Participants had any anxiety disorder, not a specific type of anxiety disorder such as generalized anxiety disorder or a panic disorder[234] , making it difficult to generalize results for other populations.

---

[231] Hoge, Elizabeth A et al. "Mindfulness-Based Stress Reduction vs Escitalopram for the Treatment of Adults With Anxiety Disorders: A Randomized Clinical Trial." JAMA psychiatry, e223679. 9 Nov. 2022, doi:10.1001/jamapsychiatry.2022.3679

[232] Hoge, Elizabeth A et al. "Mindfulness-Based Stress Reduction vs Escitalopram for the Treatment of Adults With Anxiety Disorders: A Randomized Clinical Trial." JAMA psychiatry, e223679. 9 Nov. 2022, doi:10.1001/jamapsychiatry.2022.3679

[233] Hoge, Elizabeth A et al. "Mindfulness-Based Stress Reduction vs Escitalopram for the Treatment of Adults With Anxiety Disorders: A Randomized Clinical Trial." JAMA psychiatry, e223679. 9 Nov. 2022, doi:10.1001/jamapsychiatry.2022.3679

[234] Hoge, Elizabeth A et al. "Mindfulness-Based Stress Reduction vs Escitalopram for the Treatment of Adults With Anxiety Disorders: A Randomized Clinical Trial." JAMA psychiatry, e223679. 9 Nov. 2022, doi:10.1001/jamapsychiatry.2022.3679

- Participants[235] were mostly female in their 30s, which makes it difficult to generalize results for other populations.

- The MBSR is a specific type of manualized meditation taught by qualified instructors[236] , and it may be difficult to find qualified instructors or qualified classes in your area.

- In addition to work, school, and life obligations, people may find it difficult to schedule 45 minutes of daily meditation plus 2.5 hours of weekly class and a day-long retreat.

- Different people may benefit from different types of meditation, and this area is being further researched.

- Practicing meditation regularly may lead to improved benefits, and some people may see benefits with shorter duration of meditation.

- Some people may find that mindfulness or too much mindfulness may worsen their symptoms,[237] so you should check with your

---

[235] Hoge, Elizabeth A et al. "Mindfulness-Based Stress Reduction vs Escitalopram for the Treatment of Adults With Anxiety Disorders: A Randomized Clinical Trial." JAMA psychiatry, e223679. 9 Nov. 2022, doi:10.1001/jamapsychiatry.2022.3679

[236] Santorelli SF, Kabat-Zinn J, Blacker M, Meleo-Meyer F, Koerbel L. Mindfulness-Based Stress Reduction (MBSR) Authorized Curriculum Guide. Center for Mindfulness in Medicine, Health Care, and Society at the University of Massachusetts Medical School. Revised 2017. Accessed December 14, 2017. https://www.bangor.ac.uk/mindfulness/documents/mbsr-curriculum-guide-2017.pdf

[237] Britton, W. B., Lindahl, J. R., Cooper, D. J., Canby, N. K., & Palitsky, R. (2021). Defining and Measuring Meditation-Related Adverse Effects in

mental health professional if the MBSR is appropriate for you.

- Some mental health conditions may not be appropriate for the MBSR. Check with your mental health professional.

Expanded Knowledge

Mindfulness meditation is a practice with deep roots in ancient philosophy but only recently bloomed in modern healthcare. It has been shown to help with ADHD and stress (Huang et al., 2019[238]; Galante et al., 2014).[239] Other studies have shown that mindfulness meditation can help with many other conditions.

For example, 41 trials show mindfulness meditation helped improve stress-related outcomes such as anxiety, depression, stress, positive mood,_etc. (These 41 trials show mindfulness meditation helped improve stress-related outcomes such as anxiety, depression, stress, positive mood, and more).

One must always enlist the guidance of a mental health professional before embarking on a journey with

---

Mindfulness-Based Programs. Clinical Psychological Science, 9(6), 1185–1204. https://doi.org/10.1177/2167702621996340

[238] Huang, J., Nigatu, Y. T., Smail-Crevier, R., Zhang, X., & Wang, J. (2019). Interventions for common mental health problems among university and college students: A systematic review and meta-analysis of randomized controlled trials. Journal of Psychiatric Research, 119, 129-138.

[239] Galante, J., Galante, I., Bekkers, M. J., & Gallacher, J. (2014). Effect of kindness-based meditation on health and well-being: a systematic review and meta-analysis. Journal of Consulting and Clinical Psychology, 82(6), 1101.

MBSR or any mindfulness regimen—it may not be a one-size-fits-all solution (Rocha, 2020).[240]

In summary, when possible, DECREASING/AVOIDING triggers can help reduce anxiety, and increasing certain behaviors can help DECREASE anxiety.

Common triggers for anxiety to reduce/avoid include:

- Caffeine (See Chapters 5, 6).

- Alcohol (Chapter 12).

- Nicotine/tobacco (Chapter 13).

- Cannabis withdrawal (Chapter 13).

- Unhealthy ways of using technology and media (Chapter 8).

- In my experience, processed grains and added sugars may increase anxiety in some people by causing a spike and crash in blood sugar levels.

- Anxiety-decreasing strategies include exercise, as mentioned above

- Mindfulness meditation mentioned above, and apps such as Headspace, CALM, and Virtual Hope box (Chapter 8)

- Improving nutrition and omega 3's, adequate protein intake

---

[240] Rocha, T. (2020). The dark knight of the soul: Understanding the shadow side of meditation and mindfulness practice. Journal of Spirituality in Mental Health, 1-20.

- Healthy ways of using technology and media (Chapter 8)

- Improving stress management skills (Chapter 5)

In my experience, people may find that other specific triggers increase or decrease anxiety in addition to the abovementioned factors. The key part of using life strategies to improve anxiety is to find the right combination of strategies that work best for you. As always, this book is intended for informational purposes.

Check with your healthcare professional to see if any strategies discussed are right for you. If you choose to apply them, do it under the care and guidance of your health professional.

Chapter 4: Strategies to Improve Depression

Depression is a major concern among young adults, and there are many types of depressive disorders. In a national survey of over 33 thousand college students, about 23% or about 1 in 5 college students reported being diagnosed or treated with depression in the past 12 months, and 59% of students reporting anxiety said that depression impacted their academic performance.[241]

Depression, a formidable adversary in the realm of mental health, etches deep tracks across the many facets of an individual's existence. It can impact emotional, cognitive, and physical symptoms, casting a seemingly unshakeable pall over the routine rhythms of life. Yet, as our comprehension of this multifaceted disorder grows, so does our determination to combat it.

Over the years, the focus has shifted from merely mapping symptoms and diagnoses toward exploring innovative, multi-layered strategies with the potential not only to manage but potentially alleviate the effects of depression.

Despite significant progress in psychotherapeutic and pharmaceutical treatments, a substantial proportion of individuals with depression may not fully benefit. (Rush

---

[241] American College Health Association. American College Health Association-National College Health Assessment III: Reference Group Executive Summary Fall 2022. Silver Spring, MD: American College Health Association; 2023.

et al., 2006).[242] Depression is a complex condition with many different factors. Therefore, the solution to an individual's depression may involve a variety of strategies.

Moreover, the intricate dance between lifestyle factors and mental health has become increasingly scrutinized. Research has shed light, revealing how our daily choices, from our dietary habits to our sleep patterns, can deeply influence our psychological well-being. (Lopresti et al., 2013).[243]

Depression's pervasive reach and broad impact necessitates a public health response that extends beyond individual treatment. The challenge lies in formulating strategies that are potent, yet widely accessible and adaptable to the diverse tapestry of cultural and socioeconomic contexts. These strategies might utilize resources and interventions within easy reach of individuals, such as nutritional alterations or mindfulness techniques (Firth et al., 2020).[244]

Lastly, the spotlight is increasingly turning towards the importance of personalizing interventions. Depression presents a unique face in each individual,

---

[242] Rush, A. J., Trivedi, M. H., Wisniewski, S. R., Nierenberg, A. A., Stewart, J. W., Warden, D., . . . Fava, M. (2006). Acute and longer-term outcomes in depressed outpatients requiring one or several treatment steps: a STAR*D report. American Journal of Psychiatry, 163(11), 1905-1917.

[243] Lopresti, A. L., Hood, S. D., & Drummond, P. D. (2013). A review of lifestyle factors that contribute to important pathways associated with major depression: diet, sleep and exercise. Journal of Affective Disorders, 148(1), 12-27.

[244] Firth, J., Gangwisch, J. E., Borisini, A., Wootton, R. E., & Mayer, E. A. (2020). Food and mood: how do diet and nutrition affect mental wellbeing?. BMJ, 369.

with distinct symptom profiles, underlying causes, and treatment responses. Consequently, tailoring interventions to individual needs, preferences, and contexts is a necessity, whether that involves selecting an appropriate nutritional supplement or determining the optimal light therapy protocol (Chekroud et al., 2017).[245]

This chapter embarks on an exploration of these aspects of life strategies for depression management. It is a journey that navigates through the terrain of gratitude and mindfulness, nutritional interventions, other lifestyle modifications, and beyond. The ultimate objective is not simply to present knowledge but to equip individuals, healthcare professionals, and societies with the understanding and tools necessary to manage and hopefully, alleviate depression more effectively. In my decade plus of experience, combining a personalized set of life strategies with counseling and or pharmacological approaches can have a much more powerful effect on depression than any one modality or strategy alone.

As always, this book is intended for informational purposes. Check with your healthcare professional to see if any strategies discussed are right for you. If you choose to apply them, do it under the care and guidance of your health professional. Additionally, individuals with eating

---

[245] Chekroud, S. R., Gueorguieva, R., Zheutlin, A. B., Paulus, M., Krumholz, H. M., Krystal, J. H., & Chekroud, A. M. (2017). Association between physical exercise and mental health in 1·2 million individuals in the USA between 2011 and 2015: a cross-sectional study. The Lancet Psychiatry, 5(9), 739-746.

disorders should follow their eating disorder treatment plan.

Study: Happiness, Stress, and Depression might improve with Gratitude and Mindfulness[246][247]

Many studies show that mindfulness and a positive attitude can improve mood, anxiety, and happiness.

But what exactly do you need to do?

And how often?

A recent study suggests possible clues.

What Did The Study Involve?

- Nearly 65 women aged 18-46 years, with a mean age of 28.35 years.

- They were randomly assigned to wait-list or gratitude or mindfulness groups.

- Online exercise of gratitude or mindfulness four times per week for three weeks.

What Exactly Was The Intervention?

Four times a week for three consecutive weeks:

[246] https://u.osu.edu/emotionalfitness/2015/12/23/study-happiness-stress-and-depression-might-improve-with-gratitude-and-mindfulness/
[247] Oleary K, Dockray S. The Effects of Two Novel Gratitude and Mindfulness Interventions on Well-Being. THE JOURNAL OF ALTERNATIVE AND COMPLEMENTARY MEDICINE. Volume 21, Number 4, 2015, pp. 243–245

- The gratitude group was asked to list five things they felt grateful for and one thing they were most grateful for.

- The mindfulness group kept a mindfulness diary for listing thoughts, feelings, and emotions in the present moment and did mindfulness meditation called the Body Scan.

- This took 10–15 minutes to complete.

What Did The Results Show?

By the end of the study, compared to the wait list control group, participants reported being:

- Less depressed on the Edinburgh Depression Scale.

- Less stress on The Perceived Stress Scale

- Happier on the Subjective Happiness Scale

Gratitude was more helpful for stress, and mindfulness was more helpful for depression and happiness.

What About Effect Size, Side Effects, or Drop-Out Rate?

- Overall effect size ranged from 10-20%, but the time commitment was also small (four times/week).

- Even though the intervention was a few minutes 4 times per week, only about half the participants completed the study.

- No side effects were reported.

What Are Some Caveats?

- This was a small study with specific exercises; larger studies to confirm results would be helpful.

- Since the study population was women only, we don't know how well these specific techniques would work for other populations.

- Individual responses may vary.

- For the amount of time invested, the results are impressive.

Expanded Knowledge

The intervention revealed that gratitude practices had a more profound impact on stress reduction, while mindfulness was more effective for addressing depression and enhancing happiness.

However, one should note that the effect sizes observed in this study were relatively modest despite a minimal time commitment. This highlights the challenges in fostering adherence to these practices, as only about half of the participants completed the study, even with a short duration of engagement.

While these findings are promising, they echo the need for larger, more diverse studies to verify these results. The study involved only women. Thus, the generalizability to other populations remains uncertain. Also, personal experiences with these practices may differ, underscoring the necessity for individualized approaches in mental health care.

In my experience, prior knowledge has shown that our mind tends to notice thoughts and feelings that mimic how we predominantly feel at that time.

Feeling happy?

You might be more prone to notice more positive things and might recall more positive thoughts and memories. Similarly, if you are feeling angry, sad, stressed, etc., you might be more prone to thoughts, feelings, and memories in line with that emotional state. Thus, individuals with depression might be more prone to depressive thoughts, memories, and emotions.

During this time, practicing gratitude and actively cultivating a regular gratitude practice may help some people shake off or decrease symptoms of depression.

Food Choices To Improve Depression[248]

A 2017 systematic review of 21 studies across ten countries looking at food patterns and depression found an association between food patterns and depression.[249]

---

[248] https://u.osu.edu/emotionalfitness/2018/06/28/food-choices-to-improve-depression/
[249] Li, Ye & Lv, Mei-Rong & Wei, Yan-Jin & Sun, Ling & Zhang, Ji-Xiang & Zhang, Huai-Guo & Li, Bin. (2017). Dietary patterns and depression risk: A meta-analysis. Psychiatry Research. 253. 10.1016/j.psychres.2017.04.020.

What Food Patterns Were Found To Have A DECREASED Risk Of Depression?

• The study authors[250] found that high intakes of fruit, vegetables, fish, olive oil, low-fat dairy, antioxidants, and whole grain was associated with a decreased risk of depression.[251]

• Another review found that seafood, vegetables, fruit, and nut-based food patterns were associated with a reduced risk of depression.[252]

• A study of 15,980 adults over 10.8 years found that higher consumption of fruits and nuts, while lower consumption of fast food, led to a reduced depression risk.[253]

What Food Patterns Were Found To Have An INCREASED Risk Of Depression?[254]

• The study authors[255] found that high consumption of red

---

[250] Li, Ye & Lv, Mei-Rong & Wei, Yan-Jin & Sun, Ling & Zhang, Ji-Xiang & Zhang, Huai-Guo & Li, Bin. (2017). Dietary patterns and depression risk: A meta-analysis. Psychiatry Research. 253. 10.1016/j.psychres.2017.04.020.

[251] Li, Ye & Lv, Mei-Rong & Wei, Yan-Jin & Sun, Ling & Zhang, Ji-Xiang & Zhang, Huai-Guo & Li, Bin. (2017). Dietary patterns and depression risk: A meta-analysis. Psychiatry Research. 253. 10.1016/j.psychres.2017.04.020.

[252] Martínez-González MA1, Sánchez-Villegas A2. Food patterns and the prevention of depression. Proc Nutr Soc. 2016 May;75(2):139-46. doi: 10.1017/S0029665116000045. Epub 2016 Feb 22.

[253] Fresán, U., Bes-Rastrollo, M., Segovia-Siapco, G. et al. Does the MIND diet decrease depression risk? A comparison with Mediterranean diet in the SUN cohort. Eur J Nutr (2018). https://doi.org/10.1007/s00394-018-1653-x

[254] Li, Ye & Lv, Mei-Rong & Wei, Yan-Jin & Sun, Ling & Zhang, Ji-Xiang & Zhang, Huai-Guo & Li, Bin. (2017). Dietary patterns and depression risk: A meta-analysis. Psychiatry Research. 253. 10.1016/j.psychres.2017.04.020.

[255] Li, Ye & Lv, Mei-Rong & Wei, Yan-Jin & Sun, Ling & Zhang, Ji-Xiang & Zhang, Huai-Guo & Li, Bin. (2017). Dietary patterns and depression risk: A meta-analysis. Psychiatry Research. 253. 10.1016/j.psychres.2017.04.020.

and/or processed meat, refined grains (added sugars)/sweets, high-fat dairy products, butter, potatoes, and high-fat gravy was associated with an increased risk of depression.[256]

Are There Clinical Studies Where Food Pattern Was Used To TREAT Depression?

Yes. The HELFIMED[257] and SMILES trials[258] used food as a treatment for depressive disorders.

How Effective Was This?

In both trials[259][260], the improvement was almost 50%, comparable to some therapies and some antidepressant medications, and the benefits lasted for several months afterward.

---

[256] Li, Ye & Lv, Mei-Rong & Wei, Yan-Jin & Sun, Ling & Zhang, Ji-Xiang & Zhang, Huai-Guo & Li, Bin. (2017). Dietary patterns and depression risk: A meta-analysis. Psychiatry Research. 253. 10.1016/j.psychres.2017.04.020.

[257] Natalie Parletta, Dorota Zarnowiecki, Jihyun Cho, Amy Wilson, Svetlana Bogomolova, Anthony Villani, Catherine Itsiopoulos, Theo Niyonsenga, Sarah Blunden, Barbara Meyer, Leonie Segal, Bernhard T. Baune & Kerin O'Dea (2017) A Mediterranean-style dietary intervention supplemented with fish oil improves diet quality and mental health in people with depression: A randomized controlled trial (HELFIMED),Nutritional Neuroscience, DOI: 10.1080/1028415X.2017.1411320

[258] Jacka FN, O'Neil A, Opie R, et al. A randomised controlled trial of dietary improvement for adults with major depression (the "SMILES" trial). BMC Medicine. 2017;15:23. doi:10.1186/s12916-017-0791-y.

[259] Natalie Parletta, Dorota Zarnowiecki, Jihyun Cho, Amy Wilson, Svetlana Bogomolova, Anthony Villani, Catherine Itsiopoulos, Theo Niyonsenga, Sarah Blunden, Barbara Meyer, Leonie Segal, Bernhard T. Baune & Kerin O'Dea (2017) A Mediterranean-style dietary intervention supplemented with fish oil improves diet quality and mental health in people with depression: A randomized controlled trial (HELFIMED),Nutritional Neuroscience, DOI: 10.1080/1028415X.2017.1411320

[260] Jacka FN, O'Neil A, Opie R, et al. A randomised controlled trial of dietary improvement for adults with major depression (the "SMILES" trial). BMC Medicine. 2017;15:23. doi:10.1186/s12916-017-0791-y.

What Are Some Caveats?

- These studies show that nutrition can help improve depression, but further study is needed.

- Nutritious food choices DO NOT have to be expensive; in many cases, whole foods can be more affordable than processed foods.

- Good nutrition is not enough for some people to replace counseling or medications, but it can be a useful addition.

- Different people can be healthiest on different eating styles, depending on various factors.

- Even with good food choices, getting enough calories is important; and not engaging in restriction or disordered eating behaviors.

- TDEE calculators (Total daily energy expenditure) and this[261] chart may help estimate daily calorie needs.

- When considering nutritional adjustments, individuals with eating disorders should seek professional assistance from a nutritionist or specialist.

Any Other Resources To Improve Nutrition?

- Nutrition coaching with The OSU Student Wellness Center.

---

[261] https://www.nhlbi.nih.gov/health/educational/wecan/healthy-weight-basics/balance.htm

- Nutrition books.

- Working with a nutritionist.

- Take a nutrition class.

- Take a look at the Dietary Guidelines for Americans.

- National Center of Complimentary and Integrative Health's Page on Probiotics.

- Harvard's page on nutritional psychiatry.

How is your nutrition?

What is the quality of your food choices?

Are you eating enough or too much food?

Are you eating foods that worsen or improve depression?

The HELFIMED and SMILES trials were powerful studies because they showed that the benefit of nutrition for depression was up to 50% improvement in depressive symptoms, rivaling some therapies and antidepressants (Parletta et al., 2017[262]; Jacka et al., 2017).[263]

However, we must tread carefully. While undoubtedly beneficial, good nutrition may not be a standalone treatment for all. Its role as an add-on treatment becomes significant, complementing other therapy,

---

[262] Parletta, N., et al. (2017). A Mediterranean-style dietary intervention supplemented with fish oil improves diet quality and mental health in people with depression: A randomized controlled trial (HELFIMED). Nutritional Neuroscience.

[263] Jacka, F. N., et al. (2017). A randomised controlled trial of dietary improvement for adults with major depression (the 'SMILES' trial). BMC Medicine.

medication, and life strategies. Moreover, the individual variations in dietary needs caution us against a one-size-fits-all approach and underline the critical need for personalized dietary guidelines.

Ultimately, we arrive at the heart of our journey - maintaining a balanced and nutritious way of eating isn't simply about physical well-being. It emerges as a powerful tool, an ally in our arsenal, helping us in our shared human struggle against the sad shadow of depression. Chapter 6 discusses food strategies for mental health in further detail.

As always, this book is intended for informational purposes. Check with your healthcare professional to see if any strategies discussed are right for you. If you choose to apply them, do it under the care and guidance of your health professional. Additionally, individuals with eating disorders should follow their eating disorder treatment plan.

Does Smoking [Cigarettes] Increase Anxiety And Depression? If I Quit, Will I Feel Better?[264]

Most students know about the harmful effects of smoking cigarettes, including the risk of cancer, stroke, heart disease, and breathing problems.[265] Students may

---

[264] https://u.osu.edu/emotionalfitness/2015/04/15/does-smoking-increase-anxiety-and-depression-if-i-quit-will-i-feel-better/

[265] US Department of Health and Human Services. The health consequences of smoking: a report of the Surgeon General. US Department of Health and Human Services, 2004.

also know that stopping smoking reduces these health risks.[266],[267]

Most people may not know that smoking contributes to anxiety and depression and that you can feel good and increase happiness by quitting smoking.

This study[268] analyzed mental health information across 26 studies and looked at positive and negative changes in mental health before and after quitting smoking cigarettes.

What Did The Study Show?

When compared to smokers, seven weeks to nine years *after quitting smoking*, those who quit reported a DECREASE in:

- Anxiety.

- Depression.

- Mixed anxiety and depression.

- Stress.

When compared to smokers, seven weeks to 9 years after quitting smoking, those who quit smoking reported an INCREASE in:

---

[266] US Department of Health and Human Services. The health benefits of smoking cessation. US Department of Health and Human Services, 1990.

[267] Pirie K, Peto R, Reeves G, Green J, Beral V. The 21st century hazards of smoking and benefits of stopping: a prospective study of one million women in the UK. Lancet 2013;381:133-41.

[268] Taylor G, et al. Change in mental health after smoking cessation: systematic review and meta-analysis. OPEN ACCESS. BMJ 2014;348:g1151 doi: 10.1136/bmj.g1151 (Published 13 February 2014)

- Psychological quality of life 0.22 Positive affect significantly 0.40.

- This improvement occurred whether or not participants had anxiety or depression before quitting smoking.

But I Thought People Smoke To Be Less Anxious And Depressed.

- When they have not smoked for a while, smokers experience irritability, anxiety, and depression.[269][270]

- These feelings are relieved by smoking[271] , thus creating the perception that smoking has psychological benefits, while, in fact, it is smoking that caused these psychological disturbances in the first place.

Is smoking worth anxiety, depression, and feeling bad?

Is it sapping your energy level?

How good will you feel after you stop smoking for good?

Expanded Knowledge

---

[269] Hughes JR. Effects of abstinence from tobacco: valid symptoms and time course. Nicotine Tob Res 2007;9:315-27.

[270] Guthrie SK, Ni L, Zubieta JK, Teter CJ, Domino EF. Changes in craving for a cigarette and arterial nicotine plasma concentrations in abstinent smokers. Prog NeuroPsychopharmacol Biol Psychiatry 2004;28:617-23.

[271] Parrott AC. Does cigarette smoking cause stress? Am Psychol 1999;54:817-20.

The intricate dance between smoking cigarettes, mental health, and the holistic state of well-being forms a captivating focus of numerous scientific inquiries. While the traditional narrative associates smoking cigarettes primarily with physical ailments, the spotlight is increasingly veering towards its insidious ties to psychological distress—namely, amplified levels of anxiety and depression. This reframes the prevailing belief of smoking as a tranquil activity.

By increasing the release of stress-related hormones, nicotine use can also make you feel more stressed. Nicotine and its metabolites also disrupt your sleep. In my experience, nicotine use can often leave you feeling more tired.

The studies about cigarettes point out a subtle deception about the perceived relief of using nicotine: the fleeting relief from nicotine withdrawal symptoms, including irritability, anxiety, and depression, may masquerade as the calming embrace of smoking.

Those interested in quitting can find invaluable guidance and tools, such as behavioral counseling, medication, and nicotine replacement therapies, in the expertise of healthcare professionals. In my experience, this combination of treatments is quite effective in helping people quit or reduce cigarette use.

A great place to start is the following website: https://smokefree.gov/

In my experience, people see the best results if they decrease caffeine, nicotine, and alcohol gradually by 20-

25% per week and then stay off for a few weeks before they can see the full impact of eliminating these substances and how it may help improve mood, anxiety, sleep and other aspects of health.

Warning: Eliminating these substances abruptly or cold turkey can lead to withdrawal, which in the case of alcohol can be deadly!

As with all other strategies discussed in this book, check with your healthcare professional before considering changes to your caffeine, nicotine, or alcohol intake.

Study: Male College Students Might Perceive Depression Differently[272]

In a recent national survey, about 30% of college students reported that, in a 12-month period, they felt so depressed that it impacted their functioning.[273]

But, only about 7% of male and 12% of female college students were under the care of a health professional to treat their depression.[274]

Other studies have shown that men tend to underuse healthcare services in general. Men also have a shorter lifespan than women.[275]

---

[272] https://u.osu.edu/emotionalfitness/2015/11/06/study-male-college-students-might-perceive-depression-differently-3/

[273] 1. American College Health Association. (2014). American College Health Association-National College Health Assessment II: Reference Group Executive Summary Spring 2014.

[274] 1. American College Health Association. (2014). American College Health Association-National College Health Assessment II: Reference Group Executive Summary Spring 2014.

[275] http://www.cdc.gov/nchs/data_access/Vitalstatsonline.htm

While there are many reasons why so few male college students with depression are getting treatment, a recent study had intriguing findings.

What Did The Study Involve?

Around 1577 undergraduate students, ages 18–24, responded to an online survey.

The survey assessed symptoms of depression and feelings of sadness, depression, and suicidal ideation experienced in the past two weeks.

They also asked about students' perceptions of how common these are among other students.

What Did The Results Show?

Most students, particularly male college students, underestimated the sadness and depression experienced by other college students.

Students with feelings of sadness, depression, and suicidal ideation in the past two weeks overestimated students with similar problems.

What Might This Suggest?

This study suggests that students who are not depressed might not be as good at noticing depression as their peers.

Increasing awareness might help.

Expanded Knowledge

Some work has been done on why male students might perceive depression differently. This may well be anchored in societal mores and gender expectations, which venerate stoicism and emotional self-restraint in males, thus discouraging males from recognizing emotional distress and pursuing assistance (Addis & Mahalik, 2003).[276]

Beyond this, the larger canvas of men's general health behaviors may also lend some insight. A review by Galdas et al. (2005)[277] discovered that, on average, men engaged with healthcare services less frequently than women. This trend may be contributory to their under-treatment for depression.

From a broader vantage point, the World Health Organization's 2019 report[278] casts a long shadow, declaring that men's average life expectancy trails behind women's, possibly indicative of the cumulative toll of such health behaviors. This reinforces the necessity to delve deeper into the intricate interplay of societal expectations, self-perception, and mental health among college-aged males.

These findings reinforce the urgency for robust interventions addressing misconceptions about

---

[276] Addis, M. E., & Mahalik, J. R. (2003). Men, masculinity, and the contexts of help seeking. American Psychologist, 58(1), 5–14.

[277] Galdas, P. M., Cheater, F., & Marshall, P. (2005). Men and health help-seeking behaviour: literature review. Journal of Advanced Nursing, 49(6), 616-623.

[278] World Health Organization. (2019). Life expectancy and Healthy life expectancy data by WHO region. Retrieved from https://www.who.int/data/gho/data/themes/mortality-and-global-health-estimates/ghe-life-expectancy-and-healthy-life-expectancy

depression among young men. These might involve implementing mental health literacy programs in educational institutions and encouraging open conversations about men's mental health.

The useful goal is to foster an environment where male college students can recognize and accept emotional distress without stigma or fear and seek the help they need.

Study: Men and Depression Treatment[279]

About 1 in 16 individuals experienced depression in a given year,[280] impacting both men and women.

A recent survey of about 95,000 college students had interesting information about men and depression.[281]

What Did The Study Involve?[282]

- Around 95,761 college students from 137 colleges and universities across the United States.

- Out of them, 91% of the students were 18 to 29 years old.

---

[279] https://u.osu.edu/emotionalfitness/2016/10/28/study-men-and-depression-treatment/

[280] https://www.nimh.nih.gov/health/statistics/prevalence/major-depression-among-adults.shtml

[281] American College Health Association. American College Health Association-National College Health Assessment II: Reference Group Executive Summary Spring 2016. Hanover, MD: American College Health Association; 2016.

[282] American College Health Association. American College Health Association-National College Health Assessment II: Reference Group Executive Summary Spring 2016. Hanover, MD: American College Health Association; 2016.

- This is a 30-minute survey asking a variety of questions regarding health, health-related lifestyle, etc.

- This also included questions about depression, overwhelming anxiety, receiving treatment, and suicidal ideation.

- The survey was conducted over several years.

What Did The Results Show?

A similar percentage of male and female college students (30.8, 38.8%) reported feeling so depressed that they could not function in the past 12 months.

A similar percentage of males and females reported seriously considering suicide in the past 12 months (8.5, 9.6%).

However, fewer male college students reported getting treatment for depression than female college students (8.7 % male vs. 15.6% female).

Why Might This Be The Case?

There are several possibilities. Some of them include:

- Men can experience depression differently[283] than women. Men may be more likely to feel tired and irritable, lose interest in their work, family, or hobbies, and sleep difficulties due to depression.[284]

---

[283] https://u.osu.edu/emotionalfitness/2015/11/
[284] http://www.cdc.gov/nchs/data_access/Vitalstatsonline.htm

- Many men do not recognize, acknowledge, or seek help for their depression.[285]

- Around 3/4 of all suicides in the United States are men.[286]

- Men tend to underutilize health care overall than women, and this may play a role in men dying sooner than women on average.[287]

What Is Being Done About Men's Mental Health On Campus?

- Increasing awareness might help.

- Know the signs, and encourage others you know to reach out to men about their health.

- If you are concerned, encourage them to seek help.

Expanded Knowledge

Every demographic group is susceptible to depression. Yet, the yawning gap in treatment-seeking behaviors between genders, most notably amongst young men, instigates a critical discourse on societal perceptions, behavioral norms, and the overall landscape of men's mental health.

A pivotal clue to this conundrum is in understanding how depression manifests in men and women. The National Institute of Mental Health illuminates that male-identified individuals may display other

---

[285] http://www.cdc.gov/nchs/data_access/Vitalstatsonline.htm
[286] https://us.movember.com/programs/cause
[287] https://us.movember.com/programs/cause

symptoms beyond sadness and crying spells, such as fatigue, irritability, lost interest in activities, and sleep disturbance.

This difference in symptoms could be a potential factor leading to an under-recognition of the condition in male-identified individuals (NIMH, 2017).[288]

Societal stigma and gender stereotypes might render men less inclined to acknowledge or recognize their depressive symptoms. This perspective resonates with the findings of a study conducted by Vogel et al., which suggested that men might sidestep seeking help for mental health concerns to uphold an image of self-reliance and resilience (Vogel et al., 2011).[289]

The repercussions of this chasm in treatment are far-reaching and grave. In the U.S., the somber statistic is that men represent three-quarters of suicides.[290] Further, men's pervasive underutilization of healthcare services may sow the seeds of long-term complications, potentially contributing to their lower life expectancy than women.

Undeniably, steps are being taken to address this looming crisis across campuses throughout the U.S., primarily by championing awareness about men's

---

[288] National Institute of Mental Health. (2017). Men and Depression. Retrieved from https://www.nimh.nih.gov/health/publications/men-and-depression/index.shtml

[289] Vogel, D. L., Heimerdinger-Edwards, S. R., Hammer, J. H., & Hubbard, A. (2011). "Boys don't cry": Examination of the links between endorsement of masculine norms, self-stigma, and help-seeking attitudes for men from diverse backgrounds. Journal of Counseling Psychology, 58(3), 368-382.

[290] https://www.acha.org/documents/ncha/NCHA-II_SPRING_2019_US_REFERENCE_GROUP_EXECUTIVE_SUMMARY.pdf

mental health, honing the recognition of depression's signposts, and encouraging men to venture into the domain of professional help.

Study: Could Light Therapy Help With Non-Seasonal Depression?[291]

For some students, winter can be a difficult time of year. Many people know about seasonal affective disorder (S.A.D.), which is depressive symptoms that occur often during winter months.[292][293][294] Treatments for S.A.D. can include light therapy, counseling, healthy lifestyle habits, and medications.[295]

A study[296] shows that light therapy can also help with a more common form of depression, major depressive disorder, a form of depression that is NOT seasonal.

What Was The Study Design?

- Around 122 individuals ages 19-60 were randomized to 4 different groups.

---

[291] https://u.osu.edu/emotionalfitness/2016/01/15/study-could-light-therapy-help-with-non-seasonal-depression-2/

[292] http://www.nlm.nih.gov/medlineplus/seasonalaffectivedisorder.html

[293] Magnusson A. An overview of epidemiological studies on seasonal affective disorder. Acta Psychiatr Scand 2000; 101:176.

[294] Uptodate.com Seasonal Affective disorder. Accessed 01/2016.

[295] Uptodate.com Seasonal Affective disorder. Accessed 01/2016.

[296] Lam JAMA Psychiatry. 2016 Jan 1;73(1):56-63RW, et al. Efficacy of Bright Light Treatment, Fluoxetine, and the Combination in Patients With Nonseasonal Major Depressive Disorder: A Randomized Clinical Trial. JAMA Psychiatry. 2016 Jan 1;73(1):56-63.

- Light monotherapy of 10 000-lux fluorescent white lightboxes for 30 min/d in the early morning plus placebo pill (n=32).

- Medication monotherapy of a prescription antidepressant medication, Fluoxetine 20mg per day, (n=31);

- Combination of medication and light therapy (n=29);

- Placebo, (n=30).

- The study lasted for eight weeks, using a randomized, double-masked, placebo- and sham-controlled study design.

Who Was Studied?

- The average age of the 122 participants was 19-60 years

- They had a diagnosis of Major depressive disorder in outpatient psychiatry clinics in academic medical centers.

- Results were measured by changes in the MADRS score (a validated scale to measure depressive symptoms).

What Were The Study Results?

For each group, response rates (improvement in symptoms) were:

- Placebo 33%,

- 20mg fluoxetine, alone 29%,

- Light therapy 50%,

- Combination of light therapy and medication, 75.9%.

The study authors reported that all treatments were well tolerated, with few major differences in side effects.

What Are Some Caveats?

- For various reasons, light therapy and fluoxetine are **unsuitable for everyone** (check with your prescriber).

- Combining medication with light treatment was more effective than each group alone.

- In practice, we often see medications work better if the patient is also involved in non-medication treatments like counseling and healthy lifestyle habits. The most effective treatment often combines biological, psychological, and social treatments.

- Study participants were diagnosed by undergoing a psychiatric evaluation, which is not always available to everyone.

- The maximum dose of fluoxetine is 60mg, but this study only used a 20mg dose, which could have impacted results.

- Finally, we can prescribe many different antidepressant medications, and a single dose of 1 antidepressant cannot be generalized to all combinations/doses of other antidepressant medications.

What Are Other Treatments For Depression?

- Eat a healthy balanced diet of protein/veggies/fruit/whole grains, Omega-3s.

- Don't isolate yourself from family, friends, or colleagues; get involved on campus.

- Counseling.

- Talk to your doctor about various treatment options such as light therapy, medication, etc.

- A well-balanced exercise program (check with your doctor first).

Expanded Knowledge

The efficacy of light therapy, widely accepted for seasonal affective disorder (S.A.D), has recently been examined concerning non-seasonal major depressive disorder (M.D.D). MDD is a common mental health issue affecting millions worldwide, with varying treatment responses. This recent study explored the potential benefits of light therapy, a treatment method previously associated with SAD, for MDD. Depression is a complex condition with multiple factors involved and can manifest differently. Therefore, a comprehensive and flexible approach to treatment is necessary. Balanced nutrition, maintaining social connections, counseling, and a regular exercise regimen are all established contributors to improving mental health (Mammen & Faulkner, 2013[297]; Lai et al., 2015).[298]

Practicing gratitude and mindfulness may also help. Alcohol, cannabis, and other drugs can also impact your functioning directly and indirectly, causing you to feel more depressed. Individualized treatments tailored to patients' needs can optimize outcomes. Consultation with healthcare professionals is crucial in identifying the most suitable approach, potentially incorporating treatments such as counseling, light therapy, various medications, or other treatment modalities.

There is hope, and there are many options that can help.

[297] Mammen, G., & Faulkner, G. (2013). Physical activity and the prevention of depression: a systematic review of prospective studies. American Journal of Preventive Medicine, 45(5), 649-657.
[298] Lai, J. S., Hiles, S., Bisquera, A., Hure, A. J., McEvoy, M., & Attia, J. (2015). A systematic review and meta-analysis of dietary patterns and depression in community-dwelling adults. The American journal of clinical nutrition, 99(1), 181-197.

Chapter 5: Strategies to Manage Stress

There is a universal force that plays a role in a big part of just about everyone's lives– stress. Stress can be both good and bad, allowing us to survive and thrive when it occurs occasionally and can be harmful when it's too much or when it is chronic or relentlessly sustained. It influences mental health, catalyzes or cripples performance, defines behaviors, shapes relationships, and molds physical well-being. As you will see in this chapter, stress is complex and will emerge as a dynamic and context-sensitive process, which can be sculpted, steered, and softened by various tools, strategies, and interventions. As always, this book is intended for informational purposes. Check with your healthcare professional to see if any strategies discussed are right for you. If you choose to apply them, do it under the care and guidance of your health professional.

Stress And What To Do About It[299]

As we begin the new semester, the campus is buzzing with energy. There is also stress as you adjust to new people, places/routines, class schedules, etc. Stress is unavoidable.

What will you do to manage this stress?

Many college students reported feeling highly stressed (61 percent), and more students who failed to do

---

[299] https://u.osu.edu/emotionalfitness/2014/08/15/stress-and-what-to-do-about-it/

much about it (72 percent) reported low use of stress management techniques according to a recent study1 of college students performed by King and colleagues.

Ten Effective Stress Management Techniques:

- **Pause for a moment and take a deep breath.** Relax those muscles. When you are stressed, proper breathing can be powerful. See the bigger picture. Ask yourself, *"How big a deal is this? How does this fit in the grand scheme of things?"*

- **Don't let it build up.** Reach out to a friend or a counselor and talk it out so you do not hold on to painful feelings. Seek out a professional: ccs.osu.edu

- **Daily "me time."** Just a few minutes of leisure activity can be quite relaxing.

- **Plan it out**: Take a few moments each day to plan out the rest of the day. It can bring a calm sense of control.

- **Listen to** relaxing music.

- **Physical activity.** Go for a relaxing walk, take a yoga meditation class, or spend a few minutes at the RPAC.

- **Remember the basics:** Get 7-9 hours of sleep.

- **Avoid alcohol/tobacco/drugs and avoid excessive caffeine.** These unhealthy coping methods only worsen your stress. This is further discussed in subsequent chapters.

- **Eat nutritious food.**[300]

A study of stress, social support, and perceived happiness among college students.

Expanded Knowledge

Nudging into a new semester, college campuses are brimming with energy, enthusiasm, and the inevitable component of student life - stress. While the thrill of encountering new faces, imbibing novel routines, and adapting to shifting class schedules is invigorating, it is simultaneously stress-inducing.

An enlightening study by Dusselier et al. (2005)[301] evaluated the impacts of extracurricular involvement, living arrangements, and work hours on academic success and overall stress levels of university students. The research revealed an association between these factors and increased stress levels, thus emphasizing the need for effective stress management techniques.

As you navigate this maze of stressors, it is pivotal to remember that managing stress is equally as significant as encountering it. According to a comprehensive study by Brougham, Zail, Mendoza, and Miller (2009),[302]

---

[300] King KA, et al. The Journal of Happiness & Well-Being, 2014, 2(2), 132-144

[301] Dusselier, L., Dunn, B., Wang, Y., Shelley II, M. C., & Whalen, D. F. (2005). Personal, Health, Academic, and Environmental Predictors of Stress for Residence Hall Students. Journal of American College Health, 54(1), 15-24.

[302] Brougham, R. R., Zail, C. M., Mendoza, C. M., & Miller, J. R. (2009). Stress, Sex Differences, and Coping Strategies Among College Students. Current Psychology, 28(2), 85-97.

college students who utilized stress management strategies experienced better overall mental health.

King KA, et al. The Journal of Happiness & Well-Being, 2014, 2(2), 132-144

Certain techniques have proven their mettle in the quest for holistic stress management. Mindfulness and relaxation exercises, as demonstrated by a study by Keng et al. (2011)[303], can alleviate stress and improve psychological well-being. Many other free online resources can teach you mindfulness and relaxation techniques. Other strategies include apps such as Headspace, CALM, and Virtual Hope Box (VHB is discussed later in the book).

Planning and organization can also make a significant difference. According to research by Sirois and Pychyl (2013)[304], procrastination, a prevalent trait in students, can lead to increased stress and lower well-being. Therefore, daily planning can aid in controlling stress.

Maintaining balanced nutrition, engaging in physical activity, and ensuring adequate sleep are also crucial - a trio repeatedly validated by research for its contribution to stress management (Hicks et al., 2018).[305]

---

[303] Keng, S. L., Smoski, M. J., & Robins, C. J. (2011). Effects of mindfulness on psychological health: A review of empirical studies. Clinical Psychology Review, 31(6), 1041-1056.

[304] Sirois, F. M., & Pychyl, T. A. (2013). Procrastination and the Priority of Short-Term Mood Regulation: Consequences for Future Self. Social and Personality Psychology Compass, 7(2), 115-127.

[305] Hicks, R. A., Fernandez, C., & Pellegrini, R. J. (2001). Striking changes in the sleep satisfaction of university students over the last two decades. Perceptual and motor skills, 93(3), 660.

Thus, remember that while stress is an inevitable part of the college experience, it's also manageable with the right tools.

Study: Happiness, Stress, and Depression might improve with Gratitude and Mindfulness[306]

There are many studies showing that mindfulness and a positive attitude can improve mood, anxiety, and happiness.

But what exactly do you need to do? And how often?

A recent study suggests possible clues.

What Did The Study Involve?

- Around 65 women ages 18-46 years, with a mean age of 28.35 years.

- They were randomly assigned to wait-list or gratitude or mindfulness groups.

- Online exercise of gratitude or mindfulness four times per week for three weeks.

What Exactly Was The Intervention?

Four times a week for three consecutive weeks:

---

[306] https://u.osu.edu/emotionalfitness/2015/12/23/study-happiness-stress-and-depression-might-improve-with-gratitude-and-mindfulness/

- The gratitude group was asked to list five things they felt grateful for and one thing they were most grateful for.

- The mindfulness group kept a mindfulness diary for listing thoughts, feelings, and emotions in the present moment and did mindfulness meditation called the Body Scan.

- This took 10–15 minutes to complete.

What Did The Results Show?

By the end of the study, compared to the wait list control group, participants reported being:

- Less depressed on the Edinburgh Depression Scale.

- Less stress on The Perceived Stress Scale

- Happier on the Subjective Happiness Scale

Gratitude was more helpful for stress, and mindfulness was more helpful for depression and happiness.

What About Effect Size, Side Effects, Or Drop-Out Rate?

- Overall effect size ranged from 10-20%, but the time commitment was also small (four times/week).

- Even though the intervention was a few minutes, four times per week, only about half the participants completed the study.

- No side effects were reported.

What Are Some Caveats?

- This was a small study with specific exercises; larger studies to confirm results would be helpful.

- Since the study population was women only, we don't know how well these specific techniques would work for other populations.

- Individual responses may vary.

- For the amount of time invested, the results are impressive.[307]

Expanded Knowledge

Delving deeper into the world of mindfulness and gratitude, numerous studies corroborate the potency of these practices in bolstering mental health. For instance, a research piece by Goyal et al. (2014)[308] indicated that mindfulness meditation programs could substantially affect depression and anxiety among a wide age range. Similarly, a randomized controlled trial by Khoury et al. (2015)[309] concluded that mindfulness-based therapy might be a promising intervention for treating anxiety and mood problems in clinical populations.

---

[307] Oleary K, Dockray S. The Effects of Two Novel Gratitude and Mindfulness Interventions on Well-Being. THE JOURNAL OF ALTERNATIVE AND COMPLEMENTARY MEDICINE. Volume 21, Number 4, 2015, pp. 243–245

[308] Goyal M et al. (2014). Mindfulness-based stress reduction for healthy individuals: A meta-analysis. Journal of Psychosomatic Research.

[309] Khoury B et al. (2015). Mindfulness-based stress reduction for healthy individuals: A meta-analysis. Journal of Psychosomatic Research.

Concerning gratitude, a paper published by Emmons and McCullough (2003)[310] propounds that maintaining a gratitude journal can positively impact well-being and life satisfaction. Extending the gratitude practice, a study by Wood, Froh, and Geraghty (2010)[311] found that counting one's blessings can directly enhance feelings of well-being, further reducing the symptoms of depression.

Another riveting area is how the combined practice of mindfulness and gratitude can impact stress. A study by Jackowska, Brown, Ronaldson, and Steptoe (2016)[312] showed that combining mindfulness and gratitude can help with stress and inflammation. They also reported that these interventions might have meaningful effects on aspects of physical health, complementing the psychological benefits.

As with many other studies mentioned in this book, it is important to consider individual-level scope and application when looking at the study groups of participants. For example, a study by Galante et al. (2018)[313] showed that mindfulness might have differing effects based on personal disposition and culture.

---

[310] Emmons RA, McCullough ME. (2003). Counting blessings versus burdens: an experimental investigation of gratitude and subjective well-being in daily life. Journal of Personality and Social Psychology.

[311] Wood AM, Froh JJ, Geraghty AW. (2010). Gratitude and well-being: A review and theoretical integration. Clinical Psychology Review.

[312] Jackowska M, Brown J, Ronaldson A, Steptoe A. (2016). The impact of a brief gratitude intervention on subjective well-being, biology and sleep. Journal of Health Psychology.

[313] Galante J et al. (2018). Differential impact of dispositional mindfulness on academic performance in university students of natural science and social science disciplines. Journal of Further and Higher Education.

Similarly, Kashdan, Mishra, Breen, and Froh (2009)[314] note that the influence of gratitude practices may be modulated by factors such as personality traits and cultural background.

Ultimately, the positive influence of mindfulness and gratitude on mental health is supported by a growing body of research, indicating their viability as interventions for reducing stress and depression and enhancing happiness. However, considering diverse populations and individual differences, further studies will add depth to our understanding and help refine these practices for maximum effectiveness.

Study: Is Taking Notes On Your Laptop Better Than Writing Them?[315]

For many students, academic stress can be a major factor impacting their mental health. Getting better at study skills might help students feel better. Many students take notes during class and often on their laptops.[316]

But is this more effective than writing notes by hand?

---

[314] Kashdan TB, Mishra A, Breen WE, Froh JJ. (2009). Gender differences in gratitude: examining appraisals, narratives, the willingness to express emotions, and changes in psychological needs. Journal of Personality.

[315] https://u.osu.edu/emotionalfitness/2016/09/14/study-is-taking-notes-on-your-laptop-better-than-writing-them/

[316] Fried C. B. (2008). In-class laptop use and its effects on student learning. Computers & Education, 50, 906–914.

Researchers Pam Mueller and Daniel Oppenheimer try to answer this question[317].

Special thanks to my colleague, Dr. Barbara Urbanczyk, for suggesting this study.[318]

What Was The Study?

The study authors[319] conducted three different studies.

- **Study 1:** 67 college students who watched 5 TED talks projected onto a screen and took notes on a laptop versus their usual note-taking style were quizzed 30 minutes later.

- **Study 2:** 151 college students were asked to view a lecture on an individual monitor while wearing headphones and write notes or type notes. Those who chose to type notes were instructed to take notes in their own words and not type what the lecture said, word for word. Participants were tested afterward.

- **Study 3:** 109 college students were asked to view four short lectures lasting 28 minutes in a classroom setting with an individual monitor and headphones. They were tested one week later.

---

[317] Mueller PA, Oppenheimer DM.The pen is mightier than the keyboard: advantages of longhand over laptop note taking. Psychol Sci. 2014 Jun;25(6):1159-68. doi: 10.1177/0956797614524581. Epub 2014 Apr 23.
[318] Mueller PA, Oppenheimer DM.The pen is mightier than the keyboard: advantages of longhand over laptop note taking. Psychol Sci. 2014 Jun;25(6):1159-68. doi: 10.1177/0956797614524581. Epub 2014 Apr 23.
[319] Mueller PA, Oppenheimer DM.The pen is mightier than the keyboard: advantages of longhand over laptop note taking. Psychol Sci. 2014 Jun;25(6):1159-68. doi: 10.1177/0956797614524581. Epub 2014 Apr 23.

What Were The Results?

- The authors found that laptop participants were more inclined to take notes word for word than those who wrote notes.

- One week after the presentation (study 3), even when students could review their notes, those who had taken notes with laptops performed worse on tests of factual content and conceptual understanding than those who had written notes.

- For conceptual items, those taking notes on laptops (which the authors found to be verbatim notes) performed better than written notes.

What Does This Mean?

It may be worth considering adjusting note-taking based on the type of information:

When Taking Notes Of Factual Information

It may be worthwhile to synthesize and summarize notes and to write in your own words instead of transcribing notes.

More retention might make studying more efficient, decreasing your stress and improving your mental health.

When Taking Notes Of Conceptual Information

Transcribing notes may be better.

Ultimately, for best results, it may be worth trying different styles and note-taking methods based on different types of content (factual, conceptual, mixture, etc.).

Have you figured out what is the most productive note-taking style for you?

Expanded Knowledge

Expanding upon the study by Mueller and Oppenheimer (2014)[320] regarding the effectiveness of note-taking styles, a body of research underlines the cognitive processes involved in manual versus digital note-taking. Bui, Myerson, and Hale (2013)[321] propose that the physical act of writing, with its inherent slower pace, might allow students more time to process and understand the material they're jotting down cognitively.

There is also emerging evidence emphasizing the role of retrieval practice in learning. As noted by Karpicke and Roediger (2008),[322] the act of recalling information promotes deeper learning compared to merely reviewing notes. From this perspective, taking the time to articulate thoughts in your own words - as commonly done with handwritten notes - may prove beneficial,

---

[320] Mueller PA, Oppenheimer DM. (2014). The Pen Is Mightier Than the Keyboard: Advantages of Longhand Over Laptop Note Taking. Psychological Science.

[321] Bui DC, Myerson J, Hale S. (2013). Note-taking with computers: Exploring alternative strategies for improved recall. Journal of Educational Psychology.

[322] Karpicke JD, Roediger HL. (2008). The critical importance of retrieval for learning. Science.

allowing students to practice the retrieval process during note-taking.

Furthering this argument, Mangen and Velay (2010)[323] argue that the physical sensation of writing can create a richer sensory environment, possibly aiding memory and learning. They postulate that the tactile and kinesthetic feedback provided by pen-and-paper might foster a sense of personal involvement with the learning material, which could enhance memory recall.

Nevertheless, digital note-taking might have advantages, particularly when dealing with complex or conceptual data. According to a study by Sana, Weston, and Cepeda (2013),[324] students who take notes on their laptops could effectively use tools such as search functions or digital organization, which may facilitate quick review and help students comprehend complex relationships.

Finally, it's also worth mentioning the study by Fisher and Radvansky (2018)[325], which highlights the importance of individual preferences in note-taking methods. They found that while students generally perform better when they take notes in their preferred style, this effect was especially pronounced for those who preferred writing by hand.

---

[323] Mangen A, Velay JL. (2010). Digitizing literacy: reflections on the haptics of writing. Advances in Haptics.

[324] Mangen A, Velay JL. (2010). Digitizing literacy: reflections on the haptics of writing. Advances in Haptics.

[325] Fisher, J. P., & Radvansky, G. A. (2018). The effect of note-taking medium on memory. Memory, 26(6), 796-807.

The science suggests that both laptop and handwritten notes might have their unique benefits, and the choice between them could depend on factors like the nature of the information, the learning context, and personal preference.

Study: Caffeine, Stress, and Brain Function[326]

According to the Food and Drug Administration, caffeine is widely available, and up to 80% of adults have caffeine every day, up to 200mg, which is about 10 ounces of coffee.[327]

Sometimes, caffeine is used to help stay awake and alert to keep up with academic demands, etc.

While the many benefits of caffeine have been widely documented, the problems and side effects are not as widely known.

One study looked at the impact of caffeine on stress.[328]

Who Was Involved In The Study?[329]

- Around 25 participants who used caffeine regularly or were light users of caffeine.

---

[326] https://u.osu.edu/emotionalfitness/2017/04/19/study-caffeine-stress-and-brain-function/

[327] https://www.fda.gov/downloads/ucm200805.pdf

[328] Land JD, Adcock RA, Williams RB, Kuhn CM. Caffeine effects on cardiovascular and neuroendocrine responses to acute psychosocial stress and their relationship to level of habitual caffeine consumption. Psychosom Med. 1990 May-Jun;52(3):320-36.

[329] Land JD, Adcock RA, Williams RB, Kuhn CM. Caffeine effects on cardiovascular and neuroendocrine responses to acute psychosocial stress and their relationship to level of habitual caffeine consumption. Psychosom Med. 1990 May-Jun;52(3):320-36.

RYAN PATEL DO, FAPA

- Subjects received a placebo or caffeine (3.5mg per kilogram of body weight, about 238mg for a person weighing 150 pounds)

What Was Measured?[330]

- Blood pressure, cortisol (stress hormone), norepinephrine, and epinephrine (also involved in stress response and other functions).

- Measurements were taken at rest, during a stressful laboratory task, and afterward at rest.

What Were The Results?[331]

- Compared to placebo, caffeine caused more than DOUBLE the levels of epinephrine and cortisol, both involved in stress response.

- Effects were similar in both habitual and light users.

- Habitual use of caffeine did not development of tolerance to the bodily response.

- Even at rest, caffeine increases blood pressure and plasma norepinephrine levels.

---

[330] Land JD, Adcock RA, Williams RB, Kuhn CM. Caffeine effects on cardiovascular and neuroendocrine responses to acute psychosocial stress and their relationship to level of habitual caffeine consumption. Psychosom Med. 1990 May-Jun;52(3):320-36.
[331] Land JD, Adcock RA, Williams RB, Kuhn CM. Caffeine effects on cardiovascular and neuroendocrine responses to acute psychosocial stress and their relationship to level of habitual caffeine consumption. Psychosom Med. 1990 May-Jun;52(3):320-36.

What Do The Results Mean?

Caffeine may increase your stress level whether you are using caffeine sporadically or regularly.

What Are Some Other Effects Of Too Much Caffeine?

- Having caffeine as early as 7 am led to less efficient sleep and reduced total sleep at 9 pm.[332]

- Some people have more daytime sleepiness because of caffeine-related sleep disruption.[333]

- Caffeine can reduce blood flow to the brain by up to 27%[334]

- Too much caffeine can cause:[335]

- Worsening of anxiety.

- Jitteriness.

- Nervousness.

- Sleep disturbance.

- Headaches.

- Make your heart beat faster.

- Palpitations.

---

[332] H.P. Landolt, E. Werth, A.A. Borbely, D.J. Dijk. Caffeine intake (200 mg) in the morning affects human sleep and EEG power spectra at night. Brain Research, 675 (1–2) (1995), pp. 67–74.
[333] T. Roehrs, T. Roth. Caffeine: sleep and daytime sleepiness. Sleep Med Rev, 12 (2) (2008), pp. 153–162.
[334] Addicott M.A., Yang L.L., Peiffer A.M., Burnett L.R., Burdette J.H., Chen M.Y.. et al. The effect of daily caffeine use on cerebral blood flow: how much caffeine can we tolerate? Hum. Brain Mapp. 2009;30:3102–3114.
[335] https://www.fda.gov/downloads/ucm200805.pdf

- High blood pressure.

- Abnormal heart rhythms.

What Are Some Caveats?

- This is a small study, and many studies show caffeine's positive and negative effects.

- Not everyone has the same benefits or side effects of caffeine.

- The AMOUNT of caffeine with beneficial and harmful effects can differ for different people.

- Some people can metabolize caffeine much faster or slower than others.[336]

- It can take some people days to weeks to see the benefits of reducing or eliminating caffeine.

- Stopping caffeine abruptly can lead to withdrawal headaches, irritability, and other symptoms.

Are you feeling stressed, irritable, or anxious?

How is your caffeine intake?

Could you benefit from less?

Expanded Knowledge

Caffeine, a common stimulant imbibed by millions worldwide, forms an elaborate tapestry of interactions with our stress mechanisms and cerebral activity. A study

---

[336] Cornelis, M. C. et al. Genome-wide meta-analysis identifies six novel loci associated with habitual coffee consumption. Mol. Psychiatry 20, 647–656 (2015).

by Lovallo et al. (2006)[337] showed that caffeine can stimulate stress in everyday life and controlled laboratory environments.

These findings further fortify the broad body of evidence suggesting caffeine's potent influence on the hypothalamic-pituitary-adrenal axis, the master system that choreographs our body's stress response (Kudielka et al., 2009).[338]

A study by Lara (2010)[339] showed that caffeine can disrupt sleep quality, as it imposes a delay in falling sleep initiation, reducing total sleep duration and causing nighttime awakenings. This interference can worsen our cognitive performance and mood (Alhola & Polo-Kantola, 2007).[340]

Yet, the story of caffeine's influence does not end here. Higher caffeine intake has been observed to have palpable effects on the brain's blood circulation. A study by Addicott et al. (2009)[341] showed that caffeine can decrease blood flow to the brain by 20-30%. For some people, this could worsen cognitive functions like memory and concentration.

---

[337] Lovallo, W. R., et al. (2006). Caffeine Stimulation of Cortisol Secretion Across the Waking Hours in Relation to Caffeine Intake Levels. Psychosomatic Medicine.

[338] Kudielka, B. M., et al. (2009). Acute HPA axis responses, heart rate, and mood changes to psychosocial stress (TSST) in humans at different times of day. Psychoneuroendocrinology.

[339] Lara, D. R. (2010). Caffeine, mental health, and psychiatric disorders. Journal of Alzheimer's Disease.

[340] Alhola, P., & Polo-Kantola, P. (2007). Sleep deprivation: Impact on cognitive performance. Neuropsychiatric Disease and Treatment.

[341] Addicott, M. A., et al. (2009). The effect of daily caffeine use on cerebral blood flow: How much caffeine can we tolerate? Human Brain Mapping.

Another factor to consider when looking at caffeine is a study by Lovallo et al. (2006) showing caffeine's potential to increase the physiological stress response.

Delving deeper into mental health, a double-blind placebo-controlled experiment by Rogers et al. (2013)[342] presented evidence that caffeine may stoke the flames of anxiety, nervousness, and jitteriness, particularly in individuals pre-disposed to such emotional states.

Yet, the primary study underscores that the human response to caffeine is not a one-size-fits-all phenomenon. Yang et al. (2010)[343] suggested that genetic polymorphisms in the adenosine and dopamine receptors might sway an individual's response to caffeine. This could explain some variations in mood, cognitive function, and sleep, contingent on the individual's genetic blueprint.

Despite caffeine's recognized benefits like enhanced alertness and cognitive performance, high consumption could amplify stress responses, fracture sleep continuity, and generate adverse effects on mental health.

I hope that understanding these pitfalls can help you reconsider your caffeine intake, especially if you are experiencing high stress, anxiety, or sleep problems.

In my experience, thinking of caffeine as anxiety is a useful reframe. If you are already stressed, adding

[342] Rogers, P. J., et al. (2013). The effects of low doses of caffeine on human mood, cognitive function, and blood pressure. Neuropsychopharmacology. Rogers, P. J., et al. (2013). The effects of low doses of caffeine on human mood, cognitive function, and blood pressure. Neuropsychopharmacology.
[343] Yang, A., et al. (2010). Genetics of caffeine consumption and responses to caffeine. Psychopharmacology.

caffeine to the mix will likely further worsen your anxiety.

In my experience, people see the best results if they decrease caffeine, nicotine, and alcohol gradually by 20–25% per week and then stay off for a few weeks before they can see the full impact of eliminating these substances and how it may help improve mood, anxiety, sleep and other aspects of health.

Warning: Eliminating these substances abruptly or cold turkey can lead to withdrawal, which in the case of alcohol can be deadly! As with all other strategies discussed in this book, check with your Healthcare professional before considering changes to your caffeine, nicotine, or alcohol intake.

When looking at how caffeine, nicotine, or other substances impact your mental health, its important to be substance free for a few weeks to allow your body and mind to heal, and reset to get a more accurate idea of how it impacts you.

Stopping for a few days or a couple of weeks is likely not long enough to provide you with the most useful and most accurate information, in my experience.

Dealing With Too Much Stress[344]

---

[344] https://u.osu.edu/emotionalfitness/2017/09/01/dealing-with-too-much-stress/

What Is Stress?

Stress can be considered a response by the brain and body to any demand.[345]

Some stress is useful in helping us perform in life, achieve goals, grow, etc.

Too much stress can harm physical and emotional health in many ways.

What Does *Too Much* Stress Feel Like?

Different people respond to stress in different ways.

What Are Some Common Emotional Responses To Excessive Stress?

Too much stress can cause:

- Changes in mood, sleep, irritability, body aches.[346]

- Changes in appetite, difficulty concentrating, etc.

What Are Some Unhealthy Ways Of Dealing With Too Much Stress?

- Increasing use of caffeine, alcohol, tobacco, drugs.

- Unhealthy eating habits.

- Increased behaviors of isolation/avoidance. Too much time away from the problem might make

---

[345] https://www.nimh.nih.gov/health/publications/stress/index.shtml
[346] https://medlineplus.gov/ency/article/001942.htm

the problem worse by causing you to miss deadlines, meetings, assignments, etc.

What Are Some Healthy Ways Of Dealing With Too Much Stress?

The American Psychological Association's help center suggests[347]:

• **Take a break.** A few minutes away from what is stressing you might help you have a new perspective or allow you to practice stress management techniques._

• **Smile and laugh.** This might help relieve some tension and improve the situation.

• Get social support from others or a counselor. Talking to someone might help you feel better, collect your thoughts, and gain new insights.

The following are adapted from the National Library of Medicine[348] stress management page:

• **Recognize And Accept The Things You Can't Change.** This can help you let go and not get upset. For instance, you might not change rush hour traffic, but you can look for ways to relax during your commute, such as listening to a podcast or book.

• **Avoid Stressful Triggers When Possible.** For example, if your family squabbles during the holidays, give yourself a breather and go out for a walk or drive.

---

[347] http://www.apa.org/helpcenter/manage-stress.aspx
[348] https://medlineplus.gov/ency/article/001942.htm

- **Exercise.** Regular exercise or physical activity most days for about 30 minutes can help your brain release chemicals that make you feel good and help you release built-up energy or frustration.

- **Change Your Outlook.** Are you being too negative? Work on a more positive attitude toward challenges by replacing negative thoughts with more positive ones.

- **Sleep Well.** Get 7 to 9 hours of sleep per night. This can help you think more clearly and have more energy.

- **Eat Well.** Eat enough AND eat healthy foods. This can help fuel your body and mind. Skip the high-sugar snack foods and load on vegetables, fruits, raw nuts, lean proteins, and good fats.

- **Make Room for Breaks.** Do something you enjoy, preferably daily, even if it's just for a few minutes. Examples include reading a good book, listening to music, watching a favorite movie, having dinner with a friend, a new hobby, or class.

- **Learn To Say No.** Set limits if you feel over-scheduled, cut back, or defer where possible. Ask others for help when you need it.

Expanded Knowledge

Stress is a ubiquitous part of life, defined as the brain and body's response to a demand. However, while a certain stress level is beneficial, propelling us toward our goals and facilitating growth, excessive stress can adversely affect our physical and emotional well-being.

Additional techniques that may help decrease stress include various deep breathing techniques and progressive muscle relaxation. These may be learned by working with a counselor or other health professional via the Virtual Hope Box app. This app is further described later in this chapter.

In my experience, some people may notice much benefit from these techniques the first few times they try them but for those who keep doing it, breathing techniques become more effective as you practice it regularly. The key lies in finding balance – acknowledging stress as a part of life and equipping ourselves with the skills to manage it healthily.

Graduation, Stress, and Summer[349]

As the summer nears, many students anticipate positive experiences such as a break from classes or fewer classes, study abroad, vacation, time away from academics, work, internship, job search, etc.

Some students are approaching graduation from college or graduate/professional school.

While these can be positive for most students overall, some students can experience negative emotions during this time.

---

[349] https://u.osu.edu/emotionalfitness/2018/03/28/graduation-stress-and-summer/

What Are Some Sources Of Stress That Students Can Experience As Summer Approaches?

Some examples include:

- The stress of graduation, moving, finding a job or internship.

- Major life transition from being a student to being in the workforce and related lifestyle changes.

- Increased isolation.

- Change in relationships, friendships, and environment as you move away from college.

- Changes in sleep, eating, and social schedules.

What Negative Emotions Can Students Experience As Summer/Graduation Approaches?

While very little research exists in this area, as college mental health clinicians, this time of year, we will often see students experiencing:

- Decreased motivation.

- Increase in depression and anxiety.

- Difficulty sleeping.

- Increased feelings of stress.

- Changes in appetite, irritability.

- In some cases, worsening of a pre-existing mental health condition.

What are some ways to manage this?

- Recognize the changes that you are experiencing as a result of this transition.

- Think about how you were impacted and what helped you during previous transition points, such as graduating from high school or undergrad and transitioning to the next level, other life transitions, etc.

- Consider making a plan to address the upcoming transition

- Get organized and maintain lists.

- Maintain healthy habits, now more than ever. (see links below).

- Some students might benefit from planning to maintain a connection with friends and other experiences they found meaningful during college.

- It may be helpful to think of ways to incorporate what you liked in the past into your future transition (summer, life after graduation, etc.).

- Others may find it helpful to identify positive aspects of the upcoming changes.

- Enlist the help of others.

Expanded Knowledge

As the academic year draws to a close, with the allure of the summer season and the promise of graduation on the horizon, students find themselves in a sea of contrasting emotions. Transitioning from the structured academic environment to the workforce can lead to significant lifestyle changes and increased isolation.

Relationships, friendships, and the familiar campus environment undergo shifts, and changes in sleep, eating, and social schedules add to the stress (Schlossberg, 1981).[350]

In addition to the strategies mentioned above, fostering connections with college friends and incorporating past enjoyable experiences into future transitions can aid in managing change.

Acknowledging the positive aspects of the upcoming changes and seeking assistance when necessary can also be instrumental in this transition.

Virtual Hope Box For Stress And Emotional Regulation[351]

While there are many options to help with mental health, one particular app called the Virtual Hope Box (VHB) can be useful for coping with unpleasant emotions and thoughts that can impact various mental health symptoms.

---

[350] Schlossberg, N. K. (1981). A model for analyzing human adaptation to transition. The Counseling Psychologist, 9(2), 2–18.
[351] https://u.osu.edu/emotionalfitness/2021/12/21/virtual-hope-box-for-stress-and-emotional-regulation/

Is There Research To Show That This App Is Helpful?

- According to a randomized controlled trial, this app can help regulate emotions and reduce stress.[352] Future studies are ongoing.

- Numerous research studies support many app features, like relaxation skills and distraction techniques.

What Is The Cost?

- Free. It was developed via a government grant and was awarded the DoD Innovation Award in 2014.

What Are The Features Of The VHB App?

- It comes with preloaded features like inspirational tools, relaxation skills, coping tools, distraction techniques, and emergency contact numbers.

- It can also be customized to include your music, images, phone numbers of supportive contacts, and reminders of reasons for living.

- You can fill out coping cards and activity planners with the help of a mental health professional.

- These features are shown in the image below:

---

[352] Bush NE, Smolenski DJ, Denneson LM, Williams HB, Thomas EK, Dobscha SK. A virtual hope box: randomized controlled trial of a smartphone app for emotional regulation and coping with distress. Psychiatr Serv. 2017 Apr 1;68(4):330–6. doi: 10.1176/appi.ps.201600283.

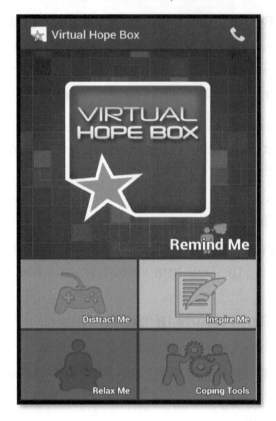

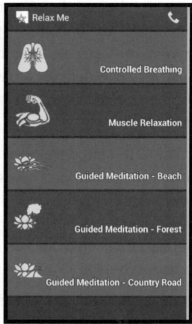

Expanded Knowledge

The Virtual Hope Box (VHB) is an innovative tool in the realm of digital mental health aid, harnessing the power of technology for psychological resilience. A critical component of the effectiveness of this app lies in its capacity to promote emotional regulation and stress management, as evidenced by a randomized controlled trial (Bush et al., 2017).[353]

Building upon these initial findings, other scientific studies have demonstrated the efficacy of similar app features. For example, research conducted by Flett et al.

---

[353] Bush, N. E., et al. (2017). A Virtual Hope Box: Randomized Controlled Trial of a Smartphone App for Emotional Regulation and Coping With Distress. Psychiatric Services.

(2019)[354] showed the effectiveness of digital relaxation techniques in reducing symptoms of anxiety and depression. Likewise, a study by Dahne et al. (2019)[355] illustrated how distraction techniques available in digital formats can aid in lowering the frequency of negative thoughts.

The VHB app, developed under a government grant, further democratizing access to mental health support tools, comes at no cost. This initiative awarded the Department of Defense Innovation Award in 2014, paves the way for a new age of mental health intervention accessibility.

Going beyond its foundational features, such as relaxation skills and distraction techniques, the VHB app is distinguished by its customizability, catering to the individual's unique needs. For instance, the app allows for the inclusion of personalized music and imagery, reminders of life's positives, and easy access to supportive contacts, which have been seen as beneficial in traditional cognitive-behavioral therapy (Hollis et al., 2017).[356]

To further enhance its effectiveness, the VHB app allows collaboration with a mental health professional to

[354] Flett, J. A., et al. (2019). Mobile mindfulness meditation: a randomised controlled trial of the effect of two popular apps on mental health. Mindfulness.

[355] Dahne, J., et al. (2019). Smartphone-Based, Momentary Intervention for Alcohol Cravings amongst Individuals with an Alcohol Use Disorder. Psychology of Addictive Behaviors.

[356] Hollis, C., et al. (2017). Annual Research Review: Digital health interventions for children and young people with mental health problems - a systematic and meta-review. Journal of Child Psychology and Psychiatry.

develop coping cards and activity plans. These features illustrate the commitment of the VHB app to provide a comprehensive suite of tools to manage and promote mental health. Other strategies using technology and mental health are discussed later in this book.

Ultimately, we all experience stress. It may not always be possible for us to decrease the stress that comes to us, but it is useful for us to learn strategies to effectively manage stress in healthy ways, as it can impact many aspects of our lives.

Chapter 6: Food Strategies to Improve Mental Health

The intersection of nutrition and mental health has emerged as a central frontier in contemporary psychiatric research. Scholars spanning the globe have dedicated themselves to elucidating the delicate balance between our nutrition and mental health. What we eat is not just an energy source; it can sculpt our emotions, steer our cognition, and significantly affect mental health disorders' progression.

The foundations of this discipline, termed nutritional psychiatry, are rooted in the realization that particular nutrient deficiencies can lead to severe psychiatric consequences. A notable example of this is niacin deficiency, which can induce pellagra, a disease with symptoms of depression, anxiety, and psychosis (Hegyi et al., 2004).[357]

Such explicit correlations represent merely the beginning of our comprehension of nutritional psychiatry. More recent research unravels a subtler narrative, disclosing that broader food-related behaviors, gut microbiota, and even the timing of meals can bear significant mental health implications.

We stand at a thrilling juncture in the journey of nutritional psychiatry, with novel findings surfacing at a remarkable pace; many challenges are still being worked

---

[357] Hegyi, J., Schwartz, R. A., & Hegyi, V. (2004). Pellagra: dermatitis, dementia, and diarrhea. International journal of dermatology, 43(1), 1-5.

out. For instance, evidence suggests that omega-3 fatty acids may ease symptoms of depression (Grosso et al., 2014),[358] yet the particulars of this relationship remain unclear.

What dosage yields optimal benefits?

Why does efficacy vary among individuals?

Should it be incorporated into a regular diet or taken as a supplement?

How do these acids interact with other dietary components and lifestyle habits?

These are but a handful of the questions that nutritional psychiatry endeavors to answer.

Another crucial consideration is tailoring dietary strategies to individual needs and preferences. Personalized healthcare has become a recurrent theme in medicine, and nutrition is no exception.

Grasping how factors like genetics, age, sex, cultural background, and others shape our dietary requirements and responses is vital for delivering effective, person-centered care. This chapter will discuss nutritional principles that could be incorporated into a personalized nutritional pattern.

Despite these hurdles, nutritional psychiatry has the potential of prevention and treatment pathways and the

---

[358] Grosso, G., Galvano, F., Marventano, S., Malaguarnera, M., Bucolo, C., Drago, F., & Caraci, F. (2014). Omega-3 fatty acids and depression: scientific evidence and biological mechanisms. Oxidative medicine and cellular longevity, 2014.

integration of mental healthcare into our day-to-day lives in a holistic and empowering manner.

As always, this book is intended for informational purposes. Check with your own healthcare professional to see if any of the strategies discussed are right for you. If you choose to apply them, do it under the care and guidance of your health professional. Additionally, individuals with eating disorders should follow their eating disorder treatment plan.

Fruits And Vegetables Might Increase Your Odds Of Mental Well-Being[359]

We all know that fruits and vegetables are good for us, but did you know that fruits and vegetables could increase our mental well-being?

In a study[360] of 13, 983 adults aged 16 years and older (56% females) were surveyed during 2010 and 2011. Mental well-being was assessed using the Warwick-Edinburgh Mental Well-being Scale (WEMWBS). The odds ratio of low and high mental well-being were estimated for body mass index (BMI), smoking, drinking habits, and fruit and vegetable intake.

---

[359] https://u.osu.edu/emotionalfitness/2015/03/25/fruits-and-vegetables-might-increase-your-odds-of-mental-well-being/

[360] Stragnes S, et al. Major health-related behaviours and mental well-being in the general population: the Health Survey for England. BMJ Open. 2014; 4(9): e005878. Published online 2014 Sep 19. doi: 10.1136/bmjopen-2014-005878 PMCID: PMC4170205

What Did The Study Show?

This study found that eating five or more portions of vegetables and fruit was associated with an increased likelihood of an elevated sense of mental well-being.

How Much Fruit And Vegetables Per Day Are Recommended?

According to the 2010 Dietary Guidelines for Americans, for an average person on a 2,000-calorie-per-day diet to maintain weight and health, approximately two measuring cups of fruit and two and a half measuring cups of vegetables per day are recommended.[361][362]

Are There Any Exceptions?

Two measuring cups count toward one cup of vegetables for lettuce and other raw leafy greens. For dried fruit, you only need to eat half a cup to get the equivalent of one cup of fruit.[363]

Are you eating enough fruit and vegetables to improve your sense of well-being?

Will that help you feel better?

How do you know?

---

[361] Agriculture USDo, Services USDoHaH. U.S. Department of Agriculture and Dietary Guidelines for Americans. 7th edn Washington, DC: US Government Printing Office, 2010.
http://health.gov/dietaryguidelines/dga2010/DietaryGuidelines2010.pdf
[362] The nutrition source. Vegetables and Fruits: Get Plenty Every Day.
http://www.hsph.harvard.edu/nutritionsource/vegetables-full-story/
[363] The nutrition source. Vegetables and Fruits: Get Plenty Every Day.
http://www.hsph.harvard.edu/nutritionsource/vegetables-full-story/

Expanded Knowledge

As we traverse the corridors of understanding our health, a novel, often overlooked sphere emerges from the shadows—the intersection of nutrition and mental wellness.

The intricate dance between nutrition and mental well-being is ripe for introspection: are we consuming enough fruits and vegetables to impact our sense of well-being positively?

Could our moods be subtly influenced by what's on our plate?

These questions are further explored later in this chapter.

Do Energy Drinks Help Or Hurt Your Attention?[364]

About 16% of young adults and teenagers consumed at least one energy drink in the past seven days.[365] Some students consume energy drinks for many perceived benefits. But what if energy drinks could actually hurt your attention?

What Does This Study Show?

A recent study[366] of 1649 middle school students found that energy drink consumption was associated with a

---

[364] https://u.osu.edu/emotionalfitness/2015/03/10/do-energy-drinks-help-or-hurt-your-attention/

[365] Emod, JA, et al. Energy Drink Consumption and the Risk of Alcohol Use Disorder among a National Sample of Adolescents and Young Adults. J Pediatr 2014;165:1194-200

[366] Schwartz DL et al. Academic Pediatrics 2015 Feb 8. Energy Drinks and Youth Self-Reported Hyperactivity/Inattention Symptoms. DOI: http://dx.doi.org/10.1016/j.acap.2014.11.006

66% greater risk for hyperactivity and inattention. In other words, energy drinks may impact inattention and hyperactivity, which could also hurt your concentration. This might be important if you are trying to study for classes, be organized to meet deadlines, conduct research, etc.

Do The Results Account For Individual Differences?

The effect remained even after accounting for differences in multiple variables. It is important to consider that energy drinks contain both caffeine and sugar.

Are Caffeine Or Sugar Causing Difficulties With Your Attention Or Hyperactivity?

How do you know? Have you tried reducing or eliminating your caffeine/sugar intake and examined the impact on your attention or hyperactivity?

Expanded Knowledge

This study points to an important possibility of energy drinks impacting your ability to pay attention. A self-reflective exercise could also illuminate our personal responses to these substances.

Have you ever attempted to reduce or eliminate caffeine and sugar intake and observed any changes in your attention span or levels of hyperactivity?

In the end, informed by scientific evidence, self-awareness is our most potent weapon in optimizing cognitive health and performance.

In my experience, people see the best results if they decrease caffeine, nicotine, and alcohol gradually by 20–25% per week and then stay off for a few weeks before they can see the full impact of eliminating these substances and how it may help improve mood, anxiety, sleep and other aspects of health.

Warning: Eliminating these substances abruptly or cold turkey can lead to withdrawal, which in the case of alcohol can be deadly!

As with all other strategies discussed in this book, check with your Healthcare professional before considering changes to your caffeine, nicotine, or alcohol intake.

Food for Academic Brain Power[367]

The end of a semester is a demanding time for most students. Most students would agree that academics are generally a demanding exercise for your brain. So, it makes sense to fuel your body to maximize your success. While many regard the Mediterranean diet as a staple for delaying dementia, the following foods have been shown

---

[367] https://u.osu.edu/emotionalfitness/2015/04/30/food-for-academic-brain-power/

in studies to be beneficial for various elements of brain functioning[368]:

- Foods rich in omega-3 fatty acids such as salmon, walnuts, flax seeds, avocados, etc.[369][370][371]

- Green vegetables.[372][373][374][375]

- Citrus fruits.[376]

---

[368] Source: Brain foods: the effects of nutrients on brain function. Fernando Gómez-Pinilla Nature Reviews Neuroscience 9, 568-578 (July 2008) doi:10.1038/nrn2421

[369] van Gelder, B. M., Tijhuis, M., Kalmijn, S. & Kromhout, D. Fish consumption, n-3 fatty acids, and subsequent 5-y cognitive decline in elderly men: the Zutphen Elderly Study. Am. J. Clin. Nutr. 85, 1142–1147 (2007).

[370] Hashimoto, M. et al. Chronic administration of docosahexaenoic acid ameliorates the impairment of spatial cognition learning ability in amyloid β-infused rats. J. Nutr. 135, 549–555 (2005).

[371] Calon, F. et al. Docosahexaenoic acid protects from dendritic pathology in an Alzheimer's disease mouse model. Neuron 43, 633–645 (2004).

[372] Wu, A., Ying, Z. & Gomez-Pinilla, F. The interplay between oxidative stress and brain-derived neurotrophic factor modulates the outcome of a saturated fat diet on synaptic plasticity and cognition. Eur. J. Neurosci. 19, 1699–1707 (2004).

[373] Wu, A., Ying, Z. & Gomez-Pinilla, F. The interplay between oxidative stress and brain-derived neurotrophic factor modulates the outcome of a saturated fat diet on synaptic plasticity and cognition. Eur. J. Neurosci. 19, 1699–1707 (2004).

[374] Holmes, G. L. et al. Seizure-induced memory impairment is reduced by choline supplementation before or after status epilepticus. Epilepsy Res. 48, 3–13 (2002).

[375] McCann, J. C., Hudes, M. & Ames, B. N. An overview of evidence for a causal relationship between dietary availability of choline during development and cognitive function in offspring. Neurosci. Biobehav. Rev. 30, 696–712 (2006).

[376] Wengreen, H. J. et al. Antioxidant intake and cognitive function of elderly men and women: the Cache County Study. J. Nutr. Health Aging 11, 230–237 (2007).

- A good balance of healthy proteins and carbohydrates to calcium, zinc, and selenium.[377378379]

- Nuts.[380381]

- B vitamin supplements.[382]

Are these part of your eating plan?

Could improving your nutrition help you feel good and perform well academically?

Expanded Knowledge

Emerging from the shadows of conventional wisdom, the scientific community increasingly acknowledges the power of certain nutrients as catalysts for brain functionality.

Despite this knowledge, sometimes young adults may find themselves looking for a quick fix —caffeine, sugar, soda, refined foods. These deceptive companions might promise instant energy, but their long-term companionship could jeopardize cognitive health

---

[377] Schram, M. T. et al. Serum calcium and cognitive function in old age. J. Am. Geriatr. Soc. 55, 1786–1792 (2007).

[378] Ortega, R. M. et al. Dietary intake and cognitive function in a group of elderly people. Am. J. Clin. Nutr. 66, 803–809 (1997).

[379] Gao, S. et al. Selenium level and cognitive function in rural elderly Chinese. Am. J. Epidemiol. 165, 955–965 (2007).

[380] Wu, A., Ying, Z. & Gomez-Pinilla, F. The interplay between oxidative stress and brain-derived neurotrophic factor modulates the outcome of a saturated fat diet on synaptic plasticity and cognition. Eur. J. Neurosci. 19, 1699–1707 (2004).

[381] Perkins, A. J. et al. Association of antioxidants with memory in a multiethnic elderly sample using the Third National Health and Nutrition Examination Survey. Am.J. Epidemiol. 150, 37–44 (1999).

[382] Gomez-Pinilla, F. The influences of diet and exercise on mental health through hormesis. Ageing Res. Rev. 7, 49–62 (2008).

(Kaplan et al., 2007).[383] In my experience, they can also cause spikes and crashes in energy, anxiety, and mood.

Would this journey of nutritional choices rekindle your spirit, stimulate your mental agility, and ultimately guide you to better academic success?

Study: Eating Fish Might Help Your Mood[384]

An increasing number of studies show that what we eat can impact our insomnia, anxiety, irritability, energy level, etc. A recent study looked at fish intake and odds of developing depression.

What Did The Study Involve?

This was a review of 26 studies involving 150,000 adults; one of the largest studies of its kind.

What Did The Results Show?

After adjusting for many variables, those who ate the most fish had a 17% lower risk of depression than those who did not.

How Much Fish Was Eaten By Those Who Had The Most Benefit?

- The exact amount of fish intake is not clearly established.

---

[383] Kaplan, B. J., Crawford, S. G., Field, C. J., & Simpson, J. S. (2007). Vitamins, minerals, and mood. Psychological Bulletin, 133(5), 747.
[384] https://u.osu.edu/emotionalfitness/2015/09/30/study-eating-fish-might-help-your-mood/

- Some people think that the benefit may also depend on what else you eat (vegetables, high-quality protein, good fats, whole grains) and what you are not eating (think junk foods, processed grains, etc.).

What Are Some Caveats?

- Reduced depression risk was statistically significant only in European countries.

- Omega-3s might help by impacting serotonin and dopamine transmission in the brain[385][386][387] since these are important transmitters involved in depression.

- Quality nutrients like protein, vitamins, and minerals might also help with depression.[388][389]

What's The Bottom Line?

For some people, fish intake and eating nutritious foods (instead of heavily processed foods) might

[385] Delion S, Chalon S, Herault J, et al. Chronic dietary alpha-linolenic acid deficiency alters dopaminergic and serotoninergic neurotransmission in rats. J Nutr 1994;124:2466–76.

[386] Zimmer L, Delpal S, Guilloteau D, et al. Chronic n-3 polyunsaturated fatty acid deficiency alters dopamine vesicle density in the rat frontal cortex. Neurosci Lett 2000;284:25–8.

[387] Su KP. Biological mechanism of antidepressant effect of omega-3 fatty acids: how does fish oil act as a 'mind-body interface'? Neurosignals 2009; 17:144–52.

[388] Kim JM, Stewart R, Kim SW, et al. Predictive value of folate, vitamin B12 and homocysteine levels in late-life depression. Br J Psychiatry 2008;192:268–74.

[389] Skarupski KA, Tangney C, Li H, et al. Longitudinal association of vitamin B-6, folate, and vitamin B-12 with depressive symptoms among older adults over time. Am J Clin Nutr 2010;92:330–5.

improve how you feel by improving brain and body functioning, hormones, etc.

How are your eating habits?

Are you feeling lousy?

Are you eating lousy?

Ready to feel better?

Expanded Knowledge

The ties that bind our mental health to the foods we consume are becoming increasingly evident in contemporary research.

One concern with seafood consumption is the negative impact of mercury on the body and the brain. For this reason, considering omega-3 from various sources may be helpful. Others may find it helpful to use purified omega-3 supplements. The United States 2020-2025 Dietary Guidelines for Americans recommend at least 8 ounces of seafood per week based on a 2,000-calorie diet.

(https://www.fda.gov/food/consumers/advice-about-eating-fish).

The same guidelines also provide the following information on types of seafood choices based on mercury content, with the best choices having lower amounts of mercury:

Best Choices			Good Choices		
Anchovy	Herring	Scallop	Bluefish	Monkfish	Tilefish (Atlantic Ocean)
Atlantic croaker	Lobster, American and spiny	Shad	Buffalofish	Rockfish	Tuna, albacore/ white tuna, canned and fresh/frozen
Atlantic mackerel		Shrimp	Carp	Sablefish	
Black sea bass	Mullet	Skate	Chilean sea bass/ Patagonian toothfish	Sheepshead	
Butterfish	Oyster	Smelt		Snapper	Tuna, yellowfin
Catfish	Pacific chub mackerel	Sole	Grouper	Spanish mackerel	Weakfish/seatrout
Clam	Perch, freshwater and ocean	Squid	Halibut	Striped bass (ocean)	White croaker/ Pacific croaker
Cod		Tilapia	Mahi mahi/dolphinfish		
Crab	Pickerel	Trout, freshwater			
Crawfish	Plaice	Tuna, canned light (includes skipjack)	**Choices to Avoid** HIGHEST MERCURY LEVELS		
Flounder	Pollock	Whitefish	King mackerel	Shark	Tilefish (Gulf of Mexico)
Haddock	Salmon	Whiting	Marlin	Swordfish	Tuna, bigeye
Hake	Sardine		Orange roughy		

Different types of omega-3s are discussed later in this chapter.

Embracing fish and nutritious foods while distancing oneself from heavily processed foods could be a dietary strategy that some individuals find enhances their mood and overall well-being.

Do your eating habits align with this?

Is there a link between how you feel and what you eat?

Perhaps it's time for a dietary recharge to feel better.

Could Vitamin D boost your Mood and Energy?[390]

Many students may be aware of Vitamin D, and with decreasing sunlight, many might not be getting enough vitamin D.

- Initially thought of as a vitamin, it is now believed to work more like a hormone and has many functions throughout the body.

[390] https://u.osu.edu/emotionalfitness/2015/12/09/could-vitamin-d-boost-your-mood-and-energy/

- Inadequate vitamin D has been implicated in fibromyalgia,[391] sleep,[392][393] athletic performance,[394] energy levels[395] , and bone disease.[396]

- A recent study discussed findings regarding vitamin D and depression.

What Did This Study Involve?

- Around 40 patients between 18 and 65 years of age with Major Depressive disorder.

- Randomly assigned to get either a single capsule of 50 kIU vitamin D per week (n = 20) or a placebo (n = 20) for eight weeks.

- This was a randomized, double-blind, placebo-controlled clinical trial.

What Did The Authors Analyze?

- Fasting blood samples before and after.

- The primary [Beck Depression Inventory (BDI) examines depressive symptoms].

---

[391] Jesus CA, Feder D, Peres MF. The role of Vitamin D in pathophysiology and treatment of fibromyalgia. Curr Pain Headache Rep. 2013 Aug;17(8):355.

[392] Bertisch SM, et al. 25-Hydroxyvitamin D Concentration and Sleep Duration and Continuity: Multi-Ethnic Study of Atherosclerosis. Sleep. 2015 Aug 1;38(8):1305-11

[393] McCarty DE, et al. The link between vitamin D metabolism and sleep medicine. Sleep Med Rev. 2014 Aug;18(4):311-9. Epub 2013 Sep 26.

[394] B Hamilton. Vitamin D and Human Skeletal Muscle. Scand J Med Sci Sports. 2010 Apr; 20(2): 182–190.

[395] Al–Dujaili E, Revuelta Iniesta R. http://www.eurekalert.org/pub_releases/2015-11/sfe-vdp102915.php Preliminary study presented Fall 2015 at the Society for Endocrinology Annual Conference in Edinburgh.

[396] https://ods.od.nih.gov/factsheets/VitaminD-Consumer/

- Secondary outcomes such as glucose homeostasis variables, lipid profiles, hs–CRP, and biomarkers of oxidative stress.

What Did The Study Show?

- After eight weeks of treatment with vitamin D, depression scores improved in the patients receiving vitamin D supplementation.

- The improvement was also related to improvement in vitamin D levels.

How Can I Get Vitamin D Tested?

There is a blood test for vitamin D, which your prescriber can order.

Can I Get Vitamin D From Food?

According to the National Institute of Health (NIH),[397] *"Very few foods naturally have vitamin D. Fortified foods provide most of the vitamin D in American diets. Fatty fish such as salmon, tuna, and mackerel are among the best sources.*

Beef liver, cheese, and egg yolks provide small amounts. Mushrooms provide some vitamin D. In some mushrooms that are newly available in stores. The vitamin D content is being boosted by exposing these mushrooms to ultraviolet light.

---

[397] https://ods.od.nih.gov/factsheets/VitaminD–Consumer/

Almost all of the U.S. milk supply is fortified with 400 IU of vitamin D per quart. But foods made from milk, like cheese and ice cream, are usually not fortified.

Vitamin D is added to many breakfast cereals and to some brands of orange juice, yogurt, margarine, and soy beverages; check the labels."

Is Too Much Vitamin D Harmful?

Too much vitamin D can be harmful.

According to the NIH[398]:

"Signs of toxicity include nausea, vomiting, poor appetite, constipation, weakness, and weight loss. And by raising blood levels of calcium, too much vitamin D can cause confusion, disorientation, and problems with heart rhythm. Excess vitamin D can also damage the kidneys."

What Is The Main Cause Of Too Much Vitamin D?

- Vitamin D toxicity almost always occurs from overuse of supplements.

- Excessive sun exposure doesn't cause vitamin D poisoning because the body limits the amount of this vitamin it produces.[399]

---

[398] https://ods.od.nih.gov/factsheets/VitaminD-Consumer/
[399] https://ods.od.nih.gov/factsheets/VitaminD-Consumer/

What Are Some Caveats?

- To avoid the risk of harm, taking Vitamin D supplements should be done under the supervision of your prescriber/doctor.

- This is the first study showing benefits on depression with high dose weekly Vitamin D supplementation.

- Further studies are needed.

- Some previous studies showed mixed results, though under-dosing and other factors may have been involved.[400]

- Vitamin D has shown benefits in some studies and clinical experience in psychiatry for select patients.

- Benefits of vitamin D may extend beyond mood.

- Treatment with vitamin D with a supplement or prescription may NOT be suitable for everyone, but it may be worth discussing with your prescriber.

Is your mood, energy level, etc., impacted by low vitamin D?

Could replacement benefit you?

Check with your healthcare provider if treatment is appropriate for you.

---

[400] Sepehrmanesh Z, et al. Vitamin D Supplementation Affects the Beck Depression Inventory, Insulin Resistance, and Biomarkers of Oxidative Stress in Patients with Major Depressive Disorder: A Randomized, Controlled Clinical Trial. J Nutr. 2015 Nov 25. pii: jn218883. [Epub ahead of print].

Expanded Knowledge

In the vast expanse of our body's inner workings, the role of Vitamin D has emerged as a quiet protagonist. Classically considered an ally of bone health, this hormone-like nutrient has now been observed to be involved in various functions, including mood and energy levels.

Getting your vitamin D levels checked via your healthcare provider will help determine how much of what type of vitamin D you need to take, if at all, and whether it would need to be a prescription or an over-the-counter supplement.

The picture of vitamin D and mental health continues to evolve. Further research promises to shed more light on its integral part in the labyrinth of our cognitive health.

Does Omega-3 Supplementation Help With Depression?[401]

Omega 3 supplements are widely available over the counter and are sold with various claims. Many studies look at omega-3 supplementation for conditions such as depressed mood, bipolar disorder, schizophrenia, ADHD, etc.

I and many psychiatrists often discuss the potential benefits of EPA fish oil omega 3 supplementation in certain cases. A recent meta-analysis (study of studies) looked at omega-3

---

[401] https://u.osu.edu/emotionalfitness/2016/04/13/does-omega-3-supplementation-help-with-depression/

supplements and major depressive disorder, a specific type of depressive disorder.[402]

What Did The Study Involve?

- The study authors[403] looked at 1,955 studies. The study authors identified 1233 individuals from 15 studies with major depressive disorder who were given omega-3 supplements. Study authors[404] factored out studies with design flaws, limitations, or other biases.

What Were Some Of The Results (1)?

- After adjusting for many variables and considering potential publication bias, this review article found that omega-3 fatty acids were helpful for Major depressive disorder.[405]

---

[402] Mocking RJT, et. al. Meta-analysis and meta-regression of omega-3 polyunsaturated fatty acid supplementation for major depressive disorder. Translational Psychiatry (2016) 6, e756; doi:10.1038/tp.2016.29 Published online 15 March 2016

[403] Mocking RJT, et. al. Meta-analysis and meta-regression of omega-3 polyunsaturated fatty acid supplementation for major depressive disorder. Translational Psychiatry (2016) 6, e756; doi:10.1038/tp.2016.29 Published online 15 March 2016

[404] Mocking RJT, et. al. Meta-analysis and meta-regression of omega-3 polyunsaturated fatty acid supplementation for major depressive disorder. Translational Psychiatry (2016) 6, e756; doi:10.1038/tp.2016.29 Published online 15 March 2016

[405] Mocking RJT, et. al. Meta-analysis and meta-regression of omega-3 polyunsaturated fatty acid supplementation for major depressive disorder. Translational Psychiatry (2016) 6, e756; doi:10.1038/tp.2016.29 Published online 15 March 2016

- Higher doses of EPA omega-3s were associated with better outcomes[406]

- Participants taking EPA omega-3s with antidepressants also benefited[407]

- DHA (another type of omega-3) to EPA ratio and DHA dose did not make a difference in Major Depressive disorder symptoms[408]

What Are Some Caveats About Omega-3 From Fish Oil?

- Omega-3s from non-seafood sources may not have the same brain impact as seafood-based omega-3s.

- Not all antidepressants have been studied with EPA omega-3 supplements.

- Long-term effects of high-dose EPA (a sub-type of omega-3) are unknown.

- Currently, there is no widely standardized way to predict who will see mood benefits from omega-3 supplementation.

---

[406] Mocking RJT, et. al. Meta-analysis and meta-regression of omega-3 polyunsaturated fatty acid supplementation for major depressive disorder. Translational Psychiatry (2016) 6, e756; doi:10.1038/tp.2016.29 Published online 15 March 2016

[407] Mocking RJT, et. al. Meta-analysis and meta-regression of omega-3 polyunsaturated fatty acid supplementation for major depressive disorder. Translational Psychiatry (2016) 6, e756; doi:10.1038/tp.2016.29 Published online 15 March 2016

[408] Mocking RJT, et. al. Meta-analysis and meta-regression of omega-3 polyunsaturated fatty acid supplementation for major depressive disorder. Translational Psychiatry (2016) 6, e756; doi:10.1038/tp.2016.29 Published online 15 March 2016

- While the exact dose of EPA omega-3 has not been identified for everyone, the studies cited in this review[409] used a dose range of up to 4400mg per day.

- It may be best to check with your prescriber before starting fish oil Omega 3 supplementation to prevent any interactions with your medications.

- Medicine and supplements are not a replacement for unhealthy lifestyle habits.

- This was a helpful study for individuals with major depression; further study is warranted for other conditions and combinations of conditions.

Expanded Knowledge

In the intricate and ever-evolving landscape of nutritional supplements, omega-3 fatty acids have emerged as potential game-changers in the field of mental health. Of these, EPA fish oil omega-3 supplements have drawn particular interest, becoming a frequent topic in professional mental health circles. Their potential reaches beyond depression, with research extending to diverse conditions such as bipolar disorder and ADHD (Hallahan et al., 2016).[410]

---

[409] Mocking RJT, et. al. Meta-analysis and meta-regression of omega-3 polyunsaturated fatty acid supplementation for major depressive disorder. Translational Psychiatry (2016) 6, e756; doi:10.1038/tp.2016.29 Published online 15 March 2016

[410] Hallahan, B., Ryan, T., Hibbeln, J. R., Murray, I. T., Glynn, S., Ramsden, C. E., SanGiovanni, J. P., & Davis, J. M. (2016). Efficacy of omega-3 highly

With regards to dosage, the studies in this review worked with amounts up to 4400mg per day, but the optimal dosage remains undetermined. It is crucial that any use of supplements, including fish oil omega-3, be discussed with a healthcare provider to avoid potential medication interactions.

Lastly, supplements should never be considered a replacement for healthy lifestyle habits. Despite these qualifications, this research opens exciting new avenues for people with MDD and invites further investigation into other mental health conditions (Grosso et al., 2014).[411]

Food Choices To Improve Depression[412]

A 2017 systematic review of 21 studies across ten countries looking at food patterns and depression found an association between food patterns and depression.[413]

unsaturated fatty acids in the treatment of depression. The British Journal of Psychiatry, 209(3), 192-201.

[411] Grosso, G., Pajak, A., Marventano, S., Castellano, S., Galvano, F., Bucolo, C., Drago, F., & Caraci, F. (2014). Role of omega-3 fatty acids in the treatment of depressive disorders: a comprehensive meta-analysis of randomized clinical trials. PloS one, 9(5), e96905.

[412] https://u.osu.edu/emotionalfitness/2018/06/28/food-choices-to-improve-depression/

[413] Li, Ye & Lv, Mei-Rong & Wei, Yan-Jin & Sun, Ling & Zhang, Ji-Xiang & Zhang, Huai-Guo & Li, Bin. (2017). Dietary patterns and depression risk: A meta-analysis. Psychiatry Research. 253. 10.1016/j.psychres.2017.04.020.

What Food Patterns Were Found To Have A DECREASED Risk Of Depression?

- The study authors[414] found that high intakes of fruit, vegetables, fish, olive oil, low-fat dairy, antioxidants, and whole grains were associated with a decreased risk of depression.[415]

- Another review found that seafood, vegetables, fruit, and nut-based food patterns were associated with a reduced risk of depression.[416]

- A study of 15,980 adults over 10.8 years found that higher consumption of fruits and nuts, while lower consumption of fast food, led to a reduced depression risk.[417]

What Food Patterns Were Found To Have An INCREASED Risk Of Depression? (1)

- The study authors[418] found that high consumption of red and/or processed meat, refined grains (added sugars)/sweets, high-fat dairy products, butter,

[414] Li, Ye & Lv, Mei-Rong & Wei, Yan-Jin & Sun, Ling & Zhang, Ji-Xiang & Zhang, Huai-Guo & Li, Bin. (2017). Dietary patterns and depression risk: A meta-analysis. Psychiatry Research. 253. 10.1016/j.psychres.2017.04.020.

[415] Li, Ye & Lv, Mei-Rong & Wei, Yan-Jin & Sun, Ling & Zhang, Ji-Xiang & Zhang, Huai-Guo & Li, Bin. (2017). Dietary patterns and depression risk: A meta-analysis. Psychiatry Research. 253. 10.1016/j.psychres.2017.04.020.

[416] Martínez-González MA1, Sánchez-Villegas A2. Food patterns and the prevention of depression. Proc Nutr Soc. 2016 May;75(2):139-46. doi: 10.1017/S0029665116000045. Epub 2016 Feb 22.

[417] Fresán, U., Bes-Rastrollo, M., Segovia-Siapco, G. et al. Does the MIND diet decrease depression risk? A comparison with Mediterranean diet in the SUN cohort. Eur J Nutr (2018). https://doi.org/10.1007/s00394-018-1653-x

[418] Li, Ye & Lv, Mei-Rong & Wei, Yan-Jin & Sun, Ling & Zhang, Ji-Xiang & Zhang, Huai-Guo & Li, Bin. (2017). Dietary patterns and depression risk: A meta-analysis. Psychiatry Research. 253. 10.1016/j.psychres.2017.04.020.

potatoes, and high-fat gravy were associated with an increased risk of depression.[419]

Are There Clinical Studies Where Food Pattern Was Used To TREAT Depression?

Yes. The HELFIMED[420] and SMILES trials[421] used food as a treatment for depressive disorders.

How Effective Was This?

In both trials,[422][423] the improvement was almost 50%, comparable to some therapies and some antidepressant medications, and the benefits lasted for several months afterward.

---

[419] Li, Ye & Lv, Mei-Rong & Wei, Yan-Jin & Sun, Ling & Zhang, Ji-Xiang & Zhang, Huai-Guo & Li, Bin. (2017). Dietary patterns and depression risk: A meta-analysis. Psychiatry Research. 253. 10.1016/j.psychres.2017.04.020.

[420] Natalie Parletta, Dorota Zarnowiecki, Jihyun Cho, Amy Wilson, Svetlana Bogomolova, Anthony Villani, Catherine Itsiopoulos, Theo Niyonsenga, Sarah Blunden, Barbara Meyer, Leonie Segal, Bernhard T. Baune & Kerin O'Dea (2017) A Mediterranean-style dietary intervention supplemented with fish oil improves diet quality and mental health in people with depression: A randomized controlled trial (HELFIMED),Nutritional Neuroscience, DOI: 10.1080/1028415X.2017.1411320

[421] Jacka FN, O'Neil A, Opie R, et al. A randomised controlled trial of dietary improvement for adults with major depression (the "SMILES" trial). BMC Medicine. 2017;15:23. doi:10.1186/s12916-017-0791-y.

[422] Natalie Parletta, Dorota Zarnowiecki, Jihyun Cho, Amy Wilson, Svetlana Bogomolova, Anthony Villani, Catherine Itsiopoulos, Theo Niyonsenga, Sarah Blunden, Barbara Meyer, Leonie Segal, Bernhard T. Baune & Kerin O'Dea (2017) A Mediterranean-style dietary intervention supplemented with fish oil improves diet quality and mental health in people with depression: A randomized controlled trial (HELFIMED),Nutritional Neuroscience, DOI: 10.1080/1028415X.2017.1411320

[423] Jacka FN, O'Neil A, Opie R, et al. A randomised controlled trial of dietary improvement for adults with major depression (the "SMILES" trial). BMC Medicine. 2017;15:23. doi:10.1186/s12916-017-0791-y.

What Are Some Caveats?

- These studies show that nutrition can be helpful in improving depression, but further study is needed.

- Nutritious food choices DO NOT have to be expensive; in many cases, whole foods can be more affordable than processed foods.

- Good nutrition is not enough for some people to replace counseling or medications, but it can be a useful addition.

- Different people can be healthiest on different eating styles, depending on various factors.

- Even with good food choices, getting enough calories is important; and not engaging in restriction or disordered eating behaviors.

- TDEE calculators and this chart[424] may help estimate daily calorie needs.

- When considering nutritional adjustments, individuals with eating disorders should seek professional assistance from a nutritionist or specialist.

Expanded Knowledge

---

[424] https://www.nhlbi.nih.gov/health/educational/wecan/healthy-weight-basics/balance.htm

The HELFIMED and SMILES trials were powerful studies because they showed that the benefit of nutrition for depression was up to 50% improvement in depressive symptoms, rivaling some therapies and antidepressants (Parletta et al., 2017[425]; Jacka et al., 2017).[426]

However, we must tread carefully. While undoubtedly beneficial, good nutrition may not be a standalone treatment for all. Its role as an add-on treatment becomes significant, complementing other forms of therapy, medication, and life strategies. Moreover, the individual variations in dietary needs caution us against a one-size-fits-all approach and underline the critical need for personalized dietary guidelines.

Ultimately, we arrive at the heart of our journey - maintaining a balanced and nutritious way of eating isn't simply about physical well-being. It emerges as a powerful tool, an ally in our arsenal, helping us in our shared human struggle against the sad shadow of depression.

As always, this book is intended for informational purposes. Check with your own healthcare professional to see if any of the strategies discussed are right for you. If you choose to apply them, do it under the care and guidance of your health professional. Additionally,

---

[425] Parletta, N., et al. (2017). A Mediterranean-style dietary intervention supplemented with fish oil improves diet quality and mental health in people with depression: A randomized controlled trial (HELFIMED). Nutritional Neuroscience.

[426] Jacka, F. N., et al. (2017). A randomised controlled trial of dietary improvement for adults with major depression (the 'SMILES' trial). BMC Medicine.

individuals with eating disorders should follow their eating disorder treatment plan.

Study: Omeg-3 May Help With Anxiety[427]

A previous blog post discussed probiotics and anxiety[428]. A recent review article examined whether omega-3 fatty acid treatment is associated with an improvement in anxiety.[429]

What are omega-3 fatty acids?

Omega-3 are polyunsaturated dietary fatty acids (PUFAs) that include alpha-linoleic acid (ALA), which is then converted to eicosapentaenoic acid (EPA) and docosahexaenoic acid (DHA)[430]

They are nutrients that the human body cannot make, so we must get them through foods or supplements.[431]

What Was The Study?

The study authors[432] reviewed 19 clinical trials, including 2240 participants from 11 countries.

---

[427] https://u.osu.edu/emotionalfitness/2019/05/29/study-omega-3s-may-help-with-anxiety/
[428] https://u.osu.edu/emotionalfitness/2016/02/05/study-can-adjusting-gu-bacteria-impact-emotions/
[429] Su KP, Tseng PT, Lin PY, et al. Association of Use of Omega-3 Polyunsaturated Fatty Acids With Changes in Severity of Anxiety Symptoms: A Systematic Review and Meta-analysis. JAMA 0Netw Open. 2018;1(5):e182327. Published 2018 Sep 14. doi:10.1001/jamanetworkopen.2018.2327
[430] https://ods.od.nih.gov/factsheets/Omega3FattyAcids-Consumer/
[431] https://ods.od.nih.gov/factsheets/Omega3FattyAcids-Consumer/
[432] Su KP, Tseng PT, Lin PY, et al. Association of Use of Omega-3 Polyunsaturated Fatty Acids With Changes in Severity of Anxiety Symptoms:

What Were The Results?

The authors[433] found an association of improved anxiety symptoms with omega-3 treatment compared with control groups in both placebo-controlled and non-placebo-controlled trials.

They also found a stronger anti-anxiety effect of omega-3 when anxiety symptoms were more severe (clinical) than less severe (subclinical) populations.[434]

How Much Omega-3 Was Used In The Studies?

In the review of 19 clinical trials,[435] anti-anxiety benefits occurred when using at least two grams per day of omega-3, DHA, and EPA combined.

The results did not differ whether the amount of EPA was more than or less than 60% of total omega-3.

A Systematic Review and Meta-analysis. JAMA ONetw Open. 2018;1(5):e182327. Published 2018 Sep 14. doi:10.1001/jamanetworkopen.2018.2327

[433] Su KP, Tseng PT, Lin PY, et al. Association of Use of Omega-3 Polyunsaturated Fatty Acids With Changes in Severity of Anxiety Symptoms: A Systematic Review and Meta-analysis. JAMA ONetw Open. 2018;1(5):e182327. Published 2018 Sep 14. doi:10.1001/jamanetworkopen.2018.2327

[434] Su KP, Tseng PT, Lin PY, et al. Association of Use of Omega-3 Polyunsaturated Fatty Acids With Changes in Severity of Anxiety Symptoms: A Systematic Review and Meta-analysis. JAMA ONetw Open. 2018;1(5):e182327. Published 2018 Sep 14. doi:10.1001/jamanetworkopen.2018.2327

[435] Su KP, Tseng PT, Lin PY, et al. Association of Use of Omega-3 Polyunsaturated Fatty Acids With Changes in Severity of Anxiety Symptoms: A Systematic Review and Meta-analysis. JAMA ONetw Open. 2018;1(5):e182327. Published 2018 Sep 14. doi:10.1001/jamanetworkopen.2018.2327

What Are Some Caveats?

- The populations studied were broad, which makes it difficult to generalize to specific populations like college students.

- Some of the studies had a small sample size.

- There was a broad range of benefits in different studies.

- Omega 3s can interact with medications and supplements.

- Talk to your health provider before considering omega-3.

Based on the research findings, not everyone will have the same benefits from omega-3.

What Are Some Sources Of Omega 3s?

According to the National Institute of Health,[436] sources of omega-3 include:

- Fish and other seafood (especially cold-water fatty fish, such as salmon, mackerel, tuna, herring, and sardines).

- Nuts and seeds (such as flaxseed, chia seeds, and walnuts).

- Plant oils (such as flaxseed oil, soybean oil, and canola oil).

---

[436] https://ods.od.nih.gov/factsheets/Omega3FattyAcids-Consumer/

- Fortified foods (such as certain brands of eggs, yogurt, juices, milk, soy beverages, and infant formulas).

- Omega-3 dietary supplements include fish oil, krill oil, cod liver oil, and algal oil (oil sourced from algae).

They come in a wide range of doses and forms.

How Much Omega-3 Do I Need Per Day?

The U.S. Food and Drug Administration recommends consuming no more than 3 grams/day of EPA and DHA combined, including up to 2 grams/day from dietary supplements.[437]

Expanded Knowledge

Omega-3 has been heavily studied for mental health. They have been implicated in memory, learning, and a range of cognitive functions, essential ingredients for the vitality of our mental lives (Innis, 2007).[438] Not stopping at that, these fatty acids also help sculpt the very nerve cells that form the physical basis of our thoughts and feelings.

Through empirical evidence, a meta-analysis of 13 studies encompassing 1,233 participants revealed the power of omega-3 as a force against anxiety (Su et al.,

---

[437] https://ods.od.nih.gov/factsheets/Omega3FattyAcids-Consumer/
[438] Innis, S. M. (2007). Dietary omega 3 fatty acids and the developing brain. Brain Research, 1187, 35–50.

2018).[439] The data show us a meaningful picture –
Omega-3 supplementation has statistically significant
effects in alleviating the clinical symptoms of anxiety.
This suggests a potential weapon in our armamentarium
against severe anxiety disorders and their subtler, often
overlooked, subclinical counterparts.

Yet, this story of omega-3 does not unfold the same
way in every individual. Just as each carries a unique
genetic blueprint, our metabolic processes and genetic
backgrounds imprint personal signatures on how we
respond to omega-3 treatments. Indeed, certain genetic
variations can impact the way these fatty acids are
metabolized and utilized in the body, ultimately
influencing the effects of supplementation (Caspi et al.,
2007).[440]

It is important to understand that many plant-based
omega-3 do not efficiently convert to the active form,
DHA and EPA.

Another important factor to remember is that the ratio
of omega-3 to non-omega-3 may also be important. This
means that, in my experience, increasing omega-3 while
decreasing non-omega-3 may provide the most benefit.

It is important to note that the journey with omega-3
fatty acids must be undertaken with prudence. The

[439] Su, K. P., Tseng, P. T., Lin, P. Y., Okubo, R., Chen, T. Y., Chen, Y. W., &
Matsuoka, Y. J. (2018). Association of Use of Omega-3 Polyunsaturated Fatty
Acids With Changes in Severity of Anxiety Symptoms: A Systematic Review
and Meta-analysis. JAMA Network Open, 1(5), e182327.
[440] Caspi, A., Williams, B., Kim-Cohen, J., Craig, I. W., Milne, B. J., Poulton,
R., ... & Moffitt, T. E. (2007). Moderation of breastfeeding effects on the IQ by
genetic variation in fatty acid metabolism. Proceedings of the National
Academy of Sciences, 104(47), 18860-18865.

promise they hold for anxiety treatment, while exciting, necessitates caution. Prior consultation with a healthcare provider is indispensable, given the potential for interactions with other medications and the natural variation in individual responses.

"Macho" Food and Mental Health[441]

Food marketing to males can sometimes include "macho food"[442] messaging associated with foods high in calories, sodium, fats, processed grains, and sugar. This can sometimes also include alcohol and nicotine products. This is significant because food can play an important role in depression, a leading cause of suicide.[443]

Previous research has looked at nutrition and depression among adults of various ages.[444]

A recent study looked at nutrition and depression among college-aged students.[445]

---

[441] https://u.osu.edu/emotionalfitness/2019/10/29/macho-food-and-mental-health/

[442] http://nymag.com/betamale/2016/06/macho-food-marketing-is-killing-men.html

[443] https://us.movember.com/about/mental-health

[444] https://u.osu.edu/emotionalfitness/category/nutrition-depression/

[445] Francis HM, Stevenson RJ, Chambers JR, Gupta D, Newey B, Lim CK (2019) A brief diet intervention can reduce symptoms of depression in young adults – A randomised controlled trial. PLoS ONE 14(10): e0222768. https://doi.org/10.1371/journal.pone.0222768

What Was The Study?

Francis and colleagues studied 100 young adults (aged 17 to 35) with moderate-to-severe depression symptoms and poor diet and were randomized to a dietary intervention or their usual diet.[446]

What Was The Intervention?[447]

The intervention group was instructed to reduce their intake of processed foods and increase their intake of vegetables, fruits, whole grains, healthy proteins, unsweetened dairy, olive oil, turmeric, and cinnamon.[448]

What Were The Results?

- At 21 days, the intervention group had lower depression, anxiety, and stress scores (DASS) than the control group after controlling for baseline scores.[449]

---

[446] Francis HM, Stevenson RJ, Chambers JR, Gupta D, Newey B, Lim CK (2019) A brief diet intervention can reduce symptoms of depression in young adults – A randomised controlled trial. PLoS ONE 14(10): e0222768. https://doi.org/10.1371/journal.pone.0222768

[447] Francis HM, Stevenson RJ, Chambers JR, Gupta D, Newey B, Lim CK (2019) A brief diet intervention can reduce symptoms of depression in young adults – A randomised controlled trial. PLoS ONE 14(10): e0222768. https://doi.org/10.1371/journal.pone.0222768

[448] Francis HM, Stevenson RJ, Chambers JR, Gupta D, Newey B, Lim CK (2019) A brief diet intervention can reduce symptoms of depression in young adults – A randomised controlled trial. PLoS ONE 14(10): e0222768. https://doi.org/10.1371/journal.pone.0222768

[449] Francis HM, Stevenson RJ, Chambers JR, Gupta D, Newey B, Lim CK (2019) A brief diet intervention can reduce symptoms of depression in young adults – A randomised controlled trial. PLoS ONE 14(10): e0222768. https://doi.org/10.1371/journal.pone.0222768

What Are Some Caveats?

- This small study builds on previous studies on nutrition for depression.[450]

- According to these studies, foods that improved depression were NOT necessarily certain foods that are sometimes marketed as "macho" foods.[451]

- This is important because males account for about 75% of suicides in the United States,[452] with depression being the leading cause of suicide.

According to the Centers for Disease Control, other health disparities experienced by men include:

- Suicide (mentioned above).

- Homicide.

- Binge drinking.

- Shorter lifespan.

- High blood pressure.

- Death by motor vehicle accidents.

Expanded Knowledge

In the labyrinthine world of food marketing, a prominent thread, typically targeting males, weaves an enticing narrative around 'macho foods.' These gastronomic indulgences are characterized by their high caloric, sodium, and fat content, often packed with

---

[450] https://u.osu.edu/emotionalfitness/category/nutrition-depression/
[451] http://nymag.com/betamale/2016/06/macho-food-marketing-is-killing-men.html
[452] https://us.movember.com/about/mental-health

processed grains and sugars, and potentially associated with alcohol and nicotine products. This narrative gains gravity when we ponder nutrition's influential role in mental health, specifically depression, a grim harbinger of suicide.

These findings compel a reevaluation of 'macho foods,' revealing a stark contrast between the foods typically associated with this marketing term. In a country where males account for an estimated 75% of suicides and where depression frequently plays the tragic lead role, the marketing and consumption of 'macho foods' warrant a deeper examination.

Further, the Centers for Disease Control and Prevention highlights[453] multiple health disparities that disproportionately affect men, including a shorter lifespan, a heightened propensity towards suicide and homicide, binge drinking, high blood pressure, and increased mortality from motor vehicle accidents. This underscores the urgent need for a comprehensive understanding of dietary patterns, which could potentially serve as a key to unlocking better health outcomes.

Energy Drinks: Side Effects And Impact On Other Substances[454]

---

[453] Centers for Disease Control and Prevention. (2022). Health Disparities in Men. CDC. https://www.cdc.gov/healthequity/lcod/men/2017/all-races-origins/index.htm

[454] https://u.osu.edu/emotionalfitness/2020/01/29/energy-drinks-side-effects-and-impact-on-other-substances/

Many young adults consume energy drinks for many perceived benefits.

A previous post discussed energy drinks worsening attention.[455] This could negatively impact academic performance.

Energy Drink Users Are At Risk Of:

- Increased energy drink-related emergency department visits.[456]

- Four times more likely than non-energy drink users to binge drink at higher intensity vs. those who do not mix energy drinks and alcohol.[457]

- More likely than drinkers who do not mix alcohol with energy drinks to report unwanted or unprotected sex, driving drunk or riding with a driver who was intoxicated, or sustaining alcohol-related injuries.[458]

What's In Energy Drinks?

Most energy drinks contain caffeine and other supplements such as sugar, other stimulants such as taurine, vitamins, etc.[459]

---

[455] https://u.osu.edu/emotionalfitness/2015/03/10/do-energy-drinks-help-or-hurt-your-attention/
[456] https://nccih.nih.gov/health/energy-drinks
[457] https://nccih.nih.gov/health/energy-drinks
[458] https://nccih.nih.gov/health/energy-drinks
[459] Alsunni A. A. (2015). Energy Drink Consumption: Beneficial and Adverse Health Effects. International journal of health sciences, 9(4), 468–474.

What Are Some Side Effects Of Energy Drinks?

While energy drinks may benefit exercise and sports performance, various side effects are also possible, such as[460]:

- **Cardiovascular side effects:** Increased heart rate, blood pressure, arrhythmia, and heart disease, including heart attacks.[461]

- **Mental health side effects:** Anxiety, insomnia, hallucinations, violent behaviors, often with doses of 300 mg or more.[462]

- Many people have side effects on much lower doses, especially when stressed.

- Other side effects are also possible.[463]

A recent study[464] of 3,071 youth aged 9 to 17 surveyed their energy drink use, alcohol, and tobacco use at baseline and 12 months later.

---

[460] Alsunni A. A. (2015). Energy Drink Consumption: Beneficial and Adverse Health Effects. International journal of health sciences, 9(4), 468–474.
[461] Alsunni A. A. (2015). Energy Drink Consumption: Beneficial and Adverse Health Effects. International journal of health sciences, 9(4), 468–474.
[462] Alsunni A. A. (2015). Energy Drink Consumption: Beneficial and Adverse Health Effects. International journal of health sciences, 9(4), 468–474.
[463] Alsunni A. A. (2015). Energy Drink Consumption: Beneficial and Adverse Health Effects. International journal of health sciences, 9(4), 468–474.
[464] Galimov, A., Hanewinkel, R., Hansen, J., Unger, J. B., Sussman, S., & Morgenstern, M. (2020). Association of energy drink consumption with substance-use initiation among adolescents: A 12-month longitudinal study. Journal of Psychopharmacology, 34(2), 221–228. https://doi.org/10.1177/0269881119895545

What Were The Results?

After one year, among energy drink users, when compared to non-energy drink users[465]:

- Around 29% started using tobacco vs. 5.6% of non-energy drink users.[466]

- Nearly 30% started using alcohol vs. 10% of non-energy drink users.[467]

- Energy drink users also reported more school stress than non-energy drink users.[468]

What Are Some Caveats?

- This association study does not tell us about cause and effect.

- Many energy drinks contain caffeine and sugar; some contain other additives that may have other side effects.

---

[465] Galimov, A., Hanewinkel, R., Hansen, J., Unger, J. B., Sussman, S., & Morgenstern, M. (2020). Association of energy drink consumption with substance-use initiation among adolescents: A 12-month longitudinal study. Journal of Psychopharmacology, 34(2), 221–228. https://doi.org/10.1177/0269881119895545

[466] Galimov, A., Hanewinkel, R., Hansen, J., Unger, J. B., Sussman, S., & Morgenstern, M. (2020). Association of energy drink consumption with substance-use initiation among adolescents: A 12-month longitudinal study. Journal of Psychopharmacology, 34(2), 221–228. https://doi.org/10.1177/0269881119895545

[467] Galimov, A., Hanewinkel, R., Hansen, J., Unger, J. B., Sussman, S., & Morgenstern, M. (2020). Association of energy drink consumption with substance-use initiation among adolescents: A 12-month longitudinal study. Journal of Psychopharmacology, 34(2), 221–228. https://doi.org/10.1177/0269881119895545

[468] Galimov, A., Hanewinkel, R., Hansen, J., Unger, J. B., Sussman, S., & Morgenstern, M. (2020). Association of energy drink consumption with substance-use initiation among adolescents: A 12-month longitudinal study. Journal of Psychopharmacology, 34(2), 221–228. https://doi.org/10.1177/0269881119895545

- Some people are more sensitive to caffeine and energy drinks' effects and side effects than others, even in lower amounts.

- Further studies are needed.

Expanded Knowledge

Among the potential risks, caffeine, a staple in most energy drinks, is a potent agent of change. In dosages exceeding 300mg, this robust stimulant has been associated with a diverse spectrum of mental health side effects. The psychic disturbances span from heightened anxiety and sleep disturbances to more alarming behavioral shifts, such as aggression.

The physical toll is no less daunting, with a host of cardiovascular side effects that include elevated heart rate, hypertension, arrhythmias, and a heightened propensity towards heart diseases and heart attacks. Beyond the realm of caffeine, energy drinks serve up a range of other ingredients like sugar, taurine, and a myriad of vitamins, each with its unique set of potential side effects.

In my experience, the amount of caffeine that can be harmful to a person's mental health can vary from person to person. Some people may notice obvious increases in anxiety, while others may simply have a poorer quality of sleep or some difficulties with focus (as described previously).

The effects and side effects of energy drinks are far from uniform, varying widely due to individual differences such as genetic predisposition and overall health. Hence, the journey towards a holistic understanding of the full range of effects that energy drinks may wield on our mental and physical health is still in progress, underscoring the urgency for further research.

Omega-3 and Stress[469]

While the role of omega-3 and inflammation has been studied,[470] omega-3 and stress are not as well studied.

This post discusses a study looking at Omega 3's and stress reduction.

Who Was In The Study?[471]

Around 138 sedentary, overweight, middle-aged participants (n = 93 women, n = 45 men) received either 2.5 grams/day of omega-3, 1.25 grams/day of omega-3, or a placebo for four months.[472]

---

[469] https://u.osu.edu/emotionalfitness/2021/07/23/omega-3-and-stress/
[470] Wall R, Ross RP, Fitzgerald GF, Stanton C. Fatty acids from fish: the anti-inflammatory potential of long-chain omega-3 fatty acids. Nutr Rev. 2010 May;68(5):280-9. doi: 10.1111/j.1753-4887.2010.00287.x. PMID: 20500789.
[471] Madison, A.A., Belury, M.A., Andridge, R. et al.Omega-3 supplementation and stress reactivity of cellular aging biomarkers: an ancillary substudy of a randomized, controlled trial in midlife adults. Mol Psychiatry (2021). https://doi.org/10.1038/s41380-021-01077-2
[472] Madison, A.A., Belury, M.A., Andridge, R. et al.Omega-3 supplementation and stress reactivity of cellular aging biomarkers: an ancillary substudy of a randomized, controlled trial in midlife adults. Mol Psychiatry (2021). https://doi.org/10.1038/s41380-021-01077-2

What Was Studied?[473]

Before and after the trial, participants underwent the Trier Social Stress Test.

Saliva and blood samples were collected once before and repeatedly after the stressor to measure salivary cortisol, telomerase in peripheral blood lymphocytes, and serum anti-inflammatory (interleukin-10; IL-10) and pro-inflammatory (interleukin-6; IL-6, interleukin-12, tumor necrosis factor-alpha) cytokines.

What Were The Results?[474]

Adjusting for pre-supplementation reactivity, age, sagittal abdominal diameter, and sex, omega-3 supplementation altered telomerase (p = 0.05) and IL-10 (p = 0.05) stress reactivity; both supplementation groups were protected from the placebo group's 24% and 26% post-stress declines in the geometric means of telomerase and IL-10, respectively.

Omega-3 Reduced Overall Cortisol (p = 0.03) and IL-6 (p = 0.03) throughout the stressor;

The group that received 2.5 grams per day of Omega 3's had 19% and 33% lower overall cortisol levels (lower

---

[473] Madison, A.A., Belury, M.A., Andridge, R. et al.Omega-3 supplementation and stress reactivity of cellular aging biomarkers: an ancillary substudy of a randomized, controlled trial in midlife adults. Mol Psychiatry (2021). https://doi.org/10.1038/s41380-021-01077-2

[474] Madison, A.A., Belury, M.A., Andridge, R. et al.Omega-3 supplementation and stress reactivity of cellular aging biomarkers: an ancillary substudy of a randomized, controlled trial in midlife adults. Mol Psychiatry (2021). https://doi.org/10.1038/s41380-021-01077-2

stress) and IL-6 geometric mean levels (lower inflammation), respectively, compared to the placebo group.

The authors[475] conclude that by lowering overall inflammation and cortisol levels during stress and boosting repair mechanisms during recovery, omega-3 may slow accelerated aging and reduce depression risk.

What Are Some Caveats?

This is a small study, and further study is needed.

The population studied was middle-aged, which makes it difficult to generalize to specific populations like college students.

Omega-3 may interact with prescription medications and supplements.

Omega-3 has other health benefits[476] as well.

Talk to your doctor or prescriber before considering omega-3.

What Are Some Sources Of Omega 3s?

According to the National Institute of Health,[477] sources of omega-3 include:

---

[475] Madison, A.A., Belury, M.A., Andridge, R. et al.Omega-3 supplementation and stress reactivity of cellular aging biomarkers: an ancillary substudy of a randomized, controlled trial in midlife adults. Mol Psychiatry (2021). https://doi.org/10.1038/s41380-021-01077-2

[476] https://ods.od.nih.gov/factsheets/Omega3FattyAcids-Consumer/

[477] https://ods.od.nih.gov/factsheets/Omega3FattyAcids-Consumer/

- Fish and other seafood (especially cold-water fatty fish, such as salmon, mackerel, tuna, herring, and sardines).

- Nuts and seeds (such as flaxseed, chia seeds, and walnuts).

- Plant oils (such as flaxseed oil, soybean oil, and canola oil).

- Fortified foods (such as certain brands of eggs, yogurt, juices, milk, soy beverages, and infant formulas).

- Omega-3 dietary supplements include fish oil, krill oil, cod liver oil, and algal oil (a vegetarian source that comes from algae).

- They come in a wide range of doses and forms.

How Much Omega-3 Do I Need Per Day?

The U.S. Food and Drug Administration recommends consuming no more than 3 grams/day of EPA and DHA combined, including up to 2 grams/day from dietary supplements.[478]

Expanded Knowledge

Omega-3 fatty acids, already renowned for their anti-inflammatory prowess, now stand on the brink of a new research frontier — the modulation of stress responses.

---

[478] https://ods.od.nih.gov/factsheets/Omega3FattyAcids-Consumer/

But the omega-3 story doesn't stop here. Su et al. (2015)[479] ventured further into its potential role, probing into stress-induced memory, mood, and cognition deficits. Their review pointed towards a possible neuroprotective role for omega-3, adding another intriguing facet to its beneficial profile.

While these findings generate optimism, it's crucial to remember their limitations. The studies often focus on specific, small groups, and the insights garnered may not translate universally. Moreover, the interaction of omega-3 with medications and supplements necessitates incorporating medical advice before its adoption.

Protein Intake And Depression Among Athletes[480]

Previous blog posts have discussed nutrition strategies for depression.

A recent study looked at depression and protein intake in young student-athletes.

---

[479] Su, K. P., Matsuoka, Y., & Pae, C. U. (2015). Omega-3 polyunsaturated fatty acids in prevention of mood and anxiety disorders. Clinical Psychopharmacology and Neuroscience, 13(2), 129.

[480] https://u.osu.edu/emotionalfitness/2023/03/27/protein-intake-and-depression-among-athletes/

What Was This Study?

Around 97 adolescent elite athletes were recruited for the study. Symptoms of depression were recorded at baseline and again during a follow-up at ten months.[481]

A three-day dietary intake log was obtained three months into the study[482]

What were the results?

Higher protein intake was associated with a reduction in symptoms of depression during the follow-up period.[483]

What Are Some General Protein Intake Guidelines?

This calculator can help get an estimate of protein intake: https://www.nal.usda.gov/human-nutrition-and-food-safety/dri-calculator

---

[481] Markus Gerber, Sarah Jakowski, Michael Kellmann, Robyn Cody, Basil Gygax, Sebastian Ludyga, Caspar Muller, Sven Ramseyer, Johanna Beckmann. Macronutrient intake as a prospective predictor of depressive symptom severity: An exploratory study with adolescent elite athletes,Psychology of Sport and Exercise, Volume 66,2023,102387, ISSN 1469-0292, https://doi.org/10.1016/j.psychsport.2023.102387. (https://www.sciencedirect.com/science/article/pii/S1469029223000110

[482] Markus Gerber, Sarah Jakowski, Michael Kellmann, Robyn Cody, Basil Gygax, Sebastian Ludyga, Caspar Muller, Sven Ramseyer, Johanna Beckmann. Macronutrient intake as a prospective predictor of depressive symptom severity: An exploratory study with adolescent elite athletes,Psychology of Sport and Exercise, Volume 66,2023,102387, ISSN 1469-0292, https://doi.org/10.1016/j.psychsport.2023.102387. (https://www.sciencedirect.com/science/article/pii/S1469029223000110

[483] Markus Gerber, Sarah Jakowski, Michael Kellmann, Robyn Cody, Basil Gygax, Sebastian Ludyga, Caspar Muller, Sven Ramseyer, Johanna Beckmann. Macronutrient intake as a prospective predictor of depressive symptom severity: An exploratory study with adolescent elite athletes,Psychology of Sport and Exercise, Volume 66,2023,102387, ISSN 1469-0292, https://doi.org/10.1016/j.psychsport.2023.102387. (https://www.sciencedirect.com/science/article/pii/S1469029223000110

However, according to the most recent dietary guidelines for Americans, almost 90 percent do not meet the recommendation for seafood, and more than half do not meet the recommendation for nuts or seeds.[484]

International Society of Sports Nutrition states that most exercising individuals should consume at minimum approximately 1.4 to 2.0 g of protein per kg of body weight per day to optimize exercise training-induced adaptations.[485]

What Are Some Caveats?

This is a small study showing association, not causation.

Study authors call for larger and more in-depth assessments and techniques.

Athletes and people who exercise regularly may require higher protein intake than Americans' Dietary guidelines.

Expanded Knowledge

As we peel back the layers of nutritional psychiatry, a recent study invites us to delve into the potential intersection between protein intake and depression, focusing particularly on young athletes.

The relationship of higher protein intake appears to correspond with reduced depressive symptoms as the

---

[484] https://www.dietaryguidelines.gov/sites/default/files/2021-03/Dietary_Guidelines_for_Americans-2020-2025.pdf
[485] https://jissn.biomedcentral.com/articles/10.1186/s12970-017-0177-8#Sec33

study progressed. This correlation builds on previous studies, suggesting the beneficial role of protein-rich diets in lessening depressive symptoms (Mikkelsen et al., 2017).[486]

However, while this pattern draws our attention, the researchers counsel measured interpretation.

Given the unique demands of athletic pursuits, athletes might require protein quantities surpassing standard dietary guidelines. These studies underscore the importance of personalized dietary plans, sculpted to cater to individual health, lifestyle, and fitness aspirations for the benefit of physical and mental health.

In my experience, I have seen patients who regularly engage in athletic activities significantly improve their mental health symptoms as they improve the quality of their nutrition, sleep, technology use, etc. While many factors beyond those discussed in this book may be impacting a person's mental health, in my experience, addressing nutrition can be beneficial for mental health.

Intermittent Fasting And Disordered Eating[487]

There are various methods of intermittent fasting, which have been reported to have many health benefits.[488]

---

[486] Mikkelsen, K., Stojanovska, L., Polenakovic, M., Bosevski, M., & Apostolopoulos, V. (2017). Exercise and mental health. Maturitas, 106, 48-56. doi: 10.1016/j.maturitas.2017.09.003.
[487] https://u.osu.edu/emotionalfitness/2023/01/31/intermittent-fasting-and-disordered-eating/
[488] https://newsinhealth.nih.gov/2019/12/fast-or-not-fast

A recent study points out the potential risks of intermittent fasting in young adults.[489]

What Was The Study?[490]

- A national study of Canadian adolescents and young adults (N = 2762) was analyzed.[491]

- Intermittent fasting participants reported, on average, 100 days of intermittent fasting over a 12-month period.[492]

- Multiple modified Poisson regression analyses were conducted to determine the association between intermittent fasting (past 12 months and 30 days) and eating disorder behaviors measured using the Eating Disorder Examination Questionnaire.[493]

---

[489] Ganson KT, Cuccolo K, Hallward L, Nagata JM. Intermittent fasting: Describing engagement and associations with eating disorder behaviors and psychopathology among Canadian adolescents and young adults. Eat Behav. 2022 Dec;47:101681. doi: 10.1016/j.eatbeh.2022.101681. Epub 2022 Nov 4. PMID: 36368052.

[490] Ganson KT, Cuccolo K, Hallward L, Nagata JM. Intermittent fasting: Describing engagement and associations with eating disorder behaviors and psychopathology among Canadian adolescents and young adults. Eat Behav. 2022 Dec;47:101681. doi: 10.1016/j.eatbeh.2022.101681. Epub 2022 Nov 4. PMID: 36368052.

[491] Ganson KT, Cuccolo K, Hallward L, Nagata JM. Intermittent fasting: Describing engagement and associations with eating disorder behaviors and psychopathology among Canadian adolescents and young adults. Eat Behav. 2022 Dec;47:101681. doi: 10.1016/j.eatbeh.2022.101681. Epub 2022 Nov 4. PMID: 36368052.

[492] Ganson KT, Cuccolo K, Hallward L, Nagata JM. Intermittent fasting: Describing engagement and associations with eating disorder behaviors and psychopathology among Canadian adolescents and young adults. Eat Behav. 2022 Dec;47:101681. doi: 10.1016/j.eatbeh.2022.101681. Epub 2022 Nov 4. PMID: 36368052.

[493] Ganson KT, Cuccolo K, Hallward L, Nagata JM. Intermittent fasting: Describing engagement and associations with eating disorder behaviors and

What Were The Results?

- Around 47 % of women, 38.4 % of men, and 52.0 % of transgender/gender non-conforming (TGNC) participants reported intermittent fasting in the past 12 months.

- Intermittent fasting in the past 12 months and 30 days was significantly associated with eating disorder psychopathology.[494]

- Varying patterns of association between intermittent fasting and eating disorder behaviors were found across genders, with the most consistent relationships between intermittent fasting and ED behaviors in women.[495]

- Women engaging in intermittent fasting were more likely to report disordered eating behaviors.[496]

psychopathology among Canadian adolescents and young adults. Eat Behav. 2022 Dec;47:101681. doi: 10.1016/j.eatbeh.2022.101681. Epub 2022 Nov 4. PMID: 36368052.

[494] Ganson KT, Cuccolo K, Hallward L, Nagata JM. Intermittent fasting: Describing engagement and associations with eating disorder behaviors and psychopathology among Canadian adolescents and young adults. Eat Behav. 2022 Dec;47:101681. doi: 10.1016/j.eatbeh.2022.101681. Epub 2022 Nov 4. PMID: 36368052.

[495] Ganson KT, Cuccolo K, Hallward L, Nagata JM. Intermittent fasting: Describing engagement and associations with eating disorder behaviors and psychopathology among Canadian adolescents and young adults. Eat Behav. 2022 Dec;47:101681. doi: 10.1016/j.eatbeh.2022.101681. Epub 2022 Nov 4. PMID: 36368052.

[496] Ganson KT, Cuccolo K, Hallward L, Nagata JM. Intermittent fasting: Describing engagement and associations with eating disorder behaviors and psychopathology among Canadian adolescents and young adults. Eat Behav. 2022 Dec;47:101681. doi: 10.1016/j.eatbeh.2022.101681. Epub 2022 Nov 4. PMID: 36368052.

- Men engaging in intermittent fasting were more likely to report compulsive exercise.[497]

Additional Thoughts

- Intermittent fasting is not without risks.

- The study design points out the association between intermittent fasting and disordered eating but does not necessarily show causation.

- The bodies and brains of young people are still developing and growing, and in this context, calorie restriction may not be ideal.

- Instead, prioritizing nutritious food may benefit physical and mental health more.[498]

- Even with good food choices, getting enough calories is important, and not engaging in restriction or disordered eating behaviors.

- TDEE calculators and this chart may help estimate daily calorie needs.

- Individuals with eating disorders should seek professional assistance via a nutritionist, eating disorder specialist, etc., when considering nutritional adjustments.

[497] Ganson KT, Cuccolo K, Hallward L, Nagata JM. Intermittent fasting: Describing engagement and associations with eating disorder behaviors and psychopathology among Canadian adolescents and young adults. Eat Behav. 2022 Dec;47:101681. doi: 10.1016/j.eatbeh.2022.101681. Epub 2022 Nov 4. PMID: 36368052.
[498] https://u.osu.edu/emotionalfitness/2018/06/28/food-choices-to-improve-depression/

- Further research is needed to understand better the risks and benefits of intermittent fasting, particularly in adolescents and young adults.

Expanded Knowledge

Intermittent fasting, though heralded as a powerful nutritional strategy, may hide a wolf in sheep's clothing, particularly regarding eating disorders in young adults.

During the transitional stage of life, when both body and mind are evolving and growing, the emphasis should ideally be on balanced, nutritious eating rather than rigid calorie restriction. Alongside this, it's crucial to maintain an adequate caloric intake to circumvent unintentional disordered eating behaviors. In addition to foods with nutritious properties such as fruits, vegetables, nutritious sources of protein and fats, 100% whole grains when appropriate, practical tools such as TDEE (Total daily energy expenditure) calculators or tailored charts could be invaluable allies in this journey toward health (Schneider et al., 2018).[499]

Importantly, anyone grappling with eating disorders should tread carefully on the path of nutritional changes and should do so only under the watchful eye of a trained professional, like a nutritionist or eating disorder specialist.

[499] Schneider, P., Börnhorst, C., Görlich, D., Traub, M., Hadjigeorgiou, C., Hebestreit, A., & Pala, V. (2018). The use of a Total Diet Quality Index to assess the diet quality in a group of German adolescents. Journal of Nutritional Science, 7.

As always, this book is intended for informational purposes. Check with your own healthcare professional to see if any of the strategies discussed are right for you. If you choose to apply them, do it under the care and guidance of a health professional.

Chapter 7: Sleep Strategies To Improve Mental Health

Sleep is a recurring state of mind and body characterized by altered consciousness, relative sensory and physical activity inhibition, and reduced interaction with the surroundings. It stands as one of life's most intricate and captivating mysteries. It launches us into a surreal realm where reality bends and contorts into the fabric of dreams.

Poor sleep quality or not sleeping enough hours is a major problem in young adults, and this has been found in various studies. One survey found that up to 60% of college students report poor sleep quality.[500]

Beyond its roles in cognitive restoration and memory consolidation, sleep has immense implications on our cognitive performance, mental health, physical health, and overall quality of life. There is very little anyone can do to make up for poor or lost sleep effectively. Insomnia can increase the risk of developing depression, anxiety, alcohol and drug use disorders.[501]

Over the centuries, sleep has gripped the interest of scientists, philosophers, and artists alike. From the ancient theories contemplating sleep as a temporary

---

[500] (Schlarb AA, Friedrich A, Claßen M. Sleep problems in university students - an intervention. Neuropsychiatr Dis Treat. 2017 Jul 26;13:1989-2001. doi: 10.2147/NDT.S142067. PMID: 287can94633; PMCID: PMC5536318.

[501] (Breslau N, Roth T, Rosenthal L, Andreski P. Sleep disturbance and psychiatric disorders: a longitudinal epidemiological study of young adults. Biol Psychiatry. 1996 Mar 15;39(6):411-8. doi: 10.1016/0006-3223(95)00188-3. PMID: 8679786.

death or an immersion into a parallel world to contemporary neuroscientific models dissecting sleep phases, our understanding of this phenomenon has significantly evolved *(Cirelli & Tononi, 2008).*[502]

As you will see, research points to a relationship between poor sleep quality, reduced hours of sleep, and academic performance. Sleep plays a critical role in a host of cognitive processes, including memory consolidation, attention, and problem-solving *(Diekelmann & Born, 2010).*[503]

As you read this chapter, I hope you realize that quality sleep, tailored to your individual needs, holds the potential to change your life in many ways: elevate your cognitive prowess, emotional well-being, and overall life quality.

As always, this book is intended for informational purposes. Check with your healthcare professional to see if any of the strategies discussed are right for you. If you choose to apply them, do it under the care and guidance of a health professional.

You May Not Need Eight Hours Per Night Of Sleep For Optimal Academic Performance.[504]

---

[502] Cirelli, C., & Tononi, G. (2008). Is sleep essential?. PLoS biology, 6(8), e216.

[503] Diekelmann, S., & Born, J. (2010). The memory function of sleep. Nature Reviews Neuroscience, 11(2), 114-126.

[504] https://u.osu.edu/emotionalfitness/2014/08/06/you-may-not-need-8-hours-per-night-of-sleep-for-optimal-academic-performance/

In a large study[505] published in 2013, researchers examined the self-reported sleeping habits of about 160,000 users of Lumnosity® who took spatial memory and matching tests and about 127,000 users who took an arithmetic test. It was found that optimal cognitive performance occurred at seven hours per night of sleep, with worse performance reported among those with more or fewer hours of sleep.

You may not need exactly eight hours of sleep per night, and guidelines for optimal sleep will likely be updated.[506] It is, however, important to remember that not everyone needs the same amount of sleep, and too little sleep, just as too much, can impact your brain and academic performance.

As the new semester approaches, have you considered how sleep impacts your academic performance and how much?

What will you do differently?

Expanded Knowledge

This narrative, shaped by an expansive collection of studies, challenges the idea of a *'one-size-fits-all'* sleep philosophy.

Shifting the focus to the age-dependent rhythm of sleep, a comprehensive report from the National Sleep

[505] 1.   Sternberg, et al. Front Hum Neurosci. 2013; 7: 292. Published online Jun 20, 2013. doi:10.3389/fnhum.2013.00292. The largest human cognitive performance dataset reveals insights into the effects of lifestyle factors and aging.

[506] 1.   http://m.us.wsj.com/articles/sleep-experts-close-in-on-the-optimal-nights-sleep-1405984970?mobile=y

Foundation, which found its home in the journal 'Sleep Health,' highlights the nuanced variations in sleep needs concerning age. The guidance indicates that young adults between the ages of 18 and 25 may find their sweet spot in a sleep duration of 7 to 9 hours.

Most importantly, the report gently warns against straying too far from this range, with both extremes—over 11 hours or under 6—posing potential perils (Hirshkowitz et al., 2015).[507] In my experience, if you are feeling low energy, napping frequently, and relying on caffeine for energy during the day despite sleeping well at night and getting good nutrition, you may need to consider increasing the amount of sleep you get. Some young adults feel much better as they sleep closer to 9 hours per night.

A fascinating study featured in the 'Journal of Sleep Research' shows[508] that sleep deprivation can impact a variety of cognitive domains and tasks that would impact your academic and work performance.

A Stanford University study found that students who adhered to a regular sleep schedule had higher GPAs than students with erratic sleep patterns—reiterating the importance of sleep consistency, even when total sleep

[507] Hirshkowitz, M., Whiton, K., Albert, S. M., Alessi, C., Bruni, O., DonCarlos, L., ... & Neubauer, D. N. (2015). National Sleep Foundation's sleep time duration recommendations: methodology and results summary. Sleep Health, 1(1), 40-43.
[508] Lim, J., & Dinges, D. F. (2010). A meta-analysis of the impact of short-term sleep deprivation on cognitive variables. Psychological bulletin, 136(3), 375–389.

duration was consistent across groups *(Diaz–Morales et al., 2017).*[509]

I hope you can appreciate the hours of sleep and the quality and consistency of sleep as important factors for cognitive and academic performance.

Ways to Improve Sleep[510]

About 30% of adults experience insomnia,[511] which can be thought of as daytime impairment caused by frequent difficulties falling or staying asleep or poor quality sleep.[512]

College students with sleep disorders are more likely to experience academic failure (GPA less than 2) than those without sleep disorders.[513]

Individuals with insomnia are more likely to suffer from depression, anxiety, alcohol, and drug abuse.[514]

---

[509] Diaz–Morales, J. F., Escribano, C., & Jankowski, K. S. (2015). Chronotype and time-of-day effects on mood during school day. Chronobiology international, 32(1), 37-42.

[510] https://u.osu.edu/emotionalfitness/2020/07/01/ways-to-improve-sleep/

[511] Roth T. (2007). Insomnia: definition, prevalence, etiology, and consequences. Journal of clinical sleep medicine : JCSM : official publication of the American Academy of Sleep Medicine, 3(5 Suppl), S7–S10.

[512] Roth T. (2007). Insomnia: definition, prevalence, etiology, and consequences. Journal of clinical sleep medicine : JCSM : official publication of the American Academy of Sleep Medicine, 3(5 Suppl), S7–S10.

[513] Gaultney JF. The prevalence of sleep disorders in college students: Impact on academic performance. J Am Coll Health. Sep-Oct 2010; 59 (2): 91-97.

[514] Breslau N et.al. Biol Psychiatry. 1996, 39: 411-418.

What Are Some Ways Of Improving Sleep?

The American Academy of Sleep Medicine suggests the following ways to improve sleep[515]:

- Keep a consistent sleep schedule.

- Get up at the same time every day, even on weekends or during vacations.

- Plan to get at least 7 hours of sleep.

- Don't go to bed unless you are sleepy.

- If you don't fall asleep after 20 minutes, get out of bed.

- Establish a relaxing bedtime routine.

- Use your bed only for sleep and sex.

- Make your bedroom quiet and relaxing. Keep the room at a comfortable, cool temperature.

- Limit exposure to bright light in the evenings.

- Turn off electronic devices at least 30 minutes before bedtime.

- Don't eat a large meal before bedtime. If you are hungry at night, eat a light, healthy snack.

- Exercise regularly and maintain good nutrition.

- Avoid consuming caffeine in the late afternoon or evening.

- Avoid consuming alcohol, nicotine, and other drugs.

---

[515] http://sleepeducation.org/essentials-in-sleep/healthy-sleep-habits

- Reduce your fluid intake before bedtime.

Anything Else?

- For some, the effects of sleep deprivation can start by missing as little as 30 minutes or more of your usual sleep time.

- Some people may need to eliminate caffeine or alcohol completely, gradually.

- If you have to use electronics in the evenings, consider using apps like <u>BLUE BLOCKERS</u>.

- Young adults should plan on 8 to 9 hours of sleep per night.

- Avoidance of things that interfere with sleep: screen time (consider using a blue light filter or night mode). Avoid large meals/snacks at bedtime.

- Practice relaxation skills such as progressive muscle relaxation, meditation, deep breathing, and guided imagery.

- Positive visualization: visualize positive past or future events.

- Consider keeping a notebook to jot down things on your mind at bedtime.

- Avoid naps when possible, sleep more at night instead, and if you take naps, keep them brief (under 20 minutes) to avoid nighttime sleep disruption.

- Professional treatment may be needed if you have had limited or no benefit from these strategies.

Expanded Knowledge

In my experience, the most important thing young adults can do to improve their sleep is to keep a consistent sleep schedule, even on their days off. If there are occasional nights where you plan to stay up later than usual, a useful strategy to consider is to go to bed a few minutes earlier than planned on a couple of nights leading up to the event and the night after the event, taking a strategic nap or two (no more than 20 minutes each to prevent sleep disruption) the day off and the following day; while keeping your wake up time the same. While not ideal, this may help reduce disruption.

Many people do not realize the impact of caffeine, nicotine, and alcohol, even in small amounts, on sleep quality. In my experience, people see the best results if they decrease caffeine, nicotine, and alcohol gradually by 20-25% per week and then stay off for a few weeks before they can see the full impact of eliminating these substances and how it may help improve mood, anxiety, sleep and other aspects of health.

Warning: Eliminating these substances abruptly or cold turkey can lead to withdrawal, which in the case of alcohol can be deadly!

As with all other strategies discussed in this book, check with your healthcare professional before considering changes to your caffeine, nicotine, or alcohol intake. Some people find that eating a large meal within three hours of bedtime can interfere with sleep as your body focuses on digestion rather than sleep processes. Exercising within three hours of bedtime may also interfere with your ability to sleep restfully.

As you can see, good sleep can impact our physical and mental health.

Poor Sleep And Poor Grades Might Go Together.[516]

College students might stay up late or have an erratic sleep schedule for various reasons.

A recent study looked at the impact of sleep patterns on grades.

Who Was Studied?[517],[518]

A total of 61 undergraduate students at Harvard College.

They were asked to keep a sleep diary for 30 days.

[516] https://u.osu.edu/emotionalfitness/2017/12/31/poor-sleep-and-poor-grades-might-go-together/

[517] https://consumer.healthday.com/sleep-disorder-information-33/misc-sleep-problems-news-626/poor-sleep-habits-61-poor-grades-723563.html

[518] Phillips AJK, Clerx WM, O'Brien CS, et al. Irregular sleep/wake patterns are associated with poorer academic performance and delayed circadian and sleep/wake timing. Scientific Reports. 2017;7:3216. doi:10.1038/s41598-017-03171-4.

What Did The Investigators Find?[519],[520]

Compared to peers, students reporting irregular patterns of sleep and wakefulness had:

- Lower grade point averages.

- Delays in the times people went to bed and woke up compared to more normal sleep/wake times.

- Up to a three-hour delay in melatonin (sleep-related hormone) release compared to students with regularly scheduled sleep and wakefulness patterns.

What Are Some Caveats?

- Poor sleep can impact almost every aspect of health and many parts of brain functioning, including learning, remembering, mood, energy level, decision-making, etc.

- This is a small study and does not prove cause and effect.[521]

---

[519] https://consumer.healthday.com/sleep-disorder-information-33/misc-sleep-problems-news-626/poor-sleep-habits-61-poor-grades-723563.html

[520] Phillips AJK, Clerx WM, O'Brien CS, et al. Irregular sleep/wake patterns are associated with poorer academic performance and delayed circadian and sleep/wake timing. Scientific Reports. 2017;7:3216. doi:10.1038/s41598-017-03171-4.

[521] Phillips AJK, Clerx WM, O'Brien CS, et al. Irregular sleep/wake patterns are associated with poorer academic performance and delayed circadian and sleep/wake timing. Scientific Reports. 2017;7:3216. doi:10.1038/s41598-017-03171-4.

- Students with erratic sleep schedules slept the same number of hours as those with a regular sleep schedule.[522][523]

- Study participants might have an erratic sleep schedule for a variety of reasons.

Anything Else?

- If you have to use electronics in the evenings, consider using apps like BLUE BLOCKERS.

Blue Blockers and other ways to reduce electronics-induced sleep disruption and daytime tiredness[524]

Blue spectrum light from electronics suppresses melatonin for several hours after use [525],[526] and disrupts your circadian (sleep-wake cycle) clock.[527] This impacts

---

[522] https://consumer.healthday.com/sleep-disorder-information-33/misc-sleep-problems-news-626/poor-sleep-habits-61-poor-grades-723563.html

[523] Phillips AJK, Clerx WM, O'Brien CS, et al. Irregular sleep/wake patterns are associated with poorer academic performance and delayed circadian and sleep/wake timing. Scientific Reports. 2017;7:3216. doi:10.1038/s41598-017-03171-4.

[524] https://u.osu.edu/emotionalfitness/2015/07/17/blue-blockers-and-other-ways-to-reduce-electronics-induced-sleep-disruption-and-daytime-tiredness/#:~:text=Blue%20Blockers%20and,sleep%20tips.

[525] Brainard GC, Hanifin JP, Greeson JM, Byrne B, Glickman G, Gerner E, et al.
Action spectrum for melatonin regulation in humans: evidence for a novel circadian photoreceptor. J Neurosci 2001;21(16):6405–12 [August 15, PMID:
11487664].

[526] Thapan K, Arendt J, Skene DJ. An action spectrum for melatonin suppression:
evidence for a novel non-rod, non-cone photoreceptor system in humans. J
Physiol 2001;535(Pt 1):261–7 [August 15, PMID: 11507175].

[527] Smith MR, Revell VL, Eastman CI. Phase advancing the human circadian clock

sleep quality and daytime tiredness.[528] Sleep disruption can also impact anxiety, depression, and many other health conditions.[529]

So it may be worth avoiding using electronic devices such as computers, TVs, tablets, smartphones, etc., 1-3 hours before bedtime.

Some suggest replacing exposure to bright light bulbs with dim light bulbs around bedtime[530] may also be helpful. There are even light bulbs that do not emit blue light.

What If I Need To Use Electronics At Bedtime?

Sometimes, it may be necessary to be on the computer, TV, smartphone, etc., right before bedtime. Blue Blockers may help prevent sleep disruption from electronics.

---

with blue-enriched polychromatic light. Sleep Med 2008 [September 18, PMID: 18805055].

[528] Fossum IN, et al. The Association Between Use of Electronic Media in Bed Before Going to Sleep and Insomnia Symptoms, Daytime Sleepiness, Morningness, and Chronotype. Behavioral Sleep Medicine. Volume 12, Issue 5, 2014, pages 343- 357. Published online: 14 Jul 2014. DOI: 10.1080/15402002.2013.819468.

[529] http://sleepfoundation.org/sleep-disorders-problems

[530] Kayumov L, et al. Blocking Low-Wavelength Light Prevents Nocturnal Melatonin Suppression with No Adverse Effect on Performance during Simulated Shift Work. The Journal of Clinical Endocrinology & Metabolism 90(5):2755–2761.

How Do Blue Blockers Work?

They block blue light emitted by electronic devices. Thus, melatonin is not disrupted.[531]

What are some examples of blue light blockers?

Some examples include blue blocker eyeglasses, software programs that prevent your device from emitting blue light, plastic filter screens placed on top of the screens to block blue light, and light bulbs that do not emit blue light. You can search for *"blue light blockers," "blue light filters," "bedtime reading software,"* etc., in a search engine or an app store.

Do Blue Blockers Work?

Small studies show blue blockers work to prevent melatonin disruption and improve the quality of sleep and mood.

For example, 20 subjects were randomized to use either blue-blocking glasses or non-blue-blocking glasses three hours before bedtime over a two-week period.[532]

---

[531] Kayumov L, et al. Blocking Low-Wavelength Light Prevents Nocturnal Melatonin Suppression with No Adverse Effect on Performance during Simulated Shift Work. The Journal of Clinical Endocrinology & Metabolism 90(5):2755–2761.

[532] Burkhart K1, Phelps JR. Amber lenses to block blue light and improve sleep: a randomized trial. Chronobiol Int. 2009 Dec;26(8):1602-12. doi: 10.3109/07420520903523719.

What Did The Results Show?

Those who used blue-blocking glasses reported better sleep quality and mood.

Words Of Caution:

- You still need to be mindful of getting enough sleep—getting four or five hours of quality sleep when you need eight will still leave you tired.

- Blue-blocking methods may not help with your sleep if your device usage is overly entertaining or emotionally intense.

- It would help if you still addressed other causes, such as caffeine, nicotine, alcohol use, etc.

- This is still a relatively new terrain, and further research is needed.

Are you sleeping poorly?

Are you tired during the day?

Are electronic devices interfering with your sleep; can you reduce your usage before bedtime?

Can blue blockers help you?

Expanded Knowledge

Electronic devices before bedtime have been identified as a significant contributor to sleep disruption and daytime tiredness due to the emission of blue spectrum light that hampers melatonin production and, subsequently, the circadian rhythm.

As evident in the abovementioned study and several other investigations, blue-blocking techniques have been introduced to counteract this disruption.

For instance, a study by Burkhart and Phelps (2009)[533] found that wearing blue-blocking glasses three hours before bedtime can improve overall sleep quality. This research involved using amber lenses that blocked blue light, demonstrating the effectiveness of physical filters in managing blue light exposure.

Beyond physical filters, various software solutions have been developed to reduce blue light emissions from electronic devices. F.lux, for instance, is a computer program that adjusts a display's color temperature according to location and time of day, reducing blue light emission during the evening. A similar study conducted by Šrámková et al. (2020)[534] endorsed the effectiveness of such software solutions in enhancing sleep quality among adolescents who were habitual electronic device users in the late evening.

Furthermore, incorporating light bulbs that do not emit blue light in your environment could be beneficial. A study conducted by *Figueiro and Rea (2010)*[535] found that using light sources with reduced or no blue light in

---

[533] Burkhart, K., & Phelps, J. R. (2009). Amber lenses to block blue light and improve sleep: a randomized trial. Chronobiology international, 26(8), 1602-1612.

[534] Šrámková, M., Dušková, M., Hill, M., Bicíková, M., Růžička, E., & Šonka, K. (2020). The effect of blue light-blocking glasses on sleep quality in computer users: a pilot study. Sleep Medicine, 72, 167-171.

[535] Figueiro, M. G., & Rea, M. S. (2010). The effects of red and blue lights on circadian variations in cortisol, alpha amylase, and melatonin. International journal of endocrinology, 2010.

the evening significantly improved sleep quality among older adults. This suggests a potentially broad application for all age groups.

Blue-blocking technology and its impact on sleep quality is a growing field and warrants further study. The next study highlights further careful consideration of screen use before bedtime.

Smartphone Use Before Bedtime Might Impact Sleep And Daytime Tiredness[536]

Smartphones or cell phones are useful tools that can benefit when used properly.

Many students frequently use cell phones and often very close to bedtime. Students may not know that cellphone use might impact their ability to sleep at night, and this might impact their daytime energy levels.

This study explored the relationship between cellphone use at bedtime and sleep.

Who Was Studied?

Around 532 students aged 18–39 were recruited from lectures or via e-mail.[537]

---

[536] https://u.osu.edu/emotionalfitness/2015/06/17/cell-phone-use-before-bedtime-might-impact-sleep-and-daytime-tiredness/

[537] Fossum IN, et al. The Association Between Use of Electronic Media in Bed Before Going to Sleep and Insomnia Symptoms, Daytime Sleepiness, Morningness, and Chronotype. Behavioral Sleep Medicine. Volume 12, Issue

The mean time of media use per night was 46.6 minutes.

What Were The Study Results?

Mobile phone usage for playing/surfing/texting was positively associated with insomnia. Computer usage for playing/surfing/reading was positively associated with insomnia.

What Do The Results Mean?

Computer or cell phone use in bed before bedtime may worsen your sleep.

How Does Screen Time Impact Sleep?

There are various potential causes:

Media use might make it take longer to fall asleep.[538] Media use might mean less time spent sleeping, thus reducing sleep.[539] The bright light emitted by electronic devices might impact sleep quality.[540] Light exposure

---

5, 2014, pages 343- 357. Published online: 14 Jul 2014. DOI: 10.1080/15402002.2013.819468.

[538] 2. Higuchi, S., Motohashi, Y., Liu, Y., & Maeda, A. (2005). Effects of playing a computer game using a bright display on presleep physiological variables, sleep latency, slow wave sleep and REM sleep. Journal of Sleep Research, 14, 267–273.

[539] 3. Van den Bulck, J. (2004). Television viewing, computer game playing, and Internet use and self-reported time to bed and time out of bed in secondary-school children. Sleep, 27, 101–104.

[540] 4. Cain, N., & Gradisar, M. (2010). Electronic media use and sleep in school-aged children and adolescents: A review. Sleep Medicine, 11, 735–742.

might be temporarily activating by increasing mental arousal [541],[542] making it harder for you to fall asleep.

Are you sleeping poorly?

Are you tired during the day?

Is screen time before bed impacting your sleep?

Will cutting down on screen time improve your sleep?

How do you know?

Expanded Knowledge

The rising prevalence of smartphone usage in the modern age, particularly among the young adult demographic, has brought about a slew of studies examining its impacts on various aspects of life, one of the most prevalent being sleep.

Expanding on this, another study by *Lemola et al. (2015)*[543] confirmed similar findings, where increased electronic media use correlated with poor sleep quality and symptoms of depression among adolescents.

This highlights a different way that electronic devices used at bedtime can interfere with your sleep in addition to blue light: by reducing your total sleep time. I would

---

[541] 5. Cajochen, C., et al. (2011). Evening exposure to a light-emitting diodes (LED)-backlit computer screen affects circadian physiology and cognitive performance. Journal of Applied Physiology, 110, 1432–1438.

[542] 6. Campbell, S. S., et al. (1995). Light treatment for sleep disorders: Consensus report. III. Alerting and activating effects. Journal of Biological Rhythms, 10, 129–132.

[543] Lemola, S., Perkinson-Gloor, N., Brand, S., Dewald-Kaufmann, J. F., & Grob, A. (2015). Adolescents' electronic media use at night, sleep disturbance, and depressive symptoms in the smartphone age. Journal of Youth and Adolescence, 44(2), 405-418.

also add that if you are choosing entertainment, intense interactions with others, thinking about stressful topics, or other stimulatory behaviors, you are sending mixed signals to your brain because these signals are inherently altering at the same time that you are trying to calm your body and mind to drift into sleep.

If you prefer to do something at bedtime to relax, consider soothing or calming activities mentioned earlier in this chapter. You can also consider adjusting your schedule to do non-screen time activities before bed and screen time earlier in the afternoon/evening.

These studies reaffirm that screen time before bedtime may substantially affect sleep quality and daytime alertness. While this subject remains a focal point of research, the initial findings certainly provide a strong rationale for managing screen time, particularly in the hours leading up to sleep.

Finally, this chapter discussed different ways sleep can impact your mental health, physical health, and cognitive/academic performance. It also showed you different strategies that may help improve sleep.

This chapter also highlights the importance of using a comprehensive, personalized set of strategies to help improve your sleep. The strategies discussed are intended to complement the work you may be doing with your health professional on improving your sleep.

Chapter 8: Social Media, Technology Use/Misuse And Mental Health

In this era of rapid technological advancement, the digital landscape has intricately woven itself into the fabric of our daily lives. This transformation has sparked a critical and pressing discourse within mental health. Indeed, the interaction between technology and mental health is as complex as it is profound, shaping our social structures, cognitive processes, and emotional well-being.

As we immerse ourselves in this multifaceted subject matter, we shall cast an investigative lens on the intricate dynamics within this digital-mental health nexus.

The pervasive integration of technology in our lives is a relatively new phenomenon. Thus, the breadth and depth of its effects on mental health remain partially unchartered territories. We are increasingly seeing more people transition from childhood to adulthood, spending the majority of their existence using technology.

The full ramifications of this are yet to be understood. The scientific exploration of this field is ongoing, fueled by an understanding of the potential implications of technology on public mental health (Twenge & Campbell, 2018).[544] This growing body of research presents a

---

[544] Twenge, J. M., & Campbell, W. K. (2018). Associations between screen time and lower psychological well-being among children and adolescents: Evidence from a population-based study. Preventive Medicine Reports, 12, 271–283. https://doi.org/10.1016/j.pmedr.2018.10.003

multifaceted picture, outlining both the potential harms and benefits of our technologically immersed lifestyles.

Concerns about the impact of technology misuse on mental health have grown in parallel with its increasing prevalence in our lives. Our collective attachment to screens has brought forth significant concerns about sleep disruption, sedentary behaviors, and the potential fostering of addictive patterns (Lin et al., 2016).[545]

Simultaneously, the intensification of digital communication platforms, particularly social media, has also been linked with a rise in symptoms of anxiety, depression, and loneliness (Primack et al., 2017).[546] Yet, despite these potential risks, it is essential to acknowledge that technology use does not invariably lead to harm. The digital era's nuances demand a more nuanced understanding and response.

As we look beyond the potential hazards, we find that technology holds substantial promise for mental health support and management. The advent of teletherapy, artificial intelligence-based mental health supports, mental health apps, monitoring tools, digital therapeutics, and online support communities are potential game-changers in mental healthcare.

---

[545] Lin, L. Y., Sidani, J. E., Shensa, A., Radovic, A., Miller, E., Colditz, J. B., ... & Primack, B. A. (2016). Association between social media use and depression among U.S. young adults. Depression and anxiety, 33(4), 323-331. https://doi.org/10.1002/da.22466s

[546] Primack, B. A., Shensa, A., Escobar-Viera, C. G., Barrett, E. L., Sidani, J. E., Colditz, J. B., & James, A. E. (2017). Use of multiple social media platforms and symptoms of depression and anxiety: A nationally-representative study among US young adults. Computers in Human Behavior, 69, 1–9. https://doi.org/10.1016/j.chb.2016.11.013

These digital tools offer increased accessibility, cost-effectiveness, and the convenience of personalized care, making mental health resources more reachable for many who might otherwise be left underserved (Torous et al., 2018).[547]

Furthermore, the utility of technology in mental health is not just limited to therapeutic interventions. The expanding field of computational psychiatry underscores the potential of digital data, from smartphone usage to social media patterns, in predicting mental health states and providing early intervention opportunities (Mohr et al., 2017).[548]

Yet, as we chart these promising waters, we must also tread carefully. There exist vital questions around privacy, data security, and ethical considerations that need our attention as we harness technology for mental health (Martinez-Martin et al., 2018).[549]

The previous chapter discussed technology use and sleep disruption. This chapter explores the intersecting pathways of technology use and misuse and other aspects of mental health.

---

[547] Torous, J., Roberts, L. W. (2018). Needed Innovation in Digital Health and Smartphone Applications for Mental Health Transparency and Trust. JAMA Psychiatry, 75(5), 437–438.
https://doi.org/10.1001/jamapsychiatry.2017.3838

[548] Mohr, D. C., Zhang, M., & Schueller, S. M. (2017). Personal Sensing: Understanding Mental Health Using Ubiquitous Sensors and Machine Learning. Annual Review of Clinical Psychology, 13, 23–47.
https://doi.org/10.1146/annurev-clinpsy-032816-044949

[549] Martinez-Martin, N., Kreitmair, K., & Char, D. (2018). Ethical issues for direct-to-consumer digital psychotherapy apps: addressing accountability, data protection, and consent. JMIR Mental Health, 5(2), e32.

As always, this book is intended for informational purposes. Check with your own healthcare professional to see if any of the strategies discussed are right for you. If you choose to apply them, do it under the care and guidance of a health professional.

Study: Could Social Media Use Increase Depression?[550]

Many students often use social media, which can have many benefits, including positive feelings. A recent study suggests that social media might worsen depressive symptoms.

Who Were The Study Participants?

- There are around 1,787 adults ages 19 to 32 were surveyed about social media use and depression.

- About 50 % of the students were female, and 57% of the participants were white.

What Was Asked In The Study?

- Participants were asked about:

- Total time per day spent on social media

- Social media visits per week

- And a global frequency score based on the Pew Internet Research Questionnaire.

---

[550] https://u.osu.edu/emotionalfitness/2016/03/04/study-could-social-media-use-increase-depression/

- Depressive symptoms were measured by using the PROMIS scale.

How Was Social Media Defined In The Study?

- Social media sites included the use of *Facebook, Twitter, Google+, YouTube, LinkedIn, Instagram, Pinterest, Tumblr, Vine, Snapchat,* and *Reddit.*

What Were The Study Results?

- The study found that social media use was associated with higher scores of depression, even after adjusting for other variables.

- Depressive scores increased with more time spent on social media, ranging from 30-135 minutes daily.

- Depressive scores increased with more sites visited, ranging from 6-17 visits per week.

What Are Some Caveats?

- This study used a survey that tells us about snapshots in time but does not tell us about cause and effect.

- The standard measure of social media use has not been established.

- Other studies have found mixed results[551],[552],[553],[554], and further study is needed.

- Investigators asked about depressive symptoms but not Major depression.

- Various social media sites are working on ways to reach at-risk students who are using social media.[555],[556],[557].

- While this study looked at risks, there may be benefits to using social media as well.

How do you feel after using social media?

Are you feeling depressed?

Are you spending a lot of time on social media?

Are you falling behind in other aspects of your life?

Expanded Knowledge

On a similar note, Lin et al. (2016) shed light on how comparison behavior on social media platforms could impact mental health. Their findings revealed that

---

[551] JelenchickLA, EickhoffJC, Moreno MA. "Facebook depression?" Social networking site use and depression in older adolescents. J Adolesc Heal 2013;52(1):128–130.

[552] Kross E, Verduyn P, Demiralp E, et al. Facebook use predicts declines in subjective well-being in young adults. PLoS One 2013;8(8):e69841.

[553] Moreno MA. Depression and Internet use among older adolescents: an experience sampling approach. Psychology2012;3:743– 748.

[554] Sagioglou C, Greitemeyer T. Facebook's emotional consequences: Why Facebook causes a decrease in mood and why people still use it. Comput Human Behav 2014;35:359–363.

[555] Lin LY, et al. Association Between Social Media use and Depression Among U.S. Young Adults. Depression And Anxiety 00:1–9 (2016).

[556] Tumblr. "Everything Okay?" 2014. Available at: http://www.webcitation.org/6aKw1PTdP.

[557] Facebook. Updates in Facebook Safety. 2015. Available at: http://www.webcitation.org/6aKw1PTdP

individuals frequently comparing themselves with others on social media were more likely to experience depressive feelings.

Going a step further, Keles et al. (2020) delved into the wider implications of social media usage. Their work drew a link between extensive social media engagement, increased anxiety levels, and disturbed sleep. Indeed, participants who invested a lot of time on these platforms reported having disturbed sleep and heightened feelings of anxiety.

These studies illuminate a complex and multi-dimensional relationship between social media usage and its potential mental health implications. There's a mounting body of evidence suggesting that time spent on these platforms might contribute to enhanced feelings of depression, isolation, and anxiety, as well as sleep disturbances.

It's critical to remember that these studies provide correlational data, not proof of causation. The intricate mechanisms and potential mitigating factors underlying this relationship call for more comprehensive research. However, it's also worth mentioning the advantages of social media, such as its role in fostering connectivity and disseminating information, which is especially crucial in an era of increased digital interaction.

Digital Media and Inattention Symptoms[558]

---

[558] https://u.osu.edu/emotionalfitness/2018/08/30/digital-media-and-inattention-symptoms/

While media consumption has many positive benefits, excessive consumption can have negative consequences.

The average American consumer spends about 4.9 hours per day watching TV, 75 minutes on their smartphone, and 62 minutes per day listening to radio.[559] Many people spend most of their workday working on a computer.

TV and video gaming has been associated with ADHD and related symptoms in a review of studies from 1987 to 2011.[560]

A recent study looked at many forms of digital media usage and ADHD-type symptoms.[561]

Who Was Involved In The Study?[562]

- Around 4100 students ages 15 and 16 years were followed for two years.

- Starting baseline and every six months, they were given surveys on digital media usage, inattention, and hyperactivity.

---

[559] https://www.statista.com/topics/1536/media-use/

[560] Nikkelen SW, Valkenburg PM, Huizinga M, Bushman BJ. Media use and ADHD-related behaviors in children and adolescents: a meta-analysis. Dev Psychol. 2014;50(9):2228-2241. doi:10.1037/a0037318

[561] Nikkelen SW, Valkenburg PM, Huizinga M, Bushman BJ. Media use and ADHD-related behaviors in children and adolescents: a meta-analysis. Dev Psychol. 2014;50(9):2228-2241. doi:10.1037/a0037318

[562] Ra CK, Cho J, Stone MD, et al. Association of Digital Media Use With Subsequent Symptoms of Attention-Deficit/Hyperactivity Disorder Among Adolescents. JAMA. 2018;320(3):255-263. doi:10.1001/jama.2018.8931

How Did The Study Define Digital Media?[563]

In this study, digital media usage included using a variety of devices for social media, smartphone usage, streaming media, web browsing, messaging/video chatting, etc.

How Did They Define Frequency Of Digital Media Usage?[564]

High-frequency (many times per day) vs. other frequency levels (0, 1-2 times per week, 1-2 times per day).

What Were The Results?[565]

- Among students with no ADHD symptoms to begin with, those who used digital media at high frequency were more likely to report symptoms of inattention and hyperactivity compared to those who use rarely used digital media.

- The most common high-frequency media activity reported was checking social media.

- Over two years of follow-up, the students who reported no high-frequency media use at baseline were half as likely to have ADHD symptoms across

[563] Ra CK, Cho J, Stone MD, et al. Association of Digital Media Use With Subsequent Symptoms of Attention-Deficit/Hyperactivity Disorder Among Adolescents. JAMA. 2018;320(3):255–263. doi:10.1001/jama.2018.8931
[564] Ra CK, Cho J, Stone MD, et al. Association of Digital Media Use With Subsequent Symptoms of Attention-Deficit/Hyperactivity Disorder Among Adolescents. JAMA. 2018;320(3):255–263. doi:10.1001/jama.2018.8931
[565] Ra CK, Cho J, Stone MD, et al. Association of Digital Media Use With Subsequent Symptoms of Attention-Deficit/Hyperactivity Disorder Among Adolescents. JAMA. 2018;320(3):255–263. doi:10.1001/jama.2018.8931

follow-ups vs. students who reported 14 high-frequency activities.

What Are Some Caveats?

- This is a large study of young adults followed over two years.

- They looked at many participants with little or no ADHD symptoms to begin with.

- While this study shows an association between digital media usage and ADHD symptoms, it does not necessarily show that one causes the other.

- This study was done on adolescents, which limits the applicability of results to other age groups.

- Further study is needed.

What Are Some Negative Consequences Of Excessive Screen Time?

Excessive screen time can[566]:

- Worse executive functioning.

- Increase aggressive behavior due to violent media content.

- Elevate depression risk.

- Decrease sleep quality.

---

[566] Reid Chassiakos Y., Radesky J., Christakis D., et al: Children and Adolescents and Digital Media. Elk Grove Village (IL): The American Academy of Pediatrics, 2016.

MENTAL HEALTH FOR COLLEGE STUDENTS

Some individuals may also spend less time sleeping because of screen usage; which can worsen daytime fatigue and productivity.

Other studies show that screen time can also worsen the physical health of adults in many different ways.

Oftentimes, excessive media consumption can take time away from other self-care activities.

Are There Some Useful Ideas Around Media Usage?

American Academy of Pediatrics guidelines on media use for children and adolescents advise to[567][568]:

- Prioritize activities that promote executive functioning and well-being, including

- Sleep

- Physical activity

- Distraction-free homework

- And positive interactions with family and friends.

- Encourages discussions about pro-social uses of media, digital citizenship, misinformation, and persuasion awareness—are relevant to the cognitive and emotional reactions to digital media of adolescents.

---

[567] Radesky J. Digital Media and Symptoms of Attention-Deficit/Hyperactivity Disorder in Adolescents. JAMA.2018;320(3):1–2. doi:10.1001/jama.2018.8932

[568] Media Use in School-Aged Children and Adolescents. COUNCIL ON COMMUNICATIONS AND MEDIA. Pediatrics Oct 2016, e20162592; DOI: 10.1542/peds.2016-2592

Consider periodic breaks and rules around how often and how much media you consume electively.

- Consider limiting elective screen time to less than 2 hours per day.[569] Focus on quality instead of quantity.

- Some people find it useful to use a timer.

- There are apps that can help you limit excessive screen time.

- In some cases excessive media consumption may be a red flag for mental health concerns.

Any Other Thoughts On Media Consumption?

- While there are no specific guidelines for adults, if most of your day studying or working in front of a screen, choosing to spend leisurely time spent on other electronic devices, phones, tablets etc. may not balance your life or your brain. It may lead to increased stress and fatigue.

- How much time are you spending on electronic devices?

- Is this making you productive or just busy?

- How do you feel during and afterward?

- How is this impacting your mental health, physical health, productivity, and academics?

---

[569] https://www.nhlbi.nih.gov/health/educational/wecan/reduce-screen-time/index.htm

- Have you set limits on **elective** media consumption, and should you cut back?

- Should you be doing other activities to balance your life, such as sleep, exercise, cooking nutritious food, spending quality time with others, etc.?

Expanded Knowledge

While opening a world of knowledge and opportunities, the ceaseless hum of digital connectivity has cast a complex, rippling shadow on our mental and physical well-being. This is particularly important for young people as their brains and bodies are still developing.

Complementing the findings above, the insightful research by Przybylski and Weinstein (2017)[570] attempts to strike a balance. Their work acknowledges the potential benefits of moderate digital technology use in a hyper-connected world yet serves as a cautionary note.

Their observations align with the American Academy of Pediatrics recommendation, indicating the ceiling for recreational screen time to be a two-hour mark per day for adolescents, any leap beyond which may start stirring the waters of mental well-being. Recreational screen time is not time doing homework, or related to one's

[570] Przybylski, A. K., & Weinstein, N. (2017). A Large-Scale Test of the Goldilocks Hypothesis: Quantifying the Relations Between Digital-Screen Use and the Mental Well-Being of Adolescents. Psychological Science, 28(2), 204-215. DOI: 10.1177/0956797616678438

RYAN PATEL DO, FAPA

occupation, though this relationship needs further investigation.

Advancing the dialogue to sleep health, a critical determinant of overall wellness, Hale and Guan's systematic review (2015)[571] shows that media use at bedtime is intricately tied to a decrease in sleep quantity, echoing the unseen nocturnal costs of digital immersion.

Further, Kim et al.'s pioneering investigation (2020)[572] showed a negative association between smartphone use duration and self-reported physical health, and an emergence of physical health issues like musculoskeletal discomfort.

In the rapidly evolving landscape of digital media research, these findings present a balanced view. They call for the judicious use of digital tools and caution against the excessive consumption that may open doors to an array of mental and physical health concerns. Unravelling these threads of research, it becomes clear that the quest for digital balance, particularly in the young adult population, holds a key to a healthier future.

Blue Blockers And Other Ways To Reduce Electronics-Induced Sleep Disruption And Daytime Tiredness[573]

[571] Hale, L., & Guan, S. (2015). Screen time and sleep among school-aged children and adolescents: a systematic literature review. Sleep Medicine Reviews, 21, 50-58. DOI: 10.1016/j.smrv.2014.07.007

[572] Kim, S. Y., Kim, M. S., Park, B., Kim, J. H., & Choi, H. G. (2020). Lack of sleep is associated with internet use for leisure. PloS One, 13(1), e0191713. DOI: 10.1371/journal.pone.0191713

[573] https://u.osu.edu/emotionalfitness/2015/07/17/blue-blockers-and-other-ways-to-reduce-electronics-induced-sleep-disruption-and-daytime-tiredness/

Blue spectrum light from electronics suppresses melatonin several hours after use[574][575] and disrupts your circadian (sleep-wake cycle) clock.[576] This impacts sleep quality and daytime tiredness.[577] Sleep disruption can also impact anxiety, depression, and many other health conditions.[578]

So it may be worth avoiding the use of electronic devices such as computers, TVs, tablets, smartphones, etc., 1-3 hours before bedtime.

Some suggest replacing exposure to bright light bulbs with dim light bulbs around bedtime[579] may also be helpful. There are even light bulbs that do not emit blue light.

---

[574] Brainard GC, Hanifin JP, Greeson JM, Byrne B, Glickman G, Gerner E, et al.
Action spectrum for melatonin regulation in humans: evidence for a novel circadian photoreceptor. J Neurosci 2001;21(16):6405–12 [August 15, PMID:
11487664].

[575] Thapan K, Arendt J, Skene DJ. An action spectrum for melatonin suppression: evidence for a novel non-rod, non-cone photoreceptor system in humans. J Physiol 2001;535(Pt 1):261–7 [August 15, PMID: 11507175].

[576] Smith MR, Revell VL, Eastman CI. Phase advancing the human circadian clock with blue-enriched polychromatic light. Sleep Med 2008 [September 18, PMID: 18805055].

[577] Fossum IN, et al. The Association Between Use of Electronic Media in Bed Before Going to Sleep and Insomnia Symptoms, Daytime Sleepiness, Morningness, and Chronotype. Behavioral Sleep Medicine. Volume 12, Issue 5, 2014, pages 343- 357. Published online: 14 Jul 2014. DOI: 10.1080/15402002.2013.819468.

[578] http://sleepfoundation.org/sleep-disorders-problems

[579] Kayumov L, et al. Blocking Low-Wavelength Light Prevents Nocturnal Melatonin Suppression with No Adverse Effect on Performance during Simulated Shift Work. The Journal of Clinical Endocrinology & Metabolism 90(5):2755–2761.

What If I Need To Use Electronics At Bedtime?

Sometimes, it may be necessary to be on the computer, TV, smartphone, etc., right before bedtime. Blue blockers may help prevent sleep disruption from electronics.

How Do Blue Blockers Work?

They block blue light emitted by electronic devices. Thus, melatonin is not disrupted.[580]

What Are Some Examples Of Blue Light Blockers?

Some examples include blue blocker eye glasses, software programs that prevent your device from emitting blue light, plastic filter screens that are placed on top of the screens to block blue light, and light bulbs that do not emit blue light. You can search for *"blue light blockers" "blue light filters"*, *"bedtime reading software"* etc. in a search engine, or in an app store.

Do Blue Blockers Work?

Small studies show blue blockers work to prevent melatonin disruption and improve the quality of sleep and mood.

For example, 20 subjects were randomized to use either blue-blocking glasses or non-blue-blocking

---

[580] Kayumov L, et al. Blocking Low-Wavelength Light Prevents Nocturnal Melatonin Suppression with No Adverse Effect on Performance during Simulated Shift Work. The Journal of Clinical Endocrinology & Metabolism 90(5):2755–2761.

glasses 3 hours before bedtime over a two weeks period.[581]

What Did The Results Show?

Those who used blue-blocking glasses reported better sleep quality and mood.

Words Of Caution

- You still need to be mindful of getting enough sleep—getting four or five hours of quality sleep when you need eight will still leave you tired.

- Blue-blocking methods may not help with your sleep if your device usage is overly entertaining or emotionally intense.

- You still need to address other causes, such as the use of caffeine, nicotine, alcohol use, etc.

- This is still a relatively new terrain, and further research is needed.

Are you sleeping poorly?

Are you tired during the day?

Are electronic devices interfering with your sleep?

Can you cut down your usage before bedtime?

Can blue blockers help you?

[581] Burkhart K1, Phelps JR. Amber lenses to block blue light and improve sleep: a randomized trial. Chronobiol Int. 2009 Dec;26(8):1602-12. doi: 10.3109/07420520903523719.

Expanded Knowledge

Digging deeper into the world of technological adaptations, Gringras et al. (2015)[582] unraveled the potential of an *"electronic sundown."* Their study indicated that employing a one-hour-long "Twilight" setting on devices specifically engineered to minimize blue-green light emissions might serve as a shield against the nighttime melatonin onset disruption commonly induced by these harmful rays, especially among the adolescent population.

However, for those wrestling with chronic sleep ailments, the path to restorative sleep may be more complicated. An eye-opening study by Casper et al. (2015)[583] underscored that the nightly use of Light Emitting e-Readers could erect formidable barriers to sleep, including prolonging sleep latency, pushing back the circadian rhythm, quelling melatonin release, reducing the crispness of morning alertness, and encumbering cognitive faculties. The implications of this study amplify the urgency of implementing a mindful bedtime tech routine, even when blue-blocking tools are at play.

---

[582] Gringras P, Middleton B, Skene DJ, Revell VL. (2015). Bigger, Brighter, Bluer-Better? Current Light-Emitting Devices – Adverse Sleep Properties and Preventative Strategies. Frontiers in Public Health, 3, 233. https://doi.org/10.3389/fpubh.2015.00233

[583] Casper DS, Caruso CC, et al. (2015). Evening use of light-emitting eReaders negatively affects sleep, circadian timing, and next-morning alertness. Proceedings of the National Academy of Sciences, 112(4), 1232–1237. https://doi.org/10.1073/pnas.1418490112

As we journey deeper into the nuances of sleep disruption, it is essential to cast light on additional nocturnal nemeses beyond blue light exposure. The research of Chang et al. (2015)[584] highlights these often-overlooked antagonists of sound sleep, revealing the disruptive role of caffeine and alcohol, the potential turmoil induced by late-night snacking, and the sleep-interfering effects of physical activity in close proximity to bedtime. See the previous chapter on strategies to improve sleep.

Despite what is already known about the impact of technology use and screen time on our sleep, further research is warranted.

Smartphone Apps for Mental Health[585]

Most people today are familiar with apps for smartphones. There are apps for many different purposes, including mental health. In fact, in 2015, mental health apps made up almost a third of disease-specific apps in app marketplaces.[586]

Some but not all apps are evidence-based, researched, and known to work, and some other apps are based on evidence-based skills.

---

[584] Chang AM, Aeschbach D, Duffy JF, Czeisler CA. (2015). Evening use of light-emitting eReaders negatively affects sleep, circadian timing, and next-morning alertness. Proceedings of the National Academy of Sciences, 112(4), 1232-1237. DOI: 10.1073/pnas.1418490112

[585] https://u.osu.edu/emotionalfitness/2017/05/17/smartphone-apps-for-mental-health/

[586] IMS Institute for Healthcare Informatics. (2015). Patient adoption of mHealth: Use, evidence and remaining barriers to mainstream acceptance. Parsippany, NJ: IMS Institute for Healthcare Informatics.

A 2017 meta review of studies looked at 190 individual papers researching 147 unique digital health tools and found that there may be some benefit of using apps for depression and anxiety but unclear benefit for other disorders at the time of publication. They also found research and method limitations for many studies.[587]

A recent study looked at an app called *"Virtual Hope Box"* (VHB).[588]

Who Was Studied?[589]

- Around 118 U.S. service veterans receiving mental health treatment and had a recent history of suicidal ideation.

- They were divided into two groups.

- One group received mental health treatment as usual, supplemented with the VHB app, and another group received treatment as usual, supplemented with printed materials about coping with suicidality over a 12-week period.

---

[587] IMS Institute for Healthcare Informatics. (2015). Patient adoption of mHealth: Use, evidence and remaining barriers to mainstream acceptance. Parsippany, NJ: IMS Institute for Healthcare Informatics.

[588] Nigel E. Bush, Ph.D., Derek J. Smolenski, Ph.D., Lauren M. Denneson, Ph.D., Holly B. Williams, B.A., Elissa K. Thomas, L.P.N., C.C.R.C., Steven K. Dobscha, M.D. A Virtual Hope Box: Randomized Controlled Trial of a Smartphone App for Emotional Regulation and Coping With Distress. Psychiatric Services 2017; 68:330–336; doi: 10.1176/appi.ps.201600283.

[589] Nigel E. Bush, Ph.D., Derek J. Smolenski, Ph.D., Lauren M. Denneson, Ph.D., Holly B. Williams, B.A., Elissa K. Thomas, L.P.N., C.C.R.C., Steven K. Dobscha, M.D. A Virtual Hope Box: Randomized Controlled Trial of a Smartphone App for Emotional Regulation and Coping With Distress. Psychiatric Services 2017; 68:330–336; doi: 10.1176/appi.ps.201600283.

What Was Measured?[590]

Using validated scales, the study authors measured coping, suicidal ideation, reasons for living, perceived stress, and interpersonal needs at various points of the study.

What Were The Results?[591]

- Participants using the virtual hope box app showed improvements in their ability to cope with unpleasant emotions and thoughts over time.

- Users found the app helpful for relaxation and distraction or inspiration when feeling distressed, when emotions were overwhelming, or when they felt like hurting themselves.

- Participants found it easy to use, helpful in dealing with stress and emotional difficulties, likely to use it in the future, and would recommend it to others.

---

[590] Nigel E. Bush, Ph.D., Derek J. Smolenski, Ph.D., Lauren M. Denneson, Ph.D., Holly B. Williams, B.A., Elissa K. Thomas, L.P.N., C.C.R.C., Steven K. Dobscha, M.D. A Virtual Hope Box: Randomized Controlled Trial of a Smartphone App for Emotional Regulation and Coping With Distress. Psychiatric Services 2017; 68:330–336; doi: 10.1176/appi.ps.201600283.

[591] Nigel E. Bush, Ph.D., Derek J. Smolenski, Ph.D., Lauren M. Denneson, Ph.D., Holly B. Williams, B.A., Elissa K. Thomas, L.P.N., C.C.R.C., Steven K. Dobscha, M.D. A Virtual Hope Box: Randomized Controlled Trial of a Smartphone App for Emotional Regulation and Coping With Distress. Psychiatric Services 2017; 68:330–336; doi: 10.1176/appi.ps.201600283.

What Are Some Caveats?

- This is a small study and may not be applicable to everyone.

- There are many apps for mental health, but research in this area is limited.

- Newer apps are being introduced frequently.

- This is a new field of research, and as we learn more, study designs and outcome measures are being improved upon.

- Not all the apps are free.

- Mental health apps do not take the place of professional treatment.

- Your mental health professional may be helpful in considering the right app mental health for you.

- Many apps use evidence-based techniques, such as apps for cognitive behavior therapy, relaxation skills, prolonged exposure, dialectical behavior therapy, mindfulness-based apps, etc.

How much time are you spending on your phone?

How are apps, in general, impacting your mental health?

Which app is helping you and which is not?

Expanded Knowledge

As noted above and in the chapter 5, virtual hope box can be useful for a variety of mental health conditions. In my experience, other apps that are extensively studied and can benefit a variety of mental health conditions include Headspace and Calm.

Electronic Gaming and Mental Health[592]

Electronic gaming is very common among young adults and comes in many forms, including smartphones, tablets, computers, game consoles, etc. By some estimates, the market size for electronic gaming is almost the same size as the movie industry. Almost 90% of people ages 16 to 24 play video games[593], and almost half are at risk of video game addiction.[594]

While many adults engage in gaming in healthy ways, gaming addiction has been linked to insomnia, anxiety, depression, and stress among college students.[595]

One study looked at gaming addiction and depression.[596]

---

[592] https://u.osu.edu/emotionalfitness/2018/10/30/gaming-and-mental-health/

[593] Brand J. (2012). Digital Australia (2012). National Research Prepared by Bond University for the Interactive Games and Entertainment Association. School of Communication and Media, Faculty of Humanities and Social Sciences, Bond University.

[594] Hussain Z, Griffiths MD, Baguley T. Online gaming addiction: classification, prediction and associated risk factors. Addict Res Theory. 2012;20:359-371.

[595] Younes F, Halawi G, Jabbour H, et al. Internet addiction and relationships with insomnia, anxiety, Depression, stress and self-esteem in university students: a cross-sectional designed study. PLoS One. 2016;11:e0161126

[596] Catherine So-Kum Tang, PhD, Yee Woen Koh, PhD, and YiQun Gan, PhD Asia Pacific Journal of Public Health Vol 29, Issue 8, pp. 673 – 682 First Published November 30, 2017 https://doi.org/10.1177/1010539517739558

Who Was Studied?

Around 3,267 undergraduate students from the United States, China, and Singapore.[597]

What Was Studied?

Rates of addictions to Internet use, online gaming, and online social networking, and their association with depressive symptoms.[598]

What Were The Results?

Around 31% of male students were addicted to online gaming, compared to 13% of female students (OR = 0.522, 95% CI = 0.440–0.620)[599]

In contrast, 37.3% of female students were addicted to social networking compared to 27.8% of male students (OR = 1.543, 95% CI = 1.329–1.791).[600]

Regarding Depression Rates

- Among students with online gaming addiction, depression rates were 65.5% for students in the

---

[597] Catherine So-Kum Tang, PhD, Yee Woen Koh, PhD, and YiQun Gan, PhD Asia Pacific Journal of Public Health Vol 29, Issue 8, pp. 673 – 682 First Published November 30, 2017 https://doi.org/10.1177/1010539517739558

[598] Catherine So-Kum Tang, PhD, Yee Woen Koh, PhD, and YiQun Gan, PhD Asia Pacific Journal of Public Health Vol 29, Issue 8, pp. 673 – 682 First Published November 30, 2017 https://doi.org/10.1177/1010539517739558

[599] Catherine So-Kum Tang, PhD, Yee Woen Koh, PhD, and YiQun Gan, PhD Asia Pacific Journal of Public Health Vol 29, Issue 8, pp. 673 – 682 First Published November 30, 2017 https://doi.org/10.1177/1010539517739558

[600] Catherine So-Kum Tang, PhD, Yee Woen Koh, PhD, and YiQun Gan, PhD Asia Pacific Journal of Public Health Vol 29, Issue 8, pp. 673 – 682 First Published November 30, 2017 https://doi.org/10.1177/1010539517739558

United States, 70.8% for China, and 69.6% for Singapore.[601]

- Among students with internet addiction, depression rates were 76.5% for students in the United States, 88.9% for China, and 75.9% for Singapore.[602]

- Among students with online social networking addiction, depression rates were 68.8% for students in the United States, 76% for China, and 71% for Singapore.[603]

What Are Some Signs Of Internet Gaming Disorder?

While there are no uniform criteria, some signs could include[604][605]:

- Preoccupation. (The individual thinks about previous gaming activity or anticipates playing the next game; internet gaming becomes the dominant activity in daily life.)

---

[601] Catherine So-Kum Tang, PhD, Yee Woen Koh, PhD, and YiQun Gan, PhD Asia Pacific Journal of Public Health Vol 29, Issue 8, pp. 673 – 682 First Published November 30, 2017 https://doi.org/10.1177/1010539517739558

[602] Catherine So-Kum Tang, PhD, Yee Woen Koh, PhD, and YiQun Gan, PhD Asia Pacific Journal of Public Health Vol 29, Issue 8, pp. 673 – 682 First Published November 30, 2017 https://doi.org/10.1177/1010539517739558

[603] Catherine So-Kum Tang, PhD, Yee Woen Koh, PhD, and YiQun Gan, PhD Asia Pacific Journal of Public Health Vol 29, Issue 8, pp. 673 – 682 First Published November 30, 2017 https://doi.org/10.1177/1010539517739558

[604] American Psychiatric Association: Diagnostic and StatisticalManual of Mental Disorders, 5th ed. Washington, DC, American Psychiatric Publishing, 2013Section III ("Emerging Measures and Models") of DSM-5 (1, pp. 795– 796).

[605] Andrew K. Przybylski, Ph.D., Netta Weinstein, Ph.D., Kou Murayama, Ph.D. Internet Gaming Disorder: Investigating the Clinical Relevance of a New Phenomenon. Am J Psychiatry 2017; 174:230–236; doi: 10.1176/appi.ajp.2016.16020224.

RYAN PATEL DO, FAPA

- Experienced withdrawal symptoms when internet gaming is taken away. (These symptoms are typically described as irritability, anxiety, or sadness, but there are no physical signs of pharmacological withdrawal.)

- Developed Tolerance—the need to spend more time engaged in games.

- Unsuccessful attempts to control the participation in gaming.

- Continued excessive use despite knowledge of psychosocial problems.

- Mislead/deceive family members, therapists, or others regarding the amount of gaming.

- Use as an escape or relieve a negative mood (e.g., feelings of helplessness, guilt, anxiety).

- Loss of interest in previous hobbies and entertainment as a result of, and with the exception of, gaming.

- Jeopardized or lost a significant relationship, job, or educational or career opportunity because of participation in electronic gaming.

What Are Some Caveats?

- Further study is needed in the area of internet and gaming addiction.

- To learn more about internet addiction, click here.

- While this study shows that males were more likely to have gaming addiction and female students were more likely to have internet addiction, newer research indicates that this gap appears to be narrowing.

Expanded Knowledge

In the vast expanse of electronic entertainment, video gaming emerges as a force of formidable influence, casting complex shadows on the landscape of mental health. From its warm glow of positive engagement to its darker corners marked by potential disorder, the impact of this technological pastime presents a multifaceted picture.

Gaining recognition in the World Health Organization's International Classification of Diseases (ICD-11)[606], the phenomenon of *'video game addiction'* or *'gaming disorder'* has risen to prominence as a subject of significant concern in contemporary mental health discourse.

Within the grip of video game addiction, the terrain of mental health is frequently marred by a slew of adversities. In a study led by Anderson et al. (2018),[607] the researchers embarked on a journey through the digital lives of 3,000 adolescents in the United States.

From this expedition emerged the disquieting statistic that 8.4% of the surveyed population met the DSM-5

[606] World Health Organization. (2019). International Statistical Classification of Diseases and Related Health Problems (11th Revision). Retrieved from https://icd.who.int/browse11/l-m/en

[607] Anderson, E. L., Steen, E., & Stavropoulos, V. (2018). Internet use and Problematic Internet Use: A systematic review of longitudinal research trends in adolescence and emergent adulthood. International Journal of Adolescence and Youth, 22(4), 430-454. DOI: 10.1080/02673843.2013.787318

criteria for Internet Gaming Disorder. Within this group, depression, anxiety, and symptoms of ADHD were more common than among those without internet gaming disorder.

Yet, the picture painted by Przybylski et al. (2017)[608] introduces a lighter shade to the complex canvas of electronic gaming. Their exploration of *'digital screen time'* revealed that, when moderated, screen time could gently illuminate the path to enhanced adolescent wellbeing. However, the study also highlighted the stark contrast between excessive gaming and screen time, both casting long, negative impact on well-being outcomes.

The mounting concern over the prevalence and potential detrimental impacts of gaming addiction highlights the importance of keen observation and prompt action. The American Psychiatric Association echoes this sentiment[609] by urging vigilance towards signs like gaming preoccupation, uncontrolled gaming habits, and persistence in gaming despite negative repercussions.

Further research is the compass guiding us toward a comprehensive understanding of gaming addiction's causes, effects, and optimal treatments. Working with a

[608] Przybylski, A. K., Weinstein, N., & Murayama, K. (2017). Internet Gaming Disorder: Investigating the Clinical Relevance of a New Phenomenon. American Journal of Psychiatry, 174(3), 230-236. DOI: 10.1176/appi.ajp.2016.16020224
[609] American Psychiatric Association. (2013). Diagnostic and statistical manual of mental disorders (5th ed.). Arlington, VA: American Psychiatric Publishing.

mental health professional would be helpful for those with concerns about potential video game addiction.

Technology, Electronics, and Mental Health[610]

With online classes, distance learning, homework time, and remote work, people are increasingly spending more time with electronic devices and technology than in the past. This increased screen time for work and school may cause previously used screen time for leisure activities not as restorative, as this may increase total screen time and sedentary behavior.

Zhai and colleague's review of 24 studies shows that too much screen time (> 6 hours per day) can impact depression.[611] Similarly, a review of 31 studies concluded that sedentary behavior may also impact anxiety.[612]

More devices are now available than ever before: computers, televisions, tablet PCs, smartphones, smart watches, etc.

While healthy technology use can have benefits of productivity, social connection, entertainment, and improved health, unhealthy technology use can worsen our distraction, isolate us socially, increase stress,

---

[610] https://u.osu.edu/emotionalfitness/2020/12/11/593/

[611] Zhai L, Zhang Y, Zhang D. Sedentary behaviour and the risk of depression: a meta-analysis. Br J Sports Med. 2015 Jun;49(11):705-9. doi: 10.1136/bjsports-2014-093613. Epub 2014 Sep 2. PMID: 25183627.

[612] Stanczykiewicz B, Banik A, Knoll N, Keller J, Hohl DH, Rosińczuk J, Luszczynska A. Sedentary behaviors and anxiety among children, adolescents and adults: a systematic review and meta-analysis. BMC Public Health. 2019 Apr 30;19(1):459. doi: 10.1186/s12889-019-6715-3. PMID: 31039760; PMCID: PMC6492316.

expose us to negative social influences, and negatively impact our health.

The American Psychological Association[613] offers the following strategies to use technology in healthy ways:

1. **Avoid distracted driving[614]:** APA advises us to turn off notifications and place our phones out of reach when driving.

2. **Avoid electronic devices before bedtime.[615]** Previous research showed blue light from electronic devices used at bedtime can impact sleep,[616] and stressful material on electronic devices can also interfere with our ability to fall asleep.[617]

3. When smartphone users turned off smartphone notifications, they reported lower levels of inattention and hyperactivity than they did during the weeks when their notifications were

---

[613] Ballard D. Connected and content: Managing healthy technology use. American Psychological Association. https://www.apa.org/topics/healthy-technology-use

[614] Ballard D. Connected and content: Managing healthy technology use. American Psychological Association. https://www.apa.org/topics/healthy-technology-use

[615] Ballard D. Connected and content: Managing healthy technology use. American Psychological Association. https://www.apa.org/topics/healthy-technology-use

[616] https://u.osu.edu/emotionalfitness/2015/07/17/blue-blockers-and-other-ways-to-reduce-electronics-induced-sleep-disruption-and-daytime-tiredness/

[617] Ballard D. Connected and content: Managing healthy technology use. American Psychological Association. https://www.apa.org/topics/healthy-technology-use

turned on.[618][619] Frequent notifications were also associated with lower levels of productivity, social connectedness, and psychological well-being.[620][621]

4. **Schedule time for email when possible.** People who checked email continuously reported more stress than those who checked email only three times per day.[622][623]

5. **Manage expectations.**[624] If possible, schedule time to check messages, email, notifications, etc., and if possible, let others (family members, boss, etc.) know how often you do this to help manage their expectations.

---

[618] Ballard D. Connected and content: Managing healthy technology use. American Psychological Association. https://www.apa.org/topics/healthy-technology-use
[619] Kostadin Kushlev, Jason Proulx, and Elizabeth W. Dunn. 2016. "Silence Your Phones": Smartphone Notifications Increase Inattention and Hyperactivity Symptoms. In Proceedings of the 2016 CHI Conference on Human Factors in Computing Systems (CHI '16). Association for Computing Machinery, New York, NY, USA, 1011–1020. DOI:https://doi.org/10.1145/2858036.2858359
[620] Ballard D. Connected and content: Managing healthy technology use. American Psychological Association. https://www.apa.org/topics/healthy-technology-use
[621] Kostadin Kushlev, Jason Proulx, and Elizabeth W. Dunn. 2016. "Silence Your Phones": Smartphone Notifications Increase Inattention and Hyperactivity Symptoms. In Proceedings of the 2016 CHI Conference on Human Factors in Computing Systems (CHI '16). Association for Computing Machinery, New York, NY, USA, 1011–1020. DOI:https://doi.org/10.1145/2858036.2858359
[622] Ballard D. Connected and content: Managing healthy technology use. American Psychological Association. https://www.apa.org/topics/healthy-technology-use
[623] Kostadin Kushlev, Elizabeth W. Dunn, Checking email less frequently reduces stress, Computers in Human Behavior, Volume 43, 2015, Pages 220-228, ISSN 0747-5632, https://doi.org/10.1016/j.chb.2014.11.005.
[624] Ballard D. Connected and content: Managing healthy technology use. American Psychological Association. https://www.apa.org/topics/healthy-technology-use

6. **While social media can help us connect with others, it can also impact** feelings of sadness or depression[625][626] ; other people may find it helpful. Consider how social media use makes you feel and adjust your use accordingly.

7. **Face-to-face interactions** are important for mental health. The 2017 Stress in America survey found that 44 percent of people who check email, texts, and social media often or constantly report feeling disconnected from their family, even when they're together.[627] When you're with friends and family, make an effort to unplug: consider silencing your phone and putting it out of reach at dinnertime or during family outings.[628]

8. **Disconnect**: Instead of grabbing your phone during spare time, disconnect from electronics to reflect, recharge, relax, and collect yourself.[629]

---

[625] Ballard D. Connected and content: Managing healthy technology use. American Psychological Association. https://www.apa.org/topics/healthy-technology-use

[626] Lin LY, Sidani JE, Shensa A, Radovic A, Miller E, Colditz JB, Hoffman BL, Giles LM, Primack BA. ASSOCIATION BETWEEN SOCIAL MEDIA USE AND DEPRESSION AMONG U.S. YOUNG ADULTS. Depress Anxiety. 2016 Apr;33(4):323-31. doi: 10.1002/da.22466. Epub 2016 Jan 19. PMID: 26783723; PMCID: PMC4853817.

[627] Ballard D. Connected and content: Managing healthy technology use. American Psychological Association. https://www.apa.org/topics/healthy-technology-use

[628] Ballard D. Connected and content: Managing healthy technology use. American Psychological Association. https://www.apa.org/topics/healthy-technology-use

[629] Ballard D. Connected and content: Managing healthy technology use. American Psychological Association. https://www.apa.org/topics/healthy-technology-use

To counteract excessive screen time and sedentary behavior from remote work/learning, consider the following:

- Periodic breaks away from the screen, even a few minutes per hour, may help.

- Stretching or walking during these breaks may be helpful.

- Instead of mindless *"infinite"* scrolling, consider your goal before starting a device or program.

- Consider time outside, in nature and other leisure activities for mental health.

- Exercise and playing sports can also help address the negative mental health effects of excessive sedentary behavior and screen time.

Expanded Knowledge

As you are seeing, the narrative of screen time and mental health is complex. Twenge and Campbell (2018)[630] showed that adolescents using electronic devices and social media reported more mental health concerns than their counterparts engrossed in non-screen activities.

---

[630] Twenge, J. M., & Campbell, W. K. (2018). Associations between screen time and lower psychological well-being among children and adolescents: Evidence from a population-based study. Preventive Medicine Reports, 12, 271-283. DOI: 10.1016/j.pmedr.2018.10.003

In a comprehensive meta-analysis, Teychenne et al. (2015)[631] found a correlation between the sedentary behavior inherent in screen time and an elevated risk of anxiety.

However, the story of technology use and mental health is not all doom and gloom. The digital world, when used judiciously, can be a fertile ground for fostering positive factors such as learning a skill, solving a problem, social connection, entertainment, humor, knowledge, creativity, etc. Navigating the digital landscape, the potential adverse effects of prolonged screen time call for prudent strategies. Researchers Harris et al. (2019)[632] present a toolkit: scheduled breaks, periodic physical activities, mindfulness exercises to anchor oneself in reality, and a deliberate prioritization of face-to-face social interactions where feasible. Furthermore, they highlight the importance of mindful engagement with electronic devices, suggesting that defining clear goals for usage before using them might allow users to exert control over their screen time and its influence on their mental health, as opposed to letting screen time control them.

Elections and Mental Health[633]

---

[631] Teychenne, M., Costigan, S. A., & Parker, K. (2015). The association between sedentary behaviour and risk of anxiety: a systematic review. BMC Public Health, 15(1), 513. DOI: 10.1186/s12889-015-1843-x

[632] Harris, C., Straker, L., & Pollock, C. (2019). A Socio-ecological Approach to Understanding the Mediators of Office Workers' Sitting Time: A Cross-sectional Analysis. Journal of Physical Activity and Health, 16(2), 106-112. DOI: 10.1123/jpah.2017-0654

[633] https://u.osu.edu/emotionalfitness/2020/09/02/elections-and-mental-health/

In the months leading up to the election, a 2019 survey of 3,617 participants showed that 45% of U.S. adults identified the 2020 presidential election as a significant stressor vs. 52% of adults who reported the 2016 presidential election as a significant source of stress.[634]

As of the summer of 2020, 77% of Democrat and 62% of Republican survey participants identified the current political climate as a significant source of stress in their lives.[635]

As the presidential election nears, this number may be even higher.

What Are Some Strategies To Manage Election-Related Stress?

The American Psychological Association[636] offers the following strategies:

- Stay informed, but know your limits[637]:

- Monitor how you feel after news consumption. Preoccupation with national events and interference with your daily life may be a sign to cut back on your news intake and limit social media discussions.

- Consider scheduling a short block of time in the morning and one in the evening to catch up on

---

[634] American Psychological Association (2019). Stress in America: Stress and Current Events. Stress in America™ Survey. Accessed August 2019.
[635] https://www.apa.org/news/press/releases/stress/2020/stress-in-america-covid-july.pdf
[636] https://www.apa.org/topics/stress-political-change
[637] https://www.apa.org/topics/stress-political-change

the news without checking for every new update during the day.

- During *"digital breaks,"* take time to focus on something enjoyable, such as a hobby, exercising, or spending time with family and friends.

- Find commonalities with others[638]:

- If political differences arise with others, instead of heated discussions, consider hearing the other person's story and look for commonalities within your views.

- (Respectfully validating someone else does not mean you have to agree with them).

- If calm and constructive conversation is difficult, it may be best to disengage from the conversation.

- Find meaningful ways to get involved in your community[639]:

- This could be through local organizations, city council or town hall meetings, local politics, etc. Sometimes, taking active steps to address your concerns can lessen feelings of stress.

- Seek solace[640]:

- Identify organizations in your community that provide emotional and spiritual support. These

[638] https://www.apa.org/topics/stress-political-change
[639] https://www.apa.org/topics/stress-political-change
[640] https://www.apa.org/topics/stress-political-change

could be faith-based or non-faith-based organizations.

- Consider meditation, progressive relaxation, or mindfulness.

- Take care of yourself[641]:

- Exercise.

- Listen to your favorite music.

- Spend time with close family and friends.

- Prioritize getting enough sleep and eating healthy foods.

- Avoid ineffective coping mechanisms such as alcohol and substance use.

Other Thoughts:

- Consider implementing healthy coping strategies that helped you cope with past stressful times in your life.

- Try the new healthy coping strategies mentioned above.

Expanded Knowledge

Navigating the turbulent waters of political events, particularly the whirlwind of elections, the ripples on our mental health landscape are palpable. Holman, Garfin,

---

[641] https://www.apa.org/topics/stress-political-change

and Silver (2014)[642] traced the undercurrents of these influences, unveiling a direct correlation between exposure to politically charged stressors and the subsequent manifestation of stress-related symptoms.

As election fever mounts, the world is awash with a tide of politically tinted information from the ubiquitous channels of news outlets and social media. This deluge, as Lin, Broström, Griffiths, and Pakpour (2020)[643] discerned, can churn the sea of emotions, instigating *'election stress disorder,'* as the relentless onslaught of social media precipitates heightened stress levels.

Political conversations, often simmering with fervor, have the potential to fan the flames of interpersonal discord and amplify stress levels. Yet, as Vezzali, Capozza, Stathi, and Giovannini (2012)[644], engaging in conversations embedded with empathy and focused on shared values can function as a soothing antidote, helping to alleviate the stress from political disagreements.

[642] Holman, E. A., Garfin, D. R., & Silver, R. C. (2014). Media's role in broadcasting acute stress following the Boston Marathon bombings. Proceedings of the National Academy of Sciences, 111(1), 93-98. DOI: 10.1073/pnas.1316265110

[643] Lin, C. Y., Broström, A., Griffiths, M. D., & Pakpour, A. H. (2020). Investigating mediated effects of fear of COVID-19 and COVID-19 misunderstanding in the association between problematic social media use, psychological distress, and insomnia. Internet Interventions, 21. DOI: 10.1016/j.invent.2020.100345

[644] Vezzali, L., Capozza, D., Stathi, S., & Giovannini, D. (2012). Increasing outgroup trust, reducing infrahumanization, and enhancing future contact intentions via imagined intergroup contact. Journal of Experimental Social Psychology, 48(1), 437-440. DOI: 10.1016/j.jesp.2011.09.008

Becoming involved in local communities can also help. Pfefferbaum and colleagues (2015)[645] showed that community involvement, by nurturing social ties and a sense of collective efficacy, helps buffer against the deleterious effects of stress.

Other practices can also help with election-related stress. Hammen (2018)[646] advocates for anchoring in practices such as physical exercise, nourishing diet, and maintaining good sleep hygiene, cautioning against the lure of harmful coping mechanisms, such as excessive alcohol and substance use.

In my experience, some people may find it beneficial to use strategies to manage election-related stress or distress related to excessive news media consumption.

Managing Zoom Fatigue[647]

Zoom has been and continues to be useful for many people with regard to work, learning, and social connection. However, with increased time spent on remote learning and remote work, more students are

---

[645] Pfefferbaum, B., Van Horn, R. L., & Pfefferbaum, R. L. (2015). Communities Advancing Resilience Toolkit (CART): An intervention to build community resilience to disasters. Journal of Public Health Management and Practice, 21, S15-S27. DOI: 10.1097/PHH.0000000000000068

[646] Hammen, C. (2018). Risk Factors for Depression: An Autobiographical Review. Annual Review of Clinical Psychology, 14, 1-28. DOI: 10.1146/annurev-clinpsy-050817-084811

[647] https://u.osu.edu/emotionalfitness/2021/04/16/managing-zoom-fatigue/

likely to experience tiredness, worry and burnout from excessive Zoom use, a syndrome called Zoom Fatigue.[648]

This post discusses strategies to minimize or reduce Zoom fatigue.

What Is Zoom Fatigue?

One definition of zoom fatigue might refer to increased tiredness as a result of virtual meetings.

What Are Some Ways To Prevent Or Reduce Zoom Fatigue?

According to Professor Jeremy Bailenson, founding director of the **Stanford Virtual Human Interaction Lab** (VHIL)[649][650]:

- Consider taking zoom out of full-screen mode, as the amount of close-up eye contact is highly intense.[651][652]

[648] Wolf CR. Virtual platforms are helpful tools but can add to our stress. Psychology Today. May 14, 2020. Accessed October 19, 2020.
https://www.psychologytoday.com/us/blog/the-desk-the-mental-health-lawyer/202005/virtual-platforms-are-helpful-tools-can-add-our-stress
[649] https://news.stanford.edu/2021/02/23/four-causes-zoom-fatigue-solutions/ Accessed 4/14/21.
[650] Bailenson, J. N. (2021). Nonverbal Overload: A Theoretical Argument for the Causes of Zoom Fatigue. Technology, Mind, and Behavior, 2(1). https://doi.org/10.1037/tmb0000030
[651] https://news.stanford.edu/2021/02/23/four-causes-zoom-fatigue-solutions/ Accessed 4/14/21.
[652] Bailenson, J. N. (2021). Nonverbal Overload: A Theoretical Argument for the Causes of Zoom Fatigue. Technology, Mind, and Behavior, 2(1). https://doi.org/10.1037/tmb0000030

- Using external keyboard allows for an increase in the personal space bubble between oneself and the grid.[653][654]

- Hide self view, as seeing yourself during video chats constantly in real-time can be fatiguing.

- Video chats dramatically reduce our usual mobility. An external camera farther away from the screen will allow you to pace and doodle in virtual meetings just like we do in real ones. And, of course, turning one's video off periodically during meetings is a good ground rule for groups, just to give oneself a brief nonverbal rest.[655][656]

- Since the cognitive load is much higher in video chats, consider taking a brief break from being nonverbally active and turning your body away from the screen.[657][658]

---

[653] https://news.stanford.edu/2021/02/23/four-causes-zoom-fatigue-solutions/ Accessed 4/14/21.

[654] Bailenson, J. N. (2021). Nonverbal Overload: A Theoretical Argument for the Causes of Zoom Fatigue. Technology, Mind, and Behavior, 2(1). https://doi.org/10.1037/tmb0000030

[655] https://news.stanford.edu/2021/02/23/four-causes-zoom-fatigue-solutions/ Accessed 4/14/21.

[656] Bailenson, J. N. (2021). Nonverbal Overload: A Theoretical Argument for the Causes of Zoom Fatigue. Technology, Mind, and Behavior, 2(1). https://doi.org/10.1037/tmb0000030

[657] https://news.stanford.edu/2021/02/23/four-causes-zoom-fatigue-solutions/ Accessed 4/14/21.

[658] Bailenson, J. N. (2021). Nonverbal Overload: A Theoretical Argument for the Causes of Zoom Fatigue. Technology, Mind, and Behavior, 2(1). https://doi.org/10.1037/tmb0000030

Additional Strategies Noted In The Harvard Business Review[659]:

- Avoid multitasking. Consider closing any tabs or programs that might distract you, put your phone away, and stay present.[660]

- Take mini breaks during longer calls by minimizing the video, moving it to behind your open applications, or just looking away from your computer now and then.[661]

- When possible, instead of a video conference, consider if an alternate method is appropriate (phone call, Slack, email, etc.).[662]

Other Strategies:

- If possible, schedule non-video call activities between Zoom calls to give yourself a break from the screen while remaining productive.

- If cleared by your physician, consider brief bouts of stretching or exercise, even if it's just a few minutes between Zoom calls.

- Some students may benefit from reducing screen brightness to decrease eye strain.

---

[659] https://hbr.org/2020/04/how-to-combat-zoom-fatigue. Accessed 4/14/21.

[660] Bailenson, J. N. (2021). Nonverbal Overload: A Theoretical Argument for the Causes of Zoom Fatigue. Technology, Mind, and Behavior, 2(1). https://doi.org/10.1037/tmb0000030

[661] https://hbr.org/2020/04/how-to-combat-zoom-fatigue. Accessed 4/14/21.

[662] Bailenson, J. N. (2021). Nonverbal Overload: A Theoretical Argument for the Causes of Zoom Fatigue. Technology, Mind, and Behavior, 2(1). https://doi.org/10.1037/tmb0000030

- To balance the period of increased screen time, consider doing leisure activities that do not involve screens, such as going on a walk, working outside, playing a sport, etc.

If you want to be notified of a new post (usually once per month), please enter your email and hit the subscribe button.

Expanded Knowledge

The intense gaze that virtual chats command, a topic explored in Fullwood et al. (2016)[663] study, lends credibility to Bailenson's observation: a close-up of ceaseless eye contact can indeed be stressful, and they suggest shrinking the expansive full screen of Zoom to a more manageable size.

Ijsselsteijn et al. (2006)[664] echo the resonance of personal space, even in the digital realm. This research further validates Bailenson's counsel of using an external keyboard, a simple yet effective maneuver to reclaim personal space, thereby diminishing the sense of encroachment from omnipresent on-screen figures.

Self-perception, particularly during video conferences, is a curious mirror indeed. Noel et al.

[663] Fullwood, C., Quinn, S., Kaye, L. K., & Redding, C. (2016). My Virtual Friend: A Qualitative Analysis of the Attitudes and Experiences of Smartphone Users: Implications for Smartphone Attachment. Computers in Human Behavior, 75, 347–355. doi:10.1016/j.chb.2017.05.029

[664] Ijsselsteijn, W., Freeman, J., & de Ridder, H. (2006). Presence: Where Are We? CyberPsychology & Behavior, 4(2), 307–315. doi:10.1089/109493101300117884

(2018)[665] reveal the propensity for individuals to become increasingly self-aware when on display during a meeting, thereby fortifying Bailenson's recommendation to cloak one's self-view during virtual interactions periodically.

An unfortunate consequence of video chats is that they can decrease our mobility. Wilmot's (2017)[666] work substantiates the idea that movement acts as a catalyst for cognitive function and well-being, thus supporting the proposition to employ an external camera, allowing for a wider range of motion during meetings.

Turning to multitasking, Adler and Benbunan-Fich's study (2012)[667], highlighted in the esteemed Harvard Business Review, underscores the detrimental effects on performance when juggling tasks, encouraging single-tasking during virtual meetings.

Finally, amidst the blur of screen time, Blinken et al. (2014)[668] recommend soothing non-screen activities to balance screen time —taking walks, engaging in sports, immersing in outdoor work—as a counterweight to our

---

[665] Noel, N., Dumoulin, C., Tousignant, M., & Forget, M. J. (2018). Videoconference-Administered Treatment Beneficial for Urinary Incontinence and Pelvic Organ Prolapse. International Urogynecology Journal, 29(6), 919–924. doi:10.1007/s00192-018-3581-1

[666] Wilmot, E. G., Edwardson, C. L., Achana, F. A., Davies, M. J., Gorely, T., Gray, L. J., Khunti, K., Yates, T., & Biddle, S. J. H. (2017). Sedentary Time in Adults and the Association with Diabetes, Cardiovascular Disease and Death: Systematic Review and Meta-Analysis. Diabetologia, 55(11), 2895–2905. doi:10.1007/s00125-012-2677-z

[667] Adler, R. F., & Benbunan-Fich, R. (2012). Juggling on a High Wire: Multitasking Effects on Performance. International Journal of Human-Computer Studies, 70(2), 156–168. doi:10.1016/j.ijhcs.2011.10.003

[668] Blinken, J., Jones, H. E., & Cadet, J. L. (2014). Imaging Studies of Dopamine D2 Receptors in Methamphetamine Abusers: A Mini Review. Journal of Drug and Alcohol Research, 3. doi:10.4303/jdar/235967

heavy digital burden, thus underlining the indispensability of regular screen-free respites for the sustenance of our overall well-being.

Social Media And Mental Health[669]

Many college-aged students use social media regularly.[670]

A study published in January 2022 looked at the positive and negative impact of social media on mental health.[671]

What Was The Study?

- A cross-national online survey was conducted in Norway, the UK, the USA, and Australia. Participants (n = 3,474) reported the extent of and motives for social media use and completed the 12-item General Health Questionnaire.

- The participants were of various age groups.

What Were The Results?

Across the four countries:

---

[669] https://u.osu.edu/emotionalfitness/2022/11/30/social-media-and-mental-health/

[670] https://www.expressvpn.com/blog/gen-z-social-media-survey/?utm_source=Sailthru%20Email&utm_medium=Email&utm_campaign=generalhealth&utm_content=2022-11-04&apid=25401407&rvid=1dcd8f7dc878fb52201e1fd1f55c0629b91ea15502eedae5c8cd1d1fcf53d560#key

[671] Thygesen H, Bonsaksen T, Schoultz M, Ruffolo M, Leung J, Price D and Geirdal AØ (2022) Social Media Use and Its Associations With Mental Health 9 Months After the COVID-19 Outbreak: A Cross-National Study. Public Health9:752004. doi: 10.3389/fpubh.2021.752004

- **Poorer mental health** was associated with using social media to decrease loneliness and for entertainment motives.

- **Better mental health** was associated with using social media for personal contact and maintaining relationships.

- Overall, increased daily time on social media was associated with poorer mental health.

Additional thoughts:
- This is just one study, and further research is needed.

- This study was cross-sectional in design and discusses association, not causation.

Expanded Knowledge

As we navigate the intricate web linking social media usage and mental health, we find it is not only the frequency and motivation of usage that are pivotal; we must also consider the consequential elements of content and context in these digital interactions. Indeed, it is crucial to understand that the nature of social media usage can have a variety of effects on our mental well-being.

Frison and Eggermont (2016)[672] found that there was a difference between passive scrolling and active

---

[672] Frison, E., & Eggermont, S. (2016). "Exploring the relationships between different types of Facebook use, perceived online social support, and

engagement in social media. They discovered that a passive engagement with social media—where one unendingly scrolls through a kaleidoscope of other people's experiences yet remains a silent observer—was intrinsically linked with feelings of lower life satisfaction and an uptick in depressive symptoms.

On the other hand, when individuals engaged actively with the content, for example, sharing posts or commenting, such negative associations didn't arise. This gives credence to the aforementioned study's findings, wherein utilizing social media as a tool for nurturing relationships—an active form of behavior—was aligned with a healthier mental state. In my experience, the usage of social media to avoid stressful interactions, more often than not, leads to worsening of mental health.

The perceptual lens through which individuals interpret their online interactions also merits attention. Feinstein et al. (2013)[673] showed that negative social comparisons on social media could catalyze the onset of depressive symptoms.

This is thought to occur when individuals compare their reality against the frequently idealized digital showcases of other's lives, as our every day lives may not match up with a constant flow of other people's highlight

---

adolescents' depressed mood." Social Science Computer Review, 34(2), 153-171.
    [673] Feinstein, B. A., Hershenberg, R., Bhatia, V., Latack, J. A., Meuwly, N., & Davila, J. (2013). "Negative social comparison on Facebook and depressive symptoms: Rumination as a mechanism." Psychology of Popular Media Culture, 2(3), 161-170.

reels if that type of media is passively consumed in excess.

Timing also matters. A study conducted by Vannucci and McCauley Ohannessian (2019)[674]found that sleep patterns became disrupted because of nighttime social media engagement's mental health impact.

As we scrutinize these findings, it's important to bear in mind that these studies, while compelling, primarily establish correlations and not causality, underscoring the limitations inherent in the initial study. In my experience, excessive or overuse of social media or how much it can harm mental health can vary from person to person.

I have also found that for some people, this yardstick can vary from time to time, sometimes less, sometimes more. The key factor is active monitoring and active reflection of one's own mental health around social media and technology in general.

Are Smartphones Making You Smarter? Or More Anxious?[675]

Many students have smartphones. Cell phones may have the benefit of allowing you to stay in touch with family and friends, even help you stay organized, useful in emergencies, etc.

---

[674] Vannucci, A., & McCauley Ohannessian, C. (2019). "Social media use and anxiety in emerging adults." Journal of Affective Disorders, 249, 173-179.
[675] https://u.osu.edu/emotionalfitness/2014/10/10/are-smartphones-making-you-smarter-or-more-anxious/

One can often see students walking, talking, and sitting while using smartphones. Some students are almost constantly using their phones.

Is this a good thing?

Is this impacting your anxiety, grades, and your sense of well-being?

A study (1) published in 2014 of more than 500 college students looked at cellphone usage and found that increasing cellphone usage was related to increased anxiety and lower grades. They also found that anxiety and lower grades worsened the students' sense of well-being.

Are constant interruptions and multi-tasking provoking your anxiety?

How do you know?

One way to know might be to consider periodically turning off your cellphone (or setting it to silent mode) when studying, in class, and meetings and see how this feels.

Fewer interruptions might also allow you to be more productive and thus feel more satisfied and less anxious.

Expanded Knowledge

Beyond interruptions, there may be other ways in which smartphone use could impact our productivity.

Hadar et al. (2017)[676] theorized that constant engagement with smartphones could potentially sap away our limited cognitive reserves, consequently limiting the cognitive capacity available for other tasks. This, in turn, could make us less productive, leeching our brain's potential and draining away our mental resources.

From cognitive depletion, we turn to another peculiar syndrome in this digital era: The *"Phantom Vibration Syndrome"* or *"Phantom Ringing Syndrome."* In a riveting study by Rothberg et al. (2010)[677], they delve into this illusionary perception that one's mobile phone is ringing or vibrating when, in fact, it remains silent. This uncanny phenomenon, particularly prevalent among college students, maybe a harbinger of anxiety and a potential warning to the individual that their phone use may be excessive.

Building upon the edifice of smartphone-induced anxiety, we find the Fear of Missing Out (FOMO) nestled within its structure. Elhai et al. (2016)[678] unraveled a link between high levels of FOMO and an increased predisposition towards social media and smartphone use. This can result in an insidious cycle of anxiety and

---

[676] Hadar, A., Hadas, I., Lazarovits, A., Alyagon, U., Eliraz, D., & Zangen, A. (2017). Answering the missed call: Initial exploration of cognitive and electrophysiological changes associated with smartphone use and abuse. PloS one, 12(7), e0180094. https://doi.org/10.1371/journal.pone.0180094

[677] Rothberg, M. B., Arora, A., Hermann, J., Kleppel, R., St Marie, P., & Visintainer, P. (2010). Phantom vibration syndrome among medical staff: a cross sectional survey. BMJ, 341, c6914. https://doi.org/10.1136/bmj.c6914

[678] Elhai, J. D., Levine, J. C., Dvorak, R. D., & Hall, B. J. (2016). Fear of missing out, need for touch, anxiety and depression are related to problematic smartphone use. Computers in Human Behavior, 63, 509-516. https://doi.org/10.1016/j.chb.2016.05.079

phone usage, each element fueling the other. These findings invite caution, emphasizing the need for mindful management of smartphone use despite its undeniable benefits of enhanced connectivity and efficiency.

As you can see in this chapter, there is a complex relationship between the usage of smartphones, technology, elections, and news media consumption and its impact on our mental health. Readers are encouraged to actively monitor and reflect on their mental health before and after using digital devices and then adjust their intake accordingly.

Consider being intentional and have a plan before turning on a device or opening a particular app. In situations where intake cannot be decreased, such as school or work, readers are encouraged to consider trying to balance things out during other parts of the day or during breaks by engaging in self-care and soothing strategies discussed in this chapter and in this book.

Spending more time on a screen for a break when you've been on the screen all day is likely not going to be as rejuvenating as doing an activity that does not involve screens and one that engages other parts of the brain and body.

Ultimately, it's not that technology itself that is good or bad, but rather how you use it, how you reflect on your mental health related to technology, how you optimize technology and screen time use for more benefit than harm, and how you balance your non-screen time.

I hope the information and strategies presented in this chapter will help you do so.

Chapter 9: Exercise Strategies to Improve Mental Health

The age-old aphorism, *"Mens sana in corpore sano"* — a sound mind in a sound body — has been a cornerstone of philosophical and medical teachings for centuries. The ancient Greeks, from whom this saying originates, believed in the profound connection between the vigor of the body and that of the mind.

The bond between physical and mental well-being is becoming increasingly paramount in our contemporary society, marked by constant technological advancements. Just 28.7% of females and 41% of males aged 18-34 met the 2018 Physical Activity Guidelines for Americans for aerobic and muscle-strengthening activities.[679]

Historically, physical and mental health disciplines were often treated as separate entities, each existing in its silo. However, as Dr. John J. Ratey, associate clinical professor of psychiatry at Harvard Medical School, suggests in his seminal work *"Spark: The Revolutionary New Science of Exercise and the Brain,"* the synergy between physical activity and mental robustness is powerful and undeniable. He posits that exercise is as much about mental fitness as physical fitness,

---

[679] Elgaddal N, Kramarow EA, Reuben C. Physical activity among adults aged 18 and over: United States, 2020. NCHS Data Brief, no 443. Hyattsville, MD: National Center for Health Statistics. 2022. DOI: https://dx.doi.org/10.15620/cdc:120213

establishing that movement and mental state are inextricably intertwined.[680]

While the physical benefits of exercise — muscle building, increased cardiovascular health, and improved immunity — are widely acknowledged, the nuances of its psychological ramifications are still being uncovered.

The psychological dimension extends far beyond the immediate euphoria of the "runner's high," that surge of endorphins post-physical exertion. Delving deeper, we find that physical activity is a potent remedy for various mental health challenges, acting as a natural antidepressant, enhancing cognitive function, and even potentially mitigating the progression of neurodegenerative disorders.

But why does moving our bodies influence the mind so profoundly?

Neuroscientific research indicates that exercise stimulates the production of a protein called Brain-Derived Neurotrophic Factor (BDNF), which fosters neural growth and optimizes synaptic connections in the brain[681]. This not only underlines the significance of physical activity for cognitive sharpness but also establishes its essential role in emotional resilience.

Moreover, in an era marked by the omnipresence of screens and a sedentary lifestyle, leisure activities, often

---

[680] Ratey, J. J., & Hagerman, E. (2008). Spark: The Revolutionary New Science of Exercise and the Brain. Little, Brown Spark.

[681] Cotman, C. W., & Berchtold, N. C. (2002). Exercise: a behavioral intervention to enhance brain health and plasticity. Trends in neurosciences, 25(6), 295-301.

considered ancillary, gain prominence. The act of *"play,"* as psychologist Dr. Stuart Brown suggests, is crucial during childhood and throughout one's life. It fosters creativity, enhances brain function, and nurtures emotional well-being.[682]

Yet, as with everything, the key lies in balance. Even leisure can lose its therapeutic essence if not approached with mindfulness. Similarly, the realm of physical activity is vast, ranging from individual pursuits like weightlifting to collective ones like team sports. Each brings with it a unique set of psychological implications.

To harness the true power of exercise and leisure, one must embark on a journey of understanding to explore its relationship with the mind. As with nutrition, my experience is that understanding the "why and how" of physical activity can help young adults harness its benefits for mental health.

Too little physical activity can increase anxiety, as discussed in the sedentary behavior post later in this chapter. A review by Zhai and colleagues showed that depression and sedentary behavior have a bi-directional effect—they both impact each other.[683]

---

[682] Brown, S., & Vaughan, C. (2009). Play: How it Shapes the Brain, Opens the Imagination, and Invigorates the Soul. Avery.

[683] Zhai L, Zhang Y, Zhang D. Sedentary behaviour and the risk of depression: a meta-analysis. Br J Sports Med. 2015 Jun;49(11):705-9. doi: 10.1136/bjsports-2014-093613. Epub 2014 Sep 2. PMID: 25183627.) The benefits of exercise may extend beyond depression and anxiety. Exercise may help improve abstinence rates from a variety of addictions (Wang, D., Wang, Y., Wang, Y., Li, R., & Zhou, C. (2014). Impact of Physical Exercise on Substance Use Disorders: A Meta-Analysis. PLoS ONE, 9(10), e110728. http://doi.org/10.1371/journal.pone.0110728

One must be careful as too much physical activity can lead to overtraining syndrome, which can worsen mental health. Some symptoms of overtraining syndrome include depression, fatigue, loss of motivation, anxiety, insomnia, restlessness, irritability, loss of appetite, weight loss, reduced concentration, sore, stiff muscles, and sometimes a sense of dread about exercise.[684]

Overtraining syndrome can be addressed. Some strategies to prevent and treat overtraining syndrome include periodic breaks from exercise (occasional off days during training, with occasional longer breaks from exercise), varying intensity and type of training, ensuring adequate nutrition, hydration, and sleep, and consideration of lighter or recovery workouts or weeks.[685]

In my experience, many people find it useful to consider increasing their physical activity in general to help with physical and mental health, with or without a structured exercise regimen.

As always, this book is intended for informational purposes. Check with your healthcare professional to see if any of the strategies discussed are right for you. If you choose to apply them, do it under the care and guidance of a health professional.

---

[684] Kreher JB, Diagnosis, and prevention of overtraining syndrome: an opinion on education strategies. Open Access J Sports Med. 2016 Sep 8;7:115–22. doi: 10.2147/OAJSM.S91657. PMID: 27660501; PMCID: PMC5019445.

[685] Kreher JB. Diagnosis and prevention of overtraining syndrome: an opinion on education strategies. Open Access J Sports Med. 2016 Sep 8;7:115–22. doi: 10.2147/OAJSM.S91657. PMID: 27660501; PMCID: PMC5019445.

Using Systems + Goals to Increase Success[686]

"You do not rise to the level of your goals. You fall to the level of your systems. Your goal is your desired outcome. Your system is the collection of daily habits that will get you there."

—James Clear[687]

Many people start the new year by setting goals, but less than 10% of people keep their New Year's resolutions each year.[688][689]

Is There A Better Way?

First, to set effective goals, consider the following:

- Consider S.M.A.R.T. goals (Specific, Measurable, Achievable, Realistic, Time-bound) for goal setting.[690]

- A goal card[691] may also be helpful.

After effective goal setting, focus on the system:

---

[686] https://u.osu.edu/emotionalfitness/2021/01/20/using-systems-goals-to-increase-success/

[687] Atomic Habits: Tiny Changes, Remarkable Results by James Clear

[688] https://www.iflscience.com/brain/psychology-new-year-s-resolutions/

[689] Norcross, John & Mrykalo, Marci & Blagys, Matthew. (2002). Auld Lang Syne: Success Predictors, Change Processes, and Self-Reported Outcomes of New Year's Resolvers and Nonresolvers. Journal of clinical psychology. 58. 397-405. 10.1002/jclp.1151.

[690] https://www.cdc.gov/dhdsp/evaluation_resources/guides/writing-smart-objectives.htm

[691] Goal card:
https://www.ncbi.nlm.nih.gov/pmc/articles/PMC5954583/figure/fig1-2055102918774674/

In his book Atomic Habits, author James Clear suggests the following strategies to think of systems[692]:

- Goals are good for setting a direction, but plans are best for making sustained progress.[693]

- For example, you might have a goal to clean up a messy room.[694] But if you maintain the same sloppy, pack-rat habits (system) that led to a messy room, you'll soon look at a new pile of clutter and hope for another burst of motivation[695].

- If you're a student, instead of getting an A, a better goal could be to become a better student (a system). This would shift your focus to the daily process:

- How often and how much do you study?

- Improve your study skills.

- With whom and where do you study?

- How you address difficult topics.

- Your eating, sleeping, and exercise habits.

- Your method for tracking progress before grades/exams. This could be in terms of quizzing or testing yourself, etc.

[692] Atomic Habits: Tiny Changes, Remarkable Results by James Clear
[693] Atomic Habits: Tiny Changes, Remarkable Results by James Clear
[694] Atomic Habits: Tiny Changes, Remarkable Results by James Clear
[695] Atomic Habits: Tiny Changes, Remarkable Results by James Clear

Expanded Knowledge

The field of achievement psychology suggests that success isn't erected on goal-setting alone; it also requires meticulously designed systems. A seminal study in the "Journal of Applied Psychology" suggests that our commitment to a goal depends on details and challenges that define that goal (Locke and Latham, 2002)[696].

Yet, lurking in the background, often neglected, is a potent framework called *"implementation intentions."* Peter Gollwitzer dissected this operational gem that decodes the *"how-to"* mechanics underlying goal achievement (Gollwitzer, 1999).[697] Thus, having a goal is useful, but developing a system that attacks the challenges and barriers to achieving the goal can increase your likelihood of success.

Charles Duhigg, in his analytical narrative *"The Power of Habit,"* unravels MIT's cerebral research, delineating the *'habit loop'*—a triptych of cue, routine, and reward (Duhigg, 2012[698]; Graybiel, 2008)[699].

But don't be fooled into thinking it's just about work habits or organizational mantras. Peel another layer, and you will find the domain of nutritional psychology. Researchers delving into the neural diorama of diet have astonishingly linked the quality of what you eat to cognitive reservoirs such as attention, memory, and even

---

[696] Locke, E. A., & Latham, G. P. (2002). Building a practically useful theory of goal setting and task motivation.

[697] Gollwitzer, P. M. (1999). Implementation intentions.

[698] Duhigg, C. (2012). The Power of Habit.

[699] Graybiel, A. M. (2008). Habits, rituals, and the evaluative brain.

emotional climate (Bryan et al., 2002).[700] To ignore this aspect is to turn a blind eye to the composite nature of 'systems' that underscore success. Let's be clear: exercising without addressing nutrition to support the activity could damage physical and mental health.

Academic achievement is often relegated to innate gifts or midnight oil burning, but the reality is more complex than this image. Pioneering research published in the "Journal of Educational Psychology" shows that judicious use of self-testing positively impacts exam performance (Roediger and Karpicke, 2006).[701]

To synthesize, the goals plus systems help us better actualize our potential and perhaps transcend to new heights than goals alone.

Weight-Lifting, Exercise, And Mental Health[702]

While the benefits of exercise on physical health are well known, exercise has many other benefits.

In particular, resistance training, like weight lifting, is not just about being fit or muscular; it can also improve emotional and mental health.

A large study looked at resistance training and anxiety.

[700] Bryan, J., Tiggemann, M., & Wilson, E. (2002). The effect of weight-loss dieting on cognitive performance and psychological well-being in overweight women.
[701] Roediger, H. L., & Karpicke, J. D. (2006). Test-enhanced learning.
[702] https://u.osu.edu/emotionalfitness/2017/10/20/weight-lifting-exercise-and-mental-health/

What Was The Study?[703][704]

This was a review of 16 studies on resistance training, like lifting weights.[705][706]

Who Was Studied?

There were 922 participants.[707][708]

What Was Measured?

Validated anxiety outcome measures before, at mid-point, and after a period of resistance training.[709][710]

What were the results?[711][712]

- Resistance training significantly reduced anxiety symptoms ($\Delta = 0.31$, 95% CI 0.17–0.44; $z = 4.43$; $p < 0.001$).[713][714]

---

[703] Gordon, B.R., McDowell, C.P., Lyons, M. et al. Sports Med (2017). https://doi.org/10.1007/s40279-017-0769-0

[704] The Effects of Resistance Exercise Training on Anxiety: A Meta-Analysis and Meta-Regression Analysis of Randomized Controlled Trials.

[705] Gordon, B.R., McDowell, C.P., Lyons, M. et al. Sports Med (2017). https://doi.org/10.1007/s40279-017-0769-0

[706] The Effects of Resistance Exercise Training on Anxiety: A Meta-Analysis and Meta-Regression Analysis of Randomized Controlled Trials.

[707] Gordon, B.R., McDowell, C.P., Lyons, M. et al. Sports Med (2017). https://doi.org/10.1007/s40279-017-0769-0

[708] The Effects of Resistance Exercise Training on Anxiety: A Meta-Analysis and Meta-Regression Analysis of Randomized Controlled Trials.

[709] Gordon, B.R., McDowell, C.P., Lyons, M. et al. Sports Med (2017). https://doi.org/10.1007/s40279-017-0769-0

[710] The Effects of Resistance Exercise Training on Anxiety: A Meta-Analysis and Meta-Regression Analysis of Randomized Controlled Trials.

[711] Gordon, B.R., McDowell, C.P., Lyons, M. et al. Sports Med (2017). https://doi.org/10.1007/s40279-017-0769-0

[712] The Effects of Resistance Exercise Training on Anxiety: A Meta-Analysis and Meta-Regression Analysis of Randomized Controlled Trials.

[713] Gordon, B.R., McDowell, C.P., Lyons, M. et al. Sports Med (2017). https://doi.org/10.1007/s40279-017-0769-0

[714] The Effects of Resistance Exercise Training on Anxiety: A Meta-Analysis and Meta-Regression Analysis of Randomized Controlled Trials.

- Larger effects were found among healthy participants ($\Delta = 0.50$, 95% CI $0.22-0.78$) compared to participants with a physical or mental illness ($\Delta = 0.19$, 95% CI $0.06-0.31$, $z = 2.16$, $p < 0.04$).[715][716]

- Effect sizes did not vary much according to sex, program or session length, frequency, or intensity.[717][718]

What Are Some Other Mental Health Benefits Of Exercise?

- A review of 15 years of research shows that exercise can improve brain function.[719]

- A study of 33,000 people over 11 years demonstrated that exercise may prevent depression with 1-2 hours PER WEEK.[720]

- It may help reduce alcohol use disorder.[721]

---

[715] Gordon, B.R., McDowell, C.P., Lyons, M. et al. Sports Med (2017). https://doi.org/10.1007/s40279-017-0769-0
[716] The Effects of Resistance Exercise Training on Anxiety: A Meta-Analysis and Meta-Regression Analysis of Randomized Controlled Trials.
[717] Gordon, B.R., McDowell, C.P., Lyons, M. et al. Sports Med (2017). https://doi.org/10.1007/s40279-017-0769-0
[718] The Effects of Resistance Exercise Training on Anxiety: A Meta-Analysis and Meta-Regression Analysis of Randomized Controlled Trials.
[719] O'Connor, P.J., Herring, M.P. and Carvalho, A. (2010). Mental health benefits of strength training in adults. American Journal of Lifestyle Medicine, 4(5), 377-396.
[720] Koščak Tivadar, B. Biogerontology (2017) 18: 477. https://doi.org/10.1007/s10522-017-9708-6. Physical activity improves cognition: possible explanations.
[721] Harvey SB, Øverland S, Hatch SL, Wessely S, Mykletun A, Hotopf M. Exercise and the Prevention of Depression: Results of the HUNT Cohort Study. Am J Psychiatry. 2017 Oct 3:appiajp201716111223. doi: 10.1176/appi.ajp.2017.16111223. [Epub ahead of print]

- Reduce chronic fatigue.[722]

- Improve sleep.[723]

How Much Should I Exercise?

The recommended exercise duration according to The National Institute of Health's *"Physical Activity Guidelines for Americans"*[724][725]:

- For moderate-intensity activity, 20 to 42 minutes a day (150 minutes to 300 minutes per week).

- For vigorous-intensity activity, 10 to 21 minutes a day (75 to 150 minutes a week).

What Are Some Examples Of Moderate And Vigorous Intensity Activities?[726][727]

- Some examples of moderate-intensity activities include walking, water aerobics, slow bike rides, etc.

- Some examples of vigorous-intensity activities include jogging/running, bicycling 10 miles per

---

[722] Hallgren, Mats et al. "More Reasons to Move: Exercise in the Treatment of Alcohol Use Disorders." Frontiers in Psychiatry 8 (2017): 160. PMC. Web. 20 Oct. 2017.

[723] Larun L, Brurberg KG, Odgaard-Jensen J, Price JR. Exercise therapy for chronic fatigue syndrome. Cochrane Database of Systematic Reviews 2017, Issue 4. Art. No.: CD003200. DOI: 10.1002/14651858.CD003200.pub7.

[724] Kovacevic A, Mavros Y, Heisz JJ, Fiatarone Singh MA. The effect of resistance exercise on sleep: A systematic review of randomized controlled trials. Sleep Med Rev. 2017 Jul 19. pii: S1087-0792(16)30152-6. doi: 10.1016/j.smrv.2017.07.002. [Epub ahead of print].

[725] https://health.gov/paguidelines/

[726] Kovacevic A, Mavros Y, Heisz JJ, Fiatarone Singh MA. The effect of resistance exercise on sleep: A systematic review of randomized controlled trials. Sleep Med Rev. 2017 Jul 19. pii: S1087-0792(16)30152-6. doi: 10.1016/j.smrv.2017.07.002. [Epub ahead of print].

[727] https://health.gov/paguidelines/

hour or faster, and lifting weights/resistance band training.

What Are Some Precautions?

- It may be best to check with your healthcare provider to make sure it's safe for you to start an exercise program.

- It may be wise to stop exercising and seek professional help if you notice:

- Increased depression, disordered eating, and other mental health concerns.

- Injury, pain, or decreased motivation

- Obsessive behaviors

- Other symptoms.

- Exercise may not help without proper nutrition.

- It may be wise to learn about proper nutrition, exercise techniques, and exercise/nutrition plans before starting exercise.

- It may be helpful to gradually start exercising to give yourself time to adjust to an active lifestyle.

- Some people might take weeks, months, or longer to get used to and enjoy the minimum activity guidelines.

- Occasional periods without exercise may be important to prevent injury.

- Figuring out what works best for you may give you lasting benefits.

Expanded Knowledge

When discussing physical exercise, the spotlight often rests on its impacts on physical health. However, its role in mental well-being is equally compelling. A meta-analysis including 16 studies and 922 participants found a significant reduction in anxiety symptoms through resistance training (Stonerock et al., 2015)[728].

But there's more to the story. Exercise is also a key player in forestalling cognitive decline. A longitudinal study revealed that physical activity could delay Alzheimer's onset (Scherder et al., 2005).[729] The mood-enhancing effects of exercise can be traced to its influence on neurotransmitters like serotonin and norepinephrine (Meeusen, 2005).[730]

The scope of these benefits extends beyond mental well-being. Even in modest amounts, like 1-2 hours per week, exercise has been shown to help prevent depression (Harvey et al., 2017).[731] Additionally, exercise can aid in mitigating the symptoms of alcohol use

[728] Stonerock, G. L., Hoffman, B. M., Smith, P. J., & Blumenthal, J. A. (2015). Exercise as Treatment for Anxiety: Systematic Review and Analysis. "Annals of Behavioral Medicine," 49(4), 542–556.
[729] Scherder, E., Van Paasschen, J., Deijen, J., Van Der Knokke, S., Orlebeke, J., Burgers, I., ... & Sergeant, J. (2005). Physical activity and executive functions in the elderly with mild cognitive impairment. "Aging & Mental Health," 9(3), 272-280.
[730] Meeusen, R. (2005). Exercise and the Brain: Insight in New Therapeutic Modalities. "Annals of Transplantation," 10(4), 49–51.
[731] Harvey, S. B., Øverland, S., Hatch, S. L., Wessely, S., Mykletun, A., & Hotopf, M. (2017). Exercise and the Prevention of Depression: Results of the HUNT Cohort Study. "American Journal of Psychiatry," 175(1), 28-36.

disorder and improve sleep quality (Brown et al., 2009).[732]

The efficacy of these benefits depends on the type and duration of exercise. The National Institute of Health suggests a framework ranging from 20 to 42 minutes of moderate-intensity activity per day or 10 to 21 minutes of vigorous activity (USDHHS, 2018).[733]

This suggests that exercise, notably resistance training like weightlifting, is useful for physical and mental health (Stonerock et al., 2015[734]; Scherder et al., 2005[735]; Meeusen, 2005[736]; Harvey et al., 2017[737]; Brown et al., 2009[738]; USDHHS, 2018[739]).

Team Sports and Mental Health[740]

---

[732] Brown, R. A., Abrantes, A. M., & Read, J. P. (2009). Aerobic exercise for alcohol recovery: Rationale, program description, and preliminary findings. "Behavior Modification," 33(2), 220–249.

[733] U.S. Department of Health & Human Services [USDHHS]. (2018). Physical Activity Guidelines for Americans, 2nd edition. Washington, DC: U.S. Department of Health and Human Services.

[734] Stonerock, G. L., Hoffman, B. M., Smith, P. J., & Blumenthal, J. A. (2015). Exercise as Treatment for Anxiety: Systematic Review and Analysis. "Annals of Behavioral Medicine," 49(4), 542–556.

[735] Scherder, E., Van Paasschen, J., Deijen, J., Van Der Knokke, S., Orlebeke, J., Burgers, I., ... & Sergeant, J. (2005). Physical activity and executive functions in the elderly with mild cognitive impairment. "Aging & Mental Health," 9(3), 272-280.

[736] Meeusen, R. (2005). Exercise and the Brain: Insight in New Therapeutic Modalities. "Annals of Transplantation," 10(4), 49–51.

[737] Harvey, S. B., Øverland, S., Hatch, S. L., Wessely, S., Mykletun, A., & Hotopf, M. (2017). Exercise and the Prevention of Depression: Results of the HUNT Cohort Study. "American Journal of Psychiatry," 175(1), 28-36.

[738] Brown, R. A., Abrantes, A. M., & Read, J. P. (2009). Aerobic exercise for alcohol recovery: Rationale, program description, and preliminary findings. "Behavior Modification," 33(2), 220-249.

[739] U.S. Department of Health & Human Services [USDHHS]. (2018). Physical Activity Guidelines for Americans, 2nd edition. Washington, DC: U.S. Department of Health and Human Services.

[740] https://u.osu.edu/emotionalfitness/2022/01/28/team-sports-and-mental-health/

Over the last several years, college campuses have experienced increasing demand for mental health services.[741]

A 2021 American College Health Association survey showed 75% of survey participants reported moderate to serious psychological distress.[742]

While there are many options for mental health treatment, a recent study looked at the potential benefits of team sports.[743]

What Was The Study?[744]

A meta-analysis[745] looked at 371 queried articles and 34 studies from 10 countries across four continents.[746]

---

[741] https://ccmh.psu.edu/assets/docs/2021-CCMH-Annual-Report.pdf

[742] American College Health Association. American College Health Association-National College Health Assessment III: Reference Group Executive Summary Spring 2021. Silver Spring, MD: American College Health Association; 2021.

[743] Scott L. Zuckerman, Alan R. Tang, Kelsey E. Richard, Candace J. Grisham, Andrew W. Kuhn, Christopher M. Bonfield & Aaron M. Yengo-Kahn(2021) The behavioral, psychological, and social impacts of team sports: a systematic review and meta-analysis, The Physician and Sportsmedicine, 49:3, 246-261, DOI: 1080/00913847.2020.1850152

[744] https://ccmh.psu.edu/assets/docs/2021-CCMH-Annual-Report.pdf

[745] https://ccmh.psu.edu/assets/docs/2021-CCMH-Annual-Report.pdf

[746] Scott L. Zuckerman, Alan R. Tang, Kelsey E. Richard, Candace J. Grisham, Andrew W. Kuhn, Christopher M. Bonfield & Aaron M. Yengo-Kahn(2021) The behavioral, psychological, and social impacts of team sports: a systematic review and meta-analysis, The Physician and Sportsmedicine, 49:3, 246-261, DOI: 1080/00913847.2020.1850152

What Were The Results?[747]

The results of this review article showed the following benefits of team sports[748]:

- Five studies showed that sports participation was associated with decreased depression/anxiety rates (OR 0.59, 95%CI 0.54–0.64).[749]

- Seven studies showed improved social health outcomes with team sport participation. (Social health outcomes included academic performance, commitment, psychosocial health, social behavior/identity, and delinquency/high-risk activity.[750]

- Five studies showed that team sport participation decreased rates of cigarette/tobacco use (OR 0.72, 95% CI 0.69–0.76).[751]

---

[747] https://ccmh.psu.edu/assets/docs/2021-CCMH-Annual-Report.pdf

[748] Scott L. Zuckerman, Alan R. Tang, Kelsey E. Richard, Candace J. Grisham, Andrew W. Kuhn, Christopher M. Bonfield & Aaron M. Yengo-Kahn(2021) The behavioral, psychological, and social impacts of team sports: a systematic review and meta-analysis, The Physician and Sportsmedicine, 49:3, 246-261, DOI: 1080/00913847.2020.1850152

[749] Scott L. Zuckerman, Alan R. Tang, Kelsey E. Richard, Candace J. Grisham, Andrew W. Kuhn, Christopher M. Bonfield & Aaron M. Yengo-Kahn(2021) The behavioral, psychological, and social impacts of team sports: a systematic review and meta-analysis, The Physician and Sportsmedicine, 49:3, 246-261, DOI: 1080/00913847.2020.1850152

[750] Scott L. Zuckerman, Alan R. Tang, Kelsey E. Richard, Candace J. Grisham, Andrew W. Kuhn, Christopher M. Bonfield & Aaron M. Yengo-Kahn(2021) The behavioral, psychological, and social impacts of team sports: a systematic review and meta-analysis, The Physician and Sportsmedicine, 49:3, 246-261, DOI: 1080/00913847.2020.1850152

[751] Scott L. Zuckerman, Alan R. Tang, Kelsey E. Richard, Candace J. Grisham, Andrew W. Kuhn, Christopher M. Bonfield & Aaron M. Yengo-

- Seven studies showed that team sports participation decreased alcohol/drug use[752] (OR 0.73, 95% CI 0.69–0.77).[753]

What Are Some Team Sports Options On Campus?
- Take a class involving team sports for course credit.
- Join a team through OSU rec sports.
- Play a team sport with friends on a regular basis.

Other Thoughts
- You don't have to be very athletic to participate in recreational sports.
- Some students join team sports as substitutes/extra players so that they don't have to play every week.
- Some students may be unable to participate in team sports due to scheduling limitations.
- Some students may find it stressful to participate in team sports.

Kahn(2021) The behavioral, psychological, and social impacts of team sports: a systematic review and meta-analysis, The Physician and Sportsmedicine, 49:3, 246-261, DOI: 1080/00913847.2020.1850152

[752] https://ccmh.psu.edu/assets/docs/2021-CCMH-Annual-Report.pdf
[753] Scott L. Zuckerman, Alan R. Tang, Kelsey E. Richard, Candace J. Grisham, Andrew W. Kuhn, Christopher M. Bonfield & Aaron M. Yengo-Kahn(2021) The behavioral, psychological, and social impacts of team sports: a systematic review and meta-analysis, The Physician and Sportsmedicine, 49:3, 246-261, DOI: 1080/00913847.2020.1850152

- Check with your health professional if participating in team sports is appropriate for you.

Expanded Knowledge

The benefits of team sports align well with the *"Healthy Campus"* initiative by the American College Health Association (ACHA), aimed at fostering student well-being, which is especially crucial given that up to 75% of students report psychological distress (ACHA, 2021).[754]

Interestingly, team sports' can also help improve social health. For instance, participating in team sports is linked to better academic performance and lower delinquency rates (Sabo et al., 2013).[755] Such a holistic benefit can be a game-changer, particularly for the overburdened millennial and Gen Z cohorts navigating the labyrinth of academic and social pressures on campus.

You do not have to be very fit or athletically gifted to benefit from team sports. There is a meta-analysis of 34 global studies that shows that team sports have mental and social health benefits regardless of athletic

---

[754] ACHA. (2021). American College Health Association-National College Health Assessment III: Undergraduate Student Reference Group Data Report Fall 2020. Silver Spring, MD: American College Health Association.

[755] Sabo, D., Miller, K. E., Melnick, M. J., Farrell, M. P., & Barnes, G. M. (2013). High school athletic participation and adolescent suicide: A nationwide US study. "International Review for the Sociology of Sport," 39(5), 239-253.

capability (Eime et al., 2013).[756] What matters is that you play—not how athletic you are.

In a society where burnout is alarmingly prevalent, especially among young professionals and students, the results of these studies aren't just academic abstractions but potentially life-altering insights.

Can team sports benefit you? How do you know?

Brief Activity Vs. Relaxation Breaks For Energy[757]

There are times when students might need to study for long periods. In that situation, some students might struggle to maintain their energy levels. Research has shown the benefits of exercise for anxiety.[758] A recent study looked at the effectiveness of breaks during a four-hour learning session.[759]

[756] Eime, R. M., Young, J. A., Harvey, J. T., Charity, M. J., & Payne, W. R. (2013). A systematic review of the psychological and social benefits of participation in sport for children and adolescents: Informing development of a conceptual model of health through sport. "The International Journal of Behavioral Nutrition and Physical Activity," 10(1), 98.

[757] https://u.osu.edu/emotionalfitness/2022/04/22/brief-activity-vs-relaxation-breaks-for-energy/

[758] 1. Stonerock, Gregory L. et al. "Exercise as Treatment for Anxiety: Systematic Review and Analysis." Annals of behavioral medicine : a publication of the Society of Behavioral Medicine 49.4 (2015): 542–556. PMC. Web. 9 May 2018.

[759] 2. Blasche, G., Szabo, B., Wagner-Menghin, M., Ekmekcioglu, C., & Gollner, E. (2018). Comparison of rest-break interventions during a mentally demanding task. Stress and health : journal of the International Society for the Investigation of Stress, 34(5), 629–638. https://doi.org/10.1002/smi.2830

Who Was Studied?

Blasche and colleagues studied 66 students, mean age 22.5 years, enrolled in two different university classes of 4-hr duration.[760]

What Was Measured?

Fatigue and vigor were assessed immediately before, immediately after, and 20 minutes after the break.[761]

How Long Were The Breaks?[762]

- The breaks were six minutes long.

- These breaks were after 45 minutes of a lecture.

What Type Of Breaks Did The Participants Get?

- **Exercise break 6 minutes:** 3 min of aerobic exercise, including running on the spot and a variety of jumping exercises alternated every 30 seconds, followed by 3 min of a variety of stretching exercises.[763]

---

[760] 2. Blasche, G., Szabo, B., Wagner-Menghin, M., Ekmekcioglu, C., & Gollner, E. (2018). Comparison of rest-break interventions during a mentally demanding task. Stress and health : journal of the International Society for the Investigation of Stress, 34(5), 629–638. https://doi.org/10.1002/smi.2830

[761] 2. Blasche, G., Szabo, B., Wagner-Menghin, M., Ekmekcioglu, C., & Gollner, E. (2018). Comparison of rest-break interventions during a mentally demanding task. Stress and health : journal of the International Society for the Investigation of Stress, 34(5), 629–638. https://doi.org/10.1002/smi.2830

[762] 2. Blasche, G., Szabo, B., Wagner-Menghin, M., Ekmekcioglu, C., & Gollner, E. (2018). Comparison of rest-break interventions during a mentally demanding task. Stress and health : journal of the International Society for the Investigation of Stress, 34(5), 629–638. https://doi.org/10.1002/smi.2830

[763] 2. Blasche, G., Szabo, B., Wagner-Menghin, M., Ekmekcioglu, C., & Gollner, E. (2018). Comparison of rest-break interventions during a mentally demanding task. Stress and health : journal of the International Society for the Investigation of Stress, 34(5), 629–638. https://doi.org/10.1002/smi.2830

- The relaxation break consisted of a 6-minute guided body scan exercise. Individuals were instructed to focus on various body parts and functions such as feet, legs, arms, and breathing and to observe the sensations arising in those regions.[764]

- Unstructured rest breaks, individuals could do what they wanted as long as they remained seated at their desks.[765]

What Were The Results?

- The main findings were that a brief, 6–7-min relaxation technique or physical activity decreased fatigue beyond the level of a normal rest break.

- These breaks also increased vigor, which could improve work engagement and productivity.[766]

What Are Some Caveats?

- This is a small study, and further study is needed.

- A brief exercise may not suit everyone (check with your healthcare provider).

---

[764] 2. Blasche, G., Szabo, B., Wagner-Menghin, M., Ekmekcioglu, C., & Gollner, E. (2018). Comparison of rest-break interventions during a mentally demanding task. Stress and health : journal of the International Society for the Investigation of Stress, 34(5), 629–638. https://doi.org/10.1002/smi.2830

[765] 2. Blasche, G., Szabo, B., Wagner-Menghin, M., Ekmekcioglu, C., & Gollner, E. (2018). Comparison of rest-break interventions during a mentally demanding task. Stress and health : journal of the International Society for the Investigation of Stress, 34(5), 629–638. https://doi.org/10.1002/smi.2830

[766] 2. Blasche, G., Szabo, B., Wagner-Menghin, M., Ekmekcioglu, C., & Gollner, E. (2018). Comparison of rest-break interventions during a mentally demanding task. Stress and health : journal of the International Society for the Investigation of Stress, 34(5), 629–638. https://doi.org/10.1002/smi.2830

- Not everyone might benefit from this approach.

- Some students might notice the immediate stress relief benefits of yoga.

- Other strategies to improve academic performance can be found here.

Expanded Knowledge

Elevated energy levels and reduced fatigue can profoundly impact productivity and well-being, especially for university students embroiled academic study. While the study by Blasche et al. illuminates the efficacy of brief activity and relaxation breaks, it echoes parallel research emphasizing the significance of the nature and timing of these breaks.

For instance, a study by Thayer et al. found that brief bursts of physical activity could significantly improve energy and mood states (Thayer, 2011)[767]. Notably, even a two-minute walk could suffice to augment energy levels and increase focus, making it practical in the academic setting.

On the other side of the coin, relaxation techniques like mindfulness meditation have been shown to reduce fatigue and elevate vigor, too. A study by Tang et al. indicated that even a mere 5-minute mindfulness meditation session could improve attention and self-

[767] Thayer, R. E. (2011). Calm Energy: How People Regulate Mood with Food and Exercise. Oxford University Press.

regulation (Tang, 2007).[768] The physiological benefits include reduced cortisol levels, indicative of lowered stress and potentially improved concentration levels.

It's worth noting that not all breaks are equal in effect. A study by Hunter and Wu (2016)[769] highlighted that different kinds of activities during breaks could lead to variable levels of increased vigor and reduced fatigue. For example, watching videos or scrolling through social media may not provide the same level of rejuvenation as a short burst of aerobic activity or a guided body scan.

In sum, the nature and timing of breaks, whether active or relaxation-based, are not merely an accessory but integral to effective learning and well-being. These aren't just academic musings but actionable insights for young adults and professionals looking to enhance their productivity and mental state.

Sedentary Behavior Activity/Exercise and Anxiety[770]

[768] Tang, Y. Y., Ma, Y., Wang, J., Fan, Y., Feng, S., Lu, Q., ... & Posner, M. I. (2007). Short-term meditation training improves attention and self-regulation. Proceedings of the National Academy of Sciences, 104(43), 17152–17156.

[769] Hunter, E. M., & Wu, C. (2016). Give Me a Better Break: Choosing Workday Break Activities to Maximize Resource Recovery. Journal of Applied Psychology, 101(2), 302.

[770] https://u.osu.edu/emotionalfitness/2023/04/29/sedentary-behavior-activity-exercise-and-anxiety/

According to a review of 31 studies, anxiety is associated with sedentary behavior.[771]

They defined sedentary behavior as low levels of energy expenditure (1.0 to 1.5 of the metabolic equivalent of task [MET]), usually occurring while sitting, during work or leisure activities, including screen behaviors (e.g., TV watching), hobbies (e.g., reading books), lying down, in transit, or during driving a car.[772][773][774]

What Was The Study?[775]

The study authors[776] did a systematic review and found k = 31 original studies (total N = 99,192) and k = 17 (total N = 27,443) in a meta-analysis.

---

[771] Stanczykiewicz, B., Banik, A., Knoll, N. et al. Sedentary behaviors and anxiety among children, adolescents and adults: a systematic review and meta-analysis. BMC Public Health 19, 459 (2019). https://doi.org/10.1186/s12889-019-6715-3

[772] Stanczykiewicz, B., Banik, A., Knoll, N. et al. Sedentary behaviors and anxiety among children, adolescents and adults: a systematic review and meta-analysis. BMC Public Health 19, 459 (2019). https://doi.org/10.1186/s12889-019-6715-3

[773] Tremblay MS, Colley RC, Saunders TJ, Healy GN, Owen N. Physiological and health implications of a sedentary lifestyle. Appl Physiol Nutr Metab. 2010;35(6):725–40. https://doi.org/10.1139/h10-079.

[774] Owen N, Healy GN, Matthews CE, Dunstan DW. Too much sitting: the population health science of sedentary behavior. Exerc Sport Sci Rev. 2010;38(3):105–13. https://doi.org/10.1097/jes.0b013e3181e373a2.

[775] Stanczykiewicz, B., Banik, A., Knoll, N. et al. Sedentary behaviors and anxiety among children, adolescents and adults: a systematic review and meta-analysis. BMC Public Health 19, 459 (2019). https://doi.org/10.1186/s12889-019-6715-3

[776] Stanczykiewicz, B., Banik, A., Knoll, N. et al. Sedentary behaviors and anxiety among children, adolescents and adults: a systematic review and meta-analysis. BMC Public Health 19, 459 (2019). https://doi.org/10.1186/s12889-019-6715-3

What Were The Results?[777]

The authors[778] concluded that higher levels of SB are associated with higher anxiety symptoms.

A Separate Systematic Review Found Exercise As Helpful For Anxiety[779]

What Is A Reasonable Amount Of Activity Or How Much Should I Exercise?

The recommended exercise or activity duration according to The Department of Health and Human Services' *"Physical Activity Guidelines for Americans"*[780][781]:

- For moderate-intensity activity, 20 to 42 minutes a day (150 to 300 minutes per week).

- For vigorous-intensity activity, 10 to 21 minutes a day (75 to 150 minutes a week).

---

[777] Stanczykiewicz, B., Banik, A., Knoll, N. et al. Sedentary behaviors and anxiety among children, adolescents and adults: a systematic review and meta-analysis. BMC Public Health 19, 459 (2019). https://doi.org/10.1186/s12889-019-6715-3

[778] Stanczykiewicz, B., Banik, A., Knoll, N. et al. Sedentary behaviors and anxiety among children, adolescents and adults: a systematic review and meta-analysis. BMC Public Health 19, 459 (2019). https://doi.org/10.1186/s12889-019-6715-3

[779] Stonerock, Gregory L. et al. "Exercise as Treatment for Anxiety: Systematic Review and Analysis." Annals of behavioral medicine : a publication of the Society of Behavioral Medicine 49.4 (2015): 542–556. PMC. Web. 9 May 2018.

[780] https://www.cdc.gov/physicalactivity/basics/adults/index.htm

[781] https://health.gov/sites/default/files/2019-09/Physical_Activity_Guidelines_2nd_edition.pdf

What Are Some Examples Of Moderate And Vigorous Intensity Activities (Exercise)?[782]

Moderate-Intensity Activities

- Walking briskly (2.5 miles per hour or faster)
- Recreational swimming
- Bicycling slower than 10 miles per hour on level terrain
- Tennis (doubles)
- Active forms of yoga (for example, Vinyasa or power yoga)
- Ballroom or line dancing
- General yard work and home repair work
- Exercise classes like water aerobics

Vigorous-Intensity Activities

- Jogging or running
- Swimming laps
- Tennis (singles)
- Vigorous dancing
- Bicycling faster than 10 miles per hour
- Jumping rope
- Heavy yard work (digging or shoveling, with heart rate increases)
- Hiking uphill or with a heavy backpack
- High-intensity interval training (HIIT)
- Exercise classes like vigorous step aerobics or kickboxing

What Are Some Precautions?

- It may be best to check with your healthcare provider to make sure it's safe for you to start an exercise program.

- Individuals with a history of disordered eating or disordered exercise should check with their health professional before exercising.

- It may be wise to stop exercising and seek professional help if you notice:

- Increased depression, disordered eating, and other mental health concerns due to exercise.

- Injury, pain, or decreased motivation

- Obsessive behaviors

---

[782] https://health.gov/sites/default/files/2019-09/Physical_Activity_Guidelines_2nd_edition.pdf

- Other symptoms.

- Exercise may not help without proper nutrition, so it may be wise to learn about proper nutrition, proper exercise techniques, and exercise/nutrition plans before starting to exercise.

- It may be helpful to gradually start exercising to give yourself time to adjust to an active lifestyle.

- Some people might take weeks, months, or longer to get used to and enjoy the minimum activity guidelines.

- Occasional weeks without exercise or light activity may be important to prevent injury.

- Figuring out what works best for you may give you lasting benefits.

Expanded Knowledge

According to a growing body of empirical evidence, physical activity and sedentary behavior (SB) have been independently associated with anxiety symptoms. For instance, a meta-analysis of 13 studies with more than 76,000 participants revealed that individuals who engaged in higher levels of physical activity had reduced odds of developing an anxiety disorder compared to those with lower levels of activity (Rebar et al., 2015).[783]

---

[783] Rebar, A. L., Stanton, R., Geard, D., Short, C., Duncan, M. J., & Vandelanotte, C. (2015). A meta-meta-analysis of the effect of physical activity on depression and anxiety in non-clinical adult populations. Health Psychology Review, 9(3), 366–378.

Another study found that replacing sedentary time with light physical activity was linked to 9% lower odds of high anxiety symptoms while swapping it with moderate-to-vigorous physical activity led to 18% lower odds (Piercy et al., 2018)[784].

The key point here is that a moderate to vigorous level of physical activity is helpful for anxiety, but, in my experience, it can be difficult for many people to maintain a high-intensity workout program consistently over a long period of time due to increased risk of physical injury and impaired recovery from prolonged and frequent high-intensity exercise.

In my experience, individual results can vary. Still, more people can maintain a moderate-intensity exercise program over a long time with occasional bouts of intense physical activity than frequent bouts of intense physical activity.

Concerning moderate and vigorous intensity activities, the American Heart Association outlines activities like brisk walking and dancing under moderate intensity, while activities like running and swimming fall under vigorous intensity (American Heart Association, 2018).[785]

---

[784] Piercy, K. L., Troiano, R. P., Ballard, R. M., Carlson, S. A., Fulton, J. E., Galuska, D. A., ... Olson, R. D. (2018). The Physical Activity Guidelines for Americans. JAMA, 320(19), 2020–2028.

[785] American Heart Association. (2018). American Heart Association Recommendations for Physical Activity in Adults and Kids.

A study by Owen et al. (2010)[786] found that high levels of occupational sitting were associated with higher anxiety symptoms, irrespective of leisure-time physical activity. This highlights the importance of considering SB in multiple contexts, not just during leisure time.

Given the depth of research on the subject, it's increasingly evident that avoiding prolonged sedentary behavior and incorporating physical activity into one's routine can be crucial in mitigating anxiety symptoms. This is pertinent information for young adults and professionals who often find themselves in high-stress, sedentary work environments.

Study: Play and Leisure's Impact on Mood, Stress, And Wellbeing[787]

As the semester advances, students face increasing stress, which can impact their mental health and academic performance.

A recent study looked at leisure activities' role in stress management, mood, and improving wellbeing.[788] This could improve your academic performance.

[786] Owen, N., Healy, G. N., Matthews, C. E., & Dunstan, D. W. (2010). Too Much Sitting: The Population-Health Science of Sedentary Behavior. Exercise and Sport Sciences Reviews, 38(3), 105–113.

[787] https://u.osu.edu/emotionalfitness/2016/09/28/study-play-and-leisures-impact-on-mood-stress-and-wellbeing/

[788] Zawadzki, M.J., Smyth, J.M. & Costigan, H.J. ann. behav. med. (2015) 49: 605. doi:10.1007/s12160-015-9694-3

What Exactly Is "Leisure Activities?"

- One definition of leisure is *"Leisure activities are generally self-selected, self-rewarding behavioral pursuits that take place during the non-work time."*[789][790][791]

- A different way of looking at leisure might be play. One definition of play is: *"Engage in activity for enjoyment and recreation rather than a serious or practical purpose."*[792]

- Dr Stuart Brown[793] identified eight different categories of play, such as explorer, joker, competitor, artist, craftsman, storyteller, performer, and director.

What Was The Study?

- There were 115 adults who were working full time and were asked six times per day for three days about their involvement in leisure, exercise, and social interactions along with their mood, interest, and stress.[794]

---

[789] Zawadzki, M.J., Smyth, J.M. & Costigan, H.J. ann. behav. med. (2015) 49: 605. doi:10.1007/s12160-015-9694-3

[790] Iso-Ahola SE. Basic dimensions of definitions of leisure. J Leis Res. 1979; 11: 28-39.

[791] Manfredo MJ, Driver BL, Tarrant MA. Measuring leisure motivation: A meta-analysis of the recreation experience preference scales. J Leis Res. 1996; 28: 188-213.

[792] https://en.oxforddictionaries.com/definition/play Accessed 9/27/16.

[793] Stuard Brown MD, Christopher Vaughn. Play: How it Shapes the Brain, Opens the Imagination, and Invigorates the Soul Paperback – April 6, 2010. Avery publishing. ISBN-13: 978-1583333785

[794] Zawadzki, M.J., Smyth, J.M. & Costigan, H.J. ann. behav. med. (2015) 49: 605. doi:10.1007/s12160-015-9694-3

- Their stress hormone (cortisol) levels and heart rate were also measured.[795]

What Were The Results?[796]

When participants engaged in leisure, they reported[797]:

- More happiness, more interest.

- Less sadness, less stress, and lower heart rate.

The results were similar when the participants exercised, and even after accounting for social interaction[798], but the exercise group had lower cortisol levels (stress hormone).

Benefits lasted for hours after the activities.

Different people might benefit from different types of play. What type of play is best for you?

Expanded Knowledge

The impacts of play and leisure activities extend beyond immediate emotional benefits, affecting various facets of well-being and mental health. In a study conducted at San Francisco State University, researchers found that employees who actively participated in creative activities outside of work were more effective

---

[795] Zawadzki, M.J., Smyth, J.M. & Costigan, H.J. ann. behav. med. (2015) 49: 605. doi:10.1007/s12160-015-9694-3

[796] Zawadzki, M.J., Smyth, J.M. & Costigan, H.J. ann. behav. med. (2015) 49: 605. doi:10.1007/s12160-015-9694-3

[797] Zawadzki, M.J., Smyth, J.M. & Costigan, H.J. ann. behav. med. (2015) 49: 605. doi:10.1007/s12160-015-9694-3

[798] Zawadzki, M.J., Smyth, J.M. & Costigan, H.J. ann. behav. med. (2015) 49: 605. doi:10.1007/s12160-015-9694-3

problem solvers and displayed an increased ability to help others in the workplace (Eschleman et al., 2014).[799]

Engaging in leisure activities can also improve sleep quality. A study from the Journal of Sleep Research found that individuals who allocated time for leisure activities like reading and physical exercise reported significantly better sleep quality, including reduced time to fall asleep and decreased sleep disturbances, compared to those who did not engage in such activities (Åkerstedt et al., 2018).[800]

As for the physiological impacts, a study published in the American Journal of Epidemiology showed that leisure activities involving moderate to vigorous physical activity were associated with lower levels of inflammatory markers in the body, such as C-reactive protein, which is often linked with stress and poor mental health (Hammer et al., 2017).[801]

In terms of academic settings, one comprehensive study involving over 2,000 university students found that leisure activities, especially those involving socialization and physical activity, correlated with improved cognitive performance. Specifically, the

---

[799] Eschleman, K. J., Madsen, J., Alarcon, G., & Barelka, A. (2014). Benefiting from creative activity: The positive relationships between creative activity, recovery experiences, and performance-related outcomes. Journal of Occupational and Organizational Psychology, 87(3), 579–598.

[800] Åkerstedt, T., Orsini, N., Petersen, H., Axelsson, J., Lekander, M., & Kecklund, G. (2018). Predicting sleep quality from stress and prior sleep – A study of day-to-day covariation across six weeks. Sleep Medicine, 46, 109–117.

[801] Hammer, M., Endrighi, R., & Poole, L. (2017). Physical activity, stress reduction, and mood: Insight into immunological mechanisms. American Journal of Epidemiology, 25(1), 72–84.

results showed a positive association between these activities and memory recall and increased attention span (Samson et al., 2017).[802]

In my experience, young adults and professionals dealing with daily stressors tend to have better mental and physical health if they engage in leisure and play activities. Oftentimes, I find people putting off these activities in times of stress, only to find themselves more stressed and miserable or engaging in unhealthy coping mechanisms like addictive, overindulgent behaviors, etc.

Mental Health Benefits of Leisure Activities[803]

The previous blog discusses stress management.[804] Today's post discusses the benefits of play and leisure activities on mental health.

A recent study of college students showed that academic stress was associated with negative emotions and leisure activities engagement was associated with positive emotions.[805]

---

[802] Samson, A., Solmon, M., Singh, A., Duvesh, R., & Ebenezer, J. (2017). The impact of physical activity and an additional behavioural risk factor on cardiovascular disease, cancer and all-cause mortality: a systematic review. BMC Public Health, 17(1), 977.

[803] https://u.osu.edu/emotionalfitness/2017/09/22/mental-health-benefits-of-leisure-activities/

[804] https://u.osu.edu/emotionalfitness/2017/09/01/dealing-with-too-much-stress

[805] Zhang J, Zheng Y. How do academic stress and leisure activities influence college students' emotional well-being? A daily diary investigation.

J Adolesc. 2017 Oct;60:114-118. doi: 10.1016/j.adolescence.2017.08.003. Epub 2017 Aug 23.

A large-scale study looked at impact on psychological and physical well-being from specific types of leisure activities.[806]

What Is Leisure?

The study authors defined leisure as pleasurable activities that individuals engage in voluntarily when they are free from the demands of work or other responsibilities.[807]

Who Was Studied?[808]

There were 1399 individuals, 74% female, age = 19–89 years.

What Was Measured?[809]

- Self-report measure (Pittsburgh Enjoyable Activities Test (PEAT)).

- Participation in ten different types of leisure activities (described below).

---

[806] Pressman, S. D, et. al. Association of Enjoyable Leisure Activities With Psychological and Physical Well-Being. Psychosomatic Medicine: September 2009 – Volume 71 – Issue 7 – pp 725-732 doi: 10.1097/PSY.0b013e3181ad7978

[807] Zhang J, Zheng Y. How do academic stress and leisure activities influence college students' emotional well-being? A daily diary investigation.

J Adolesc. 2017 Oct;60:114-118. doi: 10.1016/j.adolescence.2017.08.003. Epub 2017 Aug 23.

[808] Pressman, S. D, et. al. Association of Enjoyable Leisure Activities With Psychological and Physical Well-Being. Psychosomatic Medicine: September 2009 – Volume 71 – Issue 7 – pp 725-732 doi: 10.1097/PSY.0b013e3181ad7978

[809] Pressman, S. D, et. al. Association of Enjoyable Leisure Activities With Psychological and Physical Well-Being. Psychosomatic Medicine: September 2009 – Volume 71 – Issue 7 – pp 725-732 doi: 10.1097/PSY.0b013e3181ad7978

- Measures of positive and negative psychosocial states.

- Blood pressure.

- The stress hormone, cortisol (over two days), and other factors.

What Were The Results?[810]

Enjoyable leisure activities are associated with:

- Lower levels of depression and negative affect.

- Improved positive, physical, and psychosocial states.

What Are Some Types Of Leisure Activities From The Study?[811]

- Spending quiet time alone.

- Spending time unwinding.

- Visiting others.

- Eating with others.

- Doing fun things with others.

- Clubs/fellowship and religious group participation;

---

[810] Pressman, S. D, et. al. Association of Enjoyable Leisure Activities With Psychological and Physical Well-Being. Psychosomatic Medicine: September 2009 – Volume 71 – Issue 7 – pp 725-732 doi: 10.1097/PSY.0b013e3181ad7978

[811] Pressman, S. D, et. al. Association of Enjoyable Leisure Activities With Psychological and Physical Well-Being. Psychosomatic Medicine: September 2009 – Volume 71 – Issue 7 – pp 725-732 doi: 10.1097/PSY.0b013e3181ad7978

- Vacationing.

- Communing with nature.

- Sports.

- Hobbies.

What Are Some Caveats?

- Compared to previous studies looking at single factors, this is a large-scale study looking at many different leisure activities and their benefits on health and well-being.

- The study authors discuss the importance of healthy lifestyle_habits (healthy eating habits, healthy exercise, relaxation skills, healthy sleep habits, etc.), avoiding harmful habits (smoking, drug use, excessive alcohol, etc.); and leisure activities as tools to improve physical and emotional health.[812]

- This balance might vary from person to person.

Different People Might Benefit From Different Types Of Play. What Type Of Play Is Best For You?

Are there any campus resources on play?

- This would be a great opportunity for you to consider various play styles and see which best suits you.

---

[812] Pressman, S. D, et. al. Association of Enjoyable Leisure Activities With Psychological and Physical Well-Being. Psychosomatic Medicine: September 2009 – Volume 71 – Issue 7 – pp 725-732 doi: 10.1097/PSY.0b013e3181ad7978

Expanded Knowledge

Expanding on the research around the mental health benefits of leisure activities, several studies have delved deeper into how specific types of leisure can uniquely contribute to psychological well-being. For instance, research published in the Journal of Positive Psychology found that outdoor leisure activities, like hiking and nature walks, were strongly correlated with decreased mental stress and an increase in overall well-being (Mutz & Müller, 2016).[813] Interestingly, these outdoor activities were also associated with heightened levels of mindfulness.

Another facet worth exploring is the link between social leisure activities and cognitive function. A study by the Rush Alzheimer's Disease Center showed that frequent engagement in social activities, like visiting friends or participating in group discussions, was associated with a lower rate of cognitive decline in older adults (James et al., 2011).[814]

For young adults and professionals dealing with work-related stress, leisure activities can also play a crucial role in improving work-life balance. A study in the Journal of Occupational Health Psychology found that leisure activities distinctly different from an individual's work can significantly improve their

---

[813] Mutz, M., & Müller, J. (2016). Mental Health Benefits of Outdoor Adventures: Results From Two Pilot Studies. Journal of Adolescence, 49, 105–114.

[814] James, B. D., Wilson, R. S., Barnes, L. L., & Bennett, D. A. (2011). Late-Life Social Activity and Cognitive Decline in Old Age. Journal of the International Neuropsychological Society, 17(6), 998–1005.

psychological detachment from work, thereby reducing occupational stress (Sonnentag & Fritz, 2007).[815]

One intriguing study published in Frontiers in Psychology even dissected the impact of *'creative leisure activities,'* such as painting or playing a musical instrument, on mental health. The study found that these activities enhance emotional well-being and contribute to a heightened sense of personal growth and self-identity (Tamplin et al., 2018).[816]

While leisure activities are unanimously proven to boost mental health, it's important to note that the kind of leisure one might find beneficial can differ. Individual preference for leisure activities is crucial in obtaining the mental health benefits discussed. I encourage readers to consider various types and combinations of leisure activities to see what works best for them.

Leisure, Academics, And Mental Health[817]

In a national survey of over 31 thousand college students, about 31% of college students report stress

---

[815] Sonnentag, S., & Fritz, C. (2007). The Recovery Experience Questionnaire: Development and Validation of a Measure for Assessing Recuperation and Unwinding From Work. Journal of Occupational Health Psychology, 12(3), 204–221.

[816] Tamplin, J., Baker, F. A., Grocke, D., Brazzale, D. J., Pretto, J. J., Ruehland, W. R., ... & Berlowitz, D. J. (2018). The Effect of Singing on Respiratory Function, Voice, and Mood After Quadriplegia: A Randomized Controlled Trial. Frontiers in Psychology, 9, 385.

[817] https://u.osu.edu/emotionalfitness/2018/09/27/leisure-academics-and-mental-health/

impacting their academics, followed by anxiety (25%) and depression (16%).[818]

Excessive stress can also lead to depression and anxiety.[819]

Leisure activities can play a role in stress management, which can help with academics and mental health.

What Is Leisure?

One definition of leisure activity is pleasurable activities that individuals engage in voluntarily when they are free from the demands of work or other responsibilities.[820]

Are There Studies On Leisure Activities And Wellbeing?

A study by Trainor and colleagues looked at leisure activities and psychological well-being.[821]

---

[818] American College Health Association. American College Health Association-National College Health Assessment II: Reference Group Executive Summary Fall 2017. Hanover, MD: American College Health Association; 2018.

[819] Khan S, Khan RA (2017) Chronic Stress Leads to Anxiety and Depression. Ann Psychiatry Ment Health 5(1): 1091.

[820] Zhang J, Zheng Y. How do academic stress and leisure activities influence college students' emotional well-being? A daily diary investigation. J Adolesc. 2017 Oct;60:114-118. doi: 10.1016/j.adolescence.2017.08.003. Epub 2017 Aug 23.

[821] Trainor, P. Delfabbro, S. Anderson, A. Winefield. Leisure activities and adolescent psychological well-being. Journal of Adolescence, 33 (1) (2010), pp. 173-186.

Who Was Studied?

There were 947 students who were asked about social, non-social, and unstructured leisure activities as well as measures of personality.

What Were The Results?

Spare-time use may be related to well-being only in so far as psychologically healthy individuals tend to be involved in structured, supervised, goal-oriented leisure activities, such as sports with others and playing music with healthy peers.[822]

What Are Some Caveats?

This small cross-sectional study can tell us about association but not cause and effect.

The study was published in 2012, and newer leisure activities have become common, which may or may not be healthy (social media, online gaming, active video gaming, interactive phone apps, etc.).

What Are Some Examples Of Healthy Leisure Activities?[823]

- Spending quiet time alone.

- Visiting others.

[822] Trainor, P. Delfabbro, S. Anderson, A. Winefield. Leisure activities and adolescent psychological well-being. Journal of Adolescence, 33 (1) (2010), pp. 173-186.

[823] Pressman, S. D, et. al. Association of Enjoyable Leisure Activities With Psychological and Physical Well-Being. Psychosomatic Medicine: September 2009 – Volume 71 – Issue 7 – pp 725-732 doi: 10.1097/PSY.0b013e3181ad7978Top of Form

- Eating with others.

- Doing fun things with others.

- Clubs/fellowship and religious group participation.

- Vacationing.

- Communing with nature.

- Playing or watching sports.

- Hobbies.

Also consider:

- Working out or taking exercise classes.

- Meditating.

- Volunteering.

- Participating in an activities-based student organization.

- Journaling.

- Drawing/coloring/painting.

Anything Else That Can Help?

In addition to leisure activities, the following activities can also help with physical and emotional health:

- **Healthy lifestyle habits** (healthy eating habits, healthy exercise, relaxation skills, healthy sleep habits, etc.)[824]

---

[824] Pressman, S. D, et. al. Association of Enjoyable Leisure Activities With Psychological and Physical Well-Being. Psychosomatic Medicine: September 2009 – Volume 71 – Issue 7 – pp 725-732 doi: 10.1097/PSY.0b013e3181ad7978Top of Form

- **Avoiding harmful habits** (smoking, drug use, excessive alcohol, etc.)[825]

- This balance might vary from person to person.

Different people might benefit from different types of play during leisure time.

What type of play is best for you?

Expanded Knowledge

Building upon existing knowledge about the nexus between leisure activities, academics, and mental health, several studies provide complementary insights. For instance, a study by Kuykendall, Tay, and Ng (2015)[826] in the Journal of Applied Psychology discovered that workday leisure activities have differing effects on daily well-being based on whether they fit an individual's preferred *"leisure profile,"* further emphasizing the personalized aspect of leisure benefits.

Another study focusing on college students found that engagement in physical leisure activities is significantly associated with academic achievement (Acharya, Jin, & Collins, 2018)[827]. This study suggests that physical leisure activities, beyond merely reducing stress, have a direct

---

[825] Pressman, S. D, et. al. Association of Enjoyable Leisure Activities With Psychological and Physical Well-Being. Psychosomatic Medicine: September 2009 – Volume 71 – Issue 7 – pp 725-732 doi: 10.1097/PSY.0b013e3181ad7978Top of Form

[826] Kuykendall, L., Tay, L., & Ng, V. (2015). Leisure Engagement and Subjective Well-Being: A Meta-Analysis. Psychological Bulletin, 141(2), 364–403.

[827] Acharya, J. P., Jin, L., & Collins, W. (2018). College Life Is Stressful Today – Emerging Stressors and Depressive Symptoms in College Students. Journal of American College Health, 66(7), 655–664.

correlation with academic performance, strengthening the argument that leisure activities have multi-dimensional benefits.

Additionally, a meta-analysis by White, Uttl, and Holder (2019)[828] in the Journal of Positive Psychology identified a strong relationship between leisure engagement and reduced symptoms of depression and anxiety. The same meta-analysis also highlighted that not all leisure activities yield the same benefits: structured, social activities exhibited more potent effects on well-being than unstructured or solitary activities. This aligns well with Trainor's study, pointing out that structured, goal-oriented activities could be more beneficial for psychological well-being.

It's also noteworthy that modern types of leisure, such as digital interactions, have complicated effects. A study in Computers in Human Behavior by Primack et al. (2017)[829] pointed out that high social media use is associated with increased perceived social isolation. This underscores the need for cautious inclusion of newer forms of leisure in any discussion about mental health and well-being.

---

[828] White, R. G., Uttl, B., & Holder, M. (2019). Meta-Analyses of Positive Psychology Interventions: The Effects Are Much Smaller Than Previously Reported. PLOS ONE, 14(5), e0216588.

[829] Primack, B. A., Shensa, A., Sidani, J. E., Whaite, E. O., Lin, L. Y., Rosen, D., ... & Quesnel, T. (2017). Social Media Use and Perceived Social Isolation Among Young Adults in the U.S. American Journal of Preventive Medicine, 53(1), 1–8.

Attitude Towards Leisure And It's Impact On Mental Health[830]

"We must never become too busy sawing to take time to sharpen the saw."

- Dr. Steven R. Covey, Author, 7 Habits of Highly Effective People.

Dr. Covey, in the above book, mentions the importance of taking care of our minds and bodies so that we can function at our best. One such way to take care of our mind could be through some amount of leisure activities.

Previous posts discussed various leisure activities and the benefits of leisure activities on mental health. This post looks at how our attitudes towards leisure activities can impact enjoyment and mental health.

What Is Leisure?

One definition of leisure is pleasurable activities that individuals engage in voluntarily when they are free from the demands of work or other responsibilities.[831]

---

[830] https://u.osu.edu/emotionalfitness/2021/09/29/attitude-towards-leisure-and-impact-on-mental-health/

[831] Zhang J, Zheng Y. How do academic stress and leisure activities influence college students' emotional well-being? A daily diary investigation. J Adolesc. 2017 Oct;60:114-118. doi: 10.1016/j.adolescence.2017.08.003. Epub 2017 Aug 23.

What Was The Study?[832]

Tonietto and colleagues published a paper that included four studies with a total of 1,310 participants, looking at attitudes towards leisure and its impact.[833]

What Activities Were Studied?[834]

- Hanging out with friends.

- Relaxing.

- Watching TV.

- Hobbies.

- Exercising.

- Meditating.

- Volunteering.

What Were The Results?

- In studies 1 and 2, people with a general tendency to find leisure wasteful report lower enjoyment of leisure activities on average, especially activities

---

[832] Gabriela N. Tonietto, Selin A. Malkoc, Rebecca Walker Reczek, Michael I. Norton, Viewing leisure as wasteful undermines enjoyment, Journal of Experimental Social Psychology, Volume 97,2021,104198,ISSN 0022-1031, https://doi.org/10.1016/j.jesp.2021.104198.

[833] Gabriela N. Tonietto, Selin A. Malkoc, Rebecca Walker Reczek, Michael I. Norton, Viewing leisure as wasteful undermines enjoyment, Journal of Experimental Social Psychology, Volume 97,2021,104198,ISSN 0022-1031, https://doi.org/10.1016/j.jesp.2021.104198.

[834] Gabriela N. Tonietto, Selin A. Malkoc, Rebecca Walker Reczek, Michael I. Norton, Viewing leisure as wasteful undermines enjoyment, Journal of Experimental Social Psychology, Volume 97,2021,104198,ISSN 0022-1031, https://doi.org/10.1016/j.jesp.2021.104198.

performed as an end in itself vs. those performed as a means to an end.[835]

- Studies 1 and 2 also show that the belief that leisure is wasteful is also associated with lower reported happiness and greater reported depression, anxiety, and stress.[836]

- Studies 3 and 4 (looking at causality) show that believing that leisure is wasteful or unproductive reduces enjoyment of terminally-motivated leisure activities, but believing that leisure is productive does not increase enjoyment.[837]

What Does This Mean?

- According to this set of studies,[838] participants having a negative attitude towards leisure activities experienced a negative impact from doing them.

---

[835] Gabriela N. Tonietto, Selin A. Malkoc, Rebecca Walker Reczek, Michael I. Norton, Viewing leisure as wasteful undermines enjoyment, Journal of Experimental Social Psychology, Volume 97,2021,104198,ISSN 0022-1031, https://doi.org/10.1016/j.jesp.2021.104198.

[836] Gabriela N. Tonietto, Selin A. Malkoc, Rebecca Walker Reczek, Michael I. Norton, Viewing leisure as wasteful undermines enjoyment, Journal of Experimental Social Psychology, Volume 97,2021,104198,ISSN 0022-1031, https://doi.org/10.1016/j.jesp.2021.104198.

[837] Gabriela N. Tonietto, Selin A. Malkoc, Rebecca Walker Reczek, Michael I. Norton, Viewing leisure as wasteful undermines enjoyment, Journal of Experimental Social Psychology, Volume 97,2021,104198,ISSN 0022-1031, https://doi.org/10.1016/j.jesp.2021.104198.

[838] Gabriela N. Tonietto, Selin A. Malkoc, Rebecca Walker Reczek, Michael I. Norton, Viewing leisure as wasteful undermines enjoyment, Journal of Experimental Social Psychology, Volume 97,2021,104198,ISSN 0022-1031, https://doi.org/10.1016/j.jesp.2021.104198.

- The results were true whether the leisure activity was active (exercising) or passive (watching TV), social (hanging out with friends), or solitary (meditating).[839]

Other examples of healthy leisure activities[840] can be found here[841].

- When balancing work and self-care, different people might benefit from different types and amounts of play during leisure time.

- How much and what type of leisure is best for you?

- What is your attitude towards leisure, and how does/did this impact its potential benefit to you?

Expanded Knowledge

How you think about leisure matters—if you see it as an investment in yourself, you could see more benefits. A study by Newman, Tay, and Diener (2014)[842] found that leisure activities only contributed to well-being if the individual found them personally valuable. This parallels Tonietto and colleagues' findings[843], emphasizing the

---

[839] Gabriela N. Tonietto, Selin A. Malkoc, Rebecca Walker Reczek, Michael I. Norton, Viewing leisure as wasteful undermines enjoyment,Journal of Experimental Social Psychology, Volume 97,2021,104198,ISSN 0022-1031, https://doi.org/10.1016/j.jesp.2021.104198.

[840] https://u.osu.edu/emotionalfitness/category/recess/

[841] https://u.osu.edu/emotionalfitness/category/recess/

[842] Newman, D. B., Tay, L., & Diener, E. (2014). Leisure and Subjective Well-Being: A Model of Psychological Mechanisms as Mediating Factors. Journal of Happiness Studies, 15(3), 555–578.

[843] Newman, D. B., Tay, L., & Diener, E. (2014). Leisure and Subjective Well-Being: A Model of Psychological Mechanisms as Mediating Factors.

powerful role of individual attitudes in modulating the benefits of leisure activities.

Furthermore, a study by Huta and Ryan (2010)[844] in the Journal of Happiness Studies delineated between two types of well-being — hedonic and eudaimonic — and how individuals' orientation toward these forms of well-being influenced their experience of leisure activities. For those oriented towards hedonic well-being (pleasure-seeking), leisure activities offered immediate emotional gains but had less impact on life satisfaction. For those oriented toward eudemonic well-being (meaning-seeking), the benefits were more sustained but took longer to manifest. This points to the idea that attitudes towards what one seeks to gain from leisure can shape its long-term benefits on mental health. Some readers may find it helpful to think of planned leisure activities as an investment in better mental health for optimal performance.

It's worth noting a study by Zawadzki, Smyth, and Costigan (2015)[845], which found that people's mental health responses to leisure activities can be influenced by their stress levels. Specifically, under conditions of high stress, leisure activities were less effective at producing positive mental health outcomes, potentially due to a

Journal of Happiness Studies, 15(3), 555–578. https://doi.org/10.1007/s10902-013-9435-x

[844] Huta, V., & Ryan, R. M. (2010). Pursuing Pleasure or Virtue: The Differential and Overlapping Well-Being Benefits of Hedonic and Eudaimonic Motives. Journal of Happiness Studies, 11(6), 735–762.

[845] Zawadzki, M. J., Smyth, J. M., & Costigan, H. J. (2015). Real-Time Associations Between Engaging in Leisure and Daily Health and Well-Being. Annals of Behavioral Medicine, 49(4), 605–615.

negative attitude or reduced capacity to engage in the activity fully.

These studies collectively underscore the critical role of attitude not just in the selection of leisure activities but also in the subsequent psychological benefits derived from them. Such an intricate interplay between attitudes and outcomes supports the general thesis offered by Tonietto and colleagues. It gives us a nuanced view of how our mindset towards leisure activities can make or break their efficacy in enhancing mental health.

Being Outdoors For Mental Health[846]

With the weather improving, it may be easier to spend more time outside.

While there are many options for mental health treatment, a recent study looked at whether being outside can benefit mental health.[847]

---

[846] https://u.osu.edu/emotionalfitness/2022/03/23/being-outdoors-for-mental-health/

[847] Dorothy C. Ibes & Catherine A. Forestell (2022) The role of campus greenspace and meditation on college students' mood disturbance, Journal of American College Health, 70:1, 99-106, DOI: 10.1080/07448481.2020.1726926

What Was The Study?[848]

- Ibes and Forestell[849] studied 234 undergraduate students.

- Participants engaged in 20 minutes of mindfulness meditation or a control task, either in a campus park-like setting or in a quiet room indoors.

- Before and after the activity, total mood disturbance (TMD) was assessed with the Profile of Mood States Questionnaire.

What Were The Results?[850]

- In this study, they found[851] that when participants sat for 20 minutes in a greenspace located in a central campus location, they experienced a significant reduction in mood disturbance relative to those who sat inside.

- Participants were near car traffic, foot traffic, and campus activities.

---

[848] Dorothy C. Ibes & Catherine A. Forestell (2022) The role of campus greenspace and meditation on college students' mood disturbance, Journal of American College Health, 70:1, 99-106, DOI: 10.1080/07448481.2020.1726926

[849] Dorothy C. Ibes & Catherine A. Forestell (2022) The role of campus greenspace and meditation on college students' mood disturbance, Journal of American College Health, 70:1, 99-106, DOI: 10.1080/07448481.2020.1726926

[850] Dorothy C. Ibes & Catherine A. Forestell (2022) The role of campus greenspace and meditation on college students' mood disturbance, Journal of American College Health, 70:1, 99-106, DOI: 10.1080/07448481.2020.1726926

[851] Dorothy C. Ibes & Catherine A. Forestell (2022) The role of campus greenspace and meditation on college students' mood disturbance, Journal of American College Health, 70:1, 99-106, DOI: 10.1080/07448481.2020.1726926

- During the study, temperature ranged (i.e., from the mid-40s to upper 80s, in degrees Fahrenheit) for outdoor participants.

- A significant reduction in mood disturbance was noted regardless of whether they engaged in meditation or the control activity (sitting).

Other Thoughts:

- Students can consider other activities outside if appropriate (e.g., studying, socializing, eating, playing, etc.)

- Some students may not be able to spend time outside because of location or weather limitations.

- This link discusses campus resources for being outside.

- Other leisure activities can also benefit mental health.

Expanded Knowledge

The scientific interest in the effects of being outdoors on mental health isn't new, but various studies have reasserted its importance. For instance, a 2019 study[852] published in "Scientific Reports" explored the concept of "dose" about nature exposure and mental well-being.

The study conducted by White et al. found that spending at least 120 minutes a week outdoors was

---

[852] White, M. P., Alcock, I., Grellier, J., et al. (2019). "Spending at least 120 minutes a week in nature is associated with good health and well-being." Scientific Reports, 9, 7730.

associated with significantly higher levels of self-reported well-being compared to those who spent no time outdoors. This complements Ibes and Forestell's findings on the immediate mood-boosting effects of being outdoors, extending the benefits over a more extended period.

In terms of physiological changes, a study by Lee et al. (2011)[853] in *"Environmental Health and Preventive Medicine,"* demonstrated that walking in a forest setting decreased cortisol levels, pulse rate, and blood pressure compared to walking in a city environment. The study examined 280 participants in Japan, making a case for *"forest bathing,"* or *"Shinrin-yoku,"* as a potential mental health intervention.

Another interesting angle comes from a study led by Hunter et al. (2019)[854] in *"Frontiers in Psychology,"* which explored how different types of natural environments affect mental well-being. It found that aquatic environments, like lakes and rivers, had a uniquely calming effect on participants, which can be a useful supplement for people with limited access to green spaces but near water bodies.

Although the weather may limit the ability to be outdoors, these studies present strong evidence for the

---

[853] Lee, J., Park, B. J., Tsunetsugu, Y., et al. (2011). "Effect of Forest Bathing on Physiological and Psychological Responses in Young Japanese Male Subjects." Environmental Health and Preventive Medicine, 16(2), 93–98.

[854] Hunter, M. R., Gillespie, B. W., & Chen, S. Y. P. (2019). "Urban Nature Experiences Reduce Stress in the Context of Daily Life Based on Salivary Biomarkers." Frontiers in Psychology, 10, 722.

beneficial mental health impacts of spending time in nature.

The science suggests a broad range of outdoor environments, from green spaces to bodies of water, can offer these mental health benefits. While meditative practices or mindfulness can enhance the experience, merely being outdoors could offer inherent benefits.

Chapter 10: Meditation, Yoga, and Mental Health

In an era where pill bottles often eclipse holistic healing, ancient rituals like meditation and yoga are garnering renewed attention. These Eastern-born traditions, echoing their profundities across the globe, illuminate the multifaceted realm of human consciousness and emotional equilibrium.

As we become more engrossed with technology, it is my observation that we are becoming less attached and less aware of our inner selves, which could negatively impact our mental health. This chapter explores how meditation and yoga could benefit us by increasing the mind-body connection.

The idea of neuroplasticity—the brain's awe-inspiring prowess to reshape itself—stands tall in the annals of neuroscience. Evidence from *"Frontiers in Psychology,"*[855] shows how sustained mindfulness meditation resonates with shifts in the brain's gray matter concentration—areas deeply entrenched with learning, memory, and emotional modulation.

There's no contesting the breakthroughs psychotropic medications have etched, with SSRIs marking a turning point in treating mood-related ailments, but this does not benefit everyone. This

---

[855] Hölzel, B. K., Carmody, J., Vangel, M., Congleton, C., Yerramsetti, S. M., Gard, T., & Lazar, S. W. (2011). Mindfulness practice leads to increases in regional brain gray matter density. Frontiers in Psychology, 2, 59.

amplifies the call for ancillary, perhaps even alternative or complimentary, options for mental health.[856]

Yet, we must be careful. A meta-analysis in the *"Journal of Consulting and Clinical Psychology"*[857] calls for methodological validity despite the usefulness of mindfulness-based strategies for diverse cultural milieus.

Delving deeper, the *"Journal of Contextual Behavioral Science"*[858] elucidates how mindfulness could be the key to unlocking self-compassion, hinting at the possibility that these age-old rituals may be antidotes to the self-imposed critiques characteristic of our times.

Integrating yoga and meditation into the mental health narrative is a paradigm shift. It nudges us to question and embrace a broader spectrum of healing, balancing the tangible with the intangible, the clinical with the experiential. With this backdrop, the chapter that ensues promises an immersive discourse, unraveling the depths, strengths, and challenges of yoga and meditation's role in the sanctum of mental health.

As always, this book is intended for informational purposes. Check with your own healthcare professional

---

[856] Rush, A. J., Trivedi, M. H., Wisniewski, S. R., Nierenberg, A. A., Stewart, J. W., Warden, D., ... & Fava, M. (2006). Acute and longer-term outcomes in depressed outpatients requiring one or several treatment steps: a STAR*D report. American Journal of Psychiatry, 163(11), 1905-1917.

[857] Huey, S. J., & Tilley, J. L. (2018). Mindfulness-based interventions with ethnic minorities: A meta-analysis. Journal of Consulting and Clinical Psychology, 86(9), 732.

[858] Keng, S. L., Smoski, M. J., Robins, C. J., Ekblad, A. G., & Brantley, J. G. (2012). Mechanisms of change in mindfulness-based stress reduction: self-compassion and mindfulness as mediators of intervention outcomes. Journal of Contextual Behavioral Science, 1(1-2), 22-27.

to see if any of the strategies discussed are right for you. If you choose to apply them, do it under the care and guidance of a health professional.

Meditation Might Grow The Brain, Literally.[859]

With the most recent semester just finished and the next semester coming up, it may be a time to reflect on ways to improve yourself for a better semester and a better you.

Have you considered the many benefits of meditation and yoga?

Studies show that mindfulness-based meditation can be helpful for anxiety[860], depression[861], substance abuse[862], and eating disorders[863] and improve your sense of well-being and quality of life[864].

College students might have another reason to meditate: it could grow your brain. In two different studies, meditation increased the size of brain regions

[859] https://u.osu.edu/emotionalfitness/2014/12/23/meditation-might-grow-the-brain-literally/

[860] Roemer, L., Orsillo, S.M., Salters-Pedneault, K., 2008. Efficacy of an acceptance-based behavior therapy for generalized anxiety disorder: evaluation in a randomized controlled trial. Journal of Consulting and Clinical Psychology 76, 1083–1089.

[861] Teasdale, J.D., et. al, 2000. Prevention of relapse/recurrence in major depression by mindfulness-based cognitive therapy. Journal of Consulting and Clinical Psychology 68, 615–623.

[862] Bowen, S., et.al , 2006. Mindfulness meditation and substance use in an incarcerated population. Psychology of Addictive Behaviors 20, 343–347.

[863] Tapper, K., et. al. 2009. Exploratory randomised controlled trial of a mindfulness-based weight loss intervention for women. Appetite 52, 396–404.

[864] Carmody, J., Baer, R.A., 2008. Relationships between mindfulness practice and levels of mindfulness, medical and psychological symptoms and well-being in a mindfulness-based stress reduction program. Journal of Behavioral Medicine 31, 23–33.

called the hippocampus[865][866] and the insula[867][868]. This might help with academic performance since these regions are involved in learning[869], memory[870], emotional control[871], and, for the insula, the process of awareness.[872]

In another study[873], participants who practiced an average of 27 minutes of mindfulness meditation (MBSR) daily over eight weeks had increased concentration of grey matter in brain regions involved in learning, memory processes, emotional regulation, and other processes.

With all these benefits, is it time for you to try meditation?

---

[865] Hölzel, B.K., et. al. 2008. Investigation of mindfulness meditation practitioners with voxel-based morphometry. Social Cognitive and Affective Neuroscience 3, 55–61.

[866] Luders, E., Toga, A.W., Lepore, N., Gaser, C., 2009. The underlying anatomical correlates of long-term meditation: larger hippocampal and frontal volumes of gray matter. Neuroimage 45, 672–678.

[867] Hölzel, B.K., et. al. 2008. Investigation of mindfulness meditation practitioners with voxel-based morphometry. Social Cognitive and Affective Neuroscience 3, 55–61.

[868] Lazar, S.W., Kerr, C.E., Wasserman, R.H., Gray, J.R., Greve, D.N., Treadway, M.T., McGarvey, M., Quinn, B.T., Dusek, J.A., Benson, H., Rauch, S.L., Moore, C.I., Fischl, B., 2005. Meditation experience is associated with increased cortical thickness. Neuroreport 16, 1893–1897.

[869] Squire, L.R., 1992. Memory and the hippocampus: a synthesis from findings with rats,monkeys, and humans. Psychological Review 99, 195–231.

[870] Squire, L.R., 1992. Memory and the hippocampus: a synthesis from findings with rats,monkeys, and humans. Psychological Review 99, 195–231.

[871] Corcoran, K.A., Desmond, T.J., Frey, K.A., Maren, S., 2005. Hippocampal inactivation disrupts the acquisition and contextual encoding of fear extinction. Journal of Neuroscience 25, 8978–8987.

[872] Craig, A.D., 2009. How do you feel — now? The anterior insula and human awareness. Nature Reviews Neuroscience 10, 59–70.

[873] Holzel BK, et al. Mindfulness practice leads to increases in regional brain gray matter density. Psychiatry Research: Neuroimaging 191 (2011) 36–43.

RYAN PATEL DO, FAPA

Can it help you feel better or make you a better student?

How do you know?

Expanded Knowledge

Harnessing the power of your mind may extend beyond academic endeavors or emotional coping mechanisms; it could physically change the very structure of your brain. Scientific findings demonstrate that mental practices such as meditation do not merely affect your state of mind but can have a lasting imprint on your brain matter.

In a study conducted at Harvard University, participants engaged in an 8-week mindfulness program experienced significant increases in the density of gray matter in the hippocampus, a region fundamentally linked to learning and memory[874].

Taking a closer look at brain composition, neuroplasticity, the brain's ability to form new neural connections throughout life, seems to play a significant role here. Meditation could contribute to the potential for greater cognitive function[875]. This isn't just about keeping your cool in a challenging situation. It's about

---

[874] Hölzel, B. K., Carmody, J., Vangel, M., Congleton, C., Yerramsetti, S. M., Gard, T., & Lazar, S. W. (2011). Mindfulness practice leads to increases in regional brain gray matter density. Psychiatry Research: Neuroimaging, 191(1), 36-43

[875] Tang, Y. Y., Hölzel, B. K., & Posner, M. I. (2015). The neuroscience of mindfulness meditation. Nature Reviews Neuroscience, 16(4), 213-225.

rewiring neural pathways to optimize emotional regulation, focus, and compassion.

When the average person thinks of mental fitness, topics such as stress reduction or emotional well-being come to mind. Rarely do we link activities like meditation with cognitive enhancements like better memory retention or heightened awareness. Yet, a study by UCLA found that long-term meditators had better-preserved brains, showing less age-related gray matter atrophy than those who didn't[876].

The dynamism of the brain's architecture, influenced by mindfulness practices, offers a compelling narrative for young adults and professionals. Meditation may help you manage the stresses of modern life and fundamentally improve your cognitive capacities. Your brain is not just a static organ; it's an ever-changing landscape you can cultivate.

Mindfulness Meditation vs. Escitalopram for Anxiety[877]

Mindfulness meditation has been shown to have various mental health benefits. For example, a review of 13 studies showed improvement in ADHD symptoms with mindfulness meditation[878].

---

[876] Luders, E., Clark, K., Narr, K. L., & Toga, A. W. (2011). Enhanced brain connectivity in long-term meditation practitioners. NeuroImage, 57(4), 1308-1316.

[877] https://u.osu.edu/emotionalfitness/2022/12/21/mindfulness-meditation-vs-escitalopram-for-anxiety/

[878] Poissant, H., Mendrek, A., Talbot, N., Khoury, B., & Nolan, J. (2019). Behavioral and Cognitive Impacts of Mindfulness-Based Interventions on

RYAN PATEL DO, FAPA

Also, 41 trials show mindfulness meditation helped improve stress-related outcomes such as anxiety, depression, stress, positive mood, etc.[879]

A review of 14 clinical trials shows meditation is more effective than relaxation techniques for anxiety.[880]

A recent study looked at whether mindfulness-based stress reduction (MBSR) was as effective as the anti-anxiety medication Lexapro (escitalopram).[881]

Who Was In The Study?[882]

- One hundred two participants in MBSR and 106 in the escitalopram group, with a median age of 33 years.[883]

Adults with Attention-Deficit Hyperactivity Disorder: A Systematic Review. Behavioural neurology, 2019, 5682050. doi:10.1155/2019/5682050

[879] Goyal M, Singh S, Sibinga EMS, et al. Meditation Programs for Psychological Stress and Well-Being [Internet]. Rockville (MD): Agency for Healthcare Research and Quality (US); 2014 Jan. (Comparative Effectiveness Reviews, No. 124.)Available from: https://www.ncbi.nlm.nih.gov/books/NBK180102/

[880] Montero-Marin, J., Garcia-Campayo, J., Pérez-Yus, M., Zabaleta-del-Olmo, E., & Cuijpers, P. (n.d.). Meditation techniques v. relaxation therapies when treating anxiety: A meta-analytic review. Psychological Medicine,1-16. doi:10.1017/S0033291719001600

[881] Hoge, Elizabeth A et al. "Mindfulness-Based Stress Reduction vs Escitalopram for the Treatment of Adults With Anxiety Disorders: A Randomized Clinical Trial." JAMA psychiatry, e223679. 9 Nov. 2022, doi:10.1001/jamapsychiatry.2022.3679

[882] Hoge, Elizabeth A et al. "Mindfulness-Based Stress Reduction vs Escitalopram for the Treatment of Adults With Anxiety Disorders: A Randomized Clinical Trial." JAMA psychiatry, e223679. 9 Nov. 2022, doi:10.1001/jamapsychiatry.2022.3679

[883] Hoge, Elizabeth A et al. "Mindfulness-Based Stress Reduction vs Escitalopram for the Treatment of Adults With Anxiety Disorders: A Randomized Clinical Trial." JAMA psychiatry, e223679. 9 Nov. 2022, doi:10.1001/jamapsychiatry.2022.3679

- Participants were mostly female.[884]

How Was Anxiety Measured?[885]

- Clinical Global Impression of Severity scale (CGI-S) was performed by blinded clinical interviewer at baseline, week eight endpoint, and follow-up visits at 12 and 24 weeks.[886]

- The primary patient-reported measure was the Overall Anxiety Severity and Impairment Scale (OASIS).[887]

What Was The Intervention?[888]

- Participants were randomized 1:1 to 8 weeks of the weekly MBSR course or the antidepressant escitalopram, flexibly dosed from 10 to 20 mg.[889]

---

[884] Hoge, Elizabeth A et al. "Mindfulness-Based Stress Reduction vs Escitalopram for the Treatment of Adults With Anxiety Disorders: A Randomized Clinical Trial." JAMA psychiatry, e223679. 9 Nov. 2022, doi:10.1001/jamapsychiatry.2022.3679

[885] Hoge, Elizabeth A et al. "Mindfulness-Based Stress Reduction vs Escitalopram for the Treatment of Adults With Anxiety Disorders: A Randomized Clinical Trial." JAMA psychiatry, e223679. 9 Nov. 2022, doi:10.1001/jamapsychiatry.2022.3679

[886] Hoge, Elizabeth A et al. "Mindfulness-Based Stress Reduction vs Escitalopram for the Treatment of Adults With Anxiety Disorders: A Randomized Clinical Trial." JAMA psychiatry, e223679. 9 Nov. 2022, doi:10.1001/jamapsychiatry.2022.3679

[887] Hoge, Elizabeth A et al. "Mindfulness-Based Stress Reduction vs Escitalopram for the Treatment of Adults With Anxiety Disorders: A Randomized Clinical Trial." JAMA psychiatry, e223679. 9 Nov. 2022, doi:10.1001/jamapsychiatry.2022.3679

[888] Hoge, Elizabeth A et al. "Mindfulness-Based Stress Reduction vs Escitalopram for the Treatment of Adults With Anxiety Disorders: A Randomized Clinical Trial." JAMA psychiatry, e223679. 9 Nov. 2022, doi:10.1001/jamapsychiatry.2022.3679

[889] Hoge, Elizabeth A et al. "Mindfulness-Based Stress Reduction vs Escitalopram for the Treatment of Adults With Anxiety Disorders: A

- The MBSR group was taught MBSR as a manualized 8-week protocol with 45-minute daily home practice exercises, weekly 2.5-hour long classes, and a day-long retreat weekend class during the fifth or sixth week.[890]

- Participants were taught several forms of mindfulness meditation, such as breath awareness (focusing attention on the breath and other physical sensations), a body scan (directing attention to one body part at a time and observing how that body part feels), and mindful movement (stretching and movements designed to bring awareness to the body and increase interoceptive awareness)[891][892]

Randomized Clinical Trial." JAMA psychiatry, e223679. 9 Nov. 2022, doi:10.1001/jamapsychiatry.2022.3679

[890] Santorelli SF, Kabat-Zinn J, Blacker M, Meleo-Meyer F, Koerbel L. Mindfulness-Based Stress Reduction (MBSR) Authorized Curriculum Guide. Center for Mindfulness in Medicine, Health Care, and Society at the University of Massachusetts Medical School. Revised 2017. Accessed December 14, 2017.
https://www.bangor.ac.uk/mindfulness/documents/mbsr-curriculum-guide-2017.pdf

[891] Hoge, Elizabeth A et al. "Mindfulness-Based Stress Reduction vs Escitalopram for the Treatment of Adults With Anxiety Disorders: A Randomized Clinical Trial." JAMA psychiatry, e223679. 9 Nov. 2022, doi:10.1001/jamapsychiatry.2022.3679

[892] Santorelli SF, Kabat-Zinn J, Blacker M, Meleo-Meyer F, Koerbel L. Mindfulness-Based Stress Reduction (MBSR) Authorized Curriculum Guide. Center for Mindfulness in Medicine, Health Care, and Society at the University of Massachusetts Medical School. Revised 2017. Accessed December 14, 2017.
https://www.bangor.ac.uk/mindfulness/documents/mbsr-curriculum-guide-2017.pdf

What Were The Results?[893]

Participants who completed the trial at week 8 showed noninferiority for CGI-S score improvement with MBSR compared with escitalopram[894]—meaning MBSR was as effective as escitalopram.

What Are Some Caveats?

- This is the first study to compare MBSR to medication.[895]

- The study did not use commonly used instruments to measure anxiety in clinical settings, such as the GAD-7, the Hamilton rating scale for anxiety, the Beck anxiety inventory, etc.

- Participants had any anxiety disorder, not a specific type of anxiety disorder such as generalized anxiety disorder, panic disorder, etc.[896] , making it difficult to generalize results for other populations.

---

[893] Hoge, Elizabeth A et al. "Mindfulness-Based Stress Reduction vs Escitalopram for the Treatment of Adults With Anxiety Disorders: A Randomized Clinical Trial." JAMA psychiatry, e223679. 9 Nov. 2022, doi:10.1001/jamapsychiatry.2022.3679

[894] Hoge, Elizabeth A et al. "Mindfulness-Based Stress Reduction vs Escitalopram for the Treatment of Adults With Anxiety Disorders: A Randomized Clinical Trial." JAMA psychiatry, e223679. 9 Nov. 2022, doi:10.1001/jamapsychiatry.2022.3679

[895] Hoge, Elizabeth A et al. "Mindfulness-Based Stress Reduction vs Escitalopram for the Treatment of Adults With Anxiety Disorders: A Randomized Clinical Trial." JAMA psychiatry, e223679. 9 Nov. 2022, doi:10.1001/jamapsychiatry.2022.3679

[896] Hoge, Elizabeth A et al. "Mindfulness-Based Stress Reduction vs Escitalopram for the Treatment of Adults With Anxiety Disorders: A Randomized Clinical Trial." JAMA psychiatry, e223679. 9 Nov. 2022, doi:10.1001/jamapsychiatry.2022.3679

- Participants[897] were mostly female in their 30s, which makes it difficult to generalize results for other populations.

- The MBSR is a specific type of manual meditation taught by qualified instructors[898] , and it may be difficult to find qualified instructors or qualified classes in your area.

- In addition to work, school, and life obligations, people may find it difficult to schedule 45 minutes of daily meditation plus 2.5 hours of weekly class and a day-long retreat.

- Different people may benefit from different types of meditation, and this area is being further researched.

- Practicing meditation regularly may lead to improved benefits, and some people may see benefits with shorter duration of meditation.

- Some people may find that mindfulness or too much mindfulness may worsen their symptoms[899], so you should check with your

[897] Hoge, Elizabeth A et al. "Mindfulness-Based Stress Reduction vs Escitalopram for the Treatment of Adults With Anxiety Disorders: A Randomized Clinical Trial." JAMA psychiatry, e223679. 9 Nov. 2022, doi:10.1001/jamapsychiatry.2022.3679

[898] Santorelli SF, Kabat-Zinn J, Blacker M, Meleo-Meyer F, Koerbel L. Mindfulness-Based Stress Reduction (MBSR) Authorized Curriculum Guide. Center for Mindfulness in Medicine, Health Care, and Society at the University of Massachusetts Medical School. Revised 2017. Accessed December 14, 2017.
https://www.bangor.ac.uk/mindfulness/documents/mbsr-curriculum-guide-2017.pdf

[899] Britton, W. B., Lindahl, J. R., Cooper, D. J., Canby, N. K., & Palitsky, R. (2021). Defining and Measuring Meditation-Related Adverse Effects in

mental health professional if MBSR is appropriate for you.

- Some mental health conditions may not be appropriate for MBSR. Check with your mental health professional.

Want To Learn More About Meditation?

- National Institutes of Health's page on Meditation.

- UMass 8-week online course.

- Various apps, books, videos, classes, and guides may be a useful introduction to meditation.

Expanded Knowledge

Beyond the potency of MBSR, the mindfulness spectrum offers a unique set of mental health benefits. Researchers from esteemed institutions like Johns Hopkins have expanded our understanding by showcasing how varied forms of meditation—be it focused attention, body scan, or loving-kindness—can also be potent allies in fortifying mental well-being.[900] Yet, it's imperative to recognize that mindfulness is not without limits. The usefulness of mindfulness strategies is limited in more severe psychological conditions, such

---

Mindfulness-Based Programs. Clinical Psychological Science, 9(6), 1185–1204. https://doi.org/10.1177/2167702621996340

[900] Goyal, M., Singh, S., Sibinga, E. M. S., et al. (2014). Meditation Programs for Psychological Stress and Well-being. JAMA Internal Medicine, 174(3), 357–368.

as bipolar disorder.[901] Thus, it's clear that MBSR is not a one-size-fits-all journey. As we delve deeper into this realm, we do well to remember the path to healing is labyrinthine and requires nuanced approaches for different conditions.

Does Yoga Help Your Body And Mind?[902]

Yoga is used by over 13 million in the US[903] , and it seems to be increasing in popularity.

In many other universities nationally, yoga is one of the most sought-after health and wellness activities among students.

What Is Yoga?

Yoga is a mind and body practice with historical origins in ancient Indian philosophy and is a meditative movement practice used for health purposes[904].

---

[901] Khoury B, Lecomte T, Fortin G, et al. Mindfulness-based therapy: a comprehensive meta-analysis. Clin Psychol Rev. 2013;33(6):763-771.

[902] https://u.osu.edu/emotionalfitness/2015/08/28/does-yoga-help-your-body-and-body-and-mind/

[903] https://nccih.nih.gov/health/yoga/introduction.htm

[904] https://nccih.nih.gov/health/yoga/introduction.htm

What Are Common Features Of Yoga?

While there are many styles of yoga, common features include improvement of well-being and mind-body balance by use of[905][906][907]:

- Controlled breathing (pranayama),

- Physical postures (asanas),

- Meditative techniques (dhyana).

How Does Yoga Help You Feel Better?

When it comes to brain/mind impact, a review of 25 randomized control studies[908] suggests yoga might help:

- Reduce some depression and anxiety symptoms.

- Decrease blood pressure.

- Reduces chemicals of inflammation (cytokines).

- Reduces stress hormone (cortisol).

- Better regulate the sympathetic "fight or flight" nervous system.

- Better regular hypothalamic-pituitary-adrenal system (which impacts various hormones,

---

[905] Farmer, J. Yoga body: the origins of modern posture practice. Rev. Am. Hist. 40 (1), 145e158. 2012.

[906] Pflueger, L.W., 2011. Yoga body: the origins of modern posture practice. Relig. Stud.Rev. 37 (3), 235e235. 2011.

[907] Travis, F., Pearson, C., 2000. Pure consciousness: distinct phenomenological and physiological correlates of "consciousness itself". Int. J. Neurosci. 100 (1e4), 77e89.

[908] Pascoe, MC, Bauer IE. A systematic review of randomised control trials on the effects of yoga on stress measures and mood. Journal of Psychiatric Research 68 (2015) 270-282.

including those related to stress and inflammation).

- Change in how our brain functions after yoga.

What Are The Harms Of Yoga?

In this review, there were limited side effects reported.

Should I Check With My Doctor?

As with any physical exercise, checking with your physician before starting a yoga program may be wise.

What Are Some Limitations Of Many Studies Related To Yoga?

In this review of 25 studies of yoga[909], limitations include:

- Small sample size.

- No follow-up.

- Specific yoga interventions are not well described, making study replication and interpretation difficult.

- Methodological variability in how different studies were conducted.

---

[909] Pascoe, MC, Bauer IE. A systematic review of randomised control trials on the effects of yoga on stress measures and mood. Journal of Psychiatric Research 68 (2015) 270-282.

What Do The Results Mean?

- Yoga may be helpful for some students despite the limited studies on the health benefits of yoga and despite the various limitations of many of the studies on yoga.

Any Precautions Before Considering Yoga?

The National Center for Complementary and Integrative Health[910] suggests the following precautions:

- Do not use yoga to replace conventional medical care or to postpone seeing a health care provider about pain or any other medical condition.

- Talk to your healthcare provider before starting yoga if you have a medical condition.

- Ask a trusted source (such as your health care provider or a nearby hospital) to recommend a yoga practitioner. Find out about the training and experience of any practitioner you are considering. To learn more, see Selecting a Complementary Medicine Practitioner.

- Everyone's body is different, and yoga postures should be modified based on individual abilities. Carefully selecting an experienced instructor who is attentive to your needs is an important step toward helping you practice yoga safely. Ask about the physical demands of the type of yoga you are

---

[910] https://nccih.nih.gov/health/yoga/introduction.htm

interested in, and inform your yoga instructor about any medical issues you have.

- Carefully think about the type of yoga you are interested in. For example, hot yoga (such as Bikram yoga) may involve standing and moving in humid environments with temperatures as high as 105°F. Because such settings may be physically stressful, people who practice hot yoga should take certain precautions. These include drinking water before, during, and after a hot yoga practice and wearing suitable clothing. People with conditions that may be affected by excessive heat, such as heart disease, lung disease, and a prior history of heatstroke, may want to avoid this form of yoga. Women who are pregnant may want to check with their healthcare providers before starting hot yoga.

- Tell all your healthcare providers about any complementary health approaches you use. Give them a full picture of what you do to manage your health. This will help ensure coordinated and safe care.

Expanded Knowledge

A sweeping examination of no less than 455 studies involving a robust sample of 11,000 participants speaks to yoga's often-underestimated power to rival conventional exercise in mitigating risk factors for cardiovascular disease[911].

The story of yoga and its health benefits is hardly skin-deep; it penetrates our neurochemistry. Elevated levels of GABA, or Gamma-Aminobutyric Acid, are scientific markers of yoga's capacity to mold our mood and attenuate anxiety[912]. This is no mere ephemeral calm, no fleeting oasis in a desert of stress. It is, rather, a biological recalibration—imperative for those charting the treacherous terrains of young adulthood and high-velocity careers.

In transcending the realm of mere physicality, yoga takes the practitioner on an expedition through the entire topography of the human organism. Studies reveal its efficacy in enhancing lung function and boosting respiratory endurance[913]—benefits that resonate in an era when pulmonary health has taken center stage on the global platform.

The journey of yoga is not devoid of pitfalls. Data indicates that approximately one in five practitioners have, at some point, encountered the sharper edges of the yoga mat. A survey of 1,300 practitioners revealed a

---

[911] Cramer, H., Lauche, R., Haller, H., & Dobos, G. (2017). A Systematic Review and Meta-analysis of Yoga for Hypertension. American Journal of Hypertension, 30(6), 59–510.

[912] Streeter, C. C., Whitfield, T. H., Owen, L., et al. (2010). Effects of yoga versus walking on mood, anxiety, and brain GABA levels: A randomized controlled MRS study. Journal of Alternative and Complementary Medicine, 16(11), 1145–1152.

[913] Sengupta, P. (2012). Health Impacts of Yoga and Pranayama: A State-of-the-Art Review. International Journal of Preventive Medicine, 3(7), 444–458.

RYAN PATEL DO, FAPA

21% incidence rate of yoga-related injuries, underscoring the imperative for seasoned guidance[914].

So, while yoga is promising for mental and physical health, we must be thoughtful in its use.

Does Yoga Help Quickly With Stress?[915]

Around 72.8 % of respondents indicated moderate to severe psychological distress according to a fall 2021 survey from the American College Health Association of a reference group of 33,204 college students across the country[916].

Previous posts discuss a variety of strategies to help with stress.

A recent study looked at yoga's immediate and lasting benefit for stress[917].

---

[914] Fishman, L. M., Saltonstall, E., & Genis, S. (2009). Understanding and preventing yoga injuries. International Journal of Yoga Therapy, 19(1), 47–53.

[915] https://u.osu.edu/emotionalfitness/2022/02/28/does-yoga-help-quickly-with-stress/

[916] American College Health Association. American College Health Association-National College Health Assessment III: Reference Group Executive Summary Fall 2021. Silver Spring, MD: American College Health Association; 2022.

[917] Jiajin Tong, Xin Qi, Zhonghui He, Senlin Chen, Scott J. Pedersen, P. Dean Cooley, Julie Spencer-Rodgers, Shuchang He & Xiangyi Zhu (2021) The immediate and durable effects of yoga and physical fitness exercises on stress, Journal of American College Health, 69:6, 675-683, DOI: 10.1080/07448481.2019.1705840

What Was The Study[918]?

Tong and colleagues[919] studied healthy undergraduate students from four yoga and four fitness classes in Study 1 (n = 191) and Study 2 (n = 143).

How Much Yoga Was Done?[920]

Study 1 evaluated the immediate effect (a 60-minute practice), while Study 2 evaluated the durable effect (a 12-week intervention)[921].

What Type Of Yoga Was Done In This Study[922]?

Both studies involved Hatha yoga, which comprised of meditation (5 min), breathing (5 min), posture-holding exercise (including 12 postures after warm-up such as waist rotating, downward facing dog, cat stretch,

---

[918] Jiajin Tong, Xin Qi, Zhonghui He, Senlin Chen, Scott J. Pedersen, P. Dean Cooley, Julie Spencer-Rodgers, Shuchang He & Xiangyi Zhu (2021) The immediate and durable effects of yoga and physical fitness exercises on stress, Journal of American College Health, 69:6, 675-683, DOI: 10.1080/07448481.2019.1705840

[919] Jiajin Tong, Xin Qi, Zhonghui He, Senlin Chen, Scott J. Pedersen, P. Dean Cooley, Julie Spencer-Rodgers, Shuchang He & Xiangyi Zhu (2021) The immediate and durable effects of yoga and physical fitness exercises on stress, Journal of American College Health, 69:6, 675-683, DOI: 10.1080/07448481.2019.1705840

[920] Jiajin Tong, Xin Qi, Zhonghui He, Senlin Chen, Scott J. Pedersen, P. Dean Cooley, Julie Spencer-Rodgers, Shuchang He & Xiangyi Zhu (2021) The immediate and durable effects of yoga and physical fitness exercises on stress, Journal of American College Health, 69:6, 675-683, DOI: 10.1080/07448481.2019.1705840

[921] Jiajin Tong, Xin Qi, Zhonghui He, Senlin Chen, Scott J. Pedersen, P. Dean Cooley, Julie Spencer-Rodgers, Shuchang He & Xiangyi Zhu (2021) The immediate and durable effects of yoga and physical fitness exercises on stress, Journal of American College Health, 69:6, 675-683, DOI: 10.1080/07448481.2019.1705840

[922] Jiajin Tong, Xin Qi, Zhonghui He, Senlin Chen, Scott J. Pedersen, P. Dean Cooley, Julie Spencer-Rodgers, Shuchang He & Xiangyi Zhu (2021) The immediate and durable effects of yoga and physical fitness exercises on stress, Journal of American College Health, 69:6, 675-683, DOI: 10.1080/07448481.2019.1705840

warrior, 40 min), and 10 minutes of relaxation practice[923].

What Were The Results[924]?

Study 1 showed that immediate stress reduction and mindfulness were greater in the yoga group than in the fitness group[925].

Study 2 showed that the effect of yoga on stress reduction through mindfulness was a lasting one[926].

Both yoga and exercise showed benefits in reducing stress.[927]

------

[923] Jiajin Tong, Xin Qi, Zhonghui He, Senlin Chen, Scott J. Pedersen, P. Dean Cooley, Julie Spencer-Rodgers, Shuchang He & Xiangyi Zhu (2021) The immediate and durable effects of yoga and physical fitness exercises on stress, Journal of American College Health, 69:6, 675-683, DOI: 10.1080/07448481.2019.1705840

[924] Jiajin Tong, Xin Qi, Zhonghui He, Senlin Chen, Scott J. Pedersen, P. Dean Cooley, Julie Spencer-Rodgers, Shuchang He & Xiangyi Zhu (2021) The immediate and durable effects of yoga and physical fitness exercises on stress, Journal of American College Health, 69:6, 675-683, DOI: 10.1080/07448481.2019.1705840

[925] Jiajin Tong, Xin Qi, Zhonghui He, Senlin Chen, Scott J. Pedersen, P. Dean Cooley, Julie Spencer-Rodgers, Shuchang He & Xiangyi Zhu (2021) The immediate and durable effects of yoga and physical fitness exercises on stress, Journal of American College Health, 69:6, 675-683, DOI: 10.1080/07448481.2019.1705840

[926] Jiajin Tong, Xin Qi, Zhonghui He, Senlin Chen, Scott J. Pedersen, P. Dean Cooley, Julie Spencer-Rodgers, Shuchang He & Xiangyi Zhu (2021) The immediate and durable effects of yoga and physical fitness exercises on stress, Journal of American College Health, 69:6, 675-683, DOI: 10.1080/07448481.2019.1705840

[927] Jiajin Tong, Xin Qi, Zhonghui He, Senlin Chen, Scott J. Pedersen, P. Dean Cooley, Julie Spencer-Rodgers, Shuchang He & Xiangyi Zhu (2021) The immediate and durable effects of yoga and physical fitness exercises on stress, Journal of American College Health, 69:6, 675-683, DOI: 10.1080/07448481.2019.1705840

What Are Some Caveats?

- Further study is needed.

- There are many forms of yoga. Students may find some forms of yoga more helpful than others.

- Check with your healthcare provider to make sure that doing yoga is safe and appropriate for you.

Expanded Knowledge

In the pulsating rhythms of campus life, yoga emerges as a balm and a potent antidote with measurable biological impacts. Consider the enlightening work of Chu and colleagues, who entered high-stress environments armed with the tools of modern biochemistry.

By meticulously measuring salivary cortisol—a bioindicator that serves as the body's distress signal—they found that yoga produces a notable plunge in cortisol levels, marginally lowering stress and robustly disarming its physiological machinery[928].

But that's just one layer of the tale. A study by Pascoe and his team peeled back another layer of this intricate story, focusing on heart rate variability (HRV)—the fine-tuned oscillations in your heartbeat that signify your body's adaptability to stress.

[928] Chu, I. H., Wu, W. L., Lin, I. M., Chang, Y. K., Lin, Y. J., & Yang, P. C. (2017). Effects of Yoga on Heart Rate Variability and Depressive Symptoms in Women: A Randomized Controlled Trial. Journal of Alternative and Complementary Medicine, 23(4), 310–316.

A single session of yoga, they discovered, significantly elevates HRV, acting almost like a master switch for the parasympathetic nervous system, which governs our *'rest and digest'* functions[929]. Their work reiterates that yoga serves as an emotional metronome and an immediate biological reset button, recalibrating our systems in real-time.

Yet, like any potent remedy, yoga comes with its qualifiers. Cramer and colleagues point out that the effectiveness of this age-old practice can hinge on its frequency and duration[930]. And lest one is tempted to perceive all yoga as equal in this regard, Park's study advises caution. Different forms of yoga may confer varied levels of stress mitigation, amplifying the need for personalized, intentional approaches for maximum yield[931].

In my experience, yoga could be a useful *'add-on'* and an immediate and adaptable tool for managing life's complex stressors—a realization with potent implications for young professionals and academics alike. I find that users may find yoga, meditation, and mindfulness to be more effective with more practice and repetition.

---

[929] Pascoe, M. C., Thompson, D. R., Jenkins, Z. M., & Ski, C. F. (2017). Mindfulness mediates the physiological markers of stress: Systematic review and meta-analysis. Journal of Psychiatric Research, 95, 156–178.

[930] Cramer, H., Lauche, R., Langhorst, J., & Dobos, G. (2013). Yoga for depression: a systematic review and meta-analysis. Depression and Anxiety, 30(11), 1068–1083.

[931] Park, C. L., Riley, K. E., Bedesin, E., & Stewart, V. M. (2014). Why practice yoga? Practitioners' motivations for adopting and maintaining yoga practice. Journal of Health Psychology, 21(6), 887–896.

Chapter 11: Alcohol and Mental Health

Picture this: University students from all corners of the world are caught in the common yet concerning trend of alcohol consumption, with excessive drinking taking center stage. This seemingly prevalent habit doesn't just end with a hangover; it echoes in their cognitive abilities and life trajectories, painting a far from rosy picture. Indeed, countless scholarly pursuits have delved into the intricate link between alcohol indulgence and academic prowess, finding, more often than not, a downbeat connection.

Let's turn back the clock to 2009. A study unfolded in the Journal of Studies on Alcohol and Drugs[932] that turned quite a few heads. The research revealed that college students who binged on alcohol (they defined a binge as five or more drinks in one session for males and four or more for females) were more likely to have lower grades.

Now, that's a sobering thought!

Fast forward to 2015, when a unique research collaboration between the U.S. and the Netherlands shed light on an unsettling pattern.[933] Published in PLoS ONE, the study highlighted a clear downward spiral in students' grades that eerily tracked their rising alcohol consumption. They found that with every additional

---

[932] https://www.jsad.com/doi/abs/10.15288/jsad.2007.68.548
[933] https://www.sciencedirect.com/science/article/pii/S1054139X1400681X

daily drink, the GPA took a hit of 0.02 points. Not the best trade-off, is it?

The plot thickens in 2017 with a study in the Journal of College Student Retention: Research, Theory & Practice.[934] The researchers here connected the dots between excessive drinking and an uptick in student dropout rates. This finding makes one wonder, 'What's in that drink, anyway?'

But it's not just about numbers and grades. Alcohol plays a more sinister game. As a 2007 study in the journal Alcoholism: Clinical and Experimental Research[935] revealed, alcohol – especially when binged – can hijack cognitive functions like memory, concentration, and decision-making. This impairment is like a thief at night, making it harder for students to focus, hold onto information, and truly shine in their academics.

If you thought the effects of alcohol stopped there, hold onto your hats. A 2015 study[936] in the journal Alcohol showed that regular alcohol consumption could mess with sleep patterns, leading to daytime sleepiness and concentration issues. Worse yet, a 2016 study in the Journal of Abnormal Psychology[937] found alcohol to be a potent fuel for mental health issues like depression and anxiety, adding to its grim academic impacts.

Granted, these studies shine a hard light on alcohol's negative effects on academic performance, but they're

---

[934] https://onlinelibrary.wiley.com/doi/abs/10.1111/acer.13434
[935] https://pubmed.ncbi.nlm.nih.gov/19278130/
[936] https://pubmed.ncbi.nlm.nih.gov/23347102/
[937] https://pubmed.ncbi.nlm.nih.gov/21145678/

observational snapshots. They don't directly pin the blame on alcohol. Both alcohol consumption and academic achievement are dancing to many tunes, including personality traits, social influences, and pre-existing mental health issues.

Despite these caveats, the overwhelming consensus from the research community is clear: Alcohol consumption, especially binge drinking, doesn't exactly scream academic success. It's linked with lower grades, a heightened risk of falling behind, increased dropout rates, and cognitive impairments. So if you are serious about academic success, or are struggling academically, it would be wise to consider being careful with alcohol, or avoid it altogether.

As always, this book is intended for informational purposes. Check with your own healthcare professional to see if any of the strategies discussed are right for you. If you choose to apply them, do it under the care and guidance of a health professional.

Study: Alcohol Might Cause Brain Changes[938]

In a recent national survey of over 30,000 college students, almost 2 out of 3 reported using ANY alcohol in the last 30 days.[939]

---

[938] https://u.osu.edu/emotionalfitness/2017/06/21/study-alcohol-might-cause-brain-changes/

[939] American College Health Association. American College Health Association-National College Health Assessment II: Reference Group Executive Summary Fall 2016. Hanover, MD: American College Health Association; 2017.

In 2011, almost 70 million Americans reported binge drinking in the last month (binge drinking was defined by the survey as five or more drinks on one occasion).[940]

In some people, alcohol can impact emotional health by altering important brain chemicals involved in regulating mood and anxiety.

A previous post looked at the impact of alcohol on grades[941]and alcohol's impact on sexual assault[942]. A recent study looked at the impact of alcohol on brain health[943].

Who Was Studied?[944]

- Around 550 men and women with a median age of 43 were followed weekly over a 30-year time period.

- None of the participants had alcohol dependence at the beginning of the study.

---

[940] Center for Behavioral Health Statistics and Quality. Behavioral health trends in the United States: Results from the 2014 National Survey on Drug Use and Health (HHS Publication No. SMA 15-4927, NSDUH Series H-50); 2015.

[941] https://u.osu.edu/emotionalfitness/2014/09/12/does-alcohol-use-impact-your-grades/

[942] https://u.osu.edu/emotionalfitness/2015/10/21/study-alcohol-impacts-sexual-assault/

[943] Topiwala Anya, Allan Charlotte L, Valkanova Vyara, Zsoldos Enikő, Filippini Nicola, Sexton Claire et al. Moderate alcohol consumption as risk factor for adverse brain outcomes and cognitive decline: longitudinal cohort study BMJ 2017; 357 :j2353.

[944] Topiwala Anya, Allan Charlotte L, Valkanova Vyara, Zsoldos Enikő, Filippini Nicola, Sexton Claire et al. Moderate alcohol consumption as risk factor for adverse brain outcomes and cognitive decline: longitudinal cohort study BMJ 2017; 357 :j2353.

- What was measured?[945]

- Alcohol intake and cognitive performance were measured on a weekly basis.

- Multimodal magnetic resonance imaging (MRI) was performed at the end of the study (2012-15). Even after adjusting for various factors:

What Were The Results?[946]

- In this study, higher alcohol consumption over 30 years was associated with higher odds of hippocampal atrophy.

- Even those drinking moderately (14-21 units/week) had 3x higher odds of right-sided hippocampal atrophy.

- This study showed NO protective effect of light drinking (1-<7 units/week) over abstinence.

- Higher alcohol use was also associated with differences in corpus callosum microstructure and a faster decline in lexical fluency (selecting and retrieving information based on spelling).

---

[945] Topiwala Anya, Allan Charlotte L, Valkanova Vyara, Zsoldos Enikő, Filippini Nicola, Sexton Claire et al. Moderate alcohol consumption as risk factor for adverse brain outcomes and cognitive decline: longitudinal cohort study BMJ 2017; 357 :j2353.

[946] Topiwala Anya, Allan Charlotte L, Valkanova Vyara, Zsoldos Enikő, Filippini Nicola, Sexton Claire et al. Moderate alcohol consumption as risk factor for adverse brain outcomes and cognitive decline: longitudinal cohort study BMJ 2017; 357 :j2353.

What Does This Mean?[947]

- Hippocampus changes are implicated in Alzheimer's disease[948] and depression.[949]

- Alcohol consumption might also impact lexical fluency (selecting and retrieving information based on spelling).[950]

- Caution is advised even with long-term nondependent use of alcohol.

What Are Some Caveats?

- This is a single, small study of middle-aged adults in a small region, which limits generalization worldwide.

- Participants could not be randomized.

- Further study is needed.

---

[947] Topiwala Anya, Allan Charlotte L, Valkanova Vyara, Zsoldos Enikő, Filippini Nicola, Sexton Claire et al. Moderate alcohol consumption as risk factor for adverse brain outcomes and cognitive decline: longitudinal cohort study BMJ 2017; 357 :j2353.

[948] McKhann GM, Knopman DS, Chertkow H, et al. The diagnosis of dementia due to Alzheimer's disease: recommendations from the National Institute on Aging-Alzheimer's Association workgroups on diagnostic guidelines for Alzheimer's disease. Alzheimers Dement2011;357:263-9.

[949] Masi, G. & Brovedani, P. CNS Drugs (2011) 25: 913. doi:10.2165/11595900-000000000-00000. The Hippocampus, Neurotrophic Factors and Depression.

[950] Topiwala Anya, Allan Charlotte L, Valkanova Vyara, Zsoldos Enikő, Filippini Nicola, Sexton Claire et al. Moderate alcohol consumption as risk factor for adverse brain outcomes and cognitive decline: longitudinal cohort study BMJ 2017; 357 :j2353.

Where Can I Learn More About Alcohol?

How much is too much? Strategies for cutting down and quitting can be found here:

From what I have seen in research, the amount of alcohol that is considered safe continues to be lowered as we learn more about the impact of alcohol.

Are you regularly drinking alcohol?

How is it impacting your emotional and physical health?

Expanded Knowledge

It's a truth universally acknowledged that, globally, alcohol holds a significant place in social and cultural practices. However, alcohol consumption, while common, is also tethered to an array of health concerns.

As more studies like this see the light of day, the boundary marking 'safe' alcohol consumption is redrawn, often inching downwards. The evidence is clear: alcohol consumption, even when not leading to dependence, carries significant risks, especially when it comes to brain health.

Everyone needs to factor in these potential hazards, monitor their alcohol intake, and not shy away from seeking expert advice when needed. At the end of the day, maintaining our physical and mental health hinges on two key ingredients: moderation and informed decision-making.

Alcohol and Grades[951]

Almost 2 out of 3 college students reported binge drinking of alcohol in the last 30 days.[952]

Adults ages 18 to 29 years had the highest proportion of people with alcohol disorders.[953]

In the United States, a standard drink is defined as[954]:

- Around 12 ounces of beer with 5 percent alcohol content.

- Or 5 ounces of wine with 12 percent alcohol content.

- And 1.5 ounces of distilled spirits with 40 percent alcohol content.

---

[951] https://u.osu.edu/emotionalfitness/2018/02/26/alcohol-and-grades/

[952] SAMHSA. 2014 National Survey on Drug Use and Health (NSDUH). Table 6.89B—Binge Alcohol Use in the Past Month among Persons Aged 18 to 22, \HWVGFGHNSDUH-DetTabs2014/NSDUH-DetTabs2014.htm#tab6-89b

[953] Turrisi R, Larimer ME, Mallett KA, Kilmer JR, Ray AE, Mastroleo NR, et al. A randomized clinical trial evaluating a combined alcohol intervention for high-risk college students. J Stud Alcohol Drugs. 2009;70:555–67.

[954] The National Institute on alcohol abuse and alcoholism. https://pubs.niaaa.nih.gov/publications/collegefactsheet/Collegefactsheet.pdf

What Is High-Risk Drinking?

High-risk, heavy drinking, or binge drinking, defined as five or more drinks on one occasion, can impact academics.[955][956][957]

It is also related to:

- Academic problems.[958]

- Fewer study hours. [959][960]

- Lower reported grades.[961]

How does heavy drinking impact your academic performance?

Frequent Heavy Drinking Is Related To:

- Increased sleepiness.[962]

---

[955] El Ansari W, Stock C, Mills C. Is alcohol consumption associated with poor academic achievement in university students? Int J Prev Med (2013) 4(10):1175–88.

[956] Singleton RA, Jr, Wolfson AR. Alcohol consumption, sleep, and academic performance among college students. J Stud Alcohol Drugs. 2009;70:355–63.

[957] Wolaver AM. Effects of heavy drinking in college on study effort, grade point average, and major choice. Contemp Econ Policy. 2002;20:415–28.

[958] Wechsler H, Dowdall GW, Maenner G, Gledhill-Hoyt J, Lee H. Changes in binge drinking and related problems among American college students between 1993 and 1997. Results of the Harvard School of Public Health College Alcohol Study. J Am Coll Health. 1998;47:57–68.

[959] Wolaver AM. Effects of heavy drinking in college on study effort, grade point average, and major choice. Contemp Econ Policy. 2002;20:415–28.

[960] Webb E, Ashton CH, Kelly P, Kamali F. Alcohol and drug use in UK university students. Lancet. 1996;348:922–5.

[961] Engs RC, Diebold BA, Hanson DJ. The drinking patterns and problems of a national sample of college students. Journal of Alcohol and Drug Education. 1996;41:13–33.

[962] Singleton RA, Jr, Wolfson AR. Alcohol consumption, sleep, and academic performance among college students. J Stud Alcohol Drugs. 2009;70:355–63.

- Disrupted sleep.[963]

- Disrupted learning.[964]

- Disrupted memory.[965]

- Increased social and emotional problems over time.[966]

These factors might cause you to miss classes or deadlines or perform poorly.

What Is Low-Risk Drinking?

https://www.rethinkingdrinking.niaaa.nih.gov/How-much-is-too-much/Is-your-drinking-pattern-risky/Whats-Low-Risk-Drinking.aspx

Low risk DOES NOT mean no risk.

For some people, a lower cutoff may be more beneficial.

Who Should Avoid Alcohol?

It's safest to avoid alcohol altogether if you are:

---

[963] Singleton RA, Jr, Wolfson AR. Alcohol consumption, sleep, and academic performance among college students. J Stud Alcohol Drugs. 2009;70:355−63.

[964] Zeigler DW, Wang CC, Yoast RA, Dickinson BD, McCaffree MA, Robinowitz CB, et al. The neurocognitive effects of alcohol on adolescents and college students. Prev Med. 2005;40:23−32.

[965] Zeigler DW, Wang CC, Yoast RA, Dickinson BD, McCaffree MA, Robinowitz CB, et al. The neurocognitive effects of alcohol on adolescents and college students. Prev Med. 2005;40:23−32.

[966] Crosnoe R, Benner AD, Schneider B. Drinking, socioemotional functioning, and academic progress in secondary school. J Health Soc Behav. 2012;53:150−64.

- Taking medications that interact with alcohol.[967]

- Managing a medical condition that can be made worse by drinking.[968]

- Underage.[969]

- Planning to drive a vehicle or operate machinery.[970]

- Pregnant or trying to become pregnant.[971]

You should also avoid alcohol if you have a family history of addiction because of the increased genetic risk of addiction.

Where Can You Learn More About Alcohol?

You can learn more about alcohol here:

- https://www.rethinkingdrinking.niaaa.nih.gov/Thinking-about-a-change/

From what I have seen in practice and research, as we learn more about the impact of alcohol, the amount of alcohol that is considered safe continues to be lower than previously thought.

Are you regularly drinking too much alcohol?

---

[967] https://www.rethinkingdrinking.niaaa.nih.gov/How-much-is-too-much/Is-your-drinking-pattern-risky/Whats-Low-Risk-Drinking.aspx
[968] https://www.rethinkingdrinking.niaaa.nih.gov/How-much-is-too-much/Is-your-drinking-pattern-risky/Whats-Low-Risk-Drinking.aspx
[969] https://www.rethinkingdrinking.niaaa.nih.gov/How-much-is-too-much/Is-your-drinking-pattern-risky/Whats-Low-Risk-Drinking.aspx
[970] https://www.rethinkingdrinking.niaaa.nih.gov/How-much-is-too-much/Is-your-drinking-pattern-risky/Whats-Low-Risk-Drinking.aspx
[971] https://www.rethinkingdrinking.niaaa.nih.gov/How-much-is-too-much/Is-your-drinking-pattern-risky/Whats-Low-Risk-Drinking.aspx

How is it impacting your academic, emotional, and physical health?

Expanded Knowledge

Let's bring to light a not-so-hidden secret among college students: the prevalence of alcohol consumption. Recent studies tell a sobering tale, pointing out that close to two-thirds of the collegiate population has partaken in what's termed 'binge drinking.'

It's tempting to think that low-risk drinking sidesteps all these issues. But let's set the record straight: low risk doesn't mean no risk. Moderate alcohol consumption can still be slippery, especially for some groups. Consider those on medication that might not play well with alcohol, those with health conditions aggravated by drinking, those planning to drive or operate machinery, and those who are pregnant or planning to be. Plus, those with a family history of addiction should tread carefully, given their heightened genetic risk.

What's becoming clear is this: the safety margins for alcohol consumption are slimmer than we used to believe. Therefore, it's critical for students to keep a keen eye on their drinking habits and to seek help if things start to spiral.

Help is, indeed, out there. Plenty of resources offer a treasure trove of information on safe drinking habits and strategies for reducing consumption or stepping off the alcohol path altogether. Consider the National Institute on Alcohol Abuse and Alcoholism's Rethinking Drinking website. Alcoholics Anonymous and SMART Recovery are also options. Many campuses also have resources related to alcohol.

In my experience, people see the best results if they decrease caffeine, nicotine, and alcohol gradually by 20–25% per week and then stay off for a few weeks before they can see the full impact of eliminating these substances and how it may help improve mood, anxiety, sleep and other aspects of health.

Warning: Eliminating these substances abruptly or going cold turkey can lead to withdrawal, which can be deadly!

As with all other strategies discussed in this book, check with your healthcare professional before considering changes to your caffeine, nicotine, or alcohol intake.

To sum it up, the repercussions of regular heavy drinking on academic success, emotional stability, and physical health are significant, substantiated by a sturdy stack of research.

Therefore, informed decision-making and responsible drinking become vital keys to safeguarding one's well-being and academic journey.

Study: Alcohol Impacts Sexual Assault[972]

More attention is being given to preventing sexual assault at colleges nationwide.

---

972 https://u.osu.edu/emotionalfitness/category/sexual-assault/

While this is a complex issue with many factors, this study suggests that students might be able to reduce their risk of sexual assault by reducing or avoiding alcohol or situations that involve alcohol.

What did the study involve?

- Around 1,197 students completed an online survey.

- The study authors looked at substance use by both the victim and perpetrator at the time of sexual assault.

What did the results show?

Substance use (including alcohol) was more common for both victims and perpetrators.

Of the students reporting sexual assault or forced sexual touching:

- At least 70% reported they were drinking alcohol at the time.

- At least 70% reported that perpetrators were drinking and/or drug use during incidents of sexual assault or rape.

How Much Alcohol Was Consumed By Those Who Had The Most Harm In Terms Of Sexual Assault?

- Among victims, 40 % of females and 60% of males binge drank at least once per week over three months.

- Among victims, most of the study participants drank less than 20 drinks per week.

What Do The Results Suggest?

- Substance use is often involved in both the perpetrators and victims of sexual assault.

- This study suggests that students might be able to reduce their risk of sexual assault by reducing or avoiding alcohol or situations that involve alcohol.

What Are Some Caveats?

- Sexual assault is a complex issue with many factors involved.

- This is just 1 of many studies on the issue of alcohol and sexual assault.

Expanded Knowledge

Sexual assault on college campuses is a grim issue that has been gaining necessary attention over the years. Efforts to understand and prevent such horrifying incidents have shed light on a multitude of factors, with one consistently echoing across the board: alcohol consumption. However, let's be clear - alcohol doesn't cause sexual assault. It merely complicates the picture.

The study's findings above draw a dotted line between alcohol consumption and sexual assault prevalence. It suggests that strategies like reducing or avoiding alcohol or alcohol-involving situations could potentially lower the risk of sexual assault. This observation is not an attempt to shift blame to the victims but to highlight a common thread in many assault situations.

Of course, these findings don't exist in a vacuum. Sexual assault is a multifaceted issue, influenced by a complex web of factors, and any approach to tackle it must respect this complexity. While this study brings to the forefront the role of alcohol use in sexual assault incidents, it's just one of many exploring the tangled relationship between alcohol and sexual assault.

Addressing sexual assault on college campuses requires comprehensive strategies beyond limiting alcohol consumption. Solutions should encompass education on consent, bystander intervention training, and nurturing a culture of respect and accountability. Alcohol's role is just one piece in the larger jigsaw puzzle that requires the combined effort of academia, society, and institutions to solve.

Chapter 12: Drugs: Cannabis Cigarettes And Nicotine

The exploration of recreational drugs and their possible medicinal benefits, particularly cannabis (commonly known as marijuana), has recently captivated the attention of researchers and scholars. Against the backdrop of an evolving legal landscape where many states in the United States are embracing the decriminalization of medicinal and recreational cannabis use, a critical imperative emerges— understanding the potential ramifications and hazards entwined with prolonged and heavy drug consumption.

While other addictive things such as alcohol, food, gambling, and video gaming are also legal, they can be harmful to some people and better avoided completely, while others can use them safely. Because of increased public health awareness campaigns over the years, young adults may be aware of the dangers of many drugs that can kill you, such as heroin, opiates, methamphetamine, cocaine, etc., young adults may not be fully aware of the risks of cannabis, nicotine, tobacco on mental health.

To help you get a better idea of the potential risks and harm of cannabis usage, this chapter takes a closer look at studies that illuminate the far-reaching impact of cannabis on diverse dimensions of health, encompassing alcohol use, memory function, mental well-being, brain dynamics, and overall holistic equilibrium.

It is also important to remember that there are some health conditions where cannabis is beneficial and is used as a medicinal prescription, and this area continues to evolve as we learn more. I hope that future research will provide more guidance on the frequency, strain, concentration, and amount of cannabis use that is safe, harmful, and beneficial for different health conditions.

This chapter aims to unlock the puzzle and help you better understand the direct and indirect connections between cannabis, cigarettes, nicotine, and mental health. With this increased understanding, readers are empowered to look further and then decide what is best for them regarding these substances.

As always, this book is intended for informational purposes. Check with your healthcare professional to see if any strategies discussed are right for you. If you choose to apply them, do it under the care and guidance of a health professional.

Let's begin!

Study: Impact of Cannabis on Alcohol[973]

As of 2015, about 22 million individuals in the United States reported using cannabis/marijuana in the last month.[974] In 2011, almost 70 million Americans

---

[973] https://u.osu.edu/emotionalfitness/2017/02/08/study-impact-of-cannabis-on-alcohol/

[974] Center for Behavioral Health Statistics and Quality. Key substance use and mental health indicators in the United States: Results from the 2015 National Survey on Drug Use and Health (HHS Publication No. SMA 16-4984, NSDUH Series H-51). 2016. http://www.samhsa.gov.proxy.lib.ohio-state.edu/data/

reported binge drinking in the last month (the survey defined binge drinking as the consumption of five or more drinks on one occasion).[975]

Some individuals may consider marijuana use as they are reducing alcohol use. A recent study looked at how cannabis use might impact alcohol use.

What Was The Study?[976]

A total of 1,383 newly abstinent alcohol-dependent individuals participated in a multi-site randomized control trial for treatment options for alcohol use disorder in the landmark COMBINE study.[977],[978]

Researchers compared alcohol use among those who used cannabis to those who did not.

What Were The Results?

The authors[979] found that compared to no cannabis use, ANY cannabis use during treatment for alcohol use

---

[975] Center for Behavioral Health Statistics and Quality. Behavioral health trends in the United States: Results from the 2014 National Survey on Drug Use and Health (HHS Publication No. SMA 15-4927, NSDUH Series H-50); 2015.

[976] Subbaraman, M. S., Metrik, J., Patterson, D., and Swift, R. (2016) Cannabis use during treatment for alcohol use disorders predicts alcohol treatment outcomes. Addiction, doi: 10.1111/add.13693.

[977] Anton R. F., O'Malley S. S., Ciraulo D. A., Cisler R. A., Couper D., Donovan D. M.et al. Combined pharmacotherapies and behavioral interventions for alcohol dependence: the COMBINE study: a randomized controlled trial. JAMA 2006; 295: 2003–2017.

[978] Combine Study Research Group. Testing combined pharmacotherapies and behavioral interventions in alcohol dependence: rationale and methods. Alcohol Clin Exp Res 2003; 27: 1107–1122.

[979] Subbaraman, M. S., Metrik, J., Patterson, D., and Swift, R. (2016) Cannabis use during treatment for alcohol use disorders predicts alcohol treatment outcomes. Addiction, doi: 10.1111/add.13693.

disorder was related to LESS alcohol abstinence at the end of treatment.

They found that each additional day of cannabis use was associated with approximately 4–5 fewer days of abstinence from alcohol.[980]

In this study, cannabis use impacted how often the participants drank but not how many drinks they had.[981]

Further study in this area is needed.

What Does This Mean?

This study suggests that it may not be a good idea to use cannabis if you are trying to abstain from alcohol.

Expanded Knowledge

The prevalence of cannabis use and alcohol consumption in the United States needs to be explored in-depth to understand the intricate interplay between the use of these substances. While the preceding study has undoubtedly offered valuable insights into the impact of cannabis on alcohol use, the pursuit of knowledge in this realm persists. Additional research endeavors have expanded the boundaries of our understanding, casting light on various facets of this complex relationship.

---

[980] Subbaraman, M. S., Metrik, J., Patterson, D., and Swift, R. (2016) Cannabis use during treatment for alcohol use disorders predicts alcohol treatment outcomes. Addiction, doi: 10.1111/add.13693.

[981] Subbaraman, M. S., Metrik, J., Patterson, D., and Swift, R. (2016) Cannabis use during treatment for alcohol use disorders predicts alcohol treatment outcomes. Addiction, doi: 10.1111/add.13693.

Published in the esteemed "American Journal of Drug and Alcohol Abuse" in 2019,[982] a thought-provoking study delved into the concept of 'substitution.' This study suggested that individuals may turn to cannabis use as a means of reducing their alcohol consumption.

However, the research yielded intriguing results that defied assumptions. Contrary to expectations, the study uncovered a counterintuitive association—the simultaneous use of cannabis and alcohol heightens one's likelihood of engaging in heavy and problematic drinking.

This unexpected finding challenges the notion that co-using these substances facilitates a reduction in alcohol consumption. It also raises questions about the inadvertent contribution of such usage to escalating alcohol-related patterns.

Venturing further into the intricacies of co-use, a noteworthy investigation in the "Journal of Studies on Alcohol and Drugs" in 2020[983] delved into the dynamics of simultaneous alcohol and cannabis consumption within the same drinking event. The study found that using alcohol and cannabis together increased the risk of adverse alcohol outcomes, including blackouts.

A study showcased in the "Pharmacology Biochemistry and Behavior" journal concurrent usage of

---

[982] https://addictions.psych.ucla.edu/wp-content/uploads/sites/160/2019/05/DAD-Alcohol-tobacco-and-marijuana-consumption-is-associated-with-increased-odds-of-same-day-substance-co-and-tri-use.pdf
[983] https://www.jsad.com/doi/10.15288/jsad.2020.81.203

alcohol and cannabis on cognitive functioning. The study found that simultaneous consumption of alcohol and cannabis exacerbated the cognitive deficits attributed to each substance individually, manifesting in heightened impairment in memory, attention, and decision-making processes.[984]

It is important to remember that our current knowledge about cannabis and mental health is evolving as there is ongoing research in this area. There is a need for further comprehensive investigations to solidify these findings and understand the long-term ramifications of co-use.

Cannabis Might Worsen Memory, and Stopping It Might Improve It[985]

Since 2016, about 37 million individuals in the United States reported using cannabis/marijuana in the last year.[986] This number is projected to increase as many states move toward legalizing the medicinal and or recreational use of cannabis or marijuana.

As with many things like excessive junk food, alcohol, tobacco, etc., being legal does NOT ALWAYS mean being healthy. For example, a recent study looked at cannabis

---

984
https://www.sciencedirect.com/science/article/abs/pii/S0741832923000150
[985] https://u.osu.edu/emotionalfitness/2018/12/31/cannabis-might-worsen-memory-and-stopping-it-might-improve-it/
[986] Center for Behavioral Health Statistics and Quality, 2016 National Survey on Drug Use and Health: Detailed Tables, Substance Abuse and Mental Health Services Administration, Rockville 2017. http://www.samhsa.gov

and false memories,[987] while another looked at memory changes after stopping cannabis.[988]

What Was The First Study?[989]

- Nearly 23 healthy people aged 18 to 29 with and without tetrahydrocannabinol (THC) participated.

- They were asked to learn the material while sober.

- About two days later, researchers compared memory recall among those who had used cannabis vs. those who had not two hours before the test.

What Were The Study Results Of The First Study?[990]

In the first study, subjects who used cannabis two hours before the test were more likely to have false recognition of words and pictures that had not been presented during the sober study session.[991]

---

[987] Doss MK et al. Δ9-Tetrahydrocannibinol at retrieval drives false recollection of neutral and emotional memories. Biol Psychiatry 2018 May 9; [e-pub]. (https://doi.org/10.1016/j.biopsych.2018.04.020).

[988] Schuster RM, Gilman J, Schoenfeld D, et al. One month of cannabis abstinence in adolescents and young adults is associated with improved memory. J Clin Psychiatry. 2018;79(6):17m11977 .

[989] Doss MK et al. Δ9-Tetrahydrocannibinol at retrieval drives false recollection of neutral and emotional memories. Biol Psychiatry 2018 May 9; [e-pub]. (https://doi.org/10.1016/j.biopsych.2018.04.020).

[990] Doss MK et al. Δ9-Tetrahydrocannibinol at retrieval drives false recollection of neutral and emotional memories. Biol Psychiatry 2018 May 9; [e-pub]. (https://doi.org/10.1016/j.biopsych.2018.04.020).

[991] Doss MK et al. Δ9-Tetrahydrocannibinol at retrieval drives false recollection of neutral and emotional memories. Biol Psychiatry 2018 May 9; [e-pub]. (https://doi.org/10.1016/j.biopsych.2018.04.020).

What Does This Mean?

This small study suggests that cannabis use might impact academic performance,[992] though further research is needed.

What Was The Second Study?[993]

- A total of 88 individuals (Average age 21 years) who used cannabis at least weekly were randomized to 30 days of abstinence or to a control group, abstinence confirmed through biochemical testing.[994]

- Participants underwent cognitive testing at baseline and then weekly for four weeks.

What Were The Results Of The Second Study?[995]

This 4-week study showed that improvements in memory started at week one and continued progress through week 4.[996]

---

[992] Doss MK et al. Δ9-Tetrahydrocannibinol at retrieval drives false recollection of neutral and emotional memories. Biol Psychiatry 2018 May 9; [e-pub]. (https://doi.org/10.1016/j.biopsych.2018.04.020).

[993] Schuster RM, Gilman J, Schoenfeld D, et al. One month of cannabis abstinence in adolescents and young adults is associated with improved memory. J Clin Psychiatry. 2018;79(6):17m11977.

[994] Schuster RM, Gilman J, Schoenfeld D, et al. One month of cannabis abstinence in adolescents and young adults is associated with improved memory. J Clin Psychiatry. 2018;79(6):17m11977.

[995] Schuster RM, Gilman J, Schoenfeld D, et al. One month of cannabis abstinence in adolescents and young adults is associated with improved memory. J Clin Psychiatry. 2018;79(6):17m11977.

[996] Schuster RM, Gilman J, Schoenfeld D, et al. One month of cannabis abstinence in adolescents and young adults is associated with improved memory. J Clin Psychiatry. 2018;79(6):17m11977.

What Does This Mean?

- This small study implies stopping cannabis may improve memory, and further longer, more extensive studies are underway.[997]

- Subjects used cannabis at least weekly, and it is unclear if there is a difference in benefits among heavy vs. light users.

- These studies suggest that Cannabis or Marijuana may impact your ability to remember and may cause false recall during tests and memory improvement after stopping cannabis use. A previous post showed that cannabis might increase alcohol intake.[998]

How else is cannabis impacting you?

Expanded Knowledge

The studies presented offer a deeper glimpse into the intricate landscape of memory-related consequences associated with cannabis use. Expanding upon this, additional research endeavors have delved into the cognitive ramifications of cannabis consumption, culminating in a more comprehensive understanding of its potential impacts.

---

[997] Schuster RM, Gilman J, Schoenfeld D, et al. One month of cannabis abstinence in adolescents and young adults is associated with improved memory. J Clin Psychiatry. 2018;79(6):17m11977.
[998] https://u.osu.edu/emotionalfitness/2017/02/08/study-impact-of-cannabis-on-alcohol/

In an insightful investigation published in the "Journal of Clinical Psychiatry" in 2016[999], researchers undertook a systematic review and meta-analysis to illuminate the cognitive effects of chronic cannabis use. Their meticulous analysis revealed deficits within various cognitive domains, including learning, memory, and attention, among chronic cannabis users.

A subsequent study, published in "Neuropsychopharmacology" in 2017[1000], delved deeper into the realm of reversibility by exploring the cognitive performance of individuals after a period of cannabis abstinence. By closely monitoring 152 adults, the researchers unveiled an encouraging narrative—after a month of abstaining from cannabis, subjects exhibited significant improvements in verbal learning and memory, reinforcing the findings of the second study mentioned.

Venturing into the realm of longitudinal inquiry, the illustrious "Dunedin Study" spanning over 25 years is a testament to the profound impact of persistent cannabis use on neuropsychological decline. This seminal study, published in the "Proceedings of the National Academy of Sciences" in 2012[1001], found that individuals who engaged in persistent cannabis use from adolescence into adulthood experienced a substantial decline in IQ,

---

[999] https://jamanetwork.com/journals/jamapsychiatry/article-abstract/2678214
[1000] https://pubmed.ncbi.nlm.nih.gov/28368159/
[1001] https://www.pnas.org/doi/abs/10.1073/pnas.1206820109

with cognitive deficits more pronounced among those who initiated cannabis consumption early in life.

Shifting the focus to the academic arena, a study published in the "Review of Economic Studies" in 2017[1002] examined the effects of medical marijuana laws on student performance. The findings shed light on a disquieting reality—such legislative measures correlated with a decline in academic achievement, specifically impacting high school graduation rates. It is important to note that correlation is not causation.

These studies provide a better understanding of the direct and indirect, immediate and not-so-immediate effects of cannabis use. Hopefully, this empowers the reader to make critically informed and responsible decision-making regarding cannabis use, understanding that research in this domain is far from over, as further investigations are warranted to unravel the intricacies of these effects.

Marijuana (Cannabis) Withdrawal And Mental Health[1003]

During times of stress, people may become vulnerable to using cannabis as a way to cope. Previous posts have discussed the negative impact of cannabis on memory, cognitive performance, and PTSD.

[1002] https://academic.oup.com/restud/article-abstract/84/3/1210/3099774
[1003] https://u.osu.edu/emotionalfitness/2020/04/29/marijuana-cannabis-withdrawal-and-mental-health/

Cannabis withdrawal can cause and worsen a variety of mental health symptoms. It is essential to become aware of this connection to mental health.

What Are Some Symptoms Of Cannabis Withdrawal Syndrome (CWS)?

CWS involves three or more of the following symptoms within seven days of reduced cannabis use:[1004]

- Anxiety.

- Depression.

- Changes in sleep.

- Irritability, anger, or aggression.

- Appetite or weight disturbance.

- Restlessness.

- Somatic symptoms include headaches, sweating, nausea, vomiting, or abdominal pain.

How Common Is Cannabis Withdrawal Syndrome?

A meta-analysis[1005] of 47 studies, including 23,518 participants, found that the prevalence of cannabis withdrawal syndrome was around 47%.[1006]

[1004] American Psychiatric Association. Diagnostic and Statistical Manual of Mental Disorders. 5th ed. American Psychiatric Association Publishing; 2013.

[1005] Bahji A, Stephenson C, Tyo R, Hawken ER, Seitz DP. Prevalence of Cannabis Withdrawal Symptoms Among People With Regular or Dependent Use of Cannabinoids: A Systematic Review and Meta-analysis. JAMA Netw Open. 2020;3(4):e202370. doi:10.1001/jamanetworkopen.2020.2370.

[1006] Bahji A, Stephenson C, Tyo R, Hawken ER, Seitz DP. Prevalence of Cannabis Withdrawal Symptoms Among People With Regular or Dependent Use of Cannabinoids: A Systematic Review and Meta-analysis. JAMA Netw Open. 2020;3(4):e202370. doi:10.1001/jamanetworkopen.2020.2370.

What Are Some Factors That Were Associated With Higher Cannabis Withdrawal Syndrome?[1007]

Researchers[1008] found that daily cannabis use, concurrent tobacco use, and use of other substances were associated with higher CWS.[1009]

Other Thoughts:

- It bears repeating that daily users were more likely to have cannabis withdrawal syndrome.

- Some people may report cannabis use helping with anxiety, depression, or insomnia when it may just be masking the withdrawal symptoms caused by previous cannabis use.

- Research shows an association between cannabis use and several medical, cognitive, functional, and psychosocial problems.[1010]

[1007] Bahji A, Stephenson C, Tyo R, Hawken ER, Seitz DP. Prevalence of Cannabis Withdrawal Symptoms Among People With Regular or Dependent Use of Cannabinoids: A Systematic Review and Meta-analysis. JAMA Netw Open. 2020;3(4):e202370. doi:10.1001/jamanetworkopen.2020.2370.

[1008] Bahji A, Stephenson C, Tyo R, Hawken ER, Seitz DP. Prevalence of Cannabis Withdrawal Symptoms Among People With Regular or Dependent Use of Cannabinoids: A Systematic Review and Meta-analysis. JAMA Netw Open. 2020;3(4):e202370. doi:10.1001/jamanetworkopen.2020.2370.

[1009] Bahji A, Stephenson C, Tyo R, Hawken ER, Seitz DP. Prevalence of Cannabis Withdrawal Symptoms Among People With Regular or Dependent Use of Cannabinoids: A Systematic Review and Meta-analysis. JAMA Netw Open. 2020;3(4):e202370. doi:10.1001/jamanetworkopen.2020.2370.

[1010] Crean RD , Tapert SF , Minassian A , Macdonald K , Crane NA , Mason BJ . Effects of chronic, heavy cannabis use on executive functions. J Addict Med. 2011;5(1):9-15. doi:1097/ADM.0b013e31820cdd57

- Short-term risks of cannabis use include impaired short-term memory, motor dis-coordination, altered judgment, paranoia, and psychosis.[1011]

- Some long-term effects of cannabis use include addiction, altered brain development, poor educational outcomes, cognitive impairment, diminished quality of life, increased risk of psychotic disorders, injuries, motor vehicle collisions, and suicide.[1012],[1013]

- Further research is needed on cannabis and mental health.

Expanded Knowledge

At any amount of cannabis use, whether frequent or rare, users of cannabis might experience Cannabis Withdrawal Syndrome (CWS) and not realize it.

A comprehensive study published in the esteemed "Journal of Drug and Alcohol Dependence" in 2018[1014] revealed a noteworthy trend—the susceptibility to CWS is heightened among individuals with a history of

[1011] Volkow ND , Baler RD , Compton WM , Weiss SRB . Adverse health effects of marijuana use. N Engl J Med. 2014;370(23):2219-2227. doi:1056/NEJMra1402309

[1012] Volkow ND , Baler RD , Compton WM , Weiss SRB . Adverse health effects of marijuana use. N Engl J Med. 2014;370(23):2219-2227. doi:1056/NEJMra1402309

[1013] Carvalho AF , Stubbs B , Vancampfort D , et al. Cannabis use and suicide attempts among 86,254 adolescents aged 12-15 years from 21 low- and middle-income countries. Eur Psychiatry. 2019;56:8-13. doi:1016/j.eurpsy.2018.10.006

[1014]

https://www.sciencedirect.com/science/article/abs/pii/S0376871617308390

psychiatric disorders. This finding calls for caution for individuals using cannabis for mental health conditions.

Another critical issue is the concentration of delta-9-tetrahydrocannabinol (THC), the principal psychoactive compound in cannabis. A seminal investigation featured in the journal "Addiction" in 2019 shed light on this relationship, emphasizing that individuals using cannabis with higher THC concentrations are more prone to developing CWS. This discovery points to a dose-dependent risk, highlighting the critical interplay between THC potency and the emergence of withdrawal symptoms.

Delving into the specific consequences of CWS yields valuable insights into its profound impact on mental health. A groundbreaking study published in the "American Journal of Psychiatry" in 2019[1015] showcased compelling evidence—adolescents who engage in frequent cannabis use are at augmented risk of experiencing depression and engaging in suicidal behavior during young adulthood.

These findings evoke the possibility of enduring repercussions, underscoring the need to address the long-term effects of cannabis withdrawal comprehensively.

The ramifications of CWS extend beyond individual well-being and permeate the fabric of society itself. An incisive study in "Drug and Alcohol Dependence" in

---

[1015] https://jamanetwork.com/journals/jamapsychiatry/fullarticle/2723657

2019[1016] revealed the substantial societal costs associated with CWS. These costs manifest in various forms, including heightened healthcare expenses and decreased productivity. By elucidating the economic impact of CWS, this study highlights the imperative of addressing this issue from a broader societal perspective.

Moreover, a pioneering exploration presented in "JAMA Network Open" in 2020 opened a captivating avenue for future research. The study observed a remarkable correlation—the prevalence of CWS was more pronounced among individuals who opted for cannabis vaping as their intake mode. This finding raises intriguing questions about the potential influence of the method of cannabis consumption on the risk of developing CWS, warranting further investigation.

CWS is a substantial concern entwined with cannabis use, particularly among daily users and those contending with psychiatric disorders. Despite the increasing legalization and acceptance of cannabis, users must remain cognizant of the potential adverse effects, underscoring the pressing need for continued research and enhanced public awareness. In my experience, some people using cannabis may experience CWS, particularly anxiety in other parts, not realizing that the worsening anxiety they experience is related to cannabis use.

[1016]
https://www.samhsa.gov/data/sites/default/files/reports/rpt29393/2019NSD
UHFFRPDFWHTML/2019NSDUHFFR090120.htm

Only through an informed and comprehensive approach can we sort through the puzzle of cannabis withdrawal and its impact on mental health and society.

Cannabis (Marijuana) And Suicidal Ideation[1017]

A previous post discussed cannabis (marijuana) use memory, academic performance, and symptoms of depression and anxiety from cannabis withdrawal.

This post talks about a study looking at cannabis use and suicidal ideation.

What Was The Study?[1018]

Dr. Han and colleagues looked at data from 281,650 adult participants in the 2008-2019 National Surveys of Drug Use and Health data.

What Were Some Study Results?[1019]

- Past-year Cannabis use disorder, daily cannabis use, and nondaily cannabis use were associated with a higher prevalence of past-year suicidal ideation, plan, and attempt in both sexes (e.g.,

---

[1017] https://u.osu.edu/emotionalfitness/2021/06/30/cannabis-marijuana-and-suicidal-ideation/

[1018] Han B, Compton WM, Einstein EB, Volkow ND. Associations of Suicidality Trends With Cannabis Use as a Function of Sex and Depression Status. JAMA Netw Open. 2021;4(6):e2113025. doi:10.1001/jamanetworkopen.2021.13025

[1019] Han B, Compton WM, Einstein EB, Volkow ND. Associations of Suicidality Trends With Cannabis Use as a Function of Sex and Depression Status. JAMA Netw Open. 2021;4(6):e2113025. doi:10.1001/jamanetworkopen.2021.13025

among individuals without major depressive episodes.)

- The prevalence of suicidal ideation for those with vs. without Cannabis use disorder was 13.9% vs. 3.5% among women and 9.9% vs. 3.0% among men; P < .001).

- Suicide plan among those with Cannabis use disorder and major depressive episode was 52% higher for women [23.7%] than men [15.6%]; P < .001).

What Are Some Caveats?

- This is just one study, and further research is needed.

- While this study shows a correlation between cannabis and suicidal ideation among those with depression, it does not show direct cause and effect.

- Future research is needed to examine this increase in suicidality and to determine whether it is due to cannabis use or other overlapping risk factors.

- According to this study, cannabis use can be concerning for suicidal ideation for those with and without a major depressive disorder.

Cannabis (Marijuana) Use And Brain Functioning[1020]

[1020] https://u.osu.edu/emotionalfitness/2022/10/27/cannabis-marijuana-use-and-brain-functioning/

Many young people use marijuana for a variety of reasons.

While de-criminalized in many states, the use of cannabis is not without risks. For example, a previous post discussed the negative impact of cannabis on PTSD.

A recent study looked at the impact of cannabis use on intelligence (IQ).

What Were The Findings?[1021]

- Around 1037 individuals born in New Zealand were periodically assessed between ages 7 and 45 years for cannabis use and dependence and with intelligence quotient (IQ) testing.[1022]

- At age 45 years, the mean decline in IQ points from childhood to adulthood was greater among long-term users of cannabis (5.5 points) compared with nonusers of cannabis (0.7 points).[1023]

- Deficits were noted in processing speed, learning, and memory among adults with long-term

---

[1021] Meier MH, et. al. Long-Term Cannabis Use and Cognitive Reserves and Hippocampal Volume in Midlife. Am J Psychiatry. 2022 May;179(5):362-374. doi: 10.1176/appi.ajp.2021.21060664. Epub 2022 Mar 8. PMID: 35255711; PMCID: PMC9426660.

[1022] Meier MH, et. al. Long-Term Cannabis Use and Cognitive Reserves and Hippocampal Volume in Midlife. Am J Psychiatry. 2022 May;179(5):362-374. doi: 10.1176/appi.ajp.2021.21060664. Epub 2022 Mar 8. PMID: 35255711; PMCID: PMC9426660.

[1023] Meier MH, et. al. Long-Term Cannabis Use and Cognitive Reserves and Hippocampal Volume in Midlife. Am J Psychiatry. 2022 May;179(5):362-374. doi: 10.1176/appi.ajp.2021.21060664. Epub 2022 Mar 8. PMID: 35255711; PMCID: PMC9426660.

cannabis use relative to their childhood assessments.[1024]

Are There Studies On The Frequency Of Cannabis Use And Brain Functioning?[1025]

- The use of cannabis four or more times per month may impair brain functioning.[1026]

- In this small study, students using cannabis demonstrated poorer verbal learning ($p<.01$), verbal working memory ($p<.05$), and attention accuracy ($p<.01$) compared to non-users.[1027]

- This might translate to more time studying or less information learned, mistakes, more frustration and angst with school work, and poor academic performance.

Other thoughts:

- Some people may report cannabis use helping with anxiety, depression, or insomnia when it may just be masking the withdrawal symptoms caused by previous cannabis use.

[1024] Meier MH, et. al. Long-Term Cannabis Use and Cognitive Reserves and Hippocampal Volume in Midlife. Am J Psychiatry. 2022 May;179(5):362-374. doi: 10.1176/appi.ajp.2021.21060664. Epub 2022 Mar 8. PMID: 35255711; PMCID: PMC9426660.

[1025] Hanson KL, et al. Longitudinal study of cognition among adolescent marijuana users over three weeks of abstinence. Addict Behav. 2010 November ; 35(11): 970–976. doi:10.1016/j.addbeh.2010.06.012.

[1026] Hanson KL, et al. Longitudinal study of cognition among adolescent marijuana users over three weeks of abstinence. Addict Behav. 2010 November ; 35(11): 970–976. doi:10.1016/j.addbeh.2010.06.012.

[1027] Hanson KL, et al. Longitudinal study of cognition among adolescent marijuana users over three weeks of abstinence. Addict Behav. 2010 November ; 35(11): 970–976. doi:10.1016/j.addbeh.2010.06.012.

- Research shows an association between cannabis use and several medical, cognitive, functional, and psychosocial problems.[1028]

- Short-term risks of cannabis use include impaired short-term memory, motor dis-coordination, altered judgment, paranoia, and psychosis.[1029]

- Other long-term effects of cannabis use include addiction, poor educational outcomes, diminished quality of life, increased risk of psychotic disorders, injuries, motor vehicle collisions, and suicide.[1030],[1031]

- Further research is needed on the risks and benefits of specific types and amounts of cannabis and mental health.

- It is possible that illegally obtained cannabis may have other harmful substances added to it.

Expanded Knowledge

New studies are starting to reveal how cannabis usage affects how the brain works and relates to suicidal

---

[1028] Hanson KL, et al. Longitudinal study of cognition among adolescent marijuana users over three weeks of abstinence. Addict Behav. 2010 November; 35(11): 970–976. doi:10.1016/j.addbeh.2010.06.012.

[1029] Volkow ND , Baler RD , Compton WM , Weiss SRB . Adverse health effects of marijuana use. N Engl J Med. 2014;370(23):2219-2227. doi:1056/NEJMra1402309

[1030] Volkow ND , Baler RD , Compton WM , Weiss SRB . Adverse health effects of marijuana use. N Engl J Med. 2014;370(23):2219-2227. doi:1056/NEJMra1402309

[1031] Carvalho AF , Stubbs B , Vancampfort D , et al. Cannabis use and suicide attempts among 86,254 adolescents aged 12-15 years from 21 low-and middle-income countries. Eur Psychiatry. 2019;56:8-13. doi:1016/j.eurpsy.2018.10.006

thoughts. Such revelations highlight the necessity of an informed and circumspect approach to cannabis usage, particularly among young individuals.

Beyond the aforementioned research, a thorough 2016 review published in "JAMA Psychiatry" confirmed the findings of the aforementioned study by highlighting the link between extensive cannabis usage in youth and an elevated risk of developing depression and suicidality in early adulthood.

Additionally, the data pointed to a constant link between cannabis usage and suicidal thoughts and actions, highlighting the potential seriousness of this problem. Much research has been done on the effects of cannabis consumption over time on cognitive abilities. Intriguing research that was presented in the "Journal of Clinical Psychiatry" in 2018 showed that cannabis users had decreased hippocampus volumes and thinner cortical layers, which are linked to memory loss and cognitive decline.

In terms of frequency of use, 2018 research published in "The Lancet Psychiatry" indicated a clear correlation between daily cannabis use, particularly of high-potency cannabis, and the chance of developing psychosis. This finding adds another layer to our knowledge of the cognitive dangers related to cannabis.

Last but not least, cannabis that has been obtained illegally may provide serious risks. The "Journal of Forensic Sciences" published a paper in 2018 detailing cases of laced cannabis products that included dangerous synthetic cannabinoids or other pharmaceuticals, posing serious health hazards. The prominence of these compounds in black markets highlights the possible risks connected to the use of unrestricted cannabis.

Thus, the growing corpus of research suggests that cannabis usage, cognitive performance, and mental health are all interconnected in complicated ways. Public policies, medical procedures, and individual decisions will influence the usage of cannabis. Thus, further study in this area is necessary.

Marijuana: Four Hidden Costs to Consider[1032]

"Opportunity cost: Something a person sacrifices when they choose one option over another."[1033]

For students, the health impact of marijuana use may be understated, and its harms can be sneaky. Beyond the cost of purchase, what is marijuana use costing you?

Your Total Time In School

If you use marijuana two or more times per month, you may be 66% more likely to miss one or more semesters of class.[1034]

This was shown in a study of nearly 1,133 students over a 4-year time period, starting from their freshman year and after adjusting for variables such as demographic

---

[1032] https://u.osu.edu/emotionalfitness/2014/11/17/marijuana-4-hidden-costs-to-consider/

[1033] 1. Arria, A. M., Caldeira, K. M., Bugbee, B. A., Vincent, K. B., & O'Grady, K. E. (2013). The academic opportunity costs of substance use during college. College Park, MD: Center on Young Adult Health and Development. Available at www.cls.umd.edu/docs/AcadOppCosts.pdf.

[1034] 2. Arria AM, Garnier-Dykstra LM, Caldeira KM, Vincent KB, Winick ER, O'Grady KE. Drug use patterns and continuous enrollment in college: Results from a longitudinal study. J Stud Alcohol Drugs. 2013;74(1):71-83.

characteristics, high school GPA, fraternity/sorority involvement, personality/temperament characteristics, nicotine dependence, and alcohol use disorder.[1035]

Your Future Income

Six years after graduation, students who used marijuana infrequently during college were 3.7 times more likely to be unemployed as compared to non-users.[1036]

Your Ability To Study

The use of marijuana four or more times per month may impair brain functioning.

In this study, students demonstrated poorer verbal learning ($p<.01$), verbal working memory ($p<.05$), and attention accuracy ($p<.01$) compared to non-users.[1037]

This might translate to more time studying or less information learned, mistakes, more frustration and angst with school work, and poor academic performance.

Your Emotional Health

The cost of missing/prolonging school, poor grades due to marijuana use, reduction in future and current

---

[1035] 2. Arria AM, Garnier-Dykstra LM, Caldeira KM, Vincent KB, Winick ER, O'Grady KE. Drug use patterns and continuous enrollment in college: Results from a longitudinal study. J Stud Alcohol Drugs. 2013;74(1):71–83.

[1036] 3. Arria AM, Garnier-Dykstra LM, Cook ET, Caldeira KM, Vincent KB, Baron RA, O'Grady KE. Drug use patterns in young adulthood and post-college employment. Drug Alcohol Depend. 2013;127(1–3):23–30.

[1037] 4. Hanson KL, et al. Longitudinal study of cognition among adolescent marijuana users over three weeks of abstinence. Addict Behav. 2010 November ; 35(11): 970–976. doi:10.1016/j.addbeh.2010.06.012.

income (money spent on marijuana could be used for other things), fear of getting caught, and potential legal consequences are all stressful consequences beyond the biological impact of marijuana use.

Is it worth the extra stress?

Biologically, marijuana can impact depression, while depression can impact marijuana use.[1038]

If you can relate to any of this, you may want to ask yourself... *Are these costs worth it?*

How much better would your life be if you instead addressed your depression, anxiety, stress/time management skills in healthier ways like counseling, exercise, meditation, improving medical health, etc.?

Expanded Knowledge

In the winding paths of life, decisions we make often come cloaked in invisible ramifications, extending their reach into the future. One such choice of cannabis consumption bears a spectrum of consequences concealed in the shadows of more obvious health concerns and immediate financial expenditure.

Its silent grasp weaves into the very fabric of our lives, touching upon the realms of educational accomplishment, future earnings, cognitive function, and the emotional landscape.

[1038] 5. Pacek, LR, et al. The Bidirectional Relationships Between Alcohol, Cannabis, Cooccurring Alcohol and Cannabis Use Disorders with Major Depressive Disorder: Results From a National SampleJ Affect Disord. 2013 June ; 148(0): 188–195. doi:10.1016/j.jad.2012.11.059.

Consider an illuminating longitudinal study by Silins et al. (2014)[1039], Tracing the paths of 2,619 young adults, the study noted a poignant pattern: daily cannabis users before 17 were far less likely to don the cap and gown of high school or university graduation.

This relationship between cannabis consumption and future income was underscored by the meticulous work of Zhang et al. (2019)[1040]. Their study painted a sobering picture where regular cannabis users earned fewer dollars and climbed fewer rungs of the educational ladder. A possible link emerges here to the cognitive and motivational impairments known to shadow chronic cannabis use, silently sabotaging opportunities for advancement.

A comprehensive meta-analysis by Scott et al. (2018)[1041] synthesized findings from 69 independent studies. The amalgamation of evidence testified to significant learning, memory, and attention deficits among regular cannabis users. These cognitive roadblocks could hinder your academic and professional progress: taking a risk on job retention, promotion, future income potential, career achievements, etc.

A ground-breaking study by Gobbi et al. (2019)[1042] unveiled the stark reality of increased depression and suicidal tendencies in young adulthood following

---

[1039] https://www.thelancet.com/journals/lanpsy/article/PIIS2215-0366(14)70307-4/fulltext

[1040] https://onlinelibrary.wiley.com/doi/abs/10.1111/ajad.12357

[1041] https://jamanetwork.com/journals/jamapsychiatry/fullarticle/2678214

[1042] https://jamanetwork.com/journals/jamapsychiatry/fullarticle/2723657

adolescent cannabis consumption. The stressors entwined with cannabis use, whether academic struggles, diminished income, legal entanglements, or health predicaments, can further amplify these emotional disturbances.

The true costs of cannabis use cast a long, complex shadow beyond its immediate health effects and direct financial outlay. They seep into vital corners of our existence, such as education, future income, cognitive functioning, and emotional well-being. This reality, often under-acknowledged, holds profound implications for young adults and professionals, underscoring the need for discerning decisions regarding cannabis consumption.

While there may be some people who benefit from cannabis and see no negative health or occupational consequences, in my decade-plus of experience, people often do not make the connection between the direct and indirect impact of cannabis use and how it may be impacting their mental health and work performance.

I hope this chapter helps you see those connections as you consider the amount and frequency of cannabis that is safe for you or if it makes sense for you to use it at all.

Study: Does Marijuana Help with PTSD?[1043]

[1043] https://u.osu.edu/emotionalfitness/2016/03/18/study-does-marijuana-help-with-ptsd-2/

About 7-8 % of people may experience PTSD (or Post Traumatic Stress Disorder) at some point in their lives.[1044]

Individuals with PTSD are more likely to use marijuana to try and cope with their symptoms.[1045]

A recent study tried to look at how marijuana impacts PTSD.[1046]

What is PTSD?

- PTSD can occur after an individual witnesses or experiences a traumatic or dangerous event.[1047]

- Symptom areas can include re-experiencing trauma, avoidance behaviors, increased reactivity or "on edge" feelings, and mood and cognitive (thought) related symptoms.[1048]

- Depression, substance abuse, or other anxiety conditions can often co-occur with PTSD.[1049]

[1044] 2. http://www.ptsd.va.gov/public/PTSD-overview/basics/how-common-is-ptsd.asp

[1045] 3. Cougle, J.R., et. al. (2011). Posttraumatic stress disorder and cannabis use in a nationally representative sample. Psychology of Addictive Behaviors, 25, 554-558.

[1046] 4. Wilkinson ST et al. Marijuana use is associated with worse outcomes in symptom severity and violent behavior in patients with posttraumatic stress disorder. J Clin Psychiatry 2015 Sep; 76:1174.

[1047] http://www.nimh.nih.gov/health/topics/post-traumatic-stress-disorder-ptsd/index.shtml

[1048] http://www.nimh.nih.gov/health/topics/post-traumatic-stress-disorder-ptsd/index.shtml

[1049] http://www.nimh.nih.gov/health/topics/post-traumatic-stress-disorder-ptsd/index.shtml

Who Were The Study Participants?

- Around 2276 veterans were over a 9-year period who were admitted to specialized Veterans Affairs treatment programs.

- Participants were mostly male, and the average age was in the 50s.

- They were assessed at the beginning of PTSD treatment and 4 months after discharge from the PTSD treatment program.

What Was Asked In The Study?

- Participants were asked about the severity of PTSD symptoms, drug and alcohol use, violent behavior, and employment.

What Were The Study Results?

- After PTSD treatment, the group that stopped using marijuana or never used marijuana had the lowest levels of PTSD symptoms ($P < .0001$); − they improved the most.

- According to the study, those who kept using marijuana were significantly more likely to have:

1) Worse outcomes in PTSD symptom severity ($P < .01$),

2) Violent behavior ($P < .01$),

3) Higher use of alcohol and drugs ($P < .01$)

- Those who started using marijuana after PTSD treatment had the highest levels of violent behavior (P < .0001).

What Are Some Caveats?

- This is a large study done over the long term on this subject.

- Since most of the participants were older males, results may be different in other age groups or populations.

- This study used a survey method which tells us about snapshots in time but does not about cause and effect.

- This study did not include individuals who were using alcohol or other drugs.

- Participants may be self-medicating because they were not feeling better or the use of marijuana prevented them from feeling better.[1050]

- The amount and type of marijuana used was not identified.

- Other smaller studies show mixed results but also have different methods.

Do you have PTSD?

Are you smoking marijuana?

[1050] 4. Wilkinson ST et al. Marijuana use is associated with worse outcomes in symptom severity and violent behavior in patients with posttraumatic stress disorder. J Clin Psychiatry 2015 Sep; 76:1174.

Is it worsening your PTSD symptoms?

Expanded Knowledge

In my experience and as noted in the research, individuals who have PTSD often seek refuge in marijuana [139], particularly at night time, as cannabis can interfere with sleep architecture. But, cannabis use to cope with PTSD comes with a cost of worsening PTSD symptoms, aggressive behaviors, and substance misuse. 139.

In my experience, many factors can help reduce PTSD symptoms, so the use of illicit substances may not be necessary. Things that can help with PTSD include counseling, medications, and healthy life behaviors such as exercise, nutrition, and avoidance of alcohol, drugs, and excessive caffeine use.

Does Smoking [Cigarettes] Increase Anxiety And Depression? If I Quit, Will I Feel Better?[1051]

Most students know about the harmful effects of smoking cigarettes, including the risk of cancer, stroke, heart disease, and breathing problems.[1052] Students may

---

[1051] https://u.osu.edu/emotionalfitness/2015/04/15/does-smoking-increase-anxiety-and-depression-if-i-quit-will-i-feel-better/

[1052] US Department of Health and Human Services. The health consequences of smoking: a report of the Surgeon General. US Department of Health and Human Services, 2004.

also know that stopping smoking reduces these health risks.[1053],[1054]

Most people may not know that smoking contributes to anxiety and depression and that you can feel good and increase happiness by quitting smoking.

This study[1055] analyzed mental health information across 26 studies and looked at positive and negative changes in mental health before and after quitting smoking cigarettes.

What Did The Study Show?

When compared to smokers, seven weeks to nine years after quitting smoking, those who quit reported a DECREASE in:

- Anxiety.

- Depression.

- Mixed anxiety and depression.

- Stress.

When compared to smokers, seven weeks to 9 years after quitting smoking, those who quit smoking reported an INCREASE in:

[1053] US Department of Health and Human Services. The health benefits of smoking cessation. US Department of Health and Human Services, 1990.

[1054] Pirie K, Peto R, Reeves G, Green J, Beral V. The 21st century hazards of smoking and benefits of stopping: a prospective study of one million women in the UK. Lancet 2013;381:133-41.

[1055] Taylor G, et al. Change in mental health after smoking cessation: systematic review and meta-analysis. OPEN ACCESS. BMJ 2014;348:g1151 doi: 10.1136/bmj.g1151 (Published 13 February 2014)

- Psychological quality of life 0.22 Positive affect significantly 0.40.

- This improvement occurred whether or not participants had anxiety or depression before quitting smoking.

But I Thought People Smoke To Be Less Anxious And Depressed.

- When they have not smoked for a while, smokers experience irritability, anxiety, and depression.[1056][1057]

- These feelings are relieved by smoking[1058] , thus creating the perception that smoking has psychological benefits, while, in fact, it is smoking that caused these psychological disturbances in the first place.

How Can I Quit Smoking?

You may want to talk to your doctor/prescriber about medications and nicotine replacement as additional options to help you quit.

Is smoking worth anxiety, depression, and feeling bad?

[1056] Hughes JR. Effects of abstinence from tobacco: valid symptoms and time course. Nicotine Tob Res 2007;9:315-27.

[1057] Guthrie SK, Ni L, Zubieta JK, Teter CJ, Domino EF. Changes in craving for a cigarette and arterial nicotine plasma concentrations in abstinent smokers. Prog NeuroPsychopharmacol Biol Psychiatry 2004;28:617-23.

[1058] Parrott AC. Does cigarette smoking cause stress? Am Psychol 1999;54:817-20.

Is it sapping your energy level?

How good will you feel after you stop smoking for good?

Expanded Knowledge

The intricate dance between smoking cigarettes, mental health, and the holistic state of well-being forms a captivating focus of numerous scientific inquiries.

While the traditional narrative associates smoking cigarettes primarily with physical ailments, the spotlight is increasingly veering towards its insidious ties to psychological distress—namely, amplified levels of anxiety and depression. This reframes the prevailing belief of smoking as a tranquil port in life's stormy seas.

The cigarette studies point out a subtle deception: the fleeting relief from nicotine withdrawal symptoms, including irritability, anxiety, and depression, may masquerade as the calming embrace of smoking.

Those interested in quitting can find invaluable guidance and tools, such as behavioral counseling, medication, and nicotine replacement therapies, in the expertise of healthcare professionals. In my experience, this combination of treatments is quite effective in helping people quit or reduce cigarette use.

A great place to start is the following website: https://smokefree.gov/

In my experience, people see the best results if they decrease caffeine, nicotine, and alcohol gradually by 20-

25% per week and then stay off for a few weeks before they can see the full impact of eliminating these substances and how it may help improve mood, anxiety, sleep and other aspects of health.

Warning: Eliminating these substances abruptly or cold turkey can lead to withdrawal, which can be deadly!

As with all other strategies discussed in this book, check with your healthcare professional before considering changes to your caffeine, nicotine, or alcohol intake.

Does Smoking Increase Anxiety And Depression? If I Quit, Will I Feel Better?[1059]

Most students know about the harmful effects of smoking cigarettes, including the risk of cancer, stroke, heart disease, and breathing problems[1060]. Students may also know that stopping smoking reduces these health risks.[1061][1062]

Most people may not know that smoking contributes to anxiety and depression and that you can feel good and increase happiness by quitting smoking.

[1059] https://u.osu.edu/emotionalfitness/2015/04/15/does-smoking-increase-anxiety-and-depression-if-i-quit-will-i-feel-better/

[1060] US Department of Health and Human Services. The health benefits of smoking cessation.

US Department of Health and Human Services, 1990.

[1061] Pirie K, Peto R, Reeves G, Green J, Beral V. The 21st century hazards of smoking and

benefits of stopping: a prospective study of one million women in the UK. Lancet

2013;381:133-41.

[1062] Taylor G, et al. Change in mental health after smoking cessation: systematic review and meta-analysis. OPEN ACCESS. BMJ 2014;348:g1151 doi: 10.1136/bmj.g1151 (Published 13 February 2014)

This study[1063] analyzed mental health information across 26 studies and looked at positive and negative changes in mental health before and after quitting smoking cigarettes.

What Did The Study Show?

When compared to smokers, seven weeks to 9 years after quitting smoking, those who quit smoking reported a DECREASE in:

- Anxiety.

- Depression.

- Mixed anxiety and depression.

- Stress.

When compared to smokers, seven weeks to 9 years after quitting smoking, those who quit smoking reported an INCREASE in:

- Psychological quality of life 0.22 Positive affect significantly 0.40.

- This improvement occurred whether or not participants had anxiety or depression before quitting smoking.

[1063] Parrott AC. Does cigarette smoking cause stress? Am Psychol 1999;54:817-20.

But I Thought People Smoke To Be Less Anxious And Depressed.

- When they have not smoked for a while, smokers experience irritability, anxiety, and depression.[1064][1065]

- These feelings are relieved by smoking[1066] , thus creating the perception that smoking has psychological benefits, while, in fact, it is smoking that caused these psychological disturbances in the first place.

How Can I Quit Smoking?

http://smokefree.gov/
http://www.cancer.org/healthy/stayawayfromtobacco/guidetoquittingsmoking/index
http://www.cancer.org/cancer/cancercauses/tobaccocancer/smokelesstobaccoandhowtoquit/index

You may want to talk to your doctor/prescriber about medications and nicotine replacement as additional options to help you quit.

Is smoking worth anxiety, depression, and feeling bad?

Is it zapping your energy level?

[1064] Parrott AC. Does cigarette smoking cause stress? Am Psychol 1999;54:817-20.

[1065] Guthrie SK, Ni L, Zubieta JK, Teter CJ, Domino EF. Changes in craving for a cigarette
and arterial nicotine plasma concentrations in abstinent smokers. Prog NeuroPsychopharmacol Biol Psychiatry 2004;28:617-23.

[1066] Hughes JR. Effects of abstinence from tobacco: valid symptoms and time course. Nicotine
Tob Res 2007;9:315-27.

How good will you feel after you stop smoking for good?

Expanded Knowledge

The relationship between smoking and mental health is more complex than commonly thought. While smoking is often perceived as a stress reliever, scientific studies paint a different picture. In a study conducted by Fluharty et al., published in the British Journal of Psychiatry, the researchers found that smoking is associated with an elevated risk of developing depression and anxiety over time, indicating that the initial relief smokers feel may be temporary and deceptive (Fluharty et al., 2017).[1067]

Moreover, the misconception that smoking alleviates stress and anxiety might be linked to nicotine withdrawal symptoms. A study published in "Addiction" shows that smokers often mistake withdrawal relief for stress relief, maintaining a vicious cycle (Parrott, 1999).[1068]

As for quitting smoking, the rewards extend beyond physical health. A meta-analysis by Taylor et al. reported that quitting smoking was associated with lower levels of depression, anxiety, and stress, improved positive mood, and better quality of life compared to those who

---

[1067] Fluharty, M., Taylor, A. E., Grabski, M., & Munafò, M. R. (2017). The Association of Cigarette Smoking With Depression and Anxiety: A Systematic Review. British Journal of Psychiatry, 210(1), 3-10.

[1068] Parrott, A. C. (1999). Does cigarette smoking cause stress? Addiction, 94(10), 1411-1414.

continued smoking (Taylor et al., 2014).[1069] Importantly, these improvements in mental health occurred regardless of whether the subjects had psychiatric disorders prior to quitting, debunking the myth that quitting smoking could exacerbate mental health conditions.

Therefore, while quitting smoking can be challenging, there's compelling evidence to show that cessation improves your physical health and enhances your mental well-being. Contrary to popular belief, quitting may be a viable strategy for mental health improvement, a point often overlooked in discussions surrounding the adverse effects of smoking.

Study: Smoking Might Increase Your Alcohol Intake[1070]

Over 26 studies show[1071] that smoking contributes to anxiety and depression and that you can feel good and increase happiness by quitting tobacco.

Students might also know that smoking cigarettes raises your risk of cancer, stroke, heart disease, and

---

[1069] Taylor, G., McNeill, A., Girling, A., Farley, A., Lindson-Hawley, N., & Aveyard, P. (2014). Change in mental health after smoking cessation: systematic review and meta-analysis. British Medical Journal, 348, g1151.

[1070] https://u.osu.edu/emotionalfitness/2015/06/03/study-smoking-might-increase-your-alcohol-intake/

[1071] Taylor G, et al. Change in mental health after smoking cessation: systematic review and meta-analysis. OPEN ACCESS. BMJ 2014;348:g1151 doi: 10.1136/bmj.g1151 (Published 13 February 2014).

breathing problems[1072] and that quitting smoking can reduce these risks.[1073],[1074]

A recent study suggests smoking might increase your alcohol consumption (5-6).

What Was The Study?

In this animal study,[1075],[1076] rats were trained to press a bar to obtain alcohol and were exposed to nicotine or saline in different experimental designs.

What Did The Study Show?

- This study showed that, in alcohol-dependent animals, nicotine increased:

- The speed at which alcohol was ingested,

[1072] US Department of Health and Human Services. The health consequences of smoking: a
report of the Surgeon General. US Department of Health and Human Services, 2004.
[1073] US Department of Health and Human Services. The health benefits of smoking cessation.
US Department of Health and Human Services, 1990.
[1074] Pirie K, Peto R, Reeves G, Green J, Beral V. The 21st century hazards of smoking and
benefits of stopping: a prospective study of one million women in the UK. Lancet
2013;381:133-41.
[1075] Leão RM et al. Chronic nicotine activates stress/reward-related brain regions and facilitates the transition to compulsive alcohol drinking. J Neurosci 2015 Apr 15; 35:6241. (http://dx.doi.org/10.1523/JNEUROSCI.3302-14.2015);
[1076] May 4, 2015. Want to Stop Drinking? Don't Smoke. Steven Dubovsky MD reviewing Leão RM et al. J Neurosci 2015 Apr 15.
http://www.jwatch.org/na37661/2015/05/04/want-stop-drinking-dont-smoke?query=etoc_jwpsych#sthash.94sXS2T4.dpuf

- The amount of work that animals would do to obtain alcohol (i.e., the number of times they would press a bar to get one dose) and,

- The amount of drinking, despite adverse consequences.

What Do The Results Suggest?

Quitting smoking might help you drink less or quit alcohol completely. Further study is needed.

How Can I Quit Smoking?

- http://swc.osu.edu/alcohol-tobacco-other-drugs/quit-tobacco/

- http://tobaccofree.osu.edu/resources/

- http://smokefree.gov/

- http://www.cancer.org/healthy/stayawayfromtobacco/guidetoquittingsmoking/index

- http://www.cancer.org/cancer/cancercauses/tobaccocancer/smokelesstobaccoandhowtoquit/index

Where Can I Learn More About Alcohol?

How much is too much?

Strategies for cutting down and quitting can be found here:

- http://www.ccs.osu.edu/self-help/alcohol/

- http://rethinkingdrinking.niaaa.nih.gov/default.asp

Take the OSU Free Anonymous Mental Health Screen

Is smoking impacting your alcohol intake?

Could you stand to feel better?

Perform better academically?

What other consequences are you experiencing from smoking alcohol, or both?

Expanded Knowledge

Expanding upon the topic of smoking's potential influence on alcohol consumption, it is worth noting parallel findings in related research.

A study by Kandel, Hu, Griesler, and Wall (2007)[1077] found that nicotine activates pathways in the brain that enhance the pleasurable effects of alcohol, thus leading to increased alcohol consumption. This suggests a neurological basis for the observed interaction between smoking and drinking, bolstering the study that investigated these behaviors in rats.

Moreover, the phenomena of cross-reinforcement and cross-tolerance between tobacco and alcohol have been the subject of academic scrutiny. In a comprehensive review by McKee and Weinberger (2013),[1078] it was revealed that not only does smoking seem to increase alcohol consumption, but the reverse

[1077] Kandel, D., Hu, M.-C., Griesler, P., & Wall, M. (2007). On the Respective Contributions of Awareness of Unmet Need, Perceived Safety and Efficacy, and Consumer Advertising to Health and Mental Health Services Utilization: An Empirical Study. Journal of Health Services Research, 42(6), 3842-3863.
[1078] McKee, S. A., & Weinberger, A. H. (2013). How Can We Use Our Knowledge of Alcohol-Tobacco Interactions to Reduce Alcohol Use? Annual Review of Clinical Psychology, 9, 649-674.

appears to be true as well. Alcohol consumption can increase tobacco use, implicating a vicious cycle.

The concept of "self-medication" has also been explored in scientific research. A study by Markou et al. (1998)[1079] explored the propensity for individuals to "self-medicate" mental health symptoms with substances like alcohol and nicotine, both of which have transient anxiety-reducing properties. When combined, they may compound the reinforcing effects, explaining why individuals who smoke might also have increased alcohol intake.

Overall, while the initial animal study posits an impactful correlation between smoking and alcohol consumption, other research suggests that this relationship is bidirectional and influenced by a variety of psychological and neurochemical factors.

Hidden Consequence E-cigs[1080]

Electronic cigarettes, or E-cigs, have become popular in recent years for a variety of reasons. Some tout the tobacco-free alternative as a way to lower cancer risk. Others claim it's less addictive and less risk of lung disease.

[1079] Markou, A., Kosten, T. R., & Koob, G. F. (1998). Neurobiological Similarities in Depression and Drug Dependence: A Self-Medication Hypothesis. Neuropsychopharmacology, 18(3), 135–174.
[1080] https://u.osu.edu/emotionalfitness/2016/06/29/hidden-consequence-e-cigs/

There are also risks of much higher nicotine ingestion than traditional (tobacco-based) cigarettes, leading to nicotine toxicity.[1081]

A recent small study by Barrington-Trimis and colleagues suggests another unexpected consequence of e-cigarette use.[1082]

Who Was Studied?

Three hundred students in the 11th or 12th grade.[1083]

What Was The Study Design?[1084]

- Questionnaires were given in the 11th or 12th grade and again after they turned 18 years old.

- Some questions included whether they use e-cigarettes or traditional (tobacco) cigarettes, whether they smoke tobacco-based cigarettes now or intend to do so in the future.

What Were The Results?[1085]

- A total of 40% of participants who reported e-cigarette use at the beginning of the study ended up using traditional (tobacco) cigarettes by age 18,

---

[1081] Ordonez J, Forrester MB, Kleinschmidt K. Electronic cigarette exposures reported to poison centers. Clin Toxicology 2013;51:685

[1082] Barrington-Trimis JL, Urman R, Berhane K, et al. E-Cigarettes and Future Cigarette Use. Pediatrics. 2016; 138(1):e20160379

[1083] Barrington-Trimis JL, Urman R, Berhane K, et al. E-Cigarettes and Future Cigarette Use. Pediatrics. 2016; 138(1):e20160379

[1084] Barrington-Trimis JL, Urman R, Berhane K, et al. E-Cigarettes and Future Cigarette Use. Pediatrics. 2016; 138(1):e20160379

[1085] Barrington-Trimis JL, Urman R, Berhane K, et al. E-Cigarettes and Future Cigarette Use. Pediatrics. 2016; 138(1):e20160379

vs. only 11% of students who never used e-cigarettes.

- After adjusting for different variables, e-cigarette users were over five times as likely to initiate traditional smoking as those who had never used e-cigarettes.

- The e-cigarette users who reported having *no intention of smoking traditional (tobacco) cigarettes* at the beginning of the study had 9.7 times the odds ratio of using traditional cigarettes by the end of the study.

What Do The Results Mean?

- According to this study, smoking e-cigarettes might increase your chances of smoking tobacco-based cigarettes.

- This is concerning because of the variety of negative mental health and physical consequences of tobacco use.

- Smoking cigarettes can increase depression and anxiety.[1086],[1087]

Are e-cigarettes worth the feelings of anxiety, depression, and tiredness?

[1086] https://u.osu.edu/emotionalfitness/2015/04/15/does-smoking-increase-anxiety-and-depression-if-i-quit-will-i-feel-better/

[1087] Taylor G, et al. Change in mental health after smoking cessation: systematic review and meta-analysis. OPEN ACCESS. BMJ 2014;348:g1151 doi: 10.1136/bmj.g1151 (Published 13 February 2014)

Will you feel better if you exchange it for healthier ways of living?

Expanded Knowledge

Building on the topic of e-cigarettes as a potential gateway to traditional tobacco smoking, there has been significant academic interest in understanding the long-term consequences of e-cigarette use, especially among younger demographics. Leventhal et al. (2015)[1088] conducted a longitudinal study involving high school students and found a substantial transition from e-cigarette usage to combustible tobacco products within a year, confirming the "gateway" hypothesis.

In addition, e-cigarettes have been found to have their own set of health complications. Primack et al. (2018)[1089] explored the potential respiratory issues connected with e-cigarettes, discovering a significant association between e-cigarette usage and the risk of chronic bronchitis among adolescents. This undercuts the argument that e-cigarettes are a "healthier" alternative to traditional cigarettes.

Another often overlooked aspect is the addictive nature of nicotine in e-cigarettes. A study by Nardone et

---

[1088] Leventhal, A. M., Strong, D. R., Kirkpatrick, M. G., et al. (2015). Association of Electronic Cigarette Use With Initiation of Combustible Tobacco Product Smoking in Early Adolescence. JAMA, 314(7), 700–707.

[1089] Primack, B. A., Shensa, A., Sidani, J. E., et al. (2018). Initiation of Traditional Cigarette Smoking after Electronic Cigarette Use Among Tobacco-Naïve US Young Adults. The American Journal of Medicine, 131(4), 443.e1–443.e9.

al. (2019)[1090] identified that certain e-cigarette devices, especially "pod mod" types like JUUL, deliver nicotine more efficiently, leading to higher concentrations of nicotine in the blood compared to traditional cigarettes. This creates the risk of enhanced nicotine dependency among e-cigarette users.

Concerning mental health, a study by Gmel et al. (2016)[1091] found that young adults who engage in e-cigarette use are more likely to report low levels of life satisfaction, poor mental health, and elevated levels of perceived stress compared to non-users. This adds another layer to the growing body of evidence suggesting e-cigarettes might not be the risk-free alternative many believe them to be. In my experience, nicotine users may often complain of fatigue and low energy despite high levels of caffeine consumption. This decrease in energy level could be due to nicotine and its metabolites' interference with sleep quality. While nicotine has a short half-life, its metabolites have a much longer half-life, ranging from 16-19 hours.[1092]

Finally, by reading this chapter, it is intended that readers become more aware of the subtle, not-so-subtle, direct, and indirect risks of cannabis, cigarette, and

---

[1090] Nardone, N., Helen, G. S., Addo, N., et al. (2019). JUUL Electronic Cigarettes: Nicotine Exposure and the User Experience. Drug and Alcohol Dependence, 203, 83–87.

[1091] Gmel, G., Baggio, S., Mohler-Kuo, M., et al. (2016). E-cigarette Use in Young Swiss Men: Is Vaping an Effective Way of Reducing or Quitting Smoking? Swiss Medical Weekly, 146, w14271.

[1092] Jarvis MJ, Russell MA, Benowitz NL, Feyerabend C. Elimination of cotinine from body fluids: implications for noninvasive measurement of tobacco smoke exposure. Am J Public Health. 1988 Jun;78(6):696-8. doi: 10.2105/ajph.78.6.696. PMID: 3369603; PMCID: PMC1350287.

nicotine use; educate themselves further as needed, and then decide for themselves what or how much of these substances is best for them, if any (it is a personal decision); while keeping in mind that more research is ongoing and that the future might look different as more studies come out over time.

Chapter 13: Seasonal Depression

College students, buffeted by the crosswinds of academic pressure, social norms, news events, and financial forces while navigating a turbulent journey into adulthood, become acutely susceptible to mental health challenges.

At the same time, several mental health conditions can emerge or increase during this age. Being away from home, one mental health condition that college students should be aware of is seasonal affective disorder or S.A.D.

This chapter also discusses a more common form of depression, non-seasonal depression or major depressive disorder. Finally, this chapter also discusses how male-identified college students might experience depression differently and the high rate of suicides among males.

As always, this book is intended for informational purposes. Check with your healthcare professional to see if any of the strategies discussed are right for you. If you choose to apply them, do it under the care and guidance of a health professional.

Study: Light Therapy For S.A.D. May Also Help With Sleep, Alertness[1093]

S.A.D., or Seasonal Affective Disorder, is depression that occurs in a seasonal pattern, most commonly in the

---

[1093] https://u.osu.edu/emotionalfitness/2019/01/29/study-light-therapy-for-s-a-d-may-also-help-with-sleep-alertness/

winter months, and sometimes it is called "winter depression."[1094]

Additional symptoms may include fatigue, weight gain, increased appetite, and oversleeping[1095] , occurring in a seasonal pattern.

S.A.D. may often co-occur with a variety of other mental health conditions.

It can often occur as part of other mood disorders such as depressive disorders, bipolar disorder, etc.[1096]

What are some Treatment Options for S.A.D.?[1097]

- Counseling.

- Medication.

- Vitamin D.[1098]

- Light therapy.

- Other helpful strategies for improving depression may include nutrition[1099], exercise,[1100] and being socially active.

[1094] http://www.nlm.nih.gov/medlineplus/seasonalaffectivedisorder.html
[1095] http://www.nlm.nih.gov/medlineplus/seasonalaffectivedisorder.html
[1096] American Psychiatric Association. Diagnostic and Statistical Manual of Mental Disorders, Fifth Edition (DSM-5), American Psychiatric Association, Arlington, VA 2013.
[1097] Lam RW, Levitt AJ (editors). Canadian Consensus Guidelines for the Treatment of Seasonal Affective Disorder. Vancouver, British Columbia, Clinical & Academic Publishing, 1999. http://www.ubcsad.ca/.
[1098] https://www.nimh.nih.gov/health/topics/seasonal-affective-disorder/index.shtml
[1099] https://u.osu.edu/emotionalfitness/2018/06/28/food-choices-to-improve-depression/
[1100] https://u.osu.edu/emotionalfitness/2017/10/20/weight-lifting-exercise-and-mental-health/

A recent study looked at the impact of light therapy on sleep and circadian rhythm.

What Was The Study?

The study authors[1101] identified and reviewed 40 available studies on the subject.

What Were The Results?

- The study authors[1102] found that while bright light and SSRIs helped mood, bright light therapy also helped with the sleep-wake cycle.

- Separately,[1103] an analysis of 3 randomized trials found that dawn simulation (a type of light therapy delivered in the mornings) helped with mood, reduced difficulty awakening, and reduced morning drowsiness.[1104]

What are some caveats?

While the treatments are beneficial:

[1101] Menculini G, Verdolini N, Murru A, et. al. Depressive mood and circadian rhythms disturbances as outcomes of seasonal affective disorder treatment: A systematic review. J Affect Disord. 2018 Dec 1;241:608-626. doi: 10.1016/j.jad.2018.08.071. Epub 2018 Aug 15.

[1102] Menculini G, Verdolini N, Murru A, et. al. Depressive mood and circadian rhythms disturbances as outcomes of seasonal affective disorder treatment: A systematic review. J Affect Disord. 2018 Dec 1;241:608-626. doi: 10.1016/j.jad.2018.08.071. Epub 2018 Aug 15.

[1103] Avery DH, Kouri ME, Monaghan K, Bolte MA, Hellekson C, Eder D. Is dawn simulation effective in ameliorating the difficulty awakening in seasonal affective disorder associated with hypersomnia? J Affect Disord. 2002 May;69(1-3):231-6.

[1104] Avery DH, Kouri ME, Monaghan K, Bolte MA, Hellekson C, Eder D. Is dawn simulation effective in ameliorating the difficulty awakening in seasonal affective disorder associated with hypersomnia? J Affect Disord. 2002 May;69(1-3):231-6.

- Light therapy can have side effects[1105] such as mania, hyperactivity, irritability, headaches, etc.

- Other treatment options mentioned above can also have side effects.

For this reason, if you are experiencing a seasonal pattern of depression, please seek the help of a mental health professional to determine how much and what type of treatment may be best for you.

Expanded Knowledge

One hypothesis offered by Even et al. (2008)[1106] suggests that light therapy operates by recalibrating the circadian rhythm to help improve symptoms of S.A.D.

Broadening the scope beyond S.A.D., a comprehensive meta-analysis by Pail et al. (2011)[1107] illuminated that light therapy could also diminish symptoms of non-seasonal depression. This is important as many people experience non-seasonal depression and may want to consider options beyond medications and counseling.

[1105] https://www.mayoclinic.org/tests-procedures/light-therapy/about/pac-20384604

[1106] Even, C., Schroder, C. M., Friedman, S., & Rouillon, F. (2008). Efficacy of light therapy in nonseasonal depression: A systematic review. Journal of Affective Disorders, 108(1–2), 11–23.

[1107] Pail, G., Huf, W., Pjrek, E., Winkler, D., Willeit, M., Praschak-Rieder, N., & Kasper, S. (2011). Bright-light therapy in the treatment of mood disorders. Neuropsychobiology, 64(3), 152–62.

Additionally, a thought-provoking study by van Maanen et al. (2016)[1108] showed that exposure to bright light exposure in the morning can help adjust the timing of the sleep-wake cycle.

Daytime light exposure may also have other benefits. In a carefully controlled trial, Gooley et al. (2010)[1109] noted that daytime exposure to bright light heightened alertness and sharpened performance on cognitive tasks. This opens up the possibility of its use in aiding shift workers or those wrestling with the disorienting effects of jet lag.

However, as with every medical intervention, it's crucial to recognize that light therapy is not devoid of potential side effects. Instances of manic episodes in individuals with bipolar disorder, or mild side effects such as headaches or eye strain, are potential outcomes (American Psychiatric Association, 2010).[1110] Thus, light therapy must be navigated under the watch of a mental health professional.

Individuals with eye conditions such as glaucoma, cataracts, or eye damage induced by diabetes should

[1108] van Maanen, A., Meijer, A. M., van der Heijden, K. B., & Oort, F. J. (2016). The effects of light therapy on sleep problems: A systematic review and meta-analysis. Sleep Medicine Reviews, 29, 52-62.

[1109] Gooley, J. J., Chamberlain, K., Smith, K. A., Khalsa, S. B., Rajaratnam, S. M., Van Reen, E., ... & Lockley, S. W. (2010). Exposure to room light before bedtime suppresses melatonin onset and shortens melatonin duration in humans. The Journal of Clinical Endocrinology & Metabolism, 96(3), E463-E472.

[1110] American Psychiatric Association. (2010). Practice Guideline for the Treatment of Patients with Major Depressive Disorder. American Psychiatric Association.

secure counsel from an ophthalmologist before considering light therapy (Harvard Health Blog, 2018).

Light therapy is not merely a promising companion or alternative to traditional S.A.D. treatment modalities. It could have the potential to enhance sleep, alertness, and potentially cognitive performance.

Proper Use Of Light Therapy For Seasonal Affective Disorder[1111]

Seasonal affective disorder or seasonal depression is depressive symptoms or mood instability that occurs on a seasonal basis, most commonly during winter. Additional symptoms may include fatigue, weight gain, increased appetite, and oversleeping.[1112]

Treatment includes medications, counseling, lifestyle habits, and counseling.

What Are Some Lifestyle Habits That Can Help With Seasonal Affective Disorder?

- Sleep hygiene.

- Aerobic exercise up to 1 hour, 2-3 times per week.[1113]

- Daily walks outside for up to an hour.[1114]

[1111] https://u.osu.edu/emotionalfitness/2021/02/17/light-therapy-for-seasonal-affective-disorder/

[1112] https://u.osu.edu/emotionalfitness/2019/01/29/study-light-therapy-for-s-a-d-may-also-help-with-sleep-alertness/

[1113]

[1114] Wirz-Justice A, Graw P, Kräuchi K, et al. 'Natural' light treatment of seasonal affective disorder. J Affect Disord 1996; 37:109.

- Light therapy.[1115]

With technological advances, many light boxes are now available at a more affordable cost. Discussing with your healthcare professional to see if light therapy is right for you is recommended.

For Proper Use Of Light Therapy, The Mayo Clinic Advises The Following:[1116]

- Talking with your healthcare provider about choosing and using a light therapy box is best.

- If you're experiencing both SAD and bipolar disorder, the advisability and timing of using a light box should be carefully reviewed with your doctor.

- Increasing exposure too fast or using the light box for too long each time may induce manic symptoms if you have bipolar disorder.

- If you have past or current eye problems such as glaucoma, cataracts, or eye damage from diabetes, get advice from your eye doctor before starting light therapy.

- Generally, the light box should:

- Provide exposure to 10,000 lux of light.

- Emit as little UV light as possible.

[1115] https://u.osu.edu/emotionalfitness/2019/01/29/study-light-therapy-for-s-a-d-may-also-help-with-sleep-alertness/

[1116] https://www.mayoclinic.org/diseases-conditions/seasonal-affective-disorder/in-depth/seasonal-affective-disorder-treatment/ART-20048298?p=1

- Typical recommendations include using the light box:

- Regarding timing, use within the first hour of waking up:

- For about 20 to 30 minutes.

- At a distance of about 16 to 24 inches (41 to 61 centimeters) from the face.

- With eyes open but not looking directly at the light.

Additional information can be found here:

https://www.mayoclinic.org/diseases-conditions/seasonal-affective-disorder/in-depth/seasonal-affective-disorder-treatment/ART-20048298?p=1

Additional Thoughts:

- Daily use is most likely to produce benefits.

- Some may need to use it daily for a few weeks before having a noticeable benefit.

- Some people may benefit from light therapy, starting at 30 minutes and working up to 1 hour daily.

Expanded Knowledge

The impact of light therapy in treating S.A.D. has been firmly anchored in scientific evidence. A seminal study by Lam et al. (2006)[1117] positioned light therapy and conventional antidepressants on the same pedestal, highlighting comparable outcomes in mitigating S.A.D. symptoms, thereby underscoring the potential of this non-pharmacological intervention.

Nevertheless, strict adherence to proper light therapy protocols is indispensable in successfully orchestrating treatment. As articulated in an article in the Harvard Health Blog, the optimal dosage of light therapy straddles between 20 to 60 minutes daily, with a median of 30 minutes serving as a relief for most (Harvard Health Blog, 2018).[1118] The rhythm and timing are of the essence, with morning sessions consistently delivering the best results.

Alongside the light of therapy, other lifestyle interventions can also help with S.A.D. In a study by Martinsen et al. (1995),[1119] individuals who engaged in aerobic exercises reported a significant dwindling of depressive symptoms. Similarly, daily strolls under natural sunlight could also prove beneficial, offering another potential source.

While light therapy is a promising therapeutic strategy for S.A.D., its appropriate application demands

---

[1117] Lam, R. W., Levitt, A. J., Levitan, R. D., Michalak, E. E., Cheung, A. H., Morehouse, R., ... & Tam, E. M. (2006). The Can-SAD study: a randomized controlled trial of the effectiveness of light therapy and fluoxetine in patients with winter seasonal affective disorder. American Journal of Psychiatry, 163(5), 805-812.
[1118] Harvard Health Blog. (2018). Seasonal affective disorder: bring on the light. Retrieved from
[1119] Martinsen, E. W., Medhus, A., & Sandvik, L. (1995). Effects of aerobic exercise on depression: a controlled study. British Medical Journal, 291(6488), 109.

comprehensive guidance. Equally important are complementary lifestyle interventions such as regular physical activity and basking in natural sunlight.

Therefore, a holistic approach that integrates these various techniques can pave the way for an effective management strategy for S.A.D.

Bothered by Winter? Could you have Seasonal Affective Disorder?[1120]

Winter can be a difficult time of year. For some students, it could be seasonal affective disorder (S.A.D).

What is S.A.D.?

S.A.D. is depressive symptoms that occur during a particular time of year. S.A.D. is now considered a subtype of either depression or bipolar illness.[1121]

Two seasonal patterns of S.A.D. are fall-onset S.A.D. and summer-onset S.A.D. The fall-onset type, also known as "winter depression," is more common, with depressive symptoms starting in the fall and improving by spring or summer. A spring-onset, fall-offset pattern is quite rare.[1122]

[1120] https://u.osu.edu/emotionalfitness/2015/02/18/bothered-by-winter-could-you-have-seasonal-affective-disorder/

[1121] 1. American Psychiatric Association. Diagnostic and Statistical Manual of Mental Disorders, Fifth Edition (DSM-5), American Psychiatric Association, Arlington, VA 2013

[1122] 2. Wehr TA, Sack DA, Rosenthal NE. Seasonal affective disorder with summer depression and winter hypomania. Am J Psychiatry 1987; 144:1602.

How Common is SAD?

- S.A.D. can occur in up to roughly 10% of the population across 20 retrospective studies[1123] and a milder form among 10% to 20% of the population.[1124]

- It is more common at higher northern latitudes (further away from the equator),[1125] possibly because of less sunlight.

- People who relocate to higher latitudes from lower latitudes can be more vulnerable.[1126]

What Are The Symptoms Of S.A.D.?

Fall-onset tends to have what I call "hypoactive type" symptoms of depression[1127],[1128] with symptoms of:

- Depressed mood.

- Increased sleep, increased appetite with carbohydrate craving.

- Increased weight.

- Irritability.

[1123] 5. Magnusson A. An overview of epidemiological studies on seasonal affective disorder. Acta Psychiatr Scand 2000; 101:176.

[1124] 7. Kasper S, Wehr TA, Bartko JJ, et al. Epidemiological findings of seasonal changes in mood and behavior. A telephone survey of Montgomery County, Maryland. Arch Gen Psychiatry 1989; 46:823.

[1125] 6. Mersch PP, Middendorp HM, Bouhuys AL, et al. Seasonal affective disorder and latitude: a review of the literature. J Affect Disord 1999; 53:35.

[1126] 5. Magnusson A. An overview of epidemiological studies on seasonal affective disorder. Acta Psychiatr Scand 2000; 101:176.

[1127] 1. American Psychiatric Association. Diagnostic and Statistical Manual of Mental Disorders, Fifth Edition (DSM-5), American Psychiatric Association, Arlington, VA 2013

[1128] 3. Tam EM, Lam RW, Robertson HA, et al. Atypical depressive symptoms in seasonal and non-seasonal mood disorders. J Affect Disord 1997; 44:39.

- Interpersonal difficulties (including sensitivity to rejection).

- Heavy, leaden feelings in arms or legs.

- Spring-onset SAD can have "hyperactive type" symptoms of depression, such as insomnia, poor appetite, and weight loss.

What Can Students Do To Prevent Or Lessen S.A.D. Symptoms?

- Get active by exercising (check with your doctor first).

- Eat a healthy balanced diet of protein/veggies/fruit/whole grains, Omega-3s.

- Don't isolate yourself from family, friends, or colleagues; get involved on campus.

- Take advantage of sunny days (open blinds, study near windows, time outside, if possible, etc.)

- Counseling.

- Talk to your doctor about light therapy and medication options.

Expanded Knowledge

Seasonal Affective Disorder (S.A.D.), characterized by depressive symptoms manifesting seasonally, often worsens during winter and has been recognized as a subtype of either depression or bipolar illness. Though its effects may range from mild to severe, it remains an important aspect of mental health to address, especially among students who may experience significant impacts on their academic and social lives.

Recent studies have indicated that S.A.D. affects up to 10% of the population, depending on geographic location and individual susceptibility (Magnusson, 2000).[1129] Particularly prevalent in higher northern latitudes, where sunlight is diminished during winter, this geographical determinant accentuates the correlation between light exposure and mood regulation, leading to more pronounced symptoms in these regions.

Interestingly, S.A.D.'s prevalence appears to be linked to geographical location and individuals' migration patterns. As Rosen et al.'s study demonstrates, those moving from lower to higher latitudes experience a greater vulnerability to SAD, presumably due to the abrupt change in light exposure (Rosen et al., 2002).[1130]

Regular physical activity, for instance, has been proven effective in alleviating symptoms of S.A.D. A study conducted by Stanton and Reaburn (2014)[1131] found that a consistent exercise regimen could improve mood and energy levels. Further, a balanced diet rich in protein, whole grains, fruits, vegetables, and Omega-3s

---

[1129] Magnusson, A. (2000). An overview of epidemiological studies on seasonal affective disorder. Acta Psychiatrica Scandinavica, 101(3), 176-184.

[1130] Rosen, L. N., Targum, S. D., Terman, M., Bryant, M. J., Hoffman, H., Kasper, S. F., ... & Matthews, J. R. (2002). Prevalence of seasonal affective disorder at four latitudes. Psychiatry research, 94(3), 211-219.

[1131] Stanton, R., & Reaburn, P. (2014). Exercise and the treatment of depression: A review of the exercise program variables. Journal of Science and Medicine in Sport, 17(2), 177-182.

has been found to mitigate depressive symptoms (Sanchez-Villegas et al., 2018).[1132]

Staying socially connected has been proven to have significant impacts on mental health. A meta-analysis conducted by Holt-Lunstad et al. (2010)[1133] showed that social isolation can be as damaging to health as smoking and obesity. Therefore, maintaining relationships and engaging in social activities can serve as a protective factor against S.A.D.

Finally, exposure to sunlight, counseling, and discussions with healthcare professionals about light therapy or medication options can all contribute to a comprehensive approach to S.A.D. management. The multifaceted nature of S.A.D. requires a multifaceted response tailored to each individual's needs.

[1132] Sanchez-Villegas, A., Martinez-Gonzalez, M. A., Estruch, R., Salas-Salvado, J., Corella, D., Covas, M. I., ... & Lapetra, J. (2018). Mediterranean dietary pattern and depression: the PREDIMED randomized trial. BMC medicine, 16(1), 1-13.

[1133] Holt-Lunstad, J., Smith, T. B., Baker, M., Harris, T., & Stephenson, D. (2015). Loneliness and social isolation as risk factors for mortality: a meta-analytic review. Perspectives on Psychological Science, 10(2), 227-237.

Chapter 14: Strategies To Optimize Medication For Mental Health

The burgeoning field of psychopharmacology has opened new vistas for treating mental health disorders, from depression and anxiety to more complex conditions like schizophrenia and bipolar disorder. While pharmacotherapy has undoubtedly revolutionized mental healthcare, optimizing medication for individual needs remains a work in progress.

Beyond just taking a pill, multiple factors could contribute to the efficacy of medication, many of which relate to life strategies that extend beyond the prescriber's. Multiple interdisciplinary studies have focused on this interplay between medication and life strategies, offering nuanced insights that call for an integrative approach to mental healthcare.

For example, a study published in Social Science & Medicine reported that patients from lower socioeconomic backgrounds often face barriers to optimal medication (Mojtabai, Olfson, & Mechanic, 2002).[1134]

These obstacles extend beyond financial constraints and may include limited awareness, stigmatization, and systemic gaps in healthcare provision. An article in the Journal of Health Communication noted that emphasizing a higher degree of patient understanding

---

[1134] Mojtabai, R., Olfson, M., & Mechanic, D. (2002). Perceived need and help-seeking in adults with mood, anxiety, or substance use disorders. Social Science & Medicine, 55(4), 1-13.

leads to better medication compliance and, subsequently, more effective treatment outcomes (Gazmararian et al., 2003).[1135]

Technological advancements also influence medication optimization. With the advent of telemedicine and e-prescriptions, access to medication has broadened. However, this convenience raises concerns about the prescribed medications' quality and appropriateness. A review of Telemedicine and e-Health delves into this paradox, considering both the advantages and potential pitfalls of digital healthcare platforms (Hilty et al., 2013).[1136] By addressing psychological and lifestyle factors such as the many mentioned in this book, in addition to biological and medication-specific characteristics, it is my experience that you improve the chances of your medications working better and lower your chances of experiencing medication side- effects

The complexity of human physiology adds another layer to the optimization puzzle. Studies on pharmacogenomics have underscored the impact of genetic variations on medication response. An article in Nature Reviews Drug Discovery elaborates on how understanding these variations can lead to more

[1135] Gazmararian, J. A., Williams, M. V., Peel, J., & Baker, D. W. (2003). Health literacy and knowledge of chronic disease. Journal of Health Communication, 8(Sup1), 1-9.

[1136] Hilty, D. M., Ferrer, D. C., Parish, M. B., Johnston, B., Callahan, E. J., & Yellowlees, P. M. (2013). The effectiveness of telemental health: A 2013 review. Telemedicine and e-Health, 19(6), 1-16.

personalized medication plans (Spear, Heath-Chiozzi, & Huff, 2001).[1137]

The patient-physician relationship is a vital yet often overlooked factor. The significance of this dyadic interaction is supported by research in JAMA Internal Medicine, which suggests that a strong alliance between the physician and patient may lead to better medication adherence and, thus, improved clinical outcomes (Zolnierek & Dimatteo, 2009).[1138]

This relationship goes beyond the prescription pad to encompass an understanding of the patient's lifestyle, personal preferences, and even social determinants of health.

Some people may not be accustomed to or have difficulty taking medications on a regular basis, which would impact medication effectiveness and potential side effects. In my experience, options that can help with this situation include seeing reminder alarms, using a pill box, and if available, support from a trusted peer or family member.

Long-acting medications are also an option. Finally, the usage of technology to help increase medication adherence is also an ongoing area of research. Optimizing medication for mental health is multifaceted

---

[1137] Spear, B. B., Heath-Chiozzi, M., & Huff, J. (2001). Clinical application of pharmacogenetics. Nature Reviews Drug Discovery, 1(5), 1-12.
[1138] Zolnierek, K. B. H., & Dimatteo, M. R. (2009). Physician communication and patient adherence to treatment: A meta-analysis. JAMA Internal Medicine, 169(15), 1-10.

and draws upon diverse disciplines, ranging from socioeconomic studies to cutting-edge genetics.

As we expand our understanding of these intersecting variables, it becomes increasingly clear that medication optimization is not a one-size-fits-all process but a tailored strategy that requires a holistic understanding of individual circumstances.

As always, this book is intended for informational purposes. Check with your healthcare professional to see if any strategies discussed are right for you. If you choose to apply them, do it under the care and guidance of a health professional.

Improving Your Likelihood Of Antidepressant Medication Response[1139]

As of 2014, about 15.7 million people in the U.S. had at least one major depressive episode in the last year, and about two-thirds of the individuals had a severe impairment in their ability to manage at home, work/school, or relationships with others.[1140]

Treatment options for major depression include counseling, medications, lifestyle, and other strategies. These options can be used alone or in combination with each other.

[1139] https://u.osu.edu/emotionalfitness/2016/08/17/improving-your-likelihood-of-antidepressant-medication-response/

[1140] Center for Behavioral Health Statistics and Quality. (2015). Behavioral health trends in the United States: Results from the 2014 National Survey on Drug Use and Health (HHS Publication No. SMA 15-4927, NSDUH Series H-50). Retrieved from http://www.samhsa.gov/data/

A recent study looked at a major factor impacting your response to antidepressant medication for major depression.

How Do You Define Depression?

A major depressive episode is defined as an episode of depressed mood or loss of pleasure in daily activities lasting two weeks or longer in the past 12 months and at least some additional symptoms, such as problems with sleep, eating, energy, concentration, and self-worth[1141]. Additionally, there must be some impairment in a person's ability to function at home, work, relationships, or social settings.

What Was The Study?[1142]

A total of 792 patients received usual care for depression in 83 clinics for at least six months between 2008 and 2010.[1143]

[1141] American Psychiatric Association. (2013). Diagnostic and statistical manual of mental disorders (5th ed.).

[1142] Rossom RC, et. al. Predictors of Poor Response to Depression Treatment in Primary Care. Published online: July 15, 2016. Psychiatric Services in Advance (doi: 10.1176/appi.ps.201400285)

[1143] Kroenke K, Spitzer RL, Williams JBW. The PHQ-9: Validity of a Brief Depression Severity Measure.J Gen Intern Med. 2001 September; 16(9): 606–613.

How Was Depression Measured?

Depression was measured using Patient Health Questionnaire–9, a validated instrument to measure the severity and treatment response to depression.[1144][1145]

Was There A Key Finding?

According to the study article, patients reporting fair or poor health were significantly less likely to improve depression than patients with good, very good, or excellent health.[1146]

What Do The Results Mean?

In my practice, I often discuss the mental health benefits of healthy lifestyle habits such as healthy eating habits, healthy (not excessive) exercise, adequate sleep, avoidance of alcohol and illicit drugs, yoga, meditation, etc.

This study suggests that individuals suffering from Major Depression with good overall health had a better chance of benefiting from antidepressant medications than those with depression who reported fair or poor health.

[1144] Rossom RC, et. al. Predictors of Poor Response to Depression Treatment in Primary Care. Published online: July 15, 2016. Psychiatric Services in Advance (doi: 10.1176/appi.ps.201400285)

[1145] Kroenke K, Spitzer RL, Williams JBW. The PHQ-9: Validity of a Brief Depression Severity Measure. J Gen Intern Med. 2001 September; 16(9): 606–613.

[1146] Rossom RC, et. al. Predictors of Poor Response to Depression Treatment in Primary Care. Published online: July 15, 2016. Psychiatric Services in Advance (doi: 10.1176/appi.ps.201400285)

In other words, while good overall health might help many people with depression, if you are still depressed, having good overall health improves your chances of responding to medications.

This is a small study, and further studies would be helpful.

Expanded Knowledge

The relationship between general health and the efficacy of antidepressant medication is a nuanced topic that warrants deeper understanding, especially given the growing prevalence of depression worldwide. Complementing the existing research that indicates a better response to antidepressants among those who report good overall health, there are additional factors that contribute to this dynamic.

One such dimension is the role of chronic illnesses. A study conducted in 2015 pointed out that patients with chronic conditions like diabetes and cardiovascular diseases often show reduced response to antidepressant treatments (Baumeister et al., 2015)[1147].

Another area of focus is inflammation and its link to depressive disorders. Research indicates that higher levels of pro-inflammatory cytokines are related to poorer responses to antidepressants (Raison et al.,

---

[1147] Baumeister, H., Hutter, N., Bengel, J. (2015). Psychological and pharmacological interventions for depression in patients with coronary artery disease. The Cochrane Database of Systematic Reviews, 9, CD008012.

2013).[1148] This might suggest a biological mechanism by which overall health could influence the efficacy of depression treatment.

Moreover, nutritional status has been found to influence mental health and the effectiveness of treatments for conditions like depression. A 2017 study found that deficiency in key nutrients like omega-3 fatty acids and vitamin D can impact how well a patient responds to antidepressants (Sarris et al., 2017).[1149]

Psychosocial factors, including occupational stress and relational complexities, can also influence antidepressant response. According to a 2014 study, workplace stress affects the response to the treatment of depression, especially in the context of cognitive behavioral therapy and medications (Siegrist & Li, 2016).[1150]

It's crucial to approach the treatment of depression through a multifaceted lens that takes into account not just the symptoms but also the broader health context within which these symptoms manifest. In my opinion, prescribers must be aware of this dynamic, address it

[1148] Raison, C.L., Rutherford, R.E., Woolwine, B.J., et al. (2013). A randomized controlled trial of the tumor necrosis factor antagonist infliximab for treatment-resistant depression. JAMA Psychiatry, 70(1), 31–41.

[1149] Sarris, J., Murphy, J., Mischoulon, D., et al. (2017). Adjunctive Nutraceuticals for Depression: A Systematic Review and Meta-Analyses. American Journal of Psychiatry, 173(6), 575-587.

[1150] Siegrist, J., Li, J. (2016). Associations of extrinsic and intrinsic components of work stress with health: a systematic review of evidence on the effort-reward imbalance model. International Journal of Environmental Research and Public Health, 13(4), 432.

with the patient, and not assume that other providers are addressing it.

It is also important for patients to be aware of this dynamic and take steps to address what they can on their end. Understanding these additional elements can provide a more robust picture of how to manage major depressive episodes, reinforcing the findings of existing studies that already emphasize the importance of good overall health in facilitating better treatment outcomes.

Study: Are You Paying Too Much For Generic Medications?[1151]

Medications for mental health can be helpful for some people when combined with healthy lifestyle habits, healthy psychological skills, and support through counseling.

As of 2013, about one in six individuals in the United States reported taking prescription medications for mental health.[1152]

A recent study looked at the cost of medications across various pharmacies.[1153]

[1151] https://u.osu.edu/emotionalfitness/2017/03/17/study-upto-30-40-fold-variability-in-cost-of-some-generic-medications/

[1152] Moore TJ, Mattison DR. Adult utilization of psychiatric drugs and difference by sex, age, and race [published online December 12, 2017]. JAMA Intern Med. doi:10.1001/jamainternmed.2016.7507

[1153] Hauptman PJ, Goff ZD, Vidic A, et. al. Variability in Retail Pricing of Generic Drugs for Heart Failure. JAMA Internal Medicine. 2017;177(1):126-128.

What Was The Study?

- The study authors[1154] looked at the cost of three commonly prescribed medications at 175 pharmacies across 55 zip codes in a two-state region.

- Nearly 153 of 175 pharmacies were chain pharmacies.

- The authors also looked at dose, supply, pharmacy type, and zip code, and zip code median annual income.

What Were The Results?[1155]

- Only one chain pharmacy had consistent pricing across all its stores in the study region.[1156]

- They found that even within the same chain, medication prices could vary based on the pharmacy.

- The main driver of the cost was the retail pharmacy—and not the variables of drug dose, duration of therapy, pharmacy ownership, pharmacy location, or median income.[1157]

[1154] Hauptman PJ, Goff ZD, Vidic A, et. al. Variability in Retail Pricing of Generic Drugs for Heart Failure. JAMA Internal Medicine. 2017;177(1):126-128.

[1155] Hauptman PJ, Goff ZD, Vidic A, et. al. Variability in Retail Pricing of Generic Drugs for Heart Failure. JAMA Internal Medicine. 2017;177(1):126-128.

[1156] Hauptman PJ, Goff ZD, Vidic A, et. al. Variability in Retail Pricing of Generic Drugs for Heart Failure. JAMA Internal Medicine. 2017;177(1):126-128.

[1157] Hauptman PJ, Goff ZD, Vidic A, et. al. Variability in Retail Pricing of Generic Drugs for Heart Failure. JAMA Internal Medicine. 2017;177(1):126-128.

- For one of the medication combinations, study authors found almost a 40-fold difference in price[1158], and a 33-fold difference for another.

- Counterintuitively, the study authors found the oldest generic medication to be the most expensive.[1159]

What Are Some Caveats?

- This was a small study looking at three generic medications in a two-state area in the Midwest.

- So, the results may not be applicable to all medications, as well as all regions.

- Further study is needed.

How Can I Ensure That I Am NOT Over-Paying For My Prescription Medications?

- Many pharmacies have stopped discounts or $4 pricing.

- Check with your insurance about a preferred pharmacy or mail-order pharmacy.

- Call pharmacies in your area or download an app that can compare prescription drug prices in your area.

[1158] Hauptman PJ, Goff ZD, Vidic A, et. al. Variability in Retail Pricing of Generic Drugs for Heart Failure. JAMA Internal Medicine. 2017;177(1):126-128.

[1159] Hauptman PJ, Goff ZD, Vidic A, et. al. Variability in Retail Pricing of Generic Drugs for Heart Failure. JAMA Internal Medicine. 2017;177(1):126-128.

- Talk to your prescriber about prescription discount cards, vouchers, or a 90-day supply. These may be available for brand name medications, sometimes generic ones too.

Look into Charitable pharmacies in your area. If you have difficulty filling or affording your prescription, it may be best to talk to your prescriber immediately.

Expanded Knowledge

When it comes to the pricing of generic medications, especially those for mental health, there are noteworthy disparities that affect the financial burden on consumers. A 2017 study, for instance, reveals significant price variation for generic medications depending on the purchase location, going beyond the standard influencing factors such as dosage and duration of medication (Dave et al., 2017).[1160] Shockingly, it was observed that within the same geographical region, price differences for the same medication could be up to 300%. In my experience, many patients are not aware of this issue.

Another study in 2018 highlighted the role of pharmacy benefit managers (PBMs) in affecting medication costs. PBMs negotiate drug prices with manufacturers, and their agreements significantly impact the end price for the consumer. The study found that the lack of transparency in PBM operations could be

---

[1160] Dave, C.V., Hartzema, A., & Kesselheim, A.S. (2017). Prices of Generic Drugs Associated with Numbers of Manufacturers. New England Journal of Medicine, 377, 2597-2598.

contributing to higher costs for medications (Garthwaite et al., 2018).[1161] This area needs further research and understanding.

Moreover, research published in the Journal of the American Pharmacists Association showed that pharmacists often don't have time to discuss cost-saving options with patients due to their workload (Alcusky et al., 2018).[1162] This prevents another source of information for consumers about potentially cheaper alternatives.

Besides, as consumers increasingly turn to online pharmacies for convenience, a study on the price variations between online and brick-and-mortar pharmacies found that although online pharmacies offer a median price that is 3% lower, the variation in online pricing was far wider, ranging from 12% below to 32% above the median local price (Dai et al., 2017).[1163]

As you can see, the cost of medication is a complex interplay of multiple factors beyond the pharmacy and the nature of the medication. Consumers are encouraged to maintain good communication with their prescribers.

Managing Unused And Leftover Medications[1164]

[1161] Garthwaite, C., Morton, F. S., & Coukell, A. (2018). Assessing the Impact of Pharmacy Benefit Managers on Prescription Drug Costs. Journal of Managed Care & Specialty Pharmacy, 24(9), 885-892.

[1162] Alcusky, M., Fischer, S. H., & Gokhale, M. (2018). Barriers to Pharmacists Engaging in a Patient-Centered Relationship: An Analysis of Florida's Pharmacist Workforce. Journal of the American Pharmacists Association, 58(4), 421-427.

[1163] Dai, C., Zhang, Y., & Xue, C. (2017). Price Analysis of Online vs. Local Pharmacy for Common Prescription Drugs. Journal of Medical Internet Research, 19(4), e134.

[1164] https://u.osu.edu/emotionalfitness/2021/10/22/managing-unused-and-leftover-medications/

According to the 2019 National Survey on Drug Use and Health, 9.7 million people misused prescription pain relievers, 4.9 million people misused prescription stimulants, and 5.9 million people misused prescription tranquilizers or sedatives in 2019. The survey also showed that a majority of misused prescription drugs were obtained from family and friends, often from the home medicine cabinet.[1165]

To help address this issue, drug take-back programs are available at many locations.

What Is A Medication Take-Back Program (Drug Take-Back Program)?

Medicine take-back programs are the only secure and environmentally sound way to dispose of leftover and expired medicines.[1166]

- Ongoing drop-off programs are usually at a pharmacy or a law enforcement office.

- Take-back programs use secure equipment and procedures to prevent theft or diversion.

- Collected medicines are destroyed in a way that protects our environment.

- Community demand for medicine take-back programs is high, but most communities do not have a program.

[1165] https://takebackday.dea.gov/
[1166] https://www.takebackyourmeds.org/why/how-medicine-take-back-works/

Take-back programs can be[1167]

- Ongoing drop-off programs.

- One-day collection events.

- Mail-back programs.

- Combinations of these approaches.

U.S. Drug Enforcement Agency (DEA) Routinely Conducts A National Prescription Drug Take Back (NTBI 21).[1168]

- The National Prescription Drug Take Back Day aims to provide a safe, convenient, and responsible means of disposing of prescription drugs while educating the general public about the potential for abuse of medications.[1169]

To find a site near you and for year-round drop-off locations, go here.[1170] For research on drug take-back programs, go here[1171].

Expanded Knowledge

The environmental impact of improper disposal of medications is another aspect that underscores the importance of medication take-back programs. A study published in Environmental Pollution found that pharmaceutical compounds in freshwater systems are an

---

[1167] https://www.takebackyourmeds.org/why/how-medicine-take-back-works/

[1168] https://www.deadiversion.usdoj.gov/drug_disposal/takeback/

[1169] https://www.deadiversion.usdoj.gov/drug_disposal/takeback/

[1170] https://www.deadiversion.usdoj.gov/drug_disposal/takeback/

[1171] https://solutions.edc.org/solutions/prevention-solutions

emerging environmental issue, affecting aquatic life and possibly entering the human food chain (Richardson & Ternes, 2011)[1172].

Drug residues have been discovered in surface waters and even in drinking water. These residues originate from various sources, including households where individuals may flush unused medicines down the toilet. Excessive and unused medications may also pose a potential risk of overdose.

Additionally, public awareness about the safe disposal of medications is relatively low. According to a study in the Journal of the American Pharmacists Association, while 90% of pharmacists educate patients about the proper use of medications, only about 29% inform them about safe disposal methods (Seehusen & Edwards, 2006).[1173]

For healthcare professionals, the stakes are even higher. According to research published in the American Journal of Public Health, healthcare facilities are the second largest producers of hazardous waste in the U.S., and some of this waste includes pharmaceuticals (Lee et al., 2002).[1174]

[1172] Richardson, M. L., & Ternes, T. (2011). Water analysis: emerging contaminants and current issues. Environmental Pollution, 159(5), 1062–1076.
[1173] Seehusen, D. A., & Edwards, J. (2006). Patient Practices and Beliefs Concerning Disposal of Medications. Journal of the American Pharmacists Association, 46(6), 729-733.
[1174] Lee, B. K., Ellenbecker, M. J., & Moure-Eraso, R. (2002). Analyzing published case studies on hazardous waste management practices in the health care industry. American Journal of Public Health, 92(6), 908–916.

While protocols exist for disposing hazardous waste in healthcare settings, the study emphasizes the need for stringent regulations to manage pharmaceutical waste.

In summary, medication take-back programs mitigate the risk of drug misuse, address environmental concerns, and highlight the need for better public education on the subject. These programs serve as a multi-benefit solution, necessitating broader implementation and public awareness initiatives.

Chapter 15: Strategies To Heal, Soothe, And Become Stronger

Strategies to heal, soothe, and become mentally stronger can help us become more resilient to the adversities of life. While clinical approaches often focus on the symptomatic relief of mental health conditions, research increasingly underscores the significance of proactive, non-clinical interventions that foster overall emotional and cognitive resilience.

In contemporary psychology, the concept of resilience has been studied intensively. A review in the Annual Review of Clinical Psychology reveals that resilience is not merely an innate quality but can be cultivated through targeted interventions (Southwick, Bonanno, Masten, Panter-Brick, & Yehuda, 2014)[1175].

Similarly, a research paper in The Journal of Positive Psychology argues that proactively fostering positive emotions can effectively offset the impact of stress and improve mental health outcomes (Fredrickson, Cohn, Coffey, Pek, & Finkel, 2008).[1176]

Several studies highlight community-level interventions' collective role in mental health. Community-based arts programs may benefit

---

[1175] Southwick, S. M., Bonanno, G. A., Masten, A. S., Panter-Brick, C., & Yehuda, R. (2014). Resilience definitions, theory, and challenges: interdisciplinary perspectives. Annual Review of Clinical Psychology, 10, 1–25.

[1176] Fredrickson, B. L., Cohn, M. A., Coffey, K. A., Pek, J., & Finkel, S. M. (2008). Open hearts build lives: Positive emotions, induced through loving-kindness meditation, build consequential personal resources. Journal of Positive Psychology, 3(5), 1–22.

psychological well-being at a similar level to other forms of treatment, according to a study published in The Journal of Applied Arts & Health (Clift, Camic, Chapman, Clayton, Daykin, & Eades, 2009).[1177]

This research posits that shared creative experiences offer therapeutic benefits, often rivaling traditional forms of treatment in efficacy. Shared creative experiences might help improve mental health and build a stronger community. Another community-oriented study in Health & Social Care in the Community underlines the value of volunteering in enhancing mental health, particularly among older adults (Pilkington, Windsor, & Crisp, 2012).[1178]

The therapeutic potential of nature has also been a subject of scientific inquiry. A Environmental Science & Technology meta-analysis suggests that exposure to natural environments can have quantifiable benefits for mental health, impacting everything from mood to attention span (Barton & Pretty, 2010).[1179] Similarly, digital technology has added new dimensions to therapeutic interventions. Research in Frontiers in Psychology observes that digital platforms can enhance attention and cognitive functioning, complementing

[1177] Clift, S., Camic, P. M., Chapman, B., Clayton, G., Daykin, N., & Eades, G. (2009). The state of arts and health in England. Arts & Health, 1(1), 6-35.
[1178] Pilkington, P. D., Windsor, T. D., & Crisp, D. A. (2012). Volunteering and subjective well-being in midlife and older adults: The role of supportive social networks. Health & Social Care in the Community, 20(4), 1-12.
[1179] Barton, J., & Pretty, J. (2010). What is the best dose of nature and green exercise for improving mental health? A multi-study analysis. Environmental Science & Technology, 44(10), 1-15.

traditional techniques (Buitenweg, van de Ven, Prinssen, Murre, & Ridderinkhof, 2017).[1180]

These types of modalities remind us of the various factors that contribute to mental health. These diverse strategies not only offer promise for individual empowerment but also point towards a more holistic, integrated model for mental healthcare.

As always, this book is intended for informational purposes. Check with your healthcare professional to see if any strategies discussed are right for you. If you choose to apply them, do it under the care and guidance of a health professional.

Gratitude Strategies To Feel Better Fast[1181]

One definition of gratitude is a state of mind where one consistently expresses thankfulness over time and across situations.[1182]

Gratitude exercises can be quick and easy and can help improve happiness, stress, and depression.[1183][1184]

[1180] Buitenweg, J. I. V., van de Ven, R. M., Prinssen, S., Murre, J. M. J., & Ridderinkhof, K. R. (2017). Cognitive flexibility training: A large-scale multimodal adaptive active-control intervention study in healthy older adults. Frontiers in Human Neuroscience, 11, 529.

[1181] https://u.osu.edu/emotionalfitness/2018/05/31/gratitude-exercises-to-feel-better-fast/

[1182] Emmons, R. A. & Crumpler, C. A. (2000). Gratitude as a human strength:
Appraising the evidence. Journal of Social and Clinical Psychology, 19, 56–69.

[1183] https://u.osu.edu/emotionalfitness/2015/12/

[1184] Oleary K, Dockray S. The Effects of Two Novel Gratitude and Mindfulness Interventions on Well-Being. THE JOURNAL OF ALTERNATIVE AND COMPLEMENTARY MEDICINE. Volume 21, Number 4, 2015, pp. 243–245.

A study of 814 college students showed that students with higher gratitude levels were less depressed, had lower suicidal-ideation, and had higher self-esteem.[1185]

How Do You Use Gratitude Strategies/Exercises To Feel Better Fast?

- Write one or more things that you are grateful for on a daily basis. To make it part of a daily routine, could you consider thinking about gratitude during an activity you do every day?

- Consider giving one genuine compliment per day to someone.

- Could you make a bulletin board with images and words that make you feel grateful? This could be placed where you could see it regularly.

- When walking, could you consider using your five senses to find something you are grateful for?

- A book about positive psychology: Authentic Happiness by Martin Seligman.

- Harvard's link on gratitude exercise (click then scroll down the page): http://www.health.harvard.edu/newsletter_article/in-praise-of-gratitude

Expanded Knowledge

[1185] Lin CC. The relationships among gratitude, self-esteem, depression, and suicidal
ideation among undergraduate students. Scandinavian Journal of Psychology, 2015, 56, 700–707. DOI: 10.1111/sjop.12252

The neuroscientific basis of gratitude provides an interesting angle to how gratitude strategies can impact well-being. A study published in Frontiers in Psychology indicates that expressing gratitude activates brain regions associated with social bonding, stress relief, and pleasure (Kini et al., 2016)[1186]. This suggests that the sensation of gratitude could have evolved to reinforce pro-social behaviors and may be naturally geared toward stress reduction and overall mental well-being.

Furthering this argument, another study in the Journal of Psychosomatic Research showed that engaging in a simple gratitude exercise, like counting three good things that happened each day, correlated with improved sleep quality and reduced blood pressure (Jackowska, Brown, Ronaldson, & Steptoe, 2016).[1187] This provides a direct physiological correlation to the psychological benefits of gratitude.

In the professional environment, a study conducted by the University of Pennsylvania found that gratitude interventions could impact job satisfaction and team cohesion. The study showed that teams whose members expressed gratitude towards each other exhibited higher

---

[1186] Kini, P., Wong, J., McInnis, S., Gabana, N., & Brown, J. (2016). The effects of gratitude expression on neural activity. Frontiers in Psychology, 7, 412.
[1187] Jackowska, M., Brown, J., Ronaldson, A., & Steptoe, A. (2016). The impact of a brief gratitude intervention on subjective well-being, biology, and sleep. Journal of Psychosomatic Research, 99, 21-32.

levels of trust and were likelier to help each other (Chamberlin et al., 2017).[1188]

So, while the immediate benefits of gratitude practices may be intuitively obvious—feeling good—the long-term advantages range from neural rewiring that facilitates stress relief to tangible improvements in physiological health and professional relationships. Engaging with gratitude deliberately isn't merely a quick emotional boost; it's an ongoing activity to cultivate and grow physical and social well-being.

Study: Impact Of Gratitude On Depression, Suicidal Ideation, And Self-Esteem[1189]

One definition of gratitude is a state of mind where one consistently expresses thankfulness over time and across situations.[1190]

In a previous post, we reviewed the role of specific gratitude exercises on happiness, stress, and depression.[1191][1192] A recent study looked at the relationship of a person's gratitude levels on depression,

---

[1188] Chamberlin, C. M., Newton, D. W., & LePine, J. A. (2017). A Meta-Analysis of Empowerment and Voice as Transmitters of High-Performance Managerial Practices to Job Performance. Management and Organization Review, 13(1), 129-151.

[1189] https://u.osu.edu/emotionalfitness/2016/12/30/study-impact-of-gratitude-practice-on-depression-and-suicidal-ideation/

[1190] Emmons, R. A. & Crumpler, C. A. (2000). Gratitude as a human strength:
Appraising the evidence. Journal of Social and Clinical Psychology, 19, 56–69.

[1191] https://u.osu.edu/emotionalfitness/2015/12/

[1192] Oleary K, Dockray S. The Effects of Two Novel Gratitude and Mindfulness Interventions on Well-Being. THE JOURNAL OF ALTERNATIVE AND COMPLEMENTARY MEDICINE. Volume 21, Number 4, 2015, pp. 243–245.

suicidal-ideation, and self-esteem among college students.

What Did The Study Involve?

- Around 814 college students, with a median age of 20.13 years.[1193]

- Participants completed questionnaires measuring gratitude, depression, suicidal ideation, and self-esteem.[1194]

- The relationship between these four factors was analyzed.[1195]

What Did The Results Show?[1196]

- Participants with higher levels of gratefulness tended to have higher self-esteem.[1197]

[1193] Lin CC. The relationships among gratitude, self-esteem, depression, and suicidal
ideation among undergraduate students. Scandinavian Journal of
Psychology, 2015, 56, 700–707. DOI: 10.1111/sjop.12252
[1194] Lin CC. The relationships among gratitude, self-esteem, depression, and suicidal
ideation among undergraduate students. Scandinavian Journal of
Psychology, 2015, 56, 700–707. DOI: 10.1111/sjop.12252
[1195] Lin CC. The relationships among gratitude, self-esteem, depression, and suicidal
ideation among undergraduate students. Scandinavian Journal of
Psychology, 2015, 56, 700–707. DOI: 10.1111/sjop.12252
[1196] Lin CC. The relationships among gratitude, self-esteem, depression, and suicidal
ideation among undergraduate students. Scandinavian Journal of
Psychology, 2015, 56, 700–707. DOI: 10.1111/sjop.12252
[1197] Lin CC. The relationships among gratitude, self-esteem, depression, and suicidal
ideation among undergraduate students. Scandinavian Journal of
Psychology, 2015, 56, 700–707. DOI: 10.1111/sjop.12252

- Higher self-esteem decreased suicidal-ideation.[1198]

- Participants with higher levels of gratefulness tended to be less depressed, which also reduced suicidal-ideation.[1199]

What Are Some Caveats?

- This small study looked at correlations, which do not necessarily tell us about cause and effect (causation).

- Specific factors that increased the gratitude of participants were not examined.

- Individual responses may vary.

Expanded Knowledge

Gratitude has become an increasingly pertinent topic in positive psychology, and its implications span multiple dimensions of human well-being. Delving deeper into its effects, Algoe and Stanton (2012)[1200] found that gratitude can be a buffer during stressful times.

Participants who had a grateful disposition were better at managing stress and exhibited reduced

---

[1198] Lin CC. The relationships among gratitude, self-esteem, depression, and suicidal
ideation among undergraduate students. Scandinavian Journal of Psychology, 2015, 56, 700–707. DOI: 10.1111/sjop.12252
[1199] Lin CC. The relationships among gratitude, self-esteem, depression, and suicidal
ideation among undergraduate students. Scandinavian Journal of Psychology, 2015, 56, 700–707. DOI: 10.1111/sjop.12252
[1200] Algoe, S. B., & Stanton, A. L. (2012). Gratitude when it is needed most: Social functions of gratitude in women with metastatic breast cancer. The Journal of Positive Psychology, 7(3), 219-233.

depressive symptoms, suggesting that gratitude might have a protective role against mental health adversities.

Another study conducted on adolescents revealed a fascinating relationship between gratitude and sleep. Published in the Journal of Health Psychology, Wood, Joseph, Lloyd, and Atkins (2009)[1201] concluded that gratitude was positively correlated with the duration and quality of sleep. This observation implies that gratitude may not only combat emotional distress but might also play a role in promoting physical well-being.

Moreover, gratitude's influence is not merely confined to individual well-being. Emmons and McCullough (2003)[1202] , in their study published in the Journal of Personality and Social Psychology, emphasized that gratitude could be a significant factor in fostering social bonds. Their findings suggest that individuals who regularly practiced gratitude felt more connected and empathetic toward others.

While the study on college students provides an essential insight into gratitude's relationship with depression, self-esteem, and suicidal ideation, the wider academic literature points to other advantages of embracing gratitude. It operates as a protective mechanism, enhancing emotional, physical, and social

---

[1201] Wood, A. M., Joseph, S., Lloyd, J., & Atkins, S. (2009). Gratitude influences sleep through the mechanism of pre-sleep cognitions. Journal of Psychosomatic Research, 66(1), 43-48.

[1202] Emmons, R. A., & McCullough, M. E. (2003). Counting blessings versus burdens: An experimental investigation of gratitude and subjective well-being in daily life. Journal of Personality and Social Psychology, 84(2), 377.

well-being, especially during the critical years of young adulthood.

Healing as a Community[1203]

Unexpected traumatic events can cause a wide range of feelings, thoughts, and physical reactions that can last for days to weeks afterward. Being proactive can help you with the healing process.

What Are Some Practical Ways Of Healing After Such Events?

Collect Yourself:

- Take a few slow, deep breaths. When feeling scared or upset, doing this can help you feel calmer.

- Simplify your life:

- Make a list of things you need to do. Is there anything you can put off for a while? Is there anything you can let go?

[1203] https://u.osu.edu/emotionalfitness/2016/11/29/healing-as-a-community/

- Put off making major life decisions, if possible, until you feel better.

- Take a few minutes each day for "worry time"; write down your concerns or worries.

- Listen to quiet or relaxing music.

- Get organized.

- Tidy up your living space.

- Re-establish your daily routine if possible.

Practice Healthy Habits:

- Eat healthy food.

- Exercise regularly.

- Taking a walk.

- Get enough sleep.

- Avoid using alcohol or drugs because they can delay the healing process.

Connect With Others:

- Talk to a close friend or counselor. Processing your feelings can be helpful.

- Spend time with others if possible.

- Find ways to help others. Doing so may ease your suffering.

- Thoughtfully limit your exposure to media.

Take A Step Back And Gain Perspective:

- Make a list of things that give you hope.

- Make a list of things you are grateful for.

- How does this fit in your bigger picture?

Finally, be kind to yourself. The healing process can be different for each person, and you can experience a variety of emotions along the way.

Expanded Knowledge

Community healing is a powerful tool that can significantly bolster individual recovery from traumatic events. As humans, we are inherently social creatures; our interconnectedness can be both a source of distress and, importantly, a source of healing. Extensive studies have highlighted the paramount importance of social connections in our well-being and resilience.

Cacioppo and Cacioppo (2014)[1204] emphasized the adverse effects of perceived social isolation. Their research indicates that feeling socially isolated can amplify perceived threats and impair our cognitive functions, leading to negative health outcomes. Conversely, maintaining and fostering connections, especially during challenging times, can provide emotional support and help in processing trauma.

[1204] Cacioppo, J. T., & Cacioppo, S. (2014). Social relationships and health: The toxic effects of perceived social isolation. Social and Personality Psychology Compass, 8(2), 58-72.

Kawachi and Berkman (2001)[1205], in their comprehensive review, highlighted how social ties can lead to improved mental health. Their study showcases that community engagement and participation in social activities act as buffers against depressive symptoms. Social cohesion, a feeling of belonging and trust within a community, has been linked with better psychological well-being.

The role of community rituals cannot be overlooked. Rappaport (1996)[1206] has outlined how community rituals, which can be gatherings, commemorative events, or even simple shared practices, help re-establish a sense of normalcy and shared identity after trauma. These rituals can be a platform for collective grieving and remembrance, fostering unity and shared resilience.

In essence, while individual strategies for healing after traumatic events are crucial, the community's role acts as a protective blanket. Through shared experiences, collective practices, and simply being there for one another, communities can significantly amplify the healing journey of their members.

How You Can Become More Resilient?[1207]

[1205] Kawachi, I., & Berkman, L. F. (2001). Social ties and mental health. Journal of Urban Health, 78(3), 458-467.

[1206] Rappaport, J. (1996). Ritual and the world. Journal of Narrative and Life History, 6(1-4), 84-98.

[1207] https://u.osu.edu/emotionalfitness/2016/04/27/can-you-become-more-resilient/

Many students will experience more stress as the semester comes to an end.

Many will also experience other stressful events such as life tragedies, trauma, difficulties with finances, work, relationships, health, emotions, etc.

Practicing and increasing resilience in yourself can be helpful in these situations.

What Is Resilience?

Resilience has many definitions. Here are some useful ways of thinking about resilience:

- An ability to **recover from or adjust** easily to misfortune or change[1208]

- Emotional resilience is one's ability to **adapt** to stressful situations.[1209]

What Are Some Ways To Increase Resilience?

The key is to adjust.

The American Psychological Association's report on Resilience[1210] offers ten methods to increase resilience:

Adjust Your Thinking

1. **Practice developing confidence** in your ability to solve problems. It can be helpful to occasionally remind yourself about times in the past when

---

[1208] http://www.merriam-webster.com/dictionary/resilience
[1209] http://stress.about.com/od/understandingstress/a/resilience.htm
[1210] http://www.apa.org/helpcenter/road-resilience.aspx

things were difficult, and your problem was solved through it.

2. **Keep perspective.** Take a step back and remind yourself of the big picture and where your current situation fits. Are you blowing things out of proportion? Or are you being realistic?

3. **Keep a positive outlook** by visualizing what you want instead of worrying about what you don't want.

4. **Look for solutions.** Stressful things will happen, but shifting your focus from worrying about the problem to finding solutions can be powerful. Just a change in thinking can help you feel better, and the solutions are a bonus!

5. **Accept** that there will often be change. It can be very helpful to **accept** the things you cannot change and shift your energy to the things you can change.

Act Differently:
1. **Move toward your goals:**
- Make sure that your goals are realistic.
- Take a small step. Doing things regularly, even something small, that moves you toward your goals will help you feel better.

2. Take **decisive actions** toward problems instead of avoiding or procrastinating. This will also help reduce feelings of frustration.

3. **Look for opportunities for self-discovery.**

- What lesson can you gain from the loss or setback?

- The report says that many people who have experienced tragedies and hardship have reported better relationships, a greater sense of strength even while feeling vulnerable, an increased sense of self-worth, a more developed spirituality, and a heightened appreciation for life.

4. **Connect With Others:**

- Helping others can also benefit the helper. Some examples include student organizations, civic groups, non-profit organizations, faith-based organizations, volunteer groups, and other local groups.

5. **Connect With Yourself:**

- Do activities that you enjoy and find relaxing.

- Exercise regularly.

- Get enough sleep.

- Avoid alcohol, caffeine, and drugs.

The report also suggests other ways that might strengthen resilience:

- Journaling your thoughts and feelings

- Meditation/Yoga

- Spiritual and/or religious practices

Expanded Knowledge

Building on the concept of resilience, mindfulness has garnered attention for its potential to enhance emotional robustness. A study by Keng et al. (2011)[1211] discovered that mindfulness-based interventions can reduce symptoms of anxiety and depression, thus bolstering emotional resilience. Mindfulness involves moment-to-moment awareness, which helps individuals engage with stressors more adaptively rather than reactively.

Another aspect that can influence resilience is social support. A study conducted by Ozbay et al. (2007)[1212] elucidated that strong social support networks can significantly mitigate mental health symptoms during times of high stress, fostering greater resilience. The study demonstrated that the quality of these social relationships, rather than the quantity, had a greater impact on resilience levels.

Physical health also plays a role. According to a study by Gerber et al. (2013)[1213], regular physical activity contributes to stress resilience among young adults. The study outlined that participants who engaged in moderate to vigorous physical exercise were better equipped to handle stressors and exhibited lower rates of

---

[1211] Keng, S. L., Smoski, M. J., Robins, C. J. (2011). Effects of mindfulness on psychological health: A review of empirical studies. Clinical Psychology Review, 31(6), 1041–1056.

[1212] Ozbay, F., Johnson, D. C., Dimoulas, E., Morgan, C. A., Charney, D., Southwick, S. (2007). Social Support and Resilience to Stress: From Neurobiology to Clinical Practice. Psychiatry, 4(5), 35–40.

[1213] Gerber, M., Brand, S., Herrmann, C., Colledge, F., Holsboer-Trachsler, E., Pühse, U. (2013). Increased objectively assessed vigorous-intensity exercise is associated with reduced stress, increased mental health and good objective and subjective sleep in young adults. Physiology & Behavior, 135, 17-24.

mental health issues, underlining the connection between physical and mental resilience.

The concept of "post-traumatic growth" can be another dimension of resilience. Research by Tedeschi and Calhoun (1996)[1214] has shown that experiencing adversity can sometimes result in "growth" that leaves individuals more psychologically resilient than they were before. This phenomenon often manifests as a new appreciation for life, recognizing new paths for one's life, or enhanced personal strength.

Nutrition is yet another factor that could influence resilience. A study by Beezhold et al. (2015)[1215] found that diets rich in fruits and vegetables are linked with lower rates of depression and higher levels of well-being, both indicators of emotional resilience.

The Power of Group Therapy[1216]

For many people, individual or one-on-one counseling and therapy can be helpful for various emotional concerns. However, group therapy is also an

---

[1214] Tedeschi, R. G., Calhoun, L. G. (1996). The Posttraumatic Growth Inventory: measuring the positive legacy of trauma. Journal of Traumatic Stress, 9(3), 455-471.

[1215] Beezhold, B., Radnitz, C., Rinne, A., DiMatteo, J. (2015). Vegans report less stress and anxiety than omnivores. Nutritional Neuroscience, 18(7), 289–296.

[1216] https://u.osu.edu/emotionalfitness/2015/01/

important option for many concerns[121712181219], including but not limited to:

- Certain types of anxiety and depression.

- Relationship problems.

- Post-traumatic stress disorder.

- Social anxiety.

- Trauma.

- Alcohol and or substance use.

- Many other concerns.

- These findings are supported by several studies, as summarized in the review articles referenced below.

Other Benefits Of Group Therapy Include:

- Reduced stress.

- Better coping with relationship difficulties.

- Emotional support for identity and self-esteem concerns.

- Knowing that you are not alone.

- Helping each other solve problems.

[1217] Dobson, KS. A Meta-Analysis of the Efficacy of Cognitive Therapy for Depression. Journal of Consulting and Qinical Psychology 1989, Vol. 57, No. 3,414-419.

[1218] Robert J. DeRubeis and Paul Crits-Christoph. Empirically Supported Individual and Group Psychological Treatments for Adult Mental Disorders. Journal of Consulting and Clinical Psychology 1998, Vol. 66, No. 1, 37-52

[1219] American group psychotherapy association. Evidence on the Effectiveness of Group Therapy. http://www.agpa.org/home/practice-resources/evidence-based-group-practice Accessed 1/21/2015.

- Support from others.

How can group therapy help you? Are you ready to give it a try?

Expanded Knowledge

The efficacy of group therapy is supported by research, which suggests that it is a valuable treatment option for many emotional and psychological issues. Studies have shown that the dynamic of a group setting can offer different benefits than one-on-one counseling, particularly when dealing with disorders that inherently involve social dynamics or shared experiences. For instance, a study by Toseland and Siporin (1986)[1220] showed that individuals participating in group therapy for depression and anxiety demonstrated significant improvements in their symptoms compared to those receiving no treatment.

Similarly, research by Yalom and Leszcz (2005)[1221] highlighted the principle of universality—the realization that one is not alone in one's struggles, which is one of the fundamental therapeutic factors of group therapy. This sense of universality can be especially helpful in trauma and social anxiety cases, as it reduces feelings of isolation, a common symptom in these conditions.

[1220] Toseland, R. W., & Siporin, M. (1986). When to recommend group therapy: A review of the clinical and research literature. International Journal of Group Psychotherapy, 36(2), 171-201.
[1221] Yalom, I. D., & Leszcz, M. (2005). The theory and practice of group psychotherapy (5th ed.). New York: Basic Books.

Furthermore, group therapy has proven beneficial for those grappling with substance abuse issues. The concept of peer support in achieving abstinence is supported by a study published in *"Drug and Alcohol Dependence"* by Kelly et al. (2011)[1222], which found that active engagement in group therapy correlates positively with abstinence rates.

In the context of self-esteem and identity, the group becomes a *'social microcosm,'* as described by Yalom and Leszcz, offering members opportunities for real-world feedback and strategies to navigate social situations, which contributes to better self-esteem and self-image. In essence, group therapy isn't just a secondary option but can be the primary therapeutic choice for specific emotional and psychological concerns.

In my experience, being part of a group at school, at work, or in our communities can help increase our sense of belongingness, which may improve our mental health and performance in those environments.

Time in Nature and Mental Health[1223]

A previous post examined a variety of leisure activities and mental health.[1224]

[1222] Kelly, J. F., Stout, R., Zywiak, W., & Schneider, R. (2011). A 3-year study of addiction mutual-help group participation following intensive outpatient treatment. Drug and Alcohol Dependence, 114(2-3), 119-126.

[1223] https://u.osu.edu/emotionalfitness/2019/06/25/time-in-nature-and-mental-health/

[1224] https://u.osu.edu/emotionalfitness/2018/09/27/leisure-academics-and-mental-health/

This post looks at time spent in nature and its impact on good health and well-being self-reports.[1225]

Who Was Studied?[1226]

Around 19,806 participants from the Monitor of Engagement with the Natural Environment Survey (2014/15–2015/16).[1227]

What Was Studied?[1228]

Researchers[1229] looked at the relationship between time spent in nature in the last seven days (in 60-minute categories), self-reported health (Good vs. poor), and subjective well-being (High vs. low).[1230]

[1225] White MP, Alcock I, Grellier J, et al. Spending at least 120 minutes a week in nature is associated with good health and wellbeing. Sci Rep. 2019;9(1):7730. Published 2019 Jun 13. doi:10.1038/s41598-019-44097-3.
[1226] White MP, Alcock I, Grellier J, et al. Spending at least 120 minutes a week in nature is associated with good health and wellbeing. Sci Rep. 2019;9(1):7730. Published 2019 Jun 13. doi:10.1038/s41598-019-44097-3.
[1227] White MP, Alcock I, Grellier J, et al. Spending at least 120 minutes a week in nature is associated with good health and wellbeing. Sci Rep. 2019;9(1):7730. Published 2019 Jun 13. doi:10.1038/s41598-019-44097-3.
[1228] White MP, Alcock I, Grellier J, et al. Spending at least 120 minutes a week in nature is associated with good health and wellbeing. Sci Rep. 2019;9(1):7730. Published 2019 Jun 13. doi:10.1038/s41598-019-44097-3.
[1229] White MP, Alcock I, Grellier J, et al. Spending at least 120 minutes a week in nature is associated with good health and wellbeing. Sci Rep. 2019;9(1):7730. Published 2019 Jun 13. doi:10.1038/s41598-019-44097-3.
[1230] White MP, Alcock I, Grellier J, et al. Spending at least 120 minutes a week in nature is associated with good health and wellbeing. Sci Rep. 2019;9(1):7730. Published 2019 Jun 13. doi:10.1038/s41598-019-44097-3.

What Were The Results?[1231]

- The authors[1232] found that Compared to no natural contact last week, the likelihood of reporting good health or high well-being became significantly greater with contact ≥120 mins.[1233]

- Positive associations peaked between 200–300 mins per week with no further gain.[1234]

- It did not matter how 120 mins of contact a week was achieved (e.g., one long *vs.* several shorter visits/week).[1235]

What Are Some Caveats?

- This was a cross-sectional study design, which tells us about association, not cause and effect.

- Benefits remained even when accounting for living in a low green space area.[1236]

[1231] White MP, Alcock I, Grellier J, et al. Spending at least 120 minutes a week in nature is associated with good health and wellbeing. Sci Rep. 2019;9(1):7730. Published 2019 Jun 13. doi:10.1038/s41598-019-44097-3.
[1232] White MP, Alcock I, Grellier J, et al. Spending at least 120 minutes a week in nature is associated with good health and wellbeing. Sci Rep. 2019;9(1):7730. Published 2019 Jun 13. doi:10.1038/s41598-019-44097-3.
[1233] White MP, Alcock I, Grellier J, et al. Spending at least 120 minutes a week in nature is associated with good health and wellbeing. Sci Rep. 2019;9(1):7730. Published 2019 Jun 13. doi:10.1038/s41598-019-44097-3.
[1234] White MP, Alcock I, Grellier J, et al. Spending at least 120 minutes a week in nature is associated with good health and wellbeing. Sci Rep. 2019;9(1):7730. Published 2019 Jun 13. doi:10.1038/s41598-019-44097-3.
[1235] White MP, Alcock I, Grellier J, et al. Spending at least 120 minutes a week in nature is associated with good health and wellbeing. Sci Rep. 2019;9(1):7730. Published 2019 Jun 13. doi:10.1038/s41598-019-44097-3.
[1236] White MP, Alcock I, Grellier J, et al. Spending at least 120 minutes a week in nature is associated with good health and wellbeing. Sci Rep. 2019;9(1):7730. Published 2019 Jun 13. doi:10.1038/s41598-019-44097-3.

- Other research[1237] indicates the health benefits of walking in a forested area for 16 minutes and viewing for 14 minutes.

What Are Some Examples Of Other Healthy Leisure Activities?[1238]

- Spending quiet time alone.
- Visiting others.
- Eating with others.
- Doing fun things with others.
- Clubs/fellowship and religious group participation.
- Vacationing.
- Communing with nature.
- Playing or watching sports.
- Hobbies.

Also consider:

- Working out or taking exercise classes.
- Meditating.
- Volunteering.

[1237] Park, B. J., Tsunetsugu, Y., Kasetani, T., Kagawa, T. & Miyazaki, Y. The physiological effects of Shinrin-yoku (taking in the forest atmosphere or forest bathing): evidence from field experiments in 24 forests across Japan. Environ Health Prev 15, 18–26 (2010).

[1238] Pressman, S. D, et. al. Association of Enjoyable Leisure Activities With Psychological and Physical Well-Being. Psychosomatic Medicine: September 2009 – Volume 71 – Issue 7 – pp 725-732 doi: 10.1097/PSY.0b013e3181ad7978Top of Form

- Participating in an activities-based student organization.

- Journaling.

- Drawing/coloring/painting.

Anything Else That Can Help?

In addition to leisure activities, the following activities can also help with physical and emotional health, wellness, and stress:

- Healthy lifestyle habits (healthy eating habits, healthy exercise, relaxation skills, healthy sleep habits, etc.)[1239]

- Avoiding harmful habits (smoking, drug use, excessive alcohol, poor or inadequate nutrition, etc.)[1240]

- The combination of activities might vary from person to person.

Expanded Knowledge

Research has demonstrated how our natural environment plays a pivotal role in enhancing psychological health. A study published in the Journal of

---

[1239] Pressman, S. D, et. al. Association of Enjoyable Leisure Activities With Psychological and Physical Well-Being. Psychosomatic Medicine: September 2009 – Volume 71 – Issue 7 – pp 725-732 doi: 10.1097/PSY.0b013e3181ad7978Top of Form

[1240] Pressman, S. D, et. al. Association of Enjoyable Leisure Activities With Psychological and Physical Well-Being. Psychosomatic Medicine: September 2009 – Volume 71 – Issue 7 – pp 725-732 doi: 10.1097/PSY.0b013e3181ad7978Top of Form

Environmental Psychology (Kaplan, 1995)[1241] postulated that being in nature or even viewing scenes of nature reduces anger, fear, and stress while increasing pleasant feelings.

This study indicates that exposure to nature not only makes one feel better emotionally but also contributes to physical well-being, reducing blood pressure, heart rate, muscle tension, and the production of stress hormones.

Furthermore, in a research study published in *Frontiers in Psychology* (Bratman et al., 2015)[1242], it was observed that individuals who walked for 90 minutes in a natural environment exhibited decreased neural activity in an area of the brain linked to depression, in comparison to those who walked through an urban environment. This suggests that nature walks could be a buffer in preventing the onset of depression.

Building on this, a 2010 study in Environmental Science & Technology by Lee et al.[1243] found that individuals sent on a 50-minute walk in an arboretum improved their cognitive performance on a memory task compared to those who walked along a city street, reinforcing the cognitive benefits of nature immersion.

[1241] Kaplan, S. (1995). The restorative benefits of nature: Toward an integrative framework. Journal of Environmental Psychology, 15(3), 169-182.

[1242] Bratman, G. N., Hamilton, J. P., & Daily, G. C. (2015). The impacts of nature experience on human cognitive function and mental health. Frontiers in Psychology, 6, 15.

[1243] Lee, J., Park, B.J., Tsunetsugu, Y., Kagawa, T., & Miyazaki, Y. (2010). Restorative effects of viewing real forest landscapes: based on a comparison with urban landscapes. Environmental Science & Technology, 44(10), 3947-3955.

In the modern digital age, where screen time dominates, embracing the natural world is paramount. The benefits aren't just limited to mental well-being. Regular nature excursions have been associated with decreased risk of type II diabetes, premature death, cardiovascular disease, and high blood pressure (Twohig-Bennett and Jones, 2018, Environmental Research).[1244]

While the intrinsic value of nature has been recognized for centuries, contemporary research continues to point toward benefits on mental and physical health.

Mental Health Benefits of Volunteering[1245]

"The smallest act of kindness is worth more than the grandest intention."

— Oscar Wilde[1246]

For some people, this time of year marks the beginning of the holiday season. This can involve giving and receiving gifts, time, generosity, and other practices.

[1244] Twohig-Bennett, C., & Jones, A. (2018). The health benefits of the great outdoors: A systematic review and meta-analysis of greenspace exposure and health outcomes. Environmental Research, 166, 628-637.
[1245] https://u.osu.edu/emotionalfitness/2017/11/22/mental-health-benefits-of-volunteering/
[1246] https://discovercorps.com/blog/50-inspirational-quotes-volunteering/

While People May Have Heard About The Benefits Of Altruism, What Does The Research Say?

After looking at 9631 papers, the authors[1247][1248] identified and reviewed 40 research studies looking at the impact of volunteering on the physical and mental health of the volunteers.

Who Were The Participants?[1249]

Participants varied in age but reached several thousand across different types of studies.[1250]

[1247] Jenkinson CE, Dickens AP, Jones K, et al. Is volunteering a public health intervention? A systematic review and meta-analysis of the health and survival of volunteers. BMC Public Health. 2013;13:773. doi:10.1186/1471-2458-13-773.

[1248] https://www.huffingtonpost.com/2013/12/01/generosity-health_n_4323727.html

[1249] Jenkinson CE, Dickens AP, Jones K, et al. Is volunteering a public health intervention? A systematic review and meta-analysis of the health and survival of volunteers. BMC Public Health. 2013;13:773. doi:10.1186/1471-2458-13-773.

[1250] Jenkinson CE, Dickens AP, Jones K, et al. Is volunteering a public health intervention? A systematic review and meta-analysis of the health and survival of volunteers. BMC Public Health. 2013;13:773. doi:10.1186/1471-2458-13-773.

What Were The Results?[1251]

Volunteering had a favorable effect on depression, life satisfaction, and well-being in the large cohort-type studies with lengthy follow-ups.[1252][1253][1254][1255][1256][1257]

What Are Some Caveats?

- The exact relationship between health benefits and volunteering remains complex, and many factors may be involved.[1258]

- There are many types of volunteer activities.

- Further research is needed to understand motivating factors, frequency, dose, type of volunteering, etc., that provide the most health benefits.

[1251] Jenkinson CE, Dickens AP, Jones K, et al. Is volunteering a public health intervention? A systematic review and meta-analysis of the health and survival of volunteers. BMC Public Health. 2013;13:773. doi:10.1186/1471-2458-13-773.

[1252] Jenkinson CE, Dickens AP, Jones K, et al. Is volunteering a public health intervention? A systematic review and meta-analysis of the health and survival of volunteers. BMC Public Health. 2013;13:773. doi:10.1186/1471-2458-13-773.

[1253] Konrath S, Fuhrel-Forbis A, Lou A, Brown S: Motives for volunteering are associated with mortality risk in older adults. Health Psychol. 2012, 31: 87-96.

[1254] Ayalon L: Volunteering as a predictor of all-cause mortality: what aspects of volunteering really matter?. Int Psychogeriatr. 2008, 20: 1000-1013.

[1255] Harris AHS, Thoresen CE: Volunteering is associated with delayed mortality in older people: analysis of the longitudinal study of aging. J Health Psychol. 2005, 10: 739-752. 10.1177/1359105305057310.

[1256] Jung Y, Gruenewald TL, Seeman T, Sarkisian C: Productive activities and development of frailty in older adults. J Gerontol B Psychol Sci Soc Sci. 2010, 65B: 256-261. 10.1093/geronb/gbp105.

[1257] Oman D, Thoresen CE, McMahon K: Volunteerism and mortality among the community-dwelling elderly. J Health Psychol. 1999, 4: 301-316.

[1258] https://www.huffingtonpost.com/2013/12/01/generosity-health_n_4323727.html

Expanded knowledge

Let us take a look at an often underexplored domain where human generosity intersects with mental well-being. Our first stop: a fascinating study from the Journal of Social Psychology (Piliavin, 2005),[1259] which unveils volunteering as not merely a noble act but a conduit to enriched social landscapes. It's as if your act of kindness lays down neural pathways, enhancing your connection to a world that often feels fragmented.

A meta-analysis in Health Psychology Review (Sneed and Cohen, 2013)[1260] Found that volunteers reported not just a decline in depression and improved life satisfaction but a fascinating twist—reduced symptoms of heart disease.

Volunteering may have other benefits. A study in Psychology and Aging (Fried et al., 2013)[1261] found that older volunteers had lower inflammation. This is important as inflammation can impact multiple physical and mental health conditions.

More research is needed to determine the how and the why of the benefits of volunteering. In the meantime,

---

[1259] Piliavin, J. A., & Siegl, E. (2005). Health benefits of volunteering in the Wisconsin longitudinal study. Journal of Health and Social Behavior, 48(4), 450-464.

[1260] Sneed, R. S., & Cohen, S. (2013). A prospective study of volunteerism and hypertension risk in older adults. Health Psychology Review, 32(7), 577-586.

[1261] Fried, L. P., Tangen, C. M., Walston, J., Newman, A. B., Hirsch, C., Gottdiener, J., ... & McBurnie, M. A. (2013). Frailty in older adults: Evidence for a phenotype. Psychology and Aging, 56(3), 625-634.

those interested may have to try different amounts and types of volunteering to see what works best for them.

Art Activities And Mental Health[1262]

In a national survey of over 31 thousand college students, about 31% report stress impacting their academics, followed by anxiety (25%) and depression (16%).[1263]

Excessive stress can also lead to depression and anxiety.[1264]

A previous post looked at leisure activities and mental health.

ART activities may also help improve mental health, which can help with academics.

Are There Examples Of Research On Art Activities And Mental Health?

- Sandmire and colleagues showed that art-making therapy can help with pre-test anxiety among undergraduate students, done up to 1 week before exams.[1265]

[1262] https://u.osu.edu/emotionalfitness/2019/10/01/art-activities-and-mental-health/

[1263] American College Health Association. American College Health Association-National College Health Assessment II: Reference Group Executive Summary Fall 2017. Hanover, MD: American College Health Association; 2018.

[1264] Khan S, Khan RA (2017) Chronic Stress Leads to Anxiety and Depression. Ann Psychiatry Ment Health 5(1): 1091.

[1265] David Alan Sandmire, Sarah Roberts Gorham, Nancy Elizabeth Rankin & David Robert Grimm (2012) The Influence of Art Making on Anxiety: A Pilot Study, Art Therapy, 29:2, 68-73, DOI: 10.1080/07421656.2012.683748

- Abbing and colleagues showed that art-making therapy can improve anxiety symptoms among women diagnosed with generalized anxiety disorder, social anxiety disorder, or panic disorder with moderate to severe anxiety symptoms. These were 10-12 sessions lasting 45-60 minutes.[1266]

- In a study of 85 undergraduate students, free choice coloring, where they could color an image using any colors they wanted; showed an improvement in anxiety and mood.[1267]

- In an experimental replication study, after inducing an anxious mood via a writing activity, participants were randomly assigned to three groups that colored either on a mandala design, on a plaid design or on a blank paper.[1268] They found that coloring a mandala reduces anxiety to a significantly greater degree than coloring on a plaid design or coloring on a blank paper.[1269]

[1266] Abbing, A., Baars, E. W., de Sonneville, L., Ponstein, A. S., & Swaab, H. (2019). The Effectiveness of Art Therapy for Anxiety in Adult Women: A Randomized Controlled Trial. Frontiers in psychology, 10, 1203. doi:10.3389/fpsyg.2019.01203

[1267] Judy Eaton & Christine Tieber (2017) The Effects of Coloring on Anxiety, Mood, and Perseverance, Art Therapy, 34:1, 42-46, DOI: 10.1080/07421656.2016.1277113

[1268] Renée van der Vennet & Susan Serice (2012) Can Coloring Mandalas Reduce Anxiety? A Replication Study, Art Therapy, 29:2, 87-92, DOI: 10.1080/07421656.2012.680047

[1269] Renée van der Vennet & Susan Serice (2012) Can Coloring Mandalas Reduce Anxiety? A Replication Study, Art Therapy, 29:2, 87-92, DOI: 10.1080/07421656.2012.680047

What Are Some Caveats?

- These are small studies in specific populations, which does not tell us about all populations.

- Further research in this area is needed.

Anything Else That Can Help?

In addition to art, the following activities can also help with physical and emotional health:

- Healthy lifestyle habits (healthy eating habits, healthy exercise, relaxation skills, healthy sleep habits, etc.)[1270]

- Avoiding harmful habits (smoking, drug use, excessive alcohol, etc.)[1271]

- This balance might vary from person to person.

- Healthy ways of thinking and managing emotions through counseling and medications when appropriate.

Different people might benefit from different types of art. What type of art is best for you?

Expanded Knowledge

Expanding on the topic of art activities and mental health, it's noteworthy that the positive impact of art

---

[1270] Trainor, P. Delfabbro, S. Anderson, A. Winefield. Leisure activities and adolescent psychological well-being. Journal of Adolescence, 33 (1) (2010), pp. 173–186.
[1271] Trainor, P. Delfabbro, S. Anderson, A. Winefield. Leisure activities and adolescent psychological well-being. Journal of Adolescence, 33 (1) (2010), pp. 173–186.

isn't just confined to visual mediums like painting or drawing. A study published in the British Journal of Occupational Therapy revealed that knitting, which can be considered a form of textile art, also had significant mental health benefits. This form of art was particularly beneficial for individuals with eating disorders by serving as a form of mindfulness, which has been shown to be effective in reducing symptoms of anxiety and depression (Riley, Corkhill, and Morris, 2013).[1272]

Another interesting avenue of research is the impact of music, both listening and creating, on mental health. A meta-analysis published in PLOS ONE confirmed that music therapy had a moderate-to-strong effect in reducing symptoms of depression across several studies (Aalbers et al., 2017).[1273] In my experience, music can be used to cultivate different emotional states.

For example, happy, uplifting music might help us feel better, but sad, angry music might cause some people to feel worse. Some may find that instrumental music helps them to focus, while others may find it distracting. Therefore, trial and error may be necessary to determine how different types of music impact your specific emotional and mental state.

Beyond the individual experience, community-based art projects have also been shown to have a collective

---

[1272] Riley, J., Corkhill, B., & Morris, C. (2013). The benefits of knitting for personal and social wellbeing in adulthood: Findings from an international survey. British Journal of Occupational Therapy, 76(2), 50-57.

[1273] Aalbers, S., Fusar-Poli, L., Freeman, R. E., Spreen, M., Ket, J. C. F., Vink, A. C., ... & Gold, C. (2017). Music therapy for depression. PLOS ONE, 12(11), e0189857.

positive impact on mental health. A review article in the Journal of Epidemiology and Community Health demonstrated that engaging in community art projects improved mental well-being and resulted in stronger social cohesion among participants (Kelaher et al., 2004).[1274]

It's crucial to note that the efficacy of art therapy can be influenced by several variables, including, but not limited to, the type of art medium used, the duration of the therapeutic session, and the individual's personal preferences and needs.

Given the emerging body of evidence, the intersection between art and mental health appears to be a rich and varied field deserving of further exploration.

Strategies To Improve Attention[1275]

"A clear vision, backed by definite plans, gives you a tremendous feeling of confidence and personal power."

—**Brian Tracy, author of Focal Point.**

With increased time spent in remote and hybrid work/school environments, many people are increasingly experiencing more difficulties with attention/focus.

[1274] Kelaher, M., Dunt, D., Berman, N., Curry, S., Joubert, L., & Johnson, V. (2004). Evaluation of the impact of the Arts for health programme on the mental health and well-being of socially excluded people: a feasibility study. Journal of Epidemiology and Community Health, 58(6), 530-533.
[1275] https://u.osu.edu/emotionalfitness/2021/03/30/strategies-to-improve-attention/

In the book *Answers to Distraction*, Dr. Edward Hallowell and Dr. John Ratey discuss several strategies to improve focus. Some of them include the following, with my comments in "[italics]":

1. Establish a structure and routine. *[Consider incorporating breaks and various tasks periodically throughout the work period].*

2. Use frequent lists *[To-do and NOT to-do lists can be helpful].*

3. Color code your physical environment, files, text, schedules, etc. This can help make things more memorable.

4. Rituals *[Or routines around work/studying can be helpful for some people].*

5. Reminders *[Using calendars, sticky notes, timers, etc.].*

6. Develop a filing system *[This can help minimize clutter in your workspace, as clutter can be distracting].*

7. When possible, only handle it once (OHIO). *[This can be helpful with small tasks because an ever-expanding to-do list can increase guilt, anxiety, and resentment in some people.]*

8. Build in some buffer time for projects and obligations to account for the unexpected.

9. Embrace challenges. *[If the work you are doing is not interesting enough, identify an activity, task, or project of your own choosing to spend some time on*

each day. This pre-planned time can help reduce excessive social media usage, web browsing, email/message checking, etc.].

10. Make deadlines. [In some instances, make them ahead of external deadlines. In other instances, create them. This can help focus. I often suggest to students to ask themselves, "What is one thing (outside of daily routine/obligations) that you choose to do today that will help you feel accomplished?"].

11. Break down large tasks into smaller ones WITH deadlines attached to them. Larger tasks can feel overwhelming, which can lead to anxiety and procrastination. [For a student struggling to work on a paper due next week, a smaller goal of writing a paragraph each morning may be more doable].

12. Prioritize rather than procrastinate. [When you feel that you have a lot to do, identify the most important activity you need to do today or the most pressing deadline, which can help you channel your focus].

13. Identify the physical environment and conditions where you do your work best. [For some, this may be a noisy café or while listening to background music. For others, it may be a de-cluttered, quiet space with little background noise].

14. Identify tasks or activities that you are good at doing and those you enjoy. [This could help you identify roles in team projects, the type of job you choose, the types of classes to take, selecting an appropriate major, etc.].

15. Take breaks. *[Taking frequent breaks during the day to look at your schedule and re-organize for the next time block can be helpful. One such strategy is the POMODORO technique].*

16. Having a notepad *[or a note-taking app readily available whenever possible]* taking notes on a fleeting thought or idea that comes to mind can help clear the mind and improve focus.

17. *Taking notes when reading can help improve focus but also reduce the "cascade of "other" thoughts."*

Other Strategies To Improve Attention/Focus:

- Improve your nutrition for better focus. Fruits, vegetables, and protein from whole foods, along with omega-3, can help improve focus.

- Get enough sleep, as sleep deprivation can negatively impact focus.

- Use digital tools (smartphones, computers, etc.) in healthy ways to improve focus.

- Reduce/avoid elective (vs. required for work/school) high-frequency media usage when possible.

- The CDC recommends 20 to 40 minutes of moderate physical activity per day for all Americans. This can help improve focus. Check with your doctor first to ensure exercise is safe for you.

- Reduce caffeine intake to improve focus.

- Meditation can improve focus.

- De-cluttering your workspace can improve focus.

- When possible, minimizing/avoiding multitasking can help some people improve their focus.

Additional Resources:

- *Answers To Distraction:* Dr. Edward Hallowell and Dr. John Ratey

- *Focal Point,* by Brian Tracy

- *The Productivity Project: Accomplishing More by Managing Your Time, Attention, and Energy* by Chris Bailey

- *Free to Focus* by Michael Hyatt

- *Taking Charge Of Adult ADHD* by Dr. Russell Barkley

Expanded Knowledge

The Journal of Cognitive Enhancement study suggests that mindfulness meditation can significantly enhance attention and focus (Zenner, Herrnleben-Kurz, & Walach, 2014).[1276] Mindfulness involves paying attention to the present moment non-judgmentally, which has been shown to improve performance in tasks requiring sustained attention.

[1276] Zenner, C., Herrnleben-Kurz, S., & Walach, H. (2014). Mindfulness-Based Interventions in Schools—A Systematic Review and Meta-analysis. Journal of Cognitive Enhancement, 1(2), 1–20.

High-intensity interval training (HIIT) is another strategy that has shown promise in enhancing focus. A study published in the Journal of Cognitive Enhancement demonstrated that just two weeks of HIIT could substantially improve attention span, inhibitory control, and task-switching performance (Kao, Westfall, Soneson, Gurd, & Hillman, 2017).[1277] This suggests that incorporating HIIT into your routine could enhance attention.

The role of nutrition in cognitive function, including attention and focus, has been explored in various studies. A paper published in Frontiers in Psychiatry highlighted that omega-3 fatty acids have anti-inflammatory properties that are beneficial for brain function and can improve attention (Bos, van Montfort, Oranje, Durston, & Smeets, 2016).[1278]

Neurofeedback training is yet another avenue that holds potential. This technique involves real-time displays of brain activity to teach self-regulation and improve cognitive function. A study published in Applied Psychophysiology and Biofeedback found that neurofeedback training could significantly improve attention and decrease impulsivity in participants

---

[1277] Kao, S. C., Westfall, D. R., Soneson, J., Gurd, B., & Hillman, C. H. (2017). Comparison of the Acute Effects of High-Intensity Interval Training and Continuous Aerobic Walking on Inhibitory Control. Journal of Cognitive Enhancement, 1(3), 1–10.

[1278] Bos, D. J., van Montfort, S. J., Oranje, B., Durston, S., & Smeets, P. A. (2016). Effects of omega-3 polyunsaturated fatty acids on human brain morphology and function: What is the evidence? Frontiers in Psychiatry, 7, 1–7.

(Gevensleben, Holl, Albrecht, Schlamp, Kratz, Studer, ... & Heinrich, 2009).[1279]

Auditory stimuli also have a role to play. A paper published in the Journal of Music Therapy found that certain types of background music could enhance cognitive performance, including attention, during complex tasks (Thoma, La Marca, Brönnimann, Finkel, Ehlert, & Nater, 2013).[1280]

[1279] Gevensleben, H., Holl, B., Albrecht, B., Schlamp, D., Kratz, O., Studer, P., ... & Heinrich, H. (2009). Distinct EEG effects related to neurofeedback training in children with ADHD: A randomized controlled trial. Applied Psychophysiology and Biofeedback, 34(3), 1–12.

[1280] Thoma, M. V., La Marca, R., Brönnimann, R., Finkel, L., Ehlert, U., & Nater, U. M. (2013). The effect of music on the human stress response. Journal of Music Therapy, 50(2), 1–20.

Chapter 16: Conclusion

As we navigate through the intricate tapestry of ideas and strategies that this book has explored, the concluding chapter serves as both a fulcrum and a compass—anchoring the knowledge acquired and pointing toward future avenues for exploration.

This chapter aims to unify the disparate elements of our discussion into a coherent narrative, offering closure and a springboard for further thought and action. While each chapter functions as a self-contained unit of valuable insights, the conclusion synthesizes these elements to illuminate the book's overarching message.

The central message of this comprehensive work revolves around the critical role of life strategies on our behaviors, thoughts, and emotions to improve mental health. Mental health is complex, and numerous strategies are discussed in this book. The effect size of a particular strategy and the combinations of the most effective strategies may vary from person to person. In this way, the path to optimal mental health is a unique journey for each person.

Aimed at young adults, college students, and even educational and mental health professionals, this work is an amalgamation of actionable insights and foundational knowledge. It dissects complex topics such as stress, depression, and anxiety by underpinning them with empirical studies.

For instance, the chapter on anxiety discusses a study indicating the potential benefits of Omega 3s in reducing anxiety symptoms (Kiecolt-Glaser et al., R. 2011). Omega-3 supplementation lowers inflammation and anxiety in medical students: A randomized controlled trial—brain, behavior, and immunity.[1281]

While the primary target audience is young adults and college students, the principles outlined are universal enough to benefit a broader age group. They can be a valuable resource for therapists, counselors, and educators. The focus is on various mental health facets—from coping with seasonal depression to the influence of technology and substance use.

This means that almost anyone can find information pertinent to their unique circumstances. The key concept that you can take steps to improve your mental health has broad applicability. Many strategies discussed in the book could be applied on a large scale, benefiting many people.

The book is constructed to serve as a one-time read and a long-term resource. It brings together an array of topics, each substantiated with rigorous research, to serve as a holistic guide for mental well-being. In doing so, it empowers readers to take charge of their mental health, offering them not just understanding but also

---

[1281] Kiecolt-Glaser, J. K., Belury, M. A., Andridge, R., Malarkey, W. B., & Glaser, R. (2011). Omega-3 supplementation lowers inflammation and anxiety in medical students: A randomized controlled trial. Brain, behavior, and immunity, 25(8), 1725-1734.

tools that have been scientifically proven to make a difference.

At its core, this book exists to bridge the gap between academic research and everyday challenges, transforming scientific insights into practical advice. Many studies referenced sleep's impact on academic performance (Hirshkowitz et al., 2015)[1282]. National Sleep Foundation's updated sleep duration recommendations for the influence of leisure activities on mental health (Pressman, S. D. et al., 2009)[1283].

With an evidence-based approach combined with clinical experience, the book assimilates an array of scientifically substantiated strategies and information from diverse domains like dietary habits, exercise routines, sleep schedules, and technological usage.

One central tenet is the role of nutrition in mental well-being. For instance, consuming omega-3 fatty acids has been observed to lower anxiety symptoms (Kiecolt-Glaser et al., 2011).[1284] Likewise, eating fruits

---

[1282] Hirshkowitz, M., Whiton, K., Albert, S. M., Alessi, C., Bruni, O., DonCarlos, L., ... & Neubauer, D. N. (2015). National Sleep Foundation's updated sleep duration recommendations: final report. Sleep Health, 1(4), 233-243.

[1283] Pressman, S. D., Matthews, K. A., Cohen, S., Martire, L. M., Scheier, M., Baum, A., & Schulz, R. (2009). Association of enjoyable leisure activities with psychological and physical well-being. Psychosomatic Medicine, 71(7), 725.

[1284] Kiecolt-Glaser, J. K., Belury, M. A., Andridge, R., Malarkey, W. B., & Glaser, R. (2011). Omega-3 supplementation lowers inflammation and anxiety in medical students: A randomized controlled trial. Brain, behavior, and immunity, 25(8), 1725-1734.

and vegetables is associated with enhanced mental well-being (Conner et al., 2017).[1285]

Sleep quality is another pivotal component emphasized throughout the text. For example, sleep patterns are correlated with academic performance. Contrary to popular belief, the optimal amount of sleep required for peak academic performance may not be eight hours a night (Hirshkowitz et al., 2015).[1286]

Further on, technology's role in shaping mental health cannot be overlooked. While it offers novel tools for mental health support, like smartphone apps designed to alleviate symptoms of depression or anxiety, evidence suggests that excessive social media use might exacerbate symptoms of depression (Primack et al., 2017).[1287]

Physical exercise and leisure activities are also profiled as essential factors influencing mental health. Physical activities like weightlifting have positively affected mental health (O'Connor et al., 2010).[1288] Meanwhile, leisure activity engagement correlates with

---

[1285] Conner, T. S., Brookie, K. L., Carr, A. C., Mainvil, L. A., & Vissers, M. C. (2017). Let them eat fruit! The effect of fruit and vegetable consumption on psychological well-being in young adults: A randomized controlled trial. PloS one, 12(2), e0171206.

[1286] Hirshkowitz, M., Whiton, K., Albert, S. M., Alessi, C., Bruni, O., DonCarlos, L., ... & Neubauer, D. N. (2015). National Sleep Foundation's updated sleep duration recommendations: final report. Sleep Health, 1(4), 233-243.

[1287] Primack, B. A., Shensa, A., Sidani, J. E., Whaite, E. O., Lin, L. Y., Rosen, D., ... & Qiao, S. (2017). Social Media Use and Perceived Social Isolation Among Young Adults in the U.S. American journal of preventive medicine, 53(1), 1-8.

[1288] O'Connor, P. J., Herring, M. P., & Caravalho, A. (2010). Mental Health Benefits of Strength Training in Adults. American Journal of Lifestyle Medicine, 4(5), 377-396.

psychological and physical well-being (Pressman et al., 2009).[1289]

An invaluable adjunct to the central content of the work is a compilation of seminal studies in the realm of mental health. For example, a deeper dive into the impact of omega-3 fatty acids on mental well-being can be accessed through the research of Kiecolt-Glaser et al. (2011).[1290] Their study not only looks at anxiety but also broadly at inflammation and its relationship with stress.

Lastly, the value of leisure activities and their correlation with well-being is a topic of vast interest. The work by Pressman et al. (2009)[1291] is indispensable for those wishing to understand further how leisure activities, both passive and active, intertwine with psychological and physical health.

The text is carefully crafted to serve as an invaluable resource for a broad audience, from college students and parents to healthcare providers and educators. It does so without adopting a prescriptive tone, allowing readers to consult and apply the evidence to their unique circumstances. Instead of quick fixes or one-size-fits-all solutions, the book fosters a nuanced understanding,

---

[1289] Pressman, S. D., Matthews, K. A., Cohen, S., Martire, L. M., Scheier, M., Baum, A., & Schulz, R. (2009). Association of enjoyable leisure activities with psychological and physical well-being. Psychosomatic Medicine, 71(7), 725.

[1290] Kiecolt-Glaser, J. K., Belury, M. A., Andridge, R., Malarkey, W. B., & Glaser, R. (2011). Omega-3 supplementation lowers inflammation and anxiety in medical students: A randomized controlled trial. Brain, behavior, and immunity, 25(8), 1725-1734.

[1291] Pressman, S. D., Matthews, K. A., Cohen, S., Martire, L. M., Scheier, M., Baum, A., & Schulz, R. (2009). Association of enjoyable leisure activities with psychological and physical well-being. Psychosomatic Medicine, 71(7), 725.

urging the reader to integrate various approaches for a balanced mental health strategy.

Throughout the book, numerous strategies targeting enhanced mental well-being have been introduced. The application of these strategies is pivotal, not just in their understanding. Based on evidence from multiple studies here and closing thoughts on implementing these strategies for optimal results.

A common thread in many research studies is the significance of consistency. For instance, when embracing mindfulness techniques, practicing consistently for shorter durations is more effective than occasionally delving deep for extended periods (Kabat-Zinn, 2003).[1292]

Integrating into daily life is crucial for strategies such as dietary changes that affect mental health. According to a study in the journal "Nutritional Neuroscience," subtle and gradual incorporation of mood-enhancing foods leads to sustained positive outcomes rather than abrupt dietary overhauls (Jacka, 2017).[1293]

Technological impact on mental health, especially in the ever-evolving digital age, necessitates ongoing learning. The effects observed in a study five years ago may differ today due to rapid technological advancements. Regular updates on technological

---

[1292] Kabat-Zinn, J. (2003). Mindfulness-Based Interventions in Context: Past, Present, and Future. Clinical Psychology: Science and Practice, 10(2), 144-156.

[1293] Jacka, F. N. (2017). Nutritional Psychiatry: Where to Next? EBioMedicine, 17, 24-29.

impacts are hence advised and useful in our ever-growing and fast-paced world.

While exercise undoubtedly benefits mental health, the type and intensity of exercise that's optimal can vary among individuals. Therefore, consulting with a fitness professional or therapist who understands the mental health-exercise interplay can be invaluable. It helps you better understand why you are doing a particular exercise while also focusing on the requirements and needs of the body.

Strategies, like engaging in leisure activities, are highly personal. One size doesn't fit all. What you like is necessarily going to attract and entertain another person. It is all individualized, based on our personal experiences. It's imperative to discern what resonates individually rather than doing an exercise or activity because it is popular or the talk of the town.

Continuous self-assessment and tweaking strategies based on regular feedback are fundamental. The benefits of mindfulness are plenty, as discussed in the previous chapters.

As the final pages draw near, it's essential to acknowledge the journey embarked upon — a journey towards understanding, embracing, and enhancing mental well-being. Every reader has shown commendable commitment merely by seeking knowledge and, hopefully, will take this information to heart and into the world.

In parting, it would be remiss not to express profound gratitude. Reading, after all, is a two-way interaction. While knowledge and strategies have been shared through these pages, the true essence of the book is completed by the reader's engagement. For readers looking for more, I invite you to continue the journey with me by subscribing to my blog or newsletter on my website for future posts and updates.

As an emblem of this symbiotic relationship, remember: *Every effort, every step taken towards better mental health, no matter how small, is a testament to human resilience and the enduring spirit to thrive.*

For readers looking for more, I invite you to continue the journey with me by subscribing to my blog or newsletter on my website.

mentalhealthforcollegestudents.com.

Made in United States
Troutdale, OR
06/25/2024

20810310R00289